# Walking *in* Grace

## 2025 Daily devotions to draw you closer to God

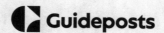

Acknowledgments

Every attempt has been made to credit the sources of copyrighted material used in this book. If any such acknowledgment has been inadvertently omitted or miscredited, receipt of such information would be appreciated.

Scripture quotations marked (AMP) are taken from the *Amplified Bible*. Copyright © 2015 by The Lockman Foundation, La Habra, California. All rights reserved.

Scripture quotations marked (ASV) are taken from the *American Standard Version Bible* (public domain).

Scripture quotations marked (CEB) are taken from the *Common English Bible*. Copyright © 2011 by Common English Bible.

Scripture quotations marked (CEV) are taken from *Holy Bible: Contemporary English Version*. Copyright © 1995 by American Bible Society.

Scripture quotations marked (CSB) are taken from *The Christian Standard Bible*. Copyright © 2017 by Holman Bible Publishers. Used by permission.

Scripture quotations marked (ESV) are taken from the *Holy Bible, English Standard Version*. Copyright © 2001 by Crossway Bibles, a division of Good News Publishers. Used by permission. All rights reserved.

Scripture quotations marked (GNT) are taken from the *Good News Translation*® (Today's English Version, Second Edition). Copyright © 1992 by American Bible Society.

Scripture quotations marked (HCSB) are taken from the *Holman Christian Standard Bible*. Copyright © 1999, 2000, 2002, 2003, 2009 by Holman Bible Publishers, Nashville, Tennessee. All rights reserved.

Scripture quotations marked (JPS) are taken from *Tanakh: A New Translation of the Holy Scriptures according to the Traditional Hebrew Text*. Copyright © 1985 by the Jewish Publication Society. All rights reserved.

Scripture quotations marked (KJV) are taken from the *King James Version of the Bible*.

Scripture quotations marked (LEB) are taken from the *Lexham English Bible*. Copyright © 2012 by Logos Bible Software. Lexham is a registered trademark of Logos Bible Software.

Scripture quotations marked (MSG) are taken from *The Message*. Copyright © 1993, 2002, 2018 by Eugene H. Peterson.

Scripture quotations marked (NASB) are taken from the *New American Standard Bible*®. Copyright © 1960, 1971, 1977, 1995, 2020 by The Lockman Foundation. All rights reserved.

Scripture quotations marked (NCV) are taken from *The Holy Bible, New Century Version*. Copyright © 2005 by Thomas Nelson.

Scripture quotations marked (NIRV) are taken from the *Holy Bible, New International Reader's Version*. Copyright © 1995, 1996, 1998, 2014 by Biblica, Inc. Used by permission. All rights reserved worldwide.

Scripture quotations marked (NIV) are taken from *The Holy Bible, New International Version*®, *NIV*®. Copyright © 1973, 1978, 1984, 2011 by Biblica, Inc. Used by permission. All rights reserved worldwide.

Scripture quotations marked (NKJV) are taken from *The Holy Bible, New King James Version*. Copyright © 1982 by Thomas Nelson. Used by permission. All rights reserved.

Scripture quotations marked (NLT) are taken from the *Holy Bible, New Living Translation*. Copyright © 1996, 2004, 2007, 2015 by Tyndale House Foundation. Used by permission of Tyndale House Publishers, Inc., Carol Stream, Illinois. All rights reserved.

Scripture quotations marked (NRSVUE) are taken from the *New Revised Standard Version, Updated Edition*. Copyright © 2021 by National Council of Churches of Christ in the United States of America. Used by permission. All rights reserved worldwide.

Scripture quotations marked (RSV) are taken from the *Revised Standard Version of the Bible*. Copyright © 1946, 1952, 1971 by the Division of Christian Education of the National Council of the Churches of Christ in the United States of America. Used by permission.

Scripture quotations marked (TLB) are taken from *The Living Bible*. Copyright © 1971 by Tyndale House Publishers, Inc., Carol Stream, Illinois. All rights reserved.

Scripture quotations marked (VOICE) are taken from *The Voice Bible*. Copyright © 2012 by Thomas Nelson, Inc. The Voice™ translation copyright © 2012 Ecclesia Bible Society. All rights reserved.

Cover design by Müllerhaus; cover photo by Andrew Soundarajan/iStock. Monthly page opener photos from Unsplash. Indexed by Kelly White. Typeset by Aptara, Inc.

ISBN 978-1-961126-10-7 (hardcover)
ISBN 978-1-961251-05-2 (softcover)
ISBN 978-1-961126-12-1 (softcover large print)
ISBN 978-1-961126-14-5 (softcover pocket edition)
ISBN 978-1-961126-11-4 (epub)

Printed and bound in the United States of America
10 9 8 7 6 5 4 3 2 1

Dear Friends,

Welcome to *Walking in Grace 2025*! We're excited to greet you as you embark upon a devotional journey that we pray will inspire and encourage you to greater faith and closeness with the living God. This beautiful annual devotional tradition connects readers from all over the country and encourages so many in their daily faith walks. *Walking in Grace 2025* is filled with 365 all-new devotions, written to refresh and enliven you as you spend quiet solitude in God's presence each day.

The theme for *Walking in Grace* this year is a balm to our weary souls. We focus on "An Everlasting Love," one of God's attributes, taken from Jeremiah 31:3 (NIV): "The LORD appeared to us in the past, saying: 'I have loved you with an everlasting love; I have drawn you with unfailing kindness.'" We see the many ways God's love, providence, and guidance cover our lives.

Brock Kidd shares the inspiring way he lives his life—as though everything were a miracle—and the encouragement that brings to him. Feeling stressed by the demands of ministry, Pablo Diaz experiences a perspective change when he watches some joyful children at play. Carla Hendricks blesses us with a beautiful story of remembrance about a beloved teenager she knew who tragically passed . . . and how God can offer comfort and hope even during heartbreaking times. Logan Eliasen recognizes that even a Christmas quarantine with a sick dog can be joyful and filled with the peace of Christ. Evelyn Bence rediscovers the joy of hosting and opening her home, and is inspired to gather more friends and serve her community after a long hiatus. Edward Grinnan reflects on the Golden Rule and reveals how good neighbors can become like family. A baking session with Ashley Kappel's daughter turns into an unexpected opportunity to witness Jesus's love. Vicki Kuyper's granddaughter lovingly reminds her how God views Vicki. Debbie Macomber recalls various waiting rooms she's spent time in and how God has provided for her in each one. One of Rick Hamlin's best friends, Jorge, leads Rick to reflect on the God-given gift of good friends.

We are delighted to bring many special series to you this year. Shawnelle Eliasen shares vulnerably about a new stage in her life—moving from full-time homeschooling to becoming a phlebotomist—in "When Change Comes" as she discerns the sustaining comfort of the Lord during a time of intense transition. Jenny Lynn Keller writes with insight about "Life Lessons from the Beach" as God uses the beauty of the seaside to reveal his truths. Patty Kirk sheds light on little-known biblical characters to remind us how precious we are to God and the wisdom we can gain from these people in "Seemingly Insignificant." Come along with Carol Knapp as she explores how twenty-first-century Christians need to be equipped when Jesus calls to us in "Journeying with Jesus." Roberta Messner shares movingly about her experience of doubt during a time of medical difficulty and how God sustained her through His faithfulness. Gail Thorell Schilling walks us through

Holy Week as she recalls her pandemic experience from Easter 2020 in "Sheltered in Grace." J. Brent Bill ushers us into a reflective Advent season in his series, "Filled with Holy Anticipation."

Jerusha Agen won't be writing for us this year; we will miss her and thank her for all of the devotional stories and insights she has shared.

We are excited to introduce you to two new writers who are joining us in the 2025 volume: Lisa Livezey and Rachel Thompson. We hope you enjoy getting to know them and find inspiration in their warm, sincere offerings.

As you begin this new year, and new devotional journey, we pray you will experience God's great blessing and promise of everlasting love in your life.

Faithfully yours,
The Editors of Guideposts

P.S. We love hearing from you! We read every letter we receive. Let us know what *Walking in Grace* means to you by emailing WIGEditors@guideposts.org or writing to Guideposts Books & Inspirational Media, 100 Reserve Road, Suite E200, Danbury, CT 06810.

# January

Beloved, let us love one another,
for love is from God, and
whoever loves has been born
of God and knows God.

—1 John 4:7 (ESV)

# New Year's Day, Wednesday, January 1

**Be still, and know that I am∫ God . . .**
**—Psalm 46:10 (NIV)**

Walking in the park on this chilly New Year's morning, my mind is overloaded with to-dos, what-ifs, and if-onlys. Yes, I'm overextended. Running the orphanage and nonprofit we developed in Zimbabwe is a bit stressful. What if people stop giving or our budget becomes unmanageable?

Back to the present moment, my "praying tree" is in sight. I consider my to-dos. We have guests coming for a New Year's celebration. The menu's in my head, but I haven't begun preparations. And the table's not set. I really relish setting a beautiful table. And my friend, who is in the hospital, I haven't called her yet. By the time I reach the tree, I'm exhausted. Ridiculous, since, apart from worrying, I haven't done a single thing.

"God?" I ask. Sometimes He answers, sometimes He doesn't (at least not immediately). Today, He's quick on the draw.

"Be still." Oh dear, not the best answer.

"Be still . . . and know . . ." He continues.

I breathe deep.

"Be still . . . and know that I am God."

I exhale slowly. "Thanks, God, I needed that. My tendency to take over Your job is at times unrelenting."

Heading home, I call my friend as I walk along. I offer her the hope that a new year brings. Next, I create a visual image of the table, dishes, flowers. I rehearse the steps of cooking the meal. By the time I'm back in the kitchen, my work is half-done in the planning.

When the guests arrive, everything's ready. I relax in the stillness of my kitchen as I plate the food. *Knowing* ... I smile to myself.

**God, please stay with me in the new year and keep that "knowing" alive.** —Pam Kidd

**Digging Deeper:** Genesis 18:14; Job 28:24

---

# Thursday, January 2

**I have fought the good fight, I have finished the race, I have kept the faith. —2 Timothy 4:7 (NIV)**

As the world celebrated the arrival of a new year, my extended family pushed through bittersweet memories of my Uncle Verdell, who had passed two days before New Year's Day. This loss had hit us hard, since my uncle was my late father's last surviving sibling. Losing Uncle Verdell represented the loss of an entire generation of our family.

I contemplated ways to assist my cousin Monisha, who had been overwhelmed by the details of her father's funeral and burial. I offered to write his obituary. In preparation, I interviewed family members, read and highlighted a decades-old professional résumé of my uncle's, and extracted correlating facts from my father's obituary.

I'd been aware of my uncle's long career as an educator but was delighted to discover his early experiences using his hands for jobs in welding, carpentry, and bricklaying. I marveled to share that back in the 1980s, he had run for mayor in Baltimore, Maryland. It was also a joy to share the story of my parents playing Cupid by transporting a lovely widow to Virginia, where my father had grown up and my uncle still lived, to introduce her to my uncle. That blind date resulted in a wedding a year later and, down the road, my cousin's birth.

Writing my uncle's obituary proved therapeutic for me, helping me to celebrate his life while simultaneously grieving the loss. Though my family had lost an entire generation, we were encouraged by their legacy and impact. We were reminded that we would not be the parents, educators, and creatives we are today without the legacy of our ancestors.

**Lord, help me honor my ancestors through a life of faith, perseverance, and love.** —Carla Hendricks

**Digging Deeper:** Proverbs 13:21–25; Acts 20:24

---

# Friday, January 3

**And we all, with unveiled face, beholding the glory of the Lord, are being transformed into the same image from one degree of glory to another. For this comes from the Lord who is the Spirit.** —2 Corinthians 3:18 (ESV)

*"She looks just like you."*

I hear the words often from people who think my daughter resembles me. Yet in my mind, she's the spitting image of my mother-in-law. I've seen the photos of her from long before I married my husband and entered her life. I think she and my daughter share the same light behind their eyes, the same high cheekbones and stunning smile.

Despite how I feel about our physical traits, I know my daughter and I share the same mannerisms and character. That's what people see. Our long strides, our posture, the way we hold our lips when we're deep in thought or concentrating on a challenging task. We think alike about most issues, and since I've raised her by my side, we share the same morals and values.

Thinking about that, it struck me: people are seeing the overflow of our intimacy. I often tell my children to watch the company they keep because they will begin to emulate and resemble the people they spend the most time with. Our time devoted to personal Bible study, prayer, worship, and being the hands and feet of God shapes us into His likeness. When people see us, they should see Him.

**Lord, let my life be a reflection of Your love. Let people see You when they see me. Change me from the inside out so that my life is a mirror of Your character. I pray that my faith journey is one that others will desire to have with You.**
—Tia McCollors

## Saturday, January 4

**. . . but I focus on this one thing: Forgetting the past and looking forward to what lies ahead.
—Philippians 3:13 (NLT)**

I stepped into my home office and stared at the pictures on my computer screen. Memories flooded my mind as each picture scrolled past, courtesy of my computer's sleep mode. Each photo recalled a certain time, place, and memory.

Pictures of the trip my husband and I took with a church group to Greece stirred my soul, seeing the smiling faces of friends. Each photo recalled a happy memory until I noticed several people who have since gone to heaven, making me want to go back to the time when they were still with us.

Many of the photos displayed trips we'd taken when Logan, my grandson, lived with us. The pictures of him remind me how much he's grown and how much I miss the little boy he used to be. And I want to go back to that time too.

Each of these memories reminds me that time has passed, and I regret not appreciating the experience back then. Now I face another new year, and I want to stop time and stay here before anything else changes.

A favorite movie scene comes to mind. In *Indiana Jones and the Last Crusade*, Indiana Jones needs to cross a deep gorge to get the sacred chalice that would save his father. There appears to be no way to get across. Yet realizing the challenge is a test of his faith, he steps off the ledge, and a bridge that hadn't been visible appears for him to cross.

Isn't that the way each new year is? In fact, every day is a step of faith, trusting God to get us through as He's done before. So, I step forward.

**Lord, thank You for being with me, now and forever.** —Marilyn Turk

**Digging Deeper:** Joshua 1:9; Jeremiah 29:11

---

# Sunday, January 5

**There is a time for everything, and a season for every activity under the heavens. —Ecclesiastes 3:1 (NIV)**

"Come into the kitchen," my grandmother said. "I made coffee."

Though I hadn't visited my grandparents' home in a while, I knew the layout of their house well. I entered the kitchen and pulled two mugs from the cupboard near the sink.

My life had changed substantially in the past few years. I graduated law school. My parents sold my childhood home. But here, at my grandparents' house, nothing ever seemed to change.

While my grandmother poured coffee, I looked out the window. I could see the pine tree my mother had planted as a girl and the garden where my grandparents grew tomatoes for canning.

But the corner of the yard was empty, save a dark ring of dirt.

"The pool," I said. "It's gone."

My grandma joined me at the window.

"Yes," she said. "After all those years, it rusted through."

I stared at the empty circle in the yard. As a child, I'd spent many summer afternoons in that pool. Now, fresh dirt was the only evidence it had existed.

"How do you feel about letting go of the pool?" I asked.

My grandma breathed deeply.

"Change is difficult," she said. She handed me a cup of coffee. We both stared at the bare circle. Then she broke the silence. "I think I'll plant a flower garden where the pool was," she said.

I thought of green things growing in that empty place. And I began to understand that goodness can spring forth from even difficult change.

**Lord, help me to embrace change as an opportunity to grow.** —Logan Eliasen

**Digging Deeper:** Isaiah 43:19;
2 Corinthians 5:17

# Epiphany, Monday, January 6

**Clap your hands, all you peoples; shout to God with loud songs of joy. —Psalm 47:1 (NRSVUE)**

Do you ever ride the city bus? I sometimes do, because my wife has the car or because my youngest daughter thinks it's fun. She's still at that wonderful age when the world is full of joy and wonder, when she doesn't see inconvenience or grime. My little one likes to bounce in the rear seats and sit up high looking out the windows.

Today, we boarded the Milwaukee bus after school, heading to the museum downtown. It was very crowded.

An older woman, seeing that we couldn't sit together, grabbed my sleeve and insisted we switch seats with her. She was in a two-seat spot by herself. With a grateful smile, I took her up on the offer.

A few minutes later, we watched a man struggle to board the bus, his arms overfull with plastic bags filled with clothes and other things. The woman reached over and insisted he take one of her cloth bags to carry his stuff more securely. I watched as she helped him transfer his things from his ripped bag to her clean bag with good handles.

There are ordinary saints all around us. I saw one today on the bus. She reminded me of the feast of Epiphany, January 6, when wise men arrived to see the Christ Child in an animal trough. They wouldn't have come if they didn't have the wonder of a child, and their gifts, like those of the woman on the bus, were gestures of grace.

**Lord, fill me with wonder. Show me Your face in the faces I see.** —Jon M. Sweeney

**Digging Deeper:** Romans 12:11–12

---

# Tuesday, January 7

**. . . And they will understand the lovingkindness of the LORD. —Psalm 107:43 (NKJV)**

I yawned and stretched as I opened the cupboard door, glancing over the rows of coffee cups from which to choose. I sighed, missing my old favorites.

My morning coffee wasn't so much about the coffee as it was about creating an experience with God. For decades, I used the same tulip-shaped, oversize cups with cheerful snowmen on them—all year round. Following a process I had down to a science, I'd make a single cup of coffee stout enough to float a horseshoe, then, over the next couple of hours, I'd snuggle in my prayer chair, sipping the brew while I prayed and read His Word. But a couple of years ago—within two months—I'd accidentally broken both snowmen cups. Although I'd diligently searched stores and online, I hadn't been able to find any of the cheery tulip-shaped, oversize cups. I pulled a regular one off the shelf.

A couple of days later, while I was finishing up my once-a-week trip to town, I glanced across the street, and my favorite thrift store seemed to glow. Something urged me to stop. I shrugged my shoulders. I had a couple of extra minutes, so why not? To my surprise, on the top shelf in the housewares section were two tulip-shaped, oversize cups. My heart skipped a beat. The same artist had drawn the cheery snowmen, only these cups each had a word on them. One said "Faith" and the other "Joy."

**Lord, oftentimes tears leak down my face when You demonstrate how much You care for me— especially with the "little things." I am so grateful. Thank You. Amen.** —Rebecca Ondov

**Digging Deeper:** Psalms 23, 103, 107:31

---

# Wednesday, January 8

**Then God opened her eyes, and she saw a well of water. —Genesis 21:19 (NRSVUE)**

I used to resent being told to drink water. No matter what the issue, water was the answer. Hot day? "Hydrate!" Flu? "Liquids!" Going for a walk? "Take water." Stubbed toe? Well, maybe not, but you get the idea.

I don't like water. Not bottled, tap, fizzy, flavored, vitamin-infused, not at all. So when I recently became ill and needed to drink water with medicine first thing in the morning, it was one more misery to go with how crummy I felt.

Then I received a letter seeking donations to provide impoverished families and villages with clean water. I read about mothers walking for miles just to get drinking water, never mind enough for cooking and bathing. I read statistics about children sickening and dying from dehydration or contaminated water. What I despised in abundance, people were dying for the lack of.

I began focusing my morning water on those people. With every swallow, I considered how they would appreciate what I disliked. I envisioned mothers, burdened by poverty and exhaustion, trudging miles for water; thirsty, hungry children without water to drink or food needing water for preparation; students missing school because they lacked water to bathe or wash their clothes.

I started praying for them, their villages, and their nations. I was careful not to pour more than I needed, avoiding waste. I considered how God created and used water for baptism and to connect us all through one life-giving resource. My dread became gratitude.

**Creator, thank You for using Your gifts of life to heal others and teach me.** —Marci Alborghetti

**Digging Deeper:** Exodus 15:22–27; Matthew 14:22–33

---

# Thursday, January 9

**Whenever you possibly can, do good to those who need it. —Proverbs 3:27 (GNT)**

The morning was bitterly cold. As I pulled into the parking lot, I noticed a woman angrily swatting at snowflakes as she walked along the icy sidewalk. I often saw homeless men and women near my workplace and had prayed for them last night as the snow began to fall. I couldn't imagine trying to stay warm through a Colorado winter without a home to call my own.

As I parked my car, the woman stepped right in front of it and yelled, "Please! Please! Do you have a couple of dollars so I can sit inside somewhere? My feet are freezing!"

Although she was dressed in a warm coat and hat, I could tell the woman was cold and desperate. I immediately opened my car door, and my wallet. I only had three dollars in cash and apologized as I held them out with my mittened hand.

The woman's frantic expression melted into a smile. Kindly assuring me I had no need to be sorry, she wrapped me in an emphatic hug that warmed us both, thanking me over and over again. She said the money would allow her to purchase a hot drink, so she could stay inside a coffee shop and out of the cold.

Throughout my workday, I could still feel the warmth of her hug and God's blessing on us both. I felt humbled by how He'd unexpectedly invited me to become an answer to my very own prayer.

**Father, help me be as free in sharing Your blessings as You've been in giving them to me.**
—Vicki Kuyper

**Digging Deeper:** Deuteronomy 15:11;
Proverbs 3:27, 22:9; Matthew 25:31–40;
2 Corinthians 9:7; Hebrews 13:2, 16

# Friday, January 10

**He has made everything beautiful in its time.**
**—Ecclesiastes 3:11 (NIV)**

When I was in college, our congregation had a ministry called "Adopt a Student." It assigned us to older members who'd see after us and maybe invite us for a home-cooked meal sometimes.

I was lucky that my adopted "mom" was Virginia, one of the congregation's best cooks. It wasn't just her food that was special, though: she always used her good china, linen napkins, crystal glasses, and fresh flowers. Always practical to a fault myself, I once asked why she went to such trouble. "I've just gotten to the point in my life where I like everything to be beautiful," she replied.

Many years later, when Virginia was spending her last days in hospice, I visited her.

"When I get well, I'll have you over for a meal," Virginia said weakly.

The two of us then planned the menu for a dinner I knew we'd never have.

I think of Virginia whenever I iron napkins that will soon be soiled and wrinkled, or buy flowers that will quickly wilt. Somehow, the extra trouble and expense don't seem like a waste.

Maybe I've reached the point in my life where I like everything to be beautiful too.

**Father, thank You for beautiful surroundings and beautiful friends.** —Ginger Rue

**Digging Deeper:** Psalm 27:4; Philippians 4:8

---

# Saturday, January 11

**Don't worry about anything; instead, pray about everything; tell God your needs, and don't forget to thank him for his answers.**
**—Philippians 4:6** (TLB)

A few years ago, in January, my beloved sister-in-law Linda and I flew to San Diego, rented a car, and explored the California coast up to San Francisco. My favorite stop was Elephant Seal Cove in Big Sur near San Simeon.

Every year, hundreds of elephant seals meet there to breed, give birth, and then head back out to sea for eleven months. It was an incredible sight watching the females, some twelve feet long and weighing up to 1,800 pounds; males up to sixteen feet long and 5,000 pounds; and babies growing from eighty pounds at birth to more than three hundred pounds in a month.

I was shocked to learn that after five weeks of nursing, the mothers return to the sea and never see their pups again, leaving the babies near the tide pools to learn how to fish and swim on their own.

What strength, determination, and resilience those babies had to have. But every year, there's a whole new generation of elephant seal pups who survive in their world after only five weeks with their mothers.

Every year, when I'm missing my four children and nine grandchildren—who live in California, Wisconsin, and Ohio, far from my home in Florida—I am reminded of the resiliency of all God's creatures, including we seniors who are fending for ourselves with no immediate family nearby. God gives us everything we need, including the ability to live on our own, make friends, travel, and find joy in the process.

**Jesus, I am so blessed and thankful to have You as my greatest support system. Keep giving me the grace to venture out on my own with You as my guide.** —Patricia Lorenz

**Digging Deeper:** Mark 4:38–41; Luke 2:43–49; 1 Peter 5:2–4

---

## Sunday, January 12

**And Nathanael said to him, "Can any good come out of Nazareth?"** —John 1:46 (NKJV)

We are traveling on a Sunday morning, so my wife and I stop for worship at some small, old Missouri town. It's a sad little village, with unpaved streets, run-down houses, and a dying downtown.

The church greeter is a cheerful woman who says, "I love this town. I grew up here, and all my family and friends live here. I can't imagine living anywhere else." Sharon and I glance at each other in disbelief, wondering how anyone could be so attached to this dismal burg.

After services, we drive on, and I am thinking about my own hometown, where I have lived for sixty years. Moberly is a typical Midwestern town of 13,000 souls, and nothing fancy. The city motto, painted on the water tower, says, "Moberly, More Than Meets the Eye," and I smile, thinking, "I certainly hope so."

And yet, when I see the Moberly skyline up ahead, my heart speeds up, and suddenly I understand what that cheerful church greeter was trying to say. It's not about the streets, the houses, the downtown. It's about the people—people I love and enjoy every day, including the thousands of my beloved Central Christian College students who have lived in this small town on their way to serving God, all over the world.

I love this town, and I can't imagine living anywhere else.

**Lord, You grew up in Nazareth, a sad little village with a bad reputation, and yet You changed the whole world with Your love. Help me to love the people I live among.** —Daniel Schantz

**Digging Deeper:** John 13:35;
Romans 13:9

# Monday, January 13

**Abraham was the father of Isaac, and Isaac the father of Jacob, and Jacob the father of Judah and his brothers . . . —Matthew 1:2 (NRSVUE)**

The babysitting detritus lingers in the house. The pots and pans on the kitchen floor that Silas likes to bang on with a spoon. The Swiffer duster he pushes around, as though he might be cleaning our floors. White Bear, his favorite stuffed animal from Gramps and Minnie's guest room (complete with crib), sits in a proud place on the sofa. And Gramps and Minnie? Those are our designated grandparent names.

We're lucky to have nineteen-month-old Silas only half a block away and get to see him often, which is a good thing, because when his parents finally took that long-delayed honeymoon trip, we could step in, dividing ourselves between his home and ours. He didn't seem too alarmed to see Minnie and Gramps there when he woke up rather than Mommy and Daddy.

Not to say it wasn't challenging. *Wait . . . where are his socks? Shouldn't he be wearing a hat outside? And with that sniffly nose and cough, shouldn't he skip daycare today? God willing, he'll be well enough to go tomorrow.*

When he sits beside me on the piano bench and pounds on the keys as I try to play the right notes, I like to think he'll have happy memories of us long after we're gone. I used to skip those lists of ancestors recorded in the Bible, but I've come to see a holy reason for them. We all come from God and belong to God, but not without generations preceding us. Thanks, Silas, for that hug. May the love be passed along.

**May I never forget, Lord, the goodness given as I try to give it back.** —Rick Hamlin

**Digging Deeper:** Psalm 145:4; Proverbs 17:6; Isaiah 46:4

---

# Tuesday, January 14

**And it shall come to pass, that before they call, I will answer; and while they are yet speaking, I will hear. —Isaiah 65:24 (KJV)**

Minor issues with the car my husband, Don, and I bought for its safety features cropped up almost immediately. The year after Don died, severe problems developed. The car was "repaired" eight times but never fixed. I needed a reliable vehicle, but car lots were almost empty. I wrote "new car" on my prayer list but doubted God would answer such a material request.

Then my friend Glenda asked me to drive her to an eye appointment in Garden City, fifty miles away. "It's a God Thing you're available," she said. "My husband had a farm emergency." God Thing?

I didn't know the term. "It's when a little miracle happens," she explained.

I dropped her at the clinic and headed downtown to shop. As I passed a car dealership, I felt a strong urge to turn around, so I did. "I need a small, reliable SUV with safety features and all-wheel drive," I told the lone salesman. "How long would an order take?"

Instead of answering, he picked up a key and took me outside. The only new car on the lot was a small gray SUV with everything I wanted. The person who had ordered it decided on a bigger car. I showed the salesman all the defects of my old car. To my amazement, I still got twice the trade-in I expected.

I was a bit late picking Glenda up. "It's because of a God Thing," I told her.

**Gracious God, I'm grateful for my miracle car.
I give You thanks every time I open the garage.**
—Penney Schwab

**Digging Deeper:** Psalm 86:6–7;
Matthew 7:7–8; Philippians 4:19

---

# Wednesday, January 15

**You make your saving help my shield, and your right hand sustains me. —Psalm 18:35 (NIV)**

I walked into our daughter Rachel's living room where she lay propped up on a couch, gauze strapped across her nose, a washcloth across her forehead. Her husband had just picked her up from outpatient sinus surgery, and I was coming over to do anything I could to help.

I sat down next to her. She was still groggy from the anesthesia, so we spoke little. Then she reached over and took hold of my hand. Emotion filled me. Though my daughter and I have a close relationship, she is grown and married and had not reached for my hand for many years.

She and I sat together for some time. Occasionally I would get up to refresh her washcloth or water glass. Each time I sat back down, she reached for my hand.

I don't know when or if Rachel will ever reach for my hand again. I do know I will never forget that afternoon when she did, or the enormity of my joy at her doing so. I had come to give her the gift of help; she had no idea of the immense gift she gave me.

Maybe that's how God feels. I know He is always there for me. But when I'm going through an especially tough time, I become acutely aware of my need for the peace of His presence. I mentally reach for His hand and am comforted, knowing He is supporting and loving me. I had not thought of the joy it must give Him as well, to have me want my hand in His.

**Heavenly Father, thank You for the gift Rachel gave me and its reminder to reach for Your hand.**
—Kim Taylor Henry

**Digging Deeper:** Psalms 63:8, 89:21

# Thursday, January 16

**Judge not according to the appearance.**
**—John 7:24 (KJV)**

*Oh dear God,* I breathe to myself as I struggle, with my arms full of packages, to open the door to the parking garage. Rushing straight toward me in the dim light is a huge burly man in a hoodie. I am alone. I am an easy target.

But the voice beneath the hood is gentle, as the big man, very near now, lifts his face and smiles at me. "Let me help you," he says. I realize that I have jumped to a terrible conclusion. I am ashamed of myself.

"Oh, you are so kind," I respond, trying to overcome the ugly taste of prejudice, which I abhor. He just laughs, a full laugh . . . a laugh tinged with something deeper.

"Oh," he says, "my grandmother would reach down and shake me if I didn't hurry to help a nice lady like you."

"Ahh," I say. "You must have had a wonderful grandmother."

"Boy, I sure did," he answers, "and I still hear her every day. She still shows me everything good that I'll ever know."

As he walks me to my car, carrying my heaviest package, we chat some more. He's a coach at a local high school, he has two boys of his own, and obviously adores his wife, Verona. He sees me safely inside my car. He reminds me to lock my door. With regret, I watch him walk away.

I see that "COACH" is written in big letters on the back of his hoodie.

*He certainly is*, I breathe to God. *He certainly is.*

**Oh Father, Your angels are ever near. Some wear hoodies. Thank You for Your goodness to me. I am safe in Your love.** —Pam Kidd

**Digging Deeper:** 1 Samuel 16:7; Matthew 7:16

---

# Friday, January 17

**She has done what she could.** —**Mark 14:8** (RSV)

Within sight of my door in Virginia, my one-way street ends at a T-intersection midway down a steep hill. So you might imagine my neighborhood's troubles last week, when the temperature dropped thirty degrees overnight. Rain turned to heavy snow, seven inches. In decades past, I've felt some satisfaction in getting out, shoveling a walk, and contributing to the community's cleanup. These days, I'm not up to the challenge. *I'm of little use here,* I thought, discouraged. Nevertheless, by force of habit, I set my snow shovel at the ready.

By nine o'clock, I saw the first of the day's drivers struggling to dislodge his wheels. I ventured onto my stoop. "Yo! Do you have a shovel?" I yelled, waving mine in the air.

"No! Oh, thank you!" he said, tromping toward me. "I need to bring my wife home from the hospital."

I lent the shovel—the only one on the block, it seemed—to five others that day, even a young policeman woefully unprepared to navigate the hill. Come evening, when the shovel didn't disengage a stranded car—still spinning on ice—I turned to my pantry. "Here, try this," I said, handing a neighbor a jar of gourmet sea salt. As that car inched free, an icicle broke loose from my weathered being. *Useless?* That feeling had melted away.

**Lord, sometimes I feel I have so little to give. This week, help me identify resources at hand— possessions, talents, or even patience—that might help lighten someone's load and brighten someone's day.** —Evelyn Bence

**Digging Deeper:** Luke 14:3–9

---

# Saturday, January 18

**I have learned to be content whatever the circumstances. —Philippians 4:11 (NIV)**

We take meals to Sherry, a shut-in. She is mostly confined to her sofa due to limited mobility from ongoing pain. She lives in an older house trailer that would benefit from some repairs. Her front door refuses to stay closed without a struggle.

When my wife, Pat, and I bring her a meal, Sherry always manages to sit up. She is unable to open the milk carton and often needs help opening the foil meal container. While I do those things, Pat makes her a cup of tea. Some days she asks Pat to toast a bagel to eat with her lunch. Her world is small. She lives alone, rarely leaves home, and only occasionally seems to have family or friends visit her.

Even though Sherry's world is small, her joy is large. Noticing the ceiling in her living room sagging, I asked how long she had lived there. "The best investment I ever made . . . been here for sixteen years . . . just love living here," she beamed. On a day when she mentioned her pain had worsened, she talked instead about the beautiful day with bright sunshine and a crystal-clear sky, saying, "It makes me feel so good inside." After Christmas, I asked her about her holidays. She said, "It was a great Christmas! My two sisters came to visit!" Once when she was a bit disappointed that the menu had changed, she didn't complain.

Sherry always finds a way to be happy. What a gift to find thankfulness in every circumstance.

**Dear Lord, my difficulties are small and few. When the hard times come, help me to find contentment, like Sherry and the Apostle Paul, rejoicing in You.**
—John Dilworth

**Digging Deeper:** Psalm 118:24; Matthew 5:12; Philippians 4:8, 12

# Sunday, January 19

**And without faith it is impossible to please God, because anyone who comes to him must believe that he exists and that he rewards those who earnestly seek him. —Hebrews 11:6 (NIV)**

Hiking with Gracie on the Appalachian Trail, I crossed over a brook that connected two marshes. I saw what I thought was a small log roll into the water and shaded my eyes against the low winter sun. Then I realized that this log had a tail. And it was swimming.

I pointed it out to Gracie. "See?" Her nose perked up. "An otter!"

I love otters—don't you?—and this was the first one I'd seen in the wild. We stood for a while watching it circle. It came closer, apparently curious, and slapped its tail on the water. I don't know if it was a greeting or a territorial warning, but I laughed, and Gracie quivered with excitement.

"Happy hunting, my friend," I said.

River otters average about twenty to forty pounds and need to eat the equivalent of 15 to 20 percent of their body weight daily, especially in winter. That's a lot of fish. Warming myself in front of the woodstove back at the house, I thought about my spiritual sustenance. I don't know what my soul weighs—if anything—but I wondered if I nourish it properly every day. Do I maintain my spiritual diet?

There are so many ways to feed my soul. I can read the Bible more intentionally. I can reserve greater quiet time to meditate fully on God's goodness. I can reach out to the less fortunate as Jesus did. I can remember that I always walk with Him and never alone. *Yes,* I thought, tossing another log on the fire, *there is so much more I can do to grow my faith.*

**You nourish my soul, Lord, in so many ways. May I consume Your love fully today and every day.** —Edward Grinnan

**Digging Deeper:** Romans 10:17; Ephesians 2:8–9; James 1:5–8

---

## Martin Luther King Jr. Day, Monday, January 20

**. . . and walk in the way of love, just as Christ loved us and gave himself up for us as a fragrant offering and sacrifice to God. —Ephesians 5:2 (NIV)**

When a sculpture honoring Dr. Martin Luther King Jr. titled *The Embrace* was unveiled in Boston, I celebrated. The sculpture itself, however, was met with both praise and criticism. Some marveled at its beauty, while others expressed disdain over the sculptor's artistic choices.

The sculptor's inspiration was a 1964 photo that depicts Dr. King embracing his wife, Coretta, as they share a smile. The two had just received news that he had been awarded the Nobel Peace Prize, and their smiles and warm hug displayed the joy and achievement of the moment.

Inspired by Mahatma Gandhi's philosophy of nonviolent civil protest, Dr. King received the Nobel Peace Prize in recognition of his leadership in the nonviolent civil rights movement for Black Americans. When notified of the award, he committed to donate the $54,123 cash award to the movement, further solidifying his leadership and integrity.

For me, the sculpture, and more importantly the photo that inspired it, reveals a beautiful, softer side of Dr. King. Historians often point to his leadership in the 1963 March on Washington, his "I Have a Dream" speech, and his "Letter from a Birmingham Jail." I applaud Dr. King for these powerful moments in history, yet I am also influenced by Martin—the husband, the father, the man. His visible love for Coretta inspires me to not only seek to leave an imprint on my community, but to also cherish and love my husband, children, and extended family.

**Lord, as I love and serve my community, may I always love and serve my family first.**
—Carla Hendricks

**Digging Deeper:** Matthew 20:25–28; Ephesians 5:21–33

---

# Tuesday, January 21

**And my soul shall be joyful in the Lord.**
**—Psalm 35:9 (KJV)**

Rain beats against the bedroom window as my alarm wakes me from a deep sleep. The house is uncharacteristically quiet. I remember that Corinne and the kids are on a mini-vacation. I'm alone. The day ahead is filled with back-to-back appointments.

It all seems so gloomy. And then I remember a quote stuck on the wall behind my desk. "There are only two ways to live your life. One is as though nothing is a miracle. The other is as though everything is a miracle."

Inspired by these great words, I find a choice for today.

And don't we all make such choices every day? The Bible helps, reminding us to "rejoice," "be joyful," "watch," and "be a cheerful giver."

So, I choose. The barista at Starbucks seems as dreary as the weather. "You serve coffee to those who need a lift," I say, as I leave a cheerful tip. I sense a bit of miracle in our exchange.

In the office, I see my assistant, already hard at work. Only a miracle could bring me someone so willing to invest herself in my work.

The office is bright with light, the numbers rolling across my computer screen . . . nothing short of a miracle. The people below my office window, passing by under bright umbrellas, the music wafting from my car radio when I break for lunch. The clients, coming to trust me with their savings. Miracles, all.

I arrive home late. My family is there to welcome me. In every face, I see a miracle.

Father, in all things, You offer us a choice. Let us take joy in the miracles You send. —Brock Kidd

**Digging Deeper:** Isaiah 44:23; Luke 10:20

---

# Wednesday, January 22

**Do not be conformed to this world, but be transformed by the renewal of your mind, that by testing you may discern what is the will of God, what is good and acceptable and perfect. —Romans 12:2 (ESV)**

I usually wear a fancy watch that tracks all sorts of fitness data: my steps, heart rate, sleep quality, and many metrics I haven't yet explored. Yet, oddly, the time doesn't show unless you tap the watch face.

I bought the watch to stay healthy, and in the same vein, earlier this year, I decided to start journaling as a way to quiet my mind. But despite my best intentions and the enticing leather-backed, lined journal I purchased, I still hadn't written one word.

Instead of putting pen to paper, I talked myself out of starting a new habit because new habits are hard for me, and then this happened—my watch broke.

The screen flashed bright static, and then went dark and died. Unfortunately, the warranty had expired, and I was on the fence about investing in a new one. In the meantime, I found myself holding out my bare wrist and tapping it. I stared at my skin and expected the time to appear before common sense kicked in.

So it dawned on me that if I could develop a crazy habit without even trying, who knows what endless possibilities I could achieve with focus and intention?

**Dear Lord, guide me to use my time well—to develop new skills and form fulfilling habits. Help me to explore beyond what I have known.**
**—Sabra Ciancanelli**

**Digging Deeper:** 1 Corinthians 10:13; 2 Timothy 1:7

---

# Thursday, January 23

**See what great love the Father has lavished on us, that we should be called children of God! And that is what we are! —1 John 3:1 (NIV)**

"Good morning, Papi," I say with a kiss on his forehead.

"Good morning, my darling," he says with a sleepy smile.

Every day that my father still remembers who I am is a good day. I move his legs over the side of the bed and help him sit up. We walk to the bathroom and I make sure he keeps his balance. He stops at the table to examine a napkin, and again at the piano to fidget with a small candle.

It reminds me of my boys when they were toddlers, touching everything in their path.

Soon my father is bathed and brushed, his dentures are in, and he's dressed for the day.

My mother, who's been making breakfast, serves him a bowl of oatmeal, then goes into the bedroom to clean up.

"Papi, eat," I say. He looks up and smiles. I feed him his first bite and celebrate when he resumes on his own.

Later in the evening, I sit near him on the sofa. He takes my head in his hands and kisses my forehead as I'd kissed him that morning.

So much has changed throughout the years, and in so many ways, my father has become my child. But as I rest on his shoulder while he caresses my curls, this truth remains—I am loved, I am treasured, I'm forever his little girl.

**Lord, in this life, where everything changes, day to day, I rest in the comfort that I am Your child forever.** —Karen Valentin

**Digging Deeper:** Exodus 20:12; Proverbs 22:6

---

# Friday, January 24

**. . . for God gave us a spirit not of fear but of power and love and self-control. —2 Timothy 1:7 (ESV)**

"Mrs. Redmond, I believe you're having a heart attack."

I arched my eyebrows when the doctor made her surprising announcement. I'd experienced heartburn but none of the chest pain one normally associates with heart attacks. I'd come to the walk-in clinic that morning hoping to get a prescription for indigestion when over-the-counter remedies had failed to provide relief. A quick blood test confirmed the diagnosis. My concerned daughter, Bethany, was soon by my side. Before I really grasped what was happening, I was in an ambulance being whisked away to the nearest heart hospital.

My panic meter revs easily. But because of my growing relationship with Jesus, I didn't panic this time. Instead, I simply prayed, "Jesus, you've got this. I'm in Your hands." After years of experiencing His faithful, loving care, I knew I could trust Him—no matter what. As the drugs began to take effect, I prayed for focus, rattling off tasks I wanted Bethany to take care of, such as notifying my husband, who was out of state on travel, gently informing my elderly mother of the situation, and looking after my dog.

Despite my scary, unexpected circumstances, I wasn't flustered—the Lord had me in His loving hands. I didn't just feel it—I *knew* it with unshakeable certainty. My husband even made it to the hospital before my scheduled surgery, which I came through with flying colors. I feel so blessed to have experienced the "peace that surpasses all understanding." It's real.

**Dear Lord, thank You for being with me always.**
—Shirley Raye Redmond

---

# Saturday, January 25

### A faithful courier brings healing.
### —Proverbs 13:17 (JPS)

When my husband, Keith, died, our greyhound, Anjin, became my companion and guard. She seemed to fill at least a small part of the gaping hole Keith's absence left in my home.

After Anjin died, that chasm of loss enveloped me again.

My friend Dawn, who was very well plugged in with the Silken Windhound community of breeders, immediately told me about Halle, a seven-year-old female whose breeder was looking to rehome. "You and Halle are perfect for each other," she assured me. She called the breeder, drove the two hundred miles to the kennel, and brought Halle to me. For some reason, feeling helpless to thank her enough, I said only, "God knows I needed a dog!"

Three years later, when Halle died, I immediately knew that I still felt the emptiness keenly. Dawn said, "Your way of grieving for a dog is to get another dog." I agreed. I didn't tell her that it was the grief about Keith's loss that a dog seemed to help me live with. This time, however, there seemed to be no older female Silkens available.

Dawn called breeder after breeder, putting out the word, and I tried to keep sadness at bay, without a lot of success. Weeks elapsed—it felt like forever—and then Dawn called to tell me she'd found Dahlia. Dawn then drove the 825 miles to Dahlia's kennel to fetch her home to me.

**I know You understood how much I need a dog, Lord of Compassion; I am just overwhelmed that You impressed it so strongly on my friend Dawn.**
—Rhoda Blecker

**Digging Deeper:** Song of Solomon 8:6; Proverbs 16:20

---

# Sunday, January 26

## SEEMINGLY INSIGNIFICANT:
### Rock of Escape
**The Lord watches over you . . .** —Psalm 121:5 (NIV)

When gyms closed during the pandemic, my husband bought an elliptical machine. To motivate myself to use it, I started working out to the podcast *The Bible in a Year*, in which Father Mike Schmitz reads and comments on some Bible chapters daily. Hearing Scripture read in a different translation than my usual one grew my faith and magnified many minor-seeming moments and people in the history of God's family—hence this series, "Seemingly Insignificant."

For example, David escapes being killed by hiding from his murderous father-in-law, Saul, on the far side of a ridge. The site acquires the baffling name

Sela Hammahlekoth in the NIV (1 Samuel 23:28). In the podcast's RSV, it's "the Rock of Escape"—commemorating, Father Mike suggested, God watching over David without his even knowing it.

This minor naming moment among many in the Bible conjured a memory of my own recent rock of escape: an overlook I nearly fell off of while trying to get a camera view of a flock of birds circling the canyon walls below. I thought they were ordinary rock pigeons; a fellow birder saw exotic terns, found only in our region in migration. I was so convinced I was right that I leaned out too far and stumbled. If that guy hadn't caught my arm, I'd have died proving (or maybe not) my birding superiority.

Like David and other psalmists, I most often find myself praying about difficulties I want God to solve. That rock of escape hinted at all the problems and even deaths that God has surely saved me from unawares. The stupid choices of my youth. My parenting failures. My know-it-all-ness. My inadequate love. I feel, in retrospect, so loved.

**Thank You, Father, for keeping watch and protecting me from myself.** —Patty Kirk

**Digging Deeper:** 1 Samuel 23; Psalm 121:3

---

# Monday, January 27

**The light shines in the darkness, and the darkness has not overcome it. —John 1:5 (NIV)**

The dishwasher gave out, again. My favorite repair guy, Kevin, arrived and got right to work in the middle of the kitchen, where Olivia, my nine-year-old, was prepping for her bake sale. Her brow furrowed as she measured, and spilled, ingredients. "That's OK! Just clean it up," she said to herself out loud. "Everyone makes mistakes. Keep going."

In no time, Kevin had fixed the dishwasher and was gathering his tools. Olivia had scampered off to find her Barbies, her cookies baking away in the oven.

"Thank you again for coming so quickly," I told him, waving my hand at the sink piled with bake-sale prep bowls. "You've saved us again."

"I was having a horrible day," he told me, setting his tools down. "I just wanted to finish and get home, but then I got here and heard her voice saying the kindest things to herself over and over, and it really helped me slow down, relax. I may need to come hear that message every day!"

Later that night, I told Olivia about how her words and attitude had witnessed to someone without her even knowing. We talk a lot at our house about letting your light for Jesus shine so that others see it and can't help but know it's His love pouring out of you. I was proud of Olivia that afternoon not only for sharing her light but also for how she spoke to herself when she made mistakes—like the beloved child of God that she is!

**Lord, thank You for the words of precious children that remind us that You are near. Help me seek and share Your joy daily.** —Ashley Kappel

**Digging Deeper:** Matthew 5:16; John 9:5

---

## Tuesday, January 28

**He put a new song in my mouth...** —**Psalm 40:3 (NIV)**

Dad had been gone twenty years when I happened upon it cleaning. I'd put the pebbled leather case that held his cherished fiddle in a safe place. One where I wouldn't be reminded of "Wildwood Flower," the last tune he'd played before the cancer took him.

At the funeral home, I'd laid out the items that told Dad's story atop a lace-covered table beside his casket. His fiddle was the centerpiece, the crumbled rosin on its strings smelling of pine. Beside it was the Baby Ben alarm clock that woke him for work on the railroad, its hands positioned at 3:30, the time he left this world.

In calligraphy, I'd penned: "The moment the music stopped."

Folks nodded and smiled as they took in the mementos. I noticed a lady I'd never met pausing to reflect. "That's beautiful," she said. "But it isn't quite true, you know." When her words took me aback, she added: "My mama took ill; I lived away. They'd turned her power off. When your daddy learned about it, he didn't just pay what she owed.

He had them add her charges to his own bill. For the rest of her life."

The lady cradled my hand inside her own. She smiled at my father, then took in his now-silent fiddle. "If you live a life like that, the music never stops."

**When grief catches up with us, Lord, You put a new song in our hearts.** —Roberta Messner

**Digging Deeper:** Psalms 30:11, 71:23; Ephesians 5:19

---

# Wednesday, January 29

**That person is like a tree planted by streams of water, which yields its fruit in season.** —Psalm 1:3 (NIV)

A ninety-something woman I know expressed to me her sense of despair. She was feeling useless. Yet her record of ministry teemed with good deeds.

Mainly known as the "soup lady" for the gallons of soup she had prepared for the sick and shut-in over the years, she had also established a small financial-aid ministry, quietly and frequently slipping offerings into the hands of those needing help. And to the delight of those who worshipped with her, she reinforced her generous lifestyle by always singing vigorously in the congregational song services.

I searched for a way to help her—to encourage her to relish the gift of what truly should be the soup lady's golden years. But somehow at that moment, she'd relegated decades of service to meaninglessness.

It occurs to me that taking note of the help we offer right now—storing the satisfying feel of it in the recesses of our hearts—has its place in God's plan. Psalm 1:3 speaks of "yielding fruit in ... [our] season"—perhaps pointing toward a future time when that season has passed; when the Lord desires contentment for us; when sweet rest should reign as a remedy against debilitating uselessness.

In a work-driven culture, where identity is tied up with productivity, this seems a bit askew, but we might do well to ponder God's provision for a period of rest that is worth enjoying, a time when we can look back and be godly proud of the cup of soup we shared.

After all, if the Lord provides for us longevity, should we not be able to peacefully recall the fruit our season has produced?

**Lord, I praise You for the ability to help someone today. Help me to rest in this blessing should the time come when I am no longer able to assist.**
—Jacqueline F. Wheelock

**Digging Deeper:** Ecclesiastes 3:1; Hebrews 4:9

---

# Thursday, January 30

**Have you visited the storehouses of the snow?**
**—Job 38:22 (NLT)**

We have a snowplow for our four-wheeler. Due to its small stature, I cannot let the snow get too deep. Sometimes it seems like expecting an ant to move a watermelon when I have to lift the blade high to shove off the snow in layers. But I admit that, normally, the worst part is my teeth hurt from the cold because I cannot keep from grinning. On our quarter-mile-long driveway, high speeds are essential to throw the snow off of the road, so what's not to love? But last night's snow fell dense and clingy. Even with the blade lifted, I couldn't shove it as hard as it shoved me. I spent half the morning shoveling out my stuck ATV.

Texting my lament to my friend Chris, she replied, "Is it OK to say, 'Lord, help me endure my blessings?'"

Our area has been gripped by drought for more years than I can count. In my immediate discomfort, I'd forgotten my promise not to complain about the desperately needed moisture in whatever form it came. My temporary burden was actually an enormous gift for our region. The wetter the snow, the better the snow for recharging the groundwater aquifer.

Chris was right. Sometimes blessings come in wet, soggy lumps. "Weather is often just a friendly reminder that humans are *not* in control," I texted back.

**Forgive me, Father God, when I look only at my little problem. You see the whole world. Thank You for providing for us.** —Erika Bentsen

**Digging Deeper:** Leviticus 26:4; Job 38:22–30; Isaiah 40:12

# Friday, January 31

**Jesus replied, "They do not need to go away. You give them something to eat."** —Matthew 14:16 (NIV)

I awakened with a jolt. I dreamed our breakfast nook had expanded to the size of a hotel ballroom and was packed with relatives. *I only bought one can of biscuits and a roll of sausage. How will I feed them?*

A series of recent events spurred the dream. My husband's ninety-three-year-old grandmother had spent the night to discuss moving in with us. My husband wanted to impress her with a breakfast of biscuits and gravy. It was too much for me to make biscuits from scratch (to my husband's disappointment), so I grabbed a can of dough at the grocery store.

My mother had been hospitalized with a fractured pelvis. She'd need to stay at our house, too, while she recovered. Spare bedrooms could accommodate two elderly women on walkers, but we were overwhelmed with cleaning out our stuff to make room for their items, putting bars on shower walls, and many other details. Preparations exhausted us, yet we knew the real work would begin once they moved in. How could we manage this impossible situation while working full time?

Lastly, my weekly Bible study had been reviewing Matthew 14, so the feeding of five thousand was on my mind.

As I stared at the ceiling, I realized the dream wasn't a jumble of random events. Yes, Jesus multiplied the food, but the disciples dispersed it to the multitude. *I still do miracles,* I heard Him say. Through His power, I knew my husband and I would manage this well.

**You are the Lord of Miracles, Dear Jesus. When all I see is impossible situations, remind me that everything is possible with You! Amen.**
—Stephanie Thompson

**Digging Deeper:** Matthew 14:15–21; Luke 1:37; 1 Corinthians 2:5

## WITH AN EVERLASTING LOVE

1 _____

2 _____

3 _____

4 _____

5 _____

6 _____

7 _____

8 _____

9 _____

10 _____

11 _____

12 _____

13 _____

14 _____

15 _____

16 _____

17 _____

18 _____

19 _____

20 _____

21 _____

22 _____

23 _____

24 _____

25 _____

26 _____

27 _____

28 _____

29 _____

30 _____

31 _____

# February

And walk in love, as Christ also has
loved us and given Himself for us,
an offering and a sacrifice to
God for a sweet-smelling aroma.

—Ephesians 5:2 (NKJV)

# Saturday, February 1

**There are friends who pretend to be friends, but there is a friend who sticks closer than a brother. —Proverbs 18:24 (RSV)**

No one really expects to hear the truth at funerals. (Imagine if they did: "Doesn't Aunt Martha look natural?" Ummm... compared to what?) But the service for Susan's dad was an exception, because he was exceptional. That's why Ralph and I—both friends of Susan—dropped everything and drove 320 miles to New York City for the midweek service. It was all very sad, very inspiring... and very tiring, to then turn around for the trip back to Pittsburgh.

On the Pennsylvania Turnpike, Ralph and I rehashed the funeral, did a recap of the Pittsburgh Pirates' season (same result, another cause for mourning), then grew quiet. I asked Ralph a passing question—to clarify something he had said earlier about our friendship—and Ralph decided to tell me the truth: that I had become an absent-minded friend, increasingly attentive to my own interests and often clueless about those closest to me. I was a nice guy, polite, funny, etc., etc., but rarely present or fully engaged.

I was stunned and angry by what he said. Was forty years of friendship going to end like this? But something stopped me. He was right. I was sometimes more considerate of my students, even total strangers, than of the people in my own orbit. He. Was. *Right*.

Somewhere near Somerset, Pennsylvania, I uncorked the lump in my throat and thanked Ralph for both his candor and his bravery. We don't expect the truth at funerals, but we should. Good friends show up at funerals, and good friends are truthful, and the truth shall set us free.

**Lord, You gave me eyes to see, yet too often I look inward. Help me see others as You see them.**
—Mark Collins

**Digging Deeper:** Luke 15:27; Romans 14:15

---

# Sunday, February 2

**Then God blessed the seventh day and made it holy, because on it he rested from all the work of creating that he had done. —Genesis 2:3 (NIV)**

"Brush your teeth so I can pack your toothbrushes," I tell my kids, who are playing video games.

"Mami, you don't need all these clothes," I tell my mother. We need to make room for an electric blanket for my father. My sister's home in the countryside is chilly, and I know he'll need it.

I remove a few handfuls of clothing and fit the blanket in the now-empty spot. My mind is racing with everyone's needs, and when it's finally time to leave, I'm the only one with any sense of urgency. "We have to go!" I shout.

Next is the circus of hailing, loading, then unloading the taxicab. My kids and I heave bags over our shoulders and guide my parents across the street. When we get to the platform, the train is just rolling in. I settle everyone in their seats, lift our things onto the overhead compartments, then finally collapse onto a seat of my own. I stare out of the window in blissful silence, watching buildings become views of trees and hills.

I breathe in deeply and intentionally, grateful for this moment to "be" without "doing." In the grind of being busy, I seldom take a moment to be grateful for what God has given me. But now my mind is clear. I look across to my parents and thank God they are still in my life. I hear my children in the seat in front of me, and I'm grateful they're mine. I look out the window and see the beauty of nature, and I'm thankful to be alive to see it. Respite, Sabbath, and rest are mentioned so many times in the Bible. It's important. As I breathe in the blessings of my life on this train, instead of dwelling on all of my responsibilities, I finally understand why.

**Thank You, Lord, for moments of respite, and reminding me how important rest is, by Your very command.** —Karen Valentin

**Digging Deeper:** Mark 6:31; Hebrews 4:9–10

---

# Monday, February 3

**Guard your heart above all else, for it determines the course of your life. —Proverbs 4:23 (NLT)**

Getting ready to feed the horses, I shrugged into my barn jacket. Normally I coveted the peace of feeding time, but the last few days I'd been stewing over a situation so much that I remained irritated. It consumed my every thought.

Snugging down my Elmer Fudd hat, I glanced at the thermometer. It was -21 degrees F. *It's a great morning for my heavy wool mittens.* When I pulled them out of the resealable bag and slipped them on, I noticed that somehow the moths had evaded the protective bag and eaten big holes in the thumbs and palms. I stormed out the door anyway.

As soon as I stepped outside, the bitter cold penetrated through those holes. *Ouch! That's like frosty laser beams . . .* not unlike the thoughts that penetrated my attitude. By replaying the negative situation over and over, it'd eaten a hole in the shield of God's love that protected my heart. Instead of rehearsing the wrong, I needed to script the answer with God's love and meditate on that.

While feeding the horses, I scrunched up the mittens to cover the gaps. Nevertheless, my hands felt frozen by the time I got back up to the house. After tossing them into the "mending" pile, I opened my Bible and read aloud 1 Corinthians 13, to mend my heart by building up God's love in me.

**Lord, thank You for reminding me to constantly wrap Your everlasting love around my heart as a shield. Amen.** —Rebecca Ondov

**Digging Deeper:** Proverbs 13:3, 18:21, 21:23

# Tuesday, February 4

**Then you will know the truth, and the truth will set you free.** —John 8:32 (NIV)

When I was twelve years old, my mother died of cancer. After her death, I remember feeling happy, but I wasn't sure why.

A few decades later, after I was diagnosed with a brain tumor, I found out why. Praying one day, the memory of feeling "happy" after my mother's death came to my mind. And with it, a familiar rush of guilt.

However, soon a different interpretation entered my mind: What I had felt as a child hadn't been happiness, it was *relief*. I was relieved that my mother's suffering had ended. And when she died, the unnamed but very real feeling of sorrow and suffering that was part of my life ended as well. I no longer had to see my mother struggle to live with an illness that soon controlled all of our lives.

One day, after my brain tumor diagnosis, I had a dream. I was at the house we lived in when Mom was alive. I was twelve and sitting on the fence in my backyard. I didn't know what to do: stay on the fence or go inside the house? Suddenly, I saw Jesus standing next to me. We looked at each other. He told me, "Adam, your mother died. You didn't. It's OK to go on with your life. I'll take care of your mother." I looked at Him. "Are you sure?" "Yes," He said.

After a moment's hesitation, I jumped off the fence and ran down the alley, happy and shouting with glee. Then the dream ended. Shortly afterward, I had a successful brain surgery and life went on. The truth had set me free.

**Dear Lord, may we always seek Your truth. Amen.** —Adam Ruiz

**Digging Deeper:** Psalm 145:18; Mark 5:33; John 1:14

---

# Wednesday, February 5

**For when I am weak, then I am strong. —2 Corinthians 12:10 (NIV)**

"Oh! I *love* your ladybugs!" exclaimed the coat claim attendant as she handed me my jacket.

"Thank you," I replied, smiling. "I do too!"

My favorite jacket is dotted with patches: ladybugs, a fluffy sheep, butterflies, a little rainbow heart, music notes. Each one marks the place of a rip or tear. And, collectively, they are what causes me to love this jacket as I do.

Displaying my own rips and tears, though? That's a different story. They're not nearly as fun as my jacket's patches, and I'd *much* rather keep them tucked safely out of sight.

*That's not what Jesus did, though, was it?* I thought. Not only did He choose to keep the wounds the Crucifixion so agonizingly inflicted, they were what He'd *led* with when He approached His suffering disciples in their locked room after His death. "Look at my hands and feet," He'd said. "See that it is I myself."

This evidence of His humanity became one of the things that helped the disciples recognize the person in their midst as the Jesus they'd known and loved.

The world would have us believe our tender, fragile places are weak and shameful. But Jesus showed us—by so readily offering His own wounds forward—that they're anything but. They are, in fact, what make it possible for us to be authentically known. And this matters, because it's only through this kind of knowing—the risky, scary, real kind—that love, the mightiest superpower of them all, can exist.

**I pray to You, God, for the courage to accept vulnerability's risks, as Jesus did, so that I'm able to live and love as You would have me do.**
—Erin Janoso

**Digging Deeper:** Hebrews 4:15; 1 John 4:16–18

---

# Thursday, February 6

**And he said: "Truly I tell you, unless you change and become like little children, you will never enter the kingdom of heaven." —Matthew 18:3 (NIV)**

One day the stress of ministry was getting the best of me. There are times the pastoral issues and demands of the ministry can weigh heavily on a pastor.

Dealing with internal conflicts and intense differences of ideas among some church members was overwhelming. A dark and heavy cloud hung over me as I worked at my desk in the church building. I was feeling down when I heard voices outside.

I walked to the window to see what was happening. The children from our preschool program were laughing, running, and playing as they waited for their parents to pick them up. Children without worries and burdens, excited about life.

The longer I watched them, the better I felt about myself and my ministry. Their angelic voices and palpable joy lifted my spirits. The dark cloud over me disappeared. I felt renewed by the sight and sound of joy coming from the children. I knew instantly that God was watching over me.

Now, whenever I hear the voices of children at church, I stop what I am doing and walk to the window. The joy, energy, laughter, and smiles of the children fill my soul.

**God, thank You for the children in our world; may their joy, laughter, and playfulness fill our hearts.** —Pablo Diaz

**Digging Deeper:** Matthew 11:29; Luke 18:16

---

# Friday, February 7

**Since we live by the Spirit, let us keep in step with the Spirit. —Galatians 5:25 (NIV)**

I hurried up the stairs at our local rec center, anxious to get to a new stretching class. I wanted to be there on time, which is the best way to start a new class. I threw open the door and stepped into a class already in progress. A roomful of very fit women were lifting heavy weights above their heads. I knew immediately I didn't belong in this class, but I was already too far into the room to sneak back out easily.

I found a tiny space on the edge of a row and quietly collected the equipment others were using. I thought maybe I could fake my way through the class, which would be less embarrassing than trying to get out of the room. But I couldn't lift the weight higher than my waist. And I'm pretty sure I couldn't do that more than a couple of times without lying down to rest.

The Voice of Wisdom began talking to me: *You stepped into the wrong class and don't belong here. Why are you making this so hard? Be real: own your mistake and leave as quietly and quickly as possible.*

With that, I returned the equipment, picked up my water bottle, and even smiled at a couple of women who watched me leave. "Wrong class," I confessed. "I don't belong here."

As soon as I closed the door behind me, a weight was lifted from me.

**Lord, sometimes I don't tell the truth to protect myself from embarrassment. Help me be more vulnerable and honest, even in small ways, to remember and be who You made me to be.**
—Carol Kuykendall

**Digging Deeper:** Psalm 138; Proverbs 4

**Jesus said to them, "I am the bread of life. Whoever comes to me will never be hungry . . . ." —John 6:35 (NRSVUE)**

A hundred years ago, Lilias Trotter wrote: "[Bread] is needed by the gray-haired and the children, by the rich man in his castle and by the poor man in his tent, in all lands and in all ages." Such a simple observation—I'm not sure why it has captured my attention. Maybe it's my recent venture in kneading and eating.

The one exception to my long-standing dislike of baking with yeast is that I occasionally make soft pretzels. Easy enough—a little kneading but no rising, punching, waiting, or guessing. Last weekend, I went for it with some neighborhood teens who were sisters. "Divide the dough into twelve balls," I said. "In your palm, roll each into a rope." They molded most of the cords into heart shapes, "for love." They claimed all but three, and I relished two of them, warm from the oven. I sent the girls home, our appetites satisfied, our bodies ready for the remains of the day, which for me included kitchen cleanup and a brief nap. At dinnertime, I enjoyed the last of the hearty goods.

At bedtime, I happened upon the Lilias Trotter line above, followed by her analogous reference to the bread of life: "As the bread satisfies the hunger of the body, so this indwelling of Christ in us satisfies the hunger of the soul, until it becomes rested through and through."

Physically sustained by heart-shaped pretzels and newly refreshed by this reminder of spiritual nourishment, I quickly fell asleep, soundly satisfied.

**Lord, Bread of Heaven, feed us today. With gratitude we pray. Amen.** —Evelyn Bence

**Digging Deeper:** Luke 4:4; John 6:35–51

---

# Sunday, February 9

**But let those who love Him be like the sun when it comes out in full strength. —Judges 5:31 (NKJV)**

Wendy was both helpful and hilarious. It was midwinter and she was leaving the next day for Jamaica but still had managed to host a lovely reception at church for those being confirmed.

We stood around, feasting on Wendy's famous meatballs complemented by her gourmet spinach ravioli. I thanked Wendy and mentioned her upcoming vacation.

Wendy quipped, "I said to my husband, 'You decide! Either we go to Jamaica for two weeks or I go to the state hospital. Which is cheaper???'" We all burst out laughing.

Wendy had a point. Many of us were feeling the winter doldrums. For some, the freezing weather was compounded by an emotional winter of sorts due to chronic illness or a difficult family situation.

At home later that day, I pulled my chair up to the window. Cold and bleak as it was outside, I could feel the sun blazing through the glass and onto my face. I remembered the delicious food seasoned with Wendy's humor, and I laughed again.

I prayed a blessing for each person standing within that circle of friendship. Although we all couldn't fly south like Wendy, we still could enjoy God's gifts of warm fellowship and the delight of humor accompanied by bright winter sunshine.

**Thank You, Lord, for laughter and the inner warmth that it brings. Please provide sources of emotional, spiritual, and physical sunshine during this winter season.** —Lisa Livezey

**Digging Deeper:** 2 Samuel 23:4; Ezekiel 1:28; Acts 6:15; Revelation 1:16–17

---

## Monday, February 10

**Well, think again . . . fools—how long before you get smart? Do you think Ear-Maker doesn't hear, Eye-Shaper doesn't see? —Psalm 94:8–9 (MSG)**

Alan told me on Monday morning that his car had been stolen on Saturday night. "I'm sorry!" I said, and then, "How did you discover the car was gone?"

Alan explained, "I was picking up takeout food, and left the car for only a minute, when someone just stole it, and drove away. The police found it trashed three hours later, after it had been joy-ridden and smashed up, on the other side of town."

The following day, I saw Alan again. I was still thinking about this. Worrying about it. *What sort of city are we living in?!*

"You were gone for only a minute?" I asked Alan. I was thinking, *Not only are people awful, but they are brazen!* But then Alan fessed up. "I actually left the car running, the keys in it, while I ran inside the restaurant. I thought it would be OK—it always has been before." Alan will never do that again.

Likewise, I think of those occasions when I have entered a situation imagining that I knew everything, that I had nothing to learn from anyone else. I was in charge. Oh, have I been full of myself at times! I need to watch more, to listen more, to talk less.

**Lord, illumine my path today, even and especially if it means realizing that I am mistaken.**
—Jon M. Sweeney

**Digging Deeper:** John 8:29–32; James 4:14

---

# Tuesday, February 11

**Do not withhold good from those to whom it is due, when it is in your power to do it.**
**—Proverbs 3:27 (NRSVUE)**

Eric is a friend from church. We sing in choir, have served on various committees. We worked hard on our stewardship campaign, and even went on a men's retreat together. He's someone I wouldn't hesitate to call if I needed something.

Except this time. I was in the hospital, waiting for a surgical procedure (that word *procedure* seems such an attempt to downplay what can be a difficult and challenging time). My wife, Carol, had come by during the day, to sit by my hospital bed. But now it was evening, and as I was getting ready for bed, I discovered a desperate need. One that couldn't be met by the nurses and aides.

Dental floss. I'd just run out. I didn't want my wife to have to come back again. Who could I call?

I thought of all the emails and texts I'd received, saying, "Let me know if there's anything I can do to help." People say that—I've said it—but do you really want to call on them at 8:00 at night? Especially when it's something as mundane as needing dental floss.

I took a deep breath and called Eric. "Great," he said. "Glad to bring you some. I just bought a package and got more than I need." Forty-five minutes later, he arrived at my hospital room door. That night, when I fell asleep, my teeth were nice and clean.

When it comes to friendship, it's the little things that add up and count. And isn't it true of godly service? Dental floss on call.

**Lord, let no one be hesitant to call on me when I can be there and serve.**
—Rick Hamlin

**Digging Deeper:** Matthew 5:16; Galatians 6:2; Hebrews 13:16

# Wednesday, February 12

**Do not conform to the pattern of this world, but be transformed by the renewing of your mind.**
**—Romans 12:2 (NIV)**

I drive slowly down the interstate. Normally, traffic on I-80 moves well above the speed limit. But last night's freezing rain has made driving dangerous. If not for a meeting this morning, I wouldn't be driving to work—I'd be working from home to avoid these icy conditions.

As I drive, I see Iowa's fields on full display. There is no snow cover. Frozen mud is laid bare. February is my least favorite month. It lacks December's magic and January's novelty. In the Midwest, February is a frigid stretch of winter. On days like today, I can't help but wish I lived somewhere else. Somewhere warmer. Where the land is not flat. Where green things grow all year.

Ahead, I see a string of trees beside a field. The trees are scraggly from tough lives lived along the interstate. Their branches are brown and bare. Then, as I draw closer, the image changes. The trees, which are coated in thick ice, catch sunlight. And they are transformed. Fine branches shimmer. The weak winter sun is refracted and thrown back in brilliant color. The beauty is distracting. I take care to focus on the road.

I pass the trees, catching a final glance of their beauty. Then I am once again driving along empty, brown fields. But I have a newfound appreciation for God's creative glory. And I am now aware of the power of perspective.

**Father, help me to see Your goodness in all You have created.** —Logan Eliasen

**Digging Deeper:** Matthew 13:44; 2 Corinthians 4:16

---

# Thursday, February 13

**But the fruit of the Spirit is love, joy, peace, forbearance, kindness, goodness, faithfulness. —Galatians 5:22 (NIV)**

I'm a list writer. Lists help me feel like I'm more organized than I actually am. They help me to maintain my focus and keep me on track. And when I've crossed off one of my goals, it gives me a feeling of accomplishment.

For more years than I can remember, every Monday morning, I list five things I hope to accomplish that week. My goals for the week aren't pie-in-the-sky ideas—they are simple goals to keep me on track. The first four are almost always the same: 1. Make progress on my current writing project. 2. Bible Study. 3. Progress on my current knitting project. 4. What I call "extra reading"—a chapter in a book that inspires my walk with the Lord, or the current book club choice. The fifth one is the one that varies from week to week. One week it might be a decluttering project or encouraging notes of appreciation to those who have touched my life—whatever the Lord puts in my mind.

I keep track each day, writing down what I did to fulfill that goal. At the end of the week, if I followed through and made progress on my list, I give myself a big red star. Success!

It seems the Lord keeps lists Himself. The Ten Commandments are one example, but He doesn't stop there. His lists continue all through Scripture: the Beatitudes (Matthew 5:3–12); the building blocks of faith (2 Peter 1:5–7); and the fruit of the Spirit, the attributes of a mature Christian (Galatians 5:22–25).

Lists, lists, and more lists. It's fun to search through Scripture and make note of the lists God has. Now *those* are lists worth noting.

**Father, thank You for the lists You have given me to guide my walk in grace.** —Debbie Macomber

**Digging Deeper:** Matthew 5:3–12; Ephesians 6:13–18

---

# Friday, February 14

**Two can accomplish more than twice as much as one . . .** —Ecclesiastes 4:9 (TLB)

Although I have been married to Sharon for a lifetime, there is another wife in my future. I know this because Sharon has told me a lot about her:

"Your next wife will pick up the clothes you leave lying around."

And, "Your next wife will make your favorite cake every day."

Obviously, my next wife is a spectacular woman, and I can hardly wait to meet her.

Somewhere in midlife I caught on to the value of this imaginary second wife, who would do all the things my current wife doesn't like to do. So, I invented "the second husband."

"Your next husband will be rich, and you can travel the world."

"Your next husband will massage your smelly feet every night."

What I have learned from this imaginary second spouse is that no one husband or wife can be everything the other needs, all the time. Sharon is not "Queen of the Amazons," and Dan is not "Master of the Universe." Sometimes Sharon will pick up after me, and sometimes she will make that burnt-sugar cake. We did travel to London for our fiftieth anniversary, and sometimes I will do her smelly feet . . . with a clothespin on my nose.

As we age, we have even less energy, but learning to work together as a couple is an ongoing process, and we have discovered that "one plus one equals three." It's about being grateful for what we have left.

For a first wife, Sharon is a rather spectacular woman.

**Remind me, Lord, not to expect from others what they cannot give.** —Daniel Schantz

**Digging Deeper:** Deuteronomy 24:5; Proverbs 18:22

# Saturday, February 15

**I know that you can do all things; no purpose of yours can be thwarted. —Job 42:2 (NIV)**

"Build a snowman," Junie, my granddaughter, declared. I didn't know how to tell her, at age three, that the winter wonderlands she had witnessed on her favorite cartoon were not possible to re-create in the middle of her neighborhood in Casa Grande, Arizona.

I stared at the dry urban landscape around us. Creosote bushes. Tall saguaro cactus. Spindly palo verde trees. Everything had barbs, thorns, and prickers. Not exactly the best snowman-building materials.

"Let me push you on the swings," I suggested, wanting to avoid disappointing her with an unrealized dream. As a former Minnesota girl, I considered myself an expert on building snowmen. I understood the importance of having snow just sticky enough to hold together. Of having charcoal eyes and a carrot nose. Of finishing with a colorful hat and mitts.

The desert sun beat down on us. The closest thing to anything cold were the ice cubes in the refrigerator. Her idea was impossible.

"Build a snowman," Junie repeated. She grabbed a small boulder and scooched it into place. She scoured the playground for the next tier—a roundish rock for the snowman's head. Tiny twig arms were next, but she was not yet satisfied. Something was missing.

"Let me help you find a hat," I said. We searched for several minutes until we found a flat black stone. Junie placed it on the top of her stone structure, tilting it until it balanced.

She stepped back. Nodded.

A desert snowman.

**Help me persevere with my dreams today, Jesus, even when others declare them to be impossible.**
—Lynne Hartke

**Digging Deeper:** Jeremiah 32:17; Matthew 19:26

---

# Sunday, February 16

**Praise be to God, who has not rejected my prayer or withheld his love from me! —Psalm 66:20 (NIV)**

I pulled up to my storage unit location the night before my movers were set to arrive. I wanted to make sure everything was prepared; I didn't want any surprises the day of the move.

To my frustration, after entering the keypad gate code several times, the gate remained shut, without any sign of movement. I begged God to please open the door by some miracle. I called the company, but because it was late, no one answered the phone. I was able to get an automated prompt to provide a temporary code to try. That didn't work either! The next day was a holiday, which meant the office would not be open the day of my move to release the gate then either.

I sat there, dwelling in the impossibility of my situation, wondering how I would reschedule my entire move. I felt so discouraged. I decided to look again at the original email confirmation, and I discovered that my storage unit was actually at a completely different, and nearby, address. I was at the wrong place. I drove to the correct one, feeling quite ridiculous but grateful for this answer to my prayer, and the door opened with ease.

**Help me, Father, to always hear Your voice, and to know when a door in my life is meant to be opened or to be left alone.** —Nicole Garcia

**Digging Deeper:** Isaiah 22:22; Colossians 4:3; Revelation 3:8

---

# Presidents' Day, Monday, February 17

**For there is no authority except from God, and those that exist have been instituted by God.** —**Romans 13:1** (ESV)

The Secret Service led us into the Rose Garden. What a surreal moment! So much green. I was a sixteen-year-old desert kid, and green was something I hadn't seen much of. But there I was, part of my high school music group, invited to meet the president of the United States. It was 1982, and Ronald Reagan was at the helm. To be honest, I didn't know a whole lot about him. Or about presidents at all. My mind was kept busy with rock bands and guitars and girls.

Still, I knew enough to sense this was an important occasion. There was a solemnity in the air, heavy and quiet. And then there he was, just like in the pictures. All these decades later I remember with real clarity the moment he smiled and shook my hand.

It's interesting now to think about what an important event meeting a sitting president was in my life. Something I'll never forget. And yet sometimes it actually slips my mind that I walk daily with the arm of the Creator of the Universe around my shoulder. A Being so much higher than any president, it's incomprehensible to the human mind.

Today I'll remember. I'll be thankful for the freedom I have in America to cast my vote for the highest office in the land. But even more so, I'll be thankful the God of the Universe loves me and still will when this earth and all it holds are only a distant memory.

> **Creator of All, no king takes his throne but by Your will. I will trust You in all things.**
> —Buck Storm

**Digging Deeper:** Isaiah 9:6–7; Romans 13:1–7

---

# Tuesday, February 18

**And this is the testimony, that God gave us eternal life, and this life is in his Son. —1 John 5:11 (ESV)**

It's time to say goodbye to our treasured friend, Jim McGimpsey. We're all believers, so we know we'll tread together again—next time on heavenly ground. But this man is dear. He's mentored my husband and reached into the lives of my boys. We've walked behind Jim and his wife for years, gleaning grain that fed our marriage, our parenting, and our relationships with the Lord.

Our friend is in the hospital and can't respond, but I believe that he can hear. My husband and I speak words of thanksgiving and words of love. Each of my boys has shared something they want me to share with their friend. "Please tell him," my grown son Logan had said, "that I remember when I was little, when we talked, Mr. McGimpsey always bent low."

I could see it with my heart. Five different boys. Jim leaning low to see them. To hear them. To make sure the connection was clear. Later, when those boys were teens, Jim spoke words of wisdom to their daddy and me. "Meet them where they are," he said. "If they play basketball, shoot hoops. If they read, get a copy of that book."

Jim's easy way made others listen. His love helped them catch a glimpse of the Lord. Once in a while, we may have the opportunity to meet someone who helps us learn of and long for Jesus. When we do, it's treasure.

But Jim knew, thanks to the gospel and grace of our Lord Jesus Christ, that the best is yet to come.

**Lord, thank You for those who share Your love in ways that leave us longing for more of You. Help me to live that way too. Amen.** —Shawnelle Eliasen

---

## Wednesday, February 19

**One of those listening was a woman from the city of Thyatira named Lydia, a dealer in purple cloth. She was a worshiper of God. The Lord opened her heart to respond to Paul's message. —Acts 16:14 (NIV)**

I had put off getting a winter coat, and the one that I was wearing had seen better days. I had decided to wait until next year when an ad appeared on my phone for a flash sale that included a beautiful coat on clearance.

The only problem was that the coat pictured was a startlingly bright fuchsia color that I would never wear. I investigated other options, but only the coat pictured was heavily discounted. Black, dark blue, and forest green were available but at double the price.

*Is it really that bright?* I asked myself. *Could I wear this?* On a whim, I bought it. The coat arrived days later. I gasped when I took it from the plastic bag. The color was even more intense in person, but the fabric was soft and super cushy. I put it on. It fit perfectly and was, without a doubt, the most comfortable coat I had ever worn.

I decided to test it out at the grocery store. As I went through the aisles, no one seemed to notice. I had forgotten about the color when the cashier handed me the receipt.

"Great coat!" she said.

I felt a little lighter on the way out and wore it the next morning. In line to get coffee, the woman behind me said, "I love your jacket."

**Lord, thank You for stretching me in silly ways. For showing me that as I grow, You will comfort me, and for the kind words of strangers encouraging me to go beyond my comfort zone and brighten up the winter.**
—Sabra Ciancanelli

**Digging Deeper:** Proverbs 31:22; Philippians 1:14

---

# Thursday, February 20

**Create in me a clean heart, O God; and renew a right spirit within me. —Psalm 51:10 (KJV)**

"Adversity introduces a man to himself." This quote, often attributed to Albert Einstein although the true source is unknown, hit home. My niece, Haley, was in the first week of her very first job. At this busy restaurant, all employees had to be proficient at every task. She scrambled to memorize menu codes and learn how to clean restrooms, fill ice machines, and prep food.

As I prayed for her to get through the challenging learning curve, I remembered my own struggles as a hotel housekeeper prior to college. I was awful. Lugging stacks of sheets, towels, cleaning supplies, complimentary items, and a vacuum cleaner up and down stairs to individual suites was exhausting. I couldn't get the knack of perfectly crisp sheets, pirouettes of towels, washcloths shaped into decorative fans. I was slower than everyone else. I made more mistakes. "Why do I need to know how to fold the first sheet of toilet paper?" I whined to Dad. "I'd rather do something else."

"You cannot quit until you have mastered the job," he said. "Otherwise it will master you."

That left me examining my heart. The person I met in my test of adversity wasn't the person I wanted to be. Once I ran from a difficulty, I might never stop running. But shifting my attitude wasn't something I could do under my own power. Fortunately, I knew the One who could help me with a total makeover. With a fresh outlook, I defeated fear. When I left for college, I was proud of what I could do.

**Lord, help us when we meet ourselves and long to be more like You.** —Erika Bentsen

**Digging Deeper:** Psalm 86:11; Proverbs 11:2

---

# Friday, February 21

**You are completely beautiful, my beloved! —Song of Solomon 4:7 (LEB)**

Looking into the face of my two-year-old grand-daughter was like looking into a mirror that reflected time gone by. Taylor had the same red hair I'd had as a child, hair that had long since turned a mélange of grays and white on my own head. Her eyes squinted almost closed when she laughed and smiled, which was often. Just like me. We both loved dancing and tapioca—and each other.

But Taylor was in the early spring of her life, while I was headed from fall into winter, the wrinkles on my face becoming more prominent with every passing year. These days, when I looked into a mirror, I was surprised to see an old woman staring back at me.

But as Taylor and I were playing together one morning, she put her hands on my cheeks, and turned my face toward hers. In her halting, toddler voice, she said gently, "Bea-u-ti-ful!" Then she gave me a kiss. I blushed like a schoolgirl.

That word hadn't been said about me in a very long time. I missed feeling pretty, let alone anything akin to beautiful. But Taylor's sweet benediction had a lasting effect. Now, when I look in the mirror, I remind myself of how my granddaughter sees me—the very same way my heavenly Father does, from the inside out.

**Father, help me feel at home in who You created me to be, uniquely beautiful, eternally loved.**
—Vicki Kuyper

**Digging Deeper:** 1 Samuel 16:7; Psalm 139:14; Proverbs 16:31, 20:29; Ecclesiastes 3:11; Isaiah 46:4–5; 1 Peter 3:3–4

# Saturday, February 22

**I rejoiced greatly in the Lord that at last you renewed your concern for me. —Philippians 4:10 (NIV)**

When my grandson Ethan was sixteen, he and I flew to Maui to visit my daughter Jeanne and her family. They had moved to Maui for fourteen months during the COVID-19 pandemic.

Since the results of our COVID tests had not come back in time, Ethan and I were told we'd be quarantined in a hotel near the airport for two weeks after our arrival. We were only planning to stay sixteen days. Horrified, my eyes filled with tears, knowing Ethan's Hawaiian vacation would be ruined by having to spend most of it in a hotel room with his grandma.

On the plane I asked Ethan, "What are you writing?"

"A list of things we can do in the hotel room," he answered cheerfully.

He shared his list: 1. Daily exercise: jumping jacks and ski motion on the bed. 2. Toga party in hotel room sheets. 3. Game night: eye spy, leapfrog, ceiling darts, card toss. 4. Crafts made from food. 5. Write funny messages on the toilet paper. 6. Reenact scenes from TV sitcoms. 7. Crash Zoom meetings. 8. Make a tent from blankets and pillows. 9. Balcony singing day. 10. Ghost stories. 11. Movie marathons.

I laughed halfway to Hawaii, thanking God that my grandson was so much more optimistic than his grandmother was.

Thankfully, our test results were waiting when we landed—I thanked God again that they were negative—so Ethan and I visited every part of the island, swam, and snorkeled with sea turtles. He even learned to surf. I learned from Ethan how to make lemonade out of turnips when things might not go as planned.

**Father, help me not to grumble or whine when things go wonky. Help me find You and joy in every situation instead.** —Patricia Lorenz

**Digging Deeper:** Psalm 37:5; Galatians 6:10; Hebrews 11:15–16

---

## Sunday, February 23

**But the tax collector, standing far off, would not even lift up his eyes to heaven but was beating his breast and saying, "God, be merciful to me, a sinner!" —Luke 18:13 (NRSVUE)**

The first time Dad left the house after Mom died was to attend church. For months afterward, it was nothing but church and grocery shopping. This surprised me for two reasons. First, Dad hadn't attended church during the last years of Mom's illness, preferring to stay with her. Second, I knew he was deeply disturbed that Mom had not been healed despite all his prayers and tears.

He had never hidden what many of us keep secret: bargaining with God. Dad felt that if he did his part, God's part was to make life gentle for those he loved. He'd prayed Mom and he would go together, gently, probably holding hands.

Don't we all?

For more than a year, I've watched Dad hold to God despite ravaging grief, added to seven years of watching Mom decline. Whatever he feels about God's will regarding my mother—or any of us as we have suffered various illnesses and loss—he has remained faithful in a way that is remarkable to me. I know he questions God, that he is angry and disappointed, lonely. I have seen him bow his head in church, as though accepting something all but impossible for him to accept.

In a way, I envy him. I hardly dare question God, much less feel anger about His will or try to bargain with Him. I'm thought of as the one in my family with great faith. I watch Dad. And I wonder.

**Almighty God, strengthen my faith so that my fear of You is not as strong as my trust in You.**
—Marci Alborghetti

**Digging Deeper:** Psalm 51:3–12; Isaiah 54:8–10

---

# Monday, February 24

**Then I heard the voice of the Lord saying, "Whom shall I send? And who will go for us?" And I said, "Here am I. Send me!" —Isaiah 6:8 (NIV)**

Ever since I heard a missionary from Africa speak at my childhood church, I've been intrigued by the idea of helping people in faraway places. These spurts of goodwill remained daydreams until I volunteered a few years ago as a local speaker on preparedness for the American Red Cross. How I admired the other volunteers who raced to help at house fires, who staffed the shelters during ice storms that knocked out power! Yes, I used my teaching skill set, but my efforts felt so mundane.

Then our church became involved in Family Promise, a nonprofit program that gives shelter and meals to a working family that has lost its home. Churches rotate weekly to provide inflatable beds, evening meals, breakfast, and bagged lunch for parent(s) and children. Parishioners contribute the food, and those who have completed safe church training sleep overnight to monitor, set up breakfast, and steer the family to lunch options. I agreed to volunteer.

After my first overnight, I joined two young boys eating cereal while their mother made lunches before heading to work and school. I found the sandwich bags for her—more mundane effort. Yet simple "thanks" as the family departed made me realize that help wouldn't have to be dramatic to be useful. Like Isaiah, I let God use me where I'm most needed, even though I don't travel—just descend a flight of stairs in my church.

**Lord, where do You need me today? I'm ready.**
—Gail Thorell Schilling

**Digging Deeper:** Jeremiah 1:7; Matthew 10:42; 1 Peter 4:10

**From heaven the LORD looks down and sees all mankind. —Psalm 33:13 (NIV)**

Excited to check an item off our bucket list, my husband and I traveled to the Dominican Republic. While there, we took excursions to see more of the country, traveling in open-air buses. Passing through small villages, I observed the locals going about their lives outside and on foot, undeterred by the oppressive heat while I was thankful our hotel had air conditioning. I felt detached from them, like we were two worlds passing each other in space, simply coexisting.

But during one trip, something wonderful happened. On a sidewalk beside the road, three little girls stood on blocks, waving to each bus that passed by. I waved back, and their faces broke into wide grins, and they jumped up and down with excitement, waving with all their might. Their joy was contagious, and my smile returned theirs.

As a result, I started waving at everyone we passed. Magically, their faces transformed from sullen to joyful as they smiled and waved back.

Such a simple gesture, but the result was powerful. We had connected by seeing each other, acknowledging each other's presence. I was no longer just a tourist, and they were no longer just locals. We were united, part of God's creation, and that fact gave us value.

Sometimes, I've felt unnoticed by others, even invisible, but I know I'm not invisible to God. One of

His names is "El Roi," which means "the God who sees me" (Genesis 16:13). He sees and values all of us.

**Thank You, Lord, for seeing me, for knowing where I am and what's going on in my life, even when no one else does.** —Marilyn Turk

**Digging Deeper:** Psalm 33:18; Proverbs 15:3; 1 Peter 3:12

---

# Wednesday, February 26

**The LORD is close to the brokenhearted and saves those who are crushed in spirit. —Psalm 34:18 (NIV)**

It happened so quickly. One Friday our pup Colby was enjoying a walk through the park. The next week, we were in the vet's office finding out he was riddled with cancer and making the really hard and sad decision to put him to sleep.

That night, the kids asked when we would die, when they would die, and what would happen next.

The first two are tricky, of course. No one knows the timing of a life or God's plan. But that last one, we spent hours on it. In the end, the kids decided that heaven must be a place of race tracks, ball fields, ice cream shops, and lazy beach afternoons.

"How can there be *no* tears in heaven, Mom?" James asked before bed. "Isn't Colby sad we aren't there?"

Sweet boy. If only you knew that there can be no sadness once you're in God's presence, something impossible to understand when you haven't stood in His glory.

We still cry about, and for, our sweet Colby. When the school does check-ins on feelings, my kids' hands go up with Colby's sad tale.

But we also remind them to remember and be thankful for the good times that God gave us and the promise of life with Him that comes with our faith. Now, I don't know if dogs get to go to heaven, but in those moments, I can't help but think that God was looking down on us with a fuzzy golden retriever right by His side.

**Lord, help me to look for the good moments while I'm in them. Give comfort to those who grieve and remind them of our eternal homecoming after death.** —Ashley Kappel

**Digging Deeper:** Isaiah 40:1–31; Matthew 5:4

---

## Thursday, February 27

# SEEMINGLY INSIGNIFICANT: Praying for Others' Faith
**I will lift up my eyes to the hills—From whence comes my help? —Psalm 121:1 (NKJV)**

The brief story of Elisha's servant in 2 Kings always thrills me. Early one morning, he leaves where he and Elisha are staying and finds "an army with horses and chariots have surrounded the city." He rushes back, wailing, "Oh no, my lord! What shall we do?" After reassuring his servant in vain, Elisha prays, "Open his eyes, Lord, so that he may see," and the servant is able to see "hills full of horses and chariots of fire" and be reassured that Elisha and he are the ones with superior forces.

In Elisha's sandals, I would've prayed a different prayer: that God would protect me. Or maybe, if I were particularly fond of my servant, that God would protect *us*. But I'd be more concerned about surviving than about my servant seeing anything. Elisha has no worry about survival at all. Rather, he prays for his servant's faith.

Who is this servant whose faith matters so much to Elisha? He's not named. Of no importance that we know of. His panicked voice sounds young, but the story doesn't say so. We get no details about him besides this word *servant*, someone whose main job would've been to "pour water on the hands of [his master]" (2 Kings 3:11).

He's just some nameless, maybe young, terrified nobody. But what he sees—that he's able to see the invisible—matters more to his master than any assistance he might provide in this moment.

That's how we are to *our* Master. Whoever we are, however unimportant, however pathetically terrified, Jesus just wants us to recognize our actual circumstances and believe.

**O Lord God, light our eyes, lest we sleep death's sleep!** —Patty Kirk

**Digging Deeper:** 2 Kings 6; Psalm 13:3

**Where can I go from your Spirit? Where can I flee from your presence? If I go up to the heavens, you are there; if I make my bed in the depths, you are there. —Psalm 139:7–8 (NIV)**

Our first vacation in three years, and the Mexican Riviera was paradise. That evening, my husband, Michael, and I visited a restaurant called 2087. With the numerical name, I wondered if it had a futuristic theme.

"It's the longitude and latitude of this place," Michael explained. "Twenty degrees north and eighty-seven degrees west."

After a delicious meal, a quick Google search revealed that longitude and latitude are the invisible lines that mapmakers have used to divide the planet horizontally and vertically, and the measurements define the precise location of a point on earth. *Of course!* I used GPS frequently while driving, but I'd never pondered the notion that each place on earth had a measurable precise location.

Back home, I discovered the longitude and latitude of our house. That got me to thinking—what precise locations could be pinpointed in other realms? What if I could determine exactly where I was emotionally, mentally, and spiritually? Better yet, was there a measurement to gauge where I was with God?

Church attendance, Bible reading, a consistent quiet time, how I treat my neighbor, and how morally upright I am are good indicators of where

I am with God, but I don't think my precise location with the Almighty can been measured outwardly. Where I am with God is a private location. Only He really knows the longitude and latitude of my heart—how spiritually near or far away I am from Him.

**Dear God, no matter where I go as I travel through life, keep my precise spiritual location on the right path—always near to You. Amen.**
—Stephanie Thompson

**Digging Deeper:** Psalms 23, 145:18; James 4:8

## WITH AN EVERLASTING LOVE

1 _____

2 _____

3 _____

4 _____

5 _____

6 _____

7 _____

8 _____

9 _____

10 _____

11 _____

12 _____

13 _____

14 _____

15 _____

16 _____

17 _____

18 _____

19 _____

20 _____

21 _____

22 _____

23 _____

24 _____

25 _____

26 _____

27 _____

28 _____

# March

Let all that you do be
done in love.

—1 Corinthians 16:14 (ESV)

**But blessed are your eyes, for they see, and your ears, for they hear. —Matthew 13:16 (ESV)**

I hadn't been on one of my jaunts around my farm, Ploughshares, and its woods lately, mostly because the weather has been frigid and my old bones preferred to stay indoors. But Lilly, our four-and-a-half-year-old great-granddaughter, came for a visit and she wanted to go on a cart ride. So, we bundled up and headed out.

Lilly loves to talk and has all sorts of questions. "What lives in the creek besides fish?"

I told her about the beavers who hang out there. I pointed out bird's nests up the trees. Squirrels scampered across our path. A hawk circled overhead.

As the trail came close to the creek, I pointed out where the beavers had been gnawing on trees. She was amazed that creatures could do that. I told her life was all around us. Even when we didn't see it.

We putt-putted around a corner of the woods, and there stood a magnificent six-point buck. He just watched us as we stopped to watch him. Then he bounded off into the woods.

Lilly was thrilled. As was I. "I can't wait to tell GiGi and Ya-Ya (her grandmother)."

As we headed to the warm house, I reflected on how, from inside the house, it didn't look like much was happening around Ploughshares. But when

I got out in it, it was teeming with activity—some I witnessed, and some I saw evidence of. That is so much like my faith life. Too often I stay someplace that feels emotionally or spiritually safe and warm instead of stepping out of my comfort zone—and so I miss the Spirit working in amazing ways.

**Oh God who is always present, slow me down so that I might behold Your eternal presence in my own life. No matter where I am, You are there. Amen.** —J. Brent Bill

**Digging Deeper:** Isaiah 42:1–9

# Sunday, March 2

**The heavens declare the glory of God, the sky proclaims His handiwork. —Psalm 19:2 (JPS)**

After my husband, Keith, died, I started using the television as white noise. I can work without really listening or watching, but the sound fills some of what could seem like an empty house.

Sometimes, though, I hear something that makes me pay attention. It's as if God installed a circuit in my brain that lights up occasionally in spite of me. That happened recently when the station that provides my local news did a new plug for some of its coverage: "Weather connects us all," one of the meteorologists said, "but nobody wants to be surprised by the sky." My brain immediately snapped to attention and said, "Wait. What?"

I love being surprised by the sky. Every morning when I go outside with the dog, the sky seems to me to be God's canvas, sometimes a deep, clear blue, other times a solid metallic gray. Clouds in various forms can hang overhead or dance by on the wind. A daytime moon is always unexpected, soft white instead of glowing. While the dog is running around, I often fancy that the sky is hinting at God's mood for the day.

I used to jokingly regret that I had not become a meteorologist "because then I could be wrong 90 percent of the time and still have everyone believe me." But if one of the aims of the weather report is to take the surprise out of the sky, I'm really glad I majored in something else in college.

**I feel Your presence so often in the open air, God of Nature, and it always surprises me.**
—Rhoda Blecker

**Digging Deeper:** Psalm 36:5–6; Daniel 12:3

---

# Monday, March 3

**At the end of forty days Noah opened the window of the ark that he had made and sent forth a raven. It went to and fro until the waters were dried up from the earth. —Genesis 8:6–7 (ESV)**

For most of a day, I'd felt overwhelmed with the humdrum responsibilities of adulthood. Late afternoon, I sighed when the phone rang. It was a neighbor girl with special needs calling for no special reason; she was bored. We often talk after school, but right then I was busy and didn't encourage conversation. "My mind is on a project. I'm doing banking and paying bills. We'll chat later, not now."

She quickly responded, "Is it an open mind or a closed mind?"

Huh? "What did you say? Do you know what those words mean?"—a question I often ask.

Despite her initial oddball, off-target question, she explained pretty well. She continued, "For example, pretend there's a substitute teacher. If you have an open mind, you'll say OK and try to learn something. If you have a closed mind, you'll think, *This is the worst day of my life.*"

I smiled. "You learned this at school? I think you've got it." I then quickly suggested that she shake off her boredom—pull out a jigsaw puzzle or dribble a ball in the park.

As for me, I pulled my mind away from my domestic chores, opened a window, and inhaled deeply—a breath of fresh air that gave my flagging spirit a second wind.

**Dear God, I think of Noah, who opened the window of the closed, stuffy ark. Show me when and how to open my heart, soul, and mind to see the hopeful possibilities of positive thinking.**
—Evelyn Bence

**Digging Deeper:** Genesis 8:6–11

# Tuesday, March 4

**I lift up my eyes to the hills. From where does my help come? My help comes from the Lord, who made heaven and earth. —Psalm 121:1–2 (ESV)**

I've recently learned that total knee replacement surgery is a boatload of fun. If your idea of fun is pain, a walker, and a bathroom that somebody moved about two hundred yards away from your bed while you were under the knife. But beat your body up long enough and eventually things wear out. What can you do?

I knew it was coming. Thought I was ready. Looking back, I'm not sure. If there's something in life I really don't like, it's feeling helpless, and the first week or two (or four) after a total knee replacement, that's exactly what you are. I'm blessed to have a family that rallied around me.

Flat on my back, my leg propped up on three or four pillows. Not going anywhere soon. I tried to read, but my mind wouldn't focus. TV, same. Forget writing. Not much to do but watch the snow fall on the other side of the window and think about that faraway bathroom.

No, I don't like helplessness, but I've found God does. How many times have I crawled out of life's latest crash site to find Him standing there?

"Finally," He says.

"That hurt."

"It was supposed to."

"All right, but that bad?"

89

A smile. "Hold still and let Me hold you."
And He does.

**Thank You, God, for always meeting me in the broken places. Thank You for Your arms around me. For lifting me out of my too-often self-imposed wreckage.** —Buck Storm

**Digging Deeper:** Psalm 34:18; Romans 15:13

---

# Ash Wednesday, Wednesday, March 5

**Then the LORD God formed a man from the dust of the ground and breathed into his nostrils the breath of life, and the man became a living being.** —Genesis 2:7 (NIV)

My mom, my husband, and I returned to our spots on the pew. The priest had just placed ashes on our heads. The organ quieted, and the priest smiled. Heavily drawn extra-large crosses spanned our foreheads.

"You might have noticed," Father Pat said. "I make my crosses bold like a plane's landing strip. Today you wear your heart on your face."

We scanned the church, smiling at one another and our shared faith-filled faces. Later that day, as I looked in the mirror, focusing my attention on the cross, I remembered something that happened years ago. A colleague at work had been critical of something I labored over, and though I didn't say a word, it was obvious that I was hurt. "I'm sorry," she went on to say. "I've upset you. Sabra, you don't wear your heart on your sleeve. You wear it on your face."

After her remark, I consciously worked on controlling my expressions. Before long, I realized the error in my thinking. Instead of putting my effort into masking my emotion, I should focus on the root of my feelings and work on finding a positive perspective—one of compassion and understanding.

**Today, on Ash Wednesday, as we usher in this season of forgiveness, I place my focus on You. Lord, guide me to mirror Your love and understanding.** —Sabra Ciancanelli

**Digging Deeper:** Ecclesiastes 3:1–20; Isaiah 58:5

---

# Thursday, March 6

**He heals the brokenhearted and binds up their wounds. —Psalm 147:3 (ESV)**

I stood in front of Julee's closet the day after Ash Wednesday. I'd lost my wife that June. I'd resisted doing something with her things. She used to say, "I don't have children, I have clothes." Said it with a smile. Julee couldn't have children, due to the lupus that would indirectly kill her.

I could use the closet space. That's what Julee would have said. I could still hear the wry note in her voice. How would Bloomingdale's survive without her?

I fingered an embroidered silk scarf in scarlet that held a trace of Joy, her perfume. Still tucked under the collar of a sleek black coat. The world was full of people who needed clothes, especially at this time of year. New York City was dealing with an influx of immigrants. There were the homeless. The people Jesus cared for and cared about. Why couldn't I undertake this task for Lent? The first without Julee.

I won't lie. A lot of this emotional paralysis about clothes and loss and guilt and so many other things is part of my grieving, a sadness like I have never known. I wonder if grief is something we learn to live through or learn to live with. Or if it is just the last act of love, of letting go.

One year, Julee said she was going to give up smoking for Lent.

"But, Jules, you quit smoking years ago," I scoffed.

"Yes, but it's a process. I think it counts."

Yes, it's a process. Letting go always is.

**Lord, grief is a shroud, so often more about the griever than the grieved. Teach me that love remains even when the loved one has gone to be with You.** —Edward Grinnan

**Digging Deeper:** Matthew 5:4; 2 Corinthians 1:3–4

---

# Friday, March 7

**The Lord God called out to the man and said to him, "Where are you?"** —Genesis 3:9 (JPS)

Even though I had visited the monastery several times during Lent, it really didn't seem any different from visits at other times during the year. All I knew about Lent was that it led up to Easter, and people gave something up. While we Jews had days on which we were supposed to fast, there really didn't seem to be any similarity. Then an interfaith group I belonged to announced it was offering a six-session workshop on Lent, and I decided to sign up out of curiosity.

The first meeting contained a discussion on whether someone should give up something that they loved or something that was hurting them, which led to an exploration of giving up something concrete or something ephemeral. As I listened, I began to realize that my rather simplistic notion of giving up chocolate or TV was only on the surface. Lent, it seemed to me, was the equivalent of the Jewish calendar month of Elul.

Elul is the month leading up to Rosh Hashanah and Yom Kippur. Jews are supposed to evaluate their lives during the past year and decide what parts of themselves they want to bring with them into the next year and what they might be better off leaving behind. I fancied that Lent was something like that. Giving something up seemed to be much more than I had thought; it helped someone who took it seriously to choose who they wanted to be. Just like Elul.

**God of All Life, You made Your children so much alike that we seek You in the same ways. I am**

grateful for the reminder of the spirit we share with each other. —Rhoda Blecker

**Digging Deeper:** Deuteronomy 4:29; Amos 5:4

---

## Saturday, March 8

**If you offer your food to the hungry and satisfy the needs of the afflicted, then your light shall rise in the darkness and your gloom be like the noonday. —Isaiah 58:10 (NRSVUE)**

Every Saturday at our church, we host a soup kitchen. There's always a main course, warm in the winter, cool in the summer, and a paper bag with some staples, not to mention something sweet: a cookie or brownie.

Volunteers sign up in advance with a last-minute push to make sure we have enough folk for cooking, bagging, passing the food out, serving coffee. The latter is my favorite task because it gives me an opportunity to talk to the guests. Though we rarely see them at Sunday worship, I think that coming here, getting sustenance, and knowing they count for something *is* church for them. We offer not just food but a taste of God's love.

On a recent Saturday, I'd shown up at 8:45 in the morning per usual, but there was a surfeit of volunteers. I helped bag some goods, had the pleasure of passing out some extra cookies while our guests waited in line, but there was plenty of help inside and out, cooking, cleaning, serving the coffee.

The door to the sanctuary was open so I slipped inside, sank into a pew, and closed my eyes. How could I best serve? If I could just say a little prayer for our guests, the ones I recognized, the ones whose needs seemed most apparent, the ones whose needs God knew better than I.

I don't know how long I was there, but when I went back outside, no one seemed to have missed me. Maybe being in prayer that day was just where I needed to be.

**Thank You, Lord, for giving me the opportunity to serve the poor and needy.** —Rick Hamlin

**Digging Deeper:** Deuteronomy 15:7; Proverbs 28:27; John 6:35

---

# Sunday, March 9

**Love is patient . . .** —1 Corinthians 13:4 (NIV)

"Patience: allowing someone to be imperfect." I underlined the passage, then closed the book by Gary Chapman and let those words resonate. I had not thought of that definition of patience before, but it spoke to me as one I need to remember.

What makes me lose patience most frequently is when someone does or says something that does not meet my needs or expectations. That is, they respond or act in a way that differs from what I think the perfect response or action should be. Not that my definition of perfect is right in the absolute sense, but it is right in my eyes. This new way of thinking about patience made me realize that I'd created a double standard. I am well aware that I am not even close to being perfect. So, when did it become OK for me to respond with impatience when others aren't either?

The day after reading this passage, I walked into my husband's study where he was, as usual, reading. He didn't respond to my entry with glee, but with frustration that I had interrupted his book.

Instead of my normal response of annoyance, I smiled, kissed him on the forehead, and whispered, "Sorry for the interruption. Let me know when you're free to talk," and walked away. My allowing him to, in my mind, be "imperfect" led to me, for once, being perfect in my response!

**Lord, I like this new definition of patience. May I live this fruit of Your Spirit by allowing others to be imperfect.** —Kim Taylor Henry

**Digging Deeper:** Galatians 5:22; Ephesians 4:2

---

# Monday, March 10

**Let each of you look not only to his own interests, but also to the interests of others.**
**—Philippians 2:4 (ESV)**

The track coach at my son's school was on a mission all year to put together the best boys' relay team he could.

The coach figured out who the fastest four sprinters were on the track team—my son Joey being one of them—and convinced all four to sign up to be on the relay team. In theory, they had everything required to be the best team the school had ever had. They were so confident that they didn't bother practicing as a team, sure that their individual blazing-fast times would bring them victory.

Then came the first track meet. You see, none of them had ever been on a relay team before. None of them knew about handoffs or exchanges or hash marks or batons. And so, while each boy's hundred-yard dash time was amazingly fast, together, they added up to a baton-dropping, collision-causing disaster.

The next day at practice, all four runners humbly came to the coach to ask for help. He taught them how to look out for each other, how each person plays a different role on the relay, and each person's individual strengths are only as good as their ability to work together.

As with any accomplishment, only by looking out for the interests of the entire group will each member be able to shine.

They still have a chance at State. We'll see if they can hold on to that baton.

**Lord, thank You that You've created us to help and encourage each other.**
—Erin MacPherson

**Digging Deeper:** Proverbs 22:9; Mark 10:21; Hebrews 12:1

# Tuesday, March 11

**Now may the Lord of peace himself give you peace at all times in every way.** —2 Thessalonians 3:16 (ESV)

You'd think I was smarter than this.

I'd left plenty of time for my golden, Gracie, and me to drive from the Berkshires for an important meeting in New York. But I am addicted to shortcuts. I've pioneered dozens of ways to the city, none of which actually save me any time. Still, I love the adventure. Except when I get lost.

Gracie popped up in the back seat. Somehow, she always knows when I'm lost.

"Relax," I said, "I got this."

But I was worried. My GPS was incoherent, and the dirt road was getting narrower. Finally, I hit a crossroads. There was a wooden sign with letters and an arrow that were meant to appear carved. The sign said *Bash Bish Falls, Five Miles.*

Bash Bish. Once considered sacred by Indigenous people. I loved Bash Bish. The water cascades more than two hundred feet into a wide pool sixty feet below, hence its onomatopoeic name. I'd scattered the ashes of my wife, Julee, and Marty, our beloved Lab, there. The falls imparted to me a profound sense of peace and well-being.

But not today. My shortcut had wasted too much time.

As I turned the Jeep around at the deserted dirt crossroads, I paused and slipped the transmission in park. Closed my eyes. Summoned the image of water tumbling over terraced rock, splashing into the serene pool below, *bash bish, bash bish* . . .

The world stopped for a moment. Peace and connectedness. Serenity and calm. I opened my eyes and put the Jeep in drive. I'd found a shortcut after all.

**Father of the waters and all the earth, thank You for the gift of imagining, so we can experience Your sacredness anytime, anywhere, to stay close to You.** —Edward Grinnan

**Digging Deeper:** Isaiah 26:3; John 14:27

---

## Wednesday, March 12

**"You do not want to leave too, do you?" Jesus asked the Twelve. —John 6:67 (NIV)**

Mike was a hospital chaplain colleague of mine. One day, sitting in his office, he casually mentioned that he didn't believe in God anymore. His words stunned me. Almost speechless, I could still squeak out, "Why?"

Mike answered, "When I prayed for patients, everyone died anyway. Also, do you remember when that baby died on Christmas? Why would a loving God allow such a thing? After that, I just couldn't believe anymore. But not believing has given me a real peace, because I don't have to figure out God anymore and I don't have to give anyone an explanation for why God does anything."

Just then, Mike received a call to visit a patient. Alone now, I tried to process his words. I wanted to change Mike's thinking. He had been a mentor and a role model for me, but now all that had changed in an instant. My heart ached.

Then I remembered the passage in John's gospel where followers of Jesus decided to leave him because his teaching was too hard. When Jesus asked if others wanted to leave him too, Peter responded, "Lord, to whom shall we go? You alone have the words of life." As I sat with this Scripture, I remembered the trials of my own faith: my mother's death and my own experience with a brain tumor, and how in these two extraordinary times in my young life, *something* had kept me going; *Someone* had kept me going.

As the evening sun drifted through the blinds in Mike's office, I gave a word of thanks to the God who has kept me close to Him all these years, the God who alone has the words of life.

**May we always stay close to you, Lord. Amen.**
—Adam Ruiz

**Digging Deeper:** Deuteronomy 4:31; Psalm 138:8; John 6:60–69

---

# Thursday, March 13

**I am astonished that you are so quickly deserting the one who called you to live in the grace of Christ and are turning to a different gospel —which is really no gospel at all. —Galatians 1:6–7 (NIV)**

When I was a child, occasionally sent to the blackboard to copy whatever the teacher instructed, I was comforted by the fact that if my letters were not constructed to the teacher's standards, there would always be a big powdery eraser nearby to guard against the permanence of my errors.

But later I was to learn that the non-erasable—the permanent, especially as it relates to walking with God—is pivotal, for it is that part of the Lord's grace that we cling to as believers, eternity and its everlasting essence being the most precious thing about our salvation.

On days when our faith hovers near rock bottom, it is easy to forget that the grace of God can never be obliterated. Unlike the popular writing instruments called permanent markers that will sometimes yield to a little bleach, God's grace for this life and eternity cannot be wiped out. His grace is there when it seems there will be no money for rent; when loneliness seems in the driver's seat; when the soul is parched and empty.

Apostle Paul cautions that no matter what is preached to us, the true and unerasable Gospel centers on Jesus, the Christ, and no matter how well-meaning, if the message we hear and the service we render do not line up with Him, then it must be regarded as "no gospel at all." Thankfully, Paul is explicit. Christ followers are called by His grace, and in that grace, there is no shadow of turning.

**Lord, help me remember that Your grace is ever-flourishing.** —Jacqueline F. Wheelock

# Friday, March 14

**For I was hungry and you gave me something to eat, I was thirsty and you gave me something to drink, I was a stranger and you invited me in. —Matthew 25:35 (NIV)**

I've been in cities where homeless people were begging for money. In San Diego, I avoided the bridge behind our hotel where dozens of homeless set up tents. In New York City, I didn't make eye contact with beggars in Times Square. In San Francisco, I walked fast in the parking garage where homeless were escaping the cold. I told myself that a monetary donation would only be used for a bottle of cheap wine.

Then one Sunday at Mass, Father Rob told about the time he and a priest friend were walking into a restaurant and they passed a homeless man sitting on the curb near the front door. Father Rob thought to himself, *Wow, Father didn't even slow down when he saw that guy. I feel bad, but, oh well, I guess we can't take care of them all.*

As soon as the two priests entered the restaurant, Father Rob's priest friend walked over to the hostess and said, "Please go out there and tell that man to come in and order whatever he wants to eat and drink. I will pay his bill. But please don't tell him who paid."

When I heard Father Rob tell that story, I had no more excuses. I certainly can be a little more creative about feeding the hungry and giving drink to the thirsty. I started by donating bags of groceries to the food ministry at church.

Baby steps.

**Heavenly Father, You have taken care of my needs. Teach me to be helpful to others.** —Patricia Lorenz

**Digging Deeper:** Genesis 24:18–19; Psalm 136:23–26

---

# Saturday, March 15

# JOURNEYING WITH JESUS: Assembling a God-Pack
**Now may the God of peace . . . equip you in every good thing to do His will.
—Hebrews 13:20–21 (NASB)**

Our grandson Isaac—then nine years old—spread the contents of his go-pack on the pine needle-strewn ground at our north Idaho campsite. The go-pack idea originated because of a book he liked called *Hatchet*. A young boy, stranded in the wilderness, must survive with only a hatchet. Isaac intended to be well equipped should such a thing ever happen to him.

His go-pack contents were impressive. There was a lantern and flashlight with extra batteries; an MRE (Meal Ready to Eat) and mess kit; a compass; a youth Bible; a water bottle; flint and steel for starting a fire; an emergency blanket and tent; matches; a rope; a hunting knife; a first aid kit; a whistle; a tackle set in a bottle; binoculars; two multi-tools; a nature guide for plants he could and could not eat; a toothbrush and toothpaste; and packets of garden seeds.

We grinned at that last inclusion. If he was lost long enough, he planned to grow a garden! Isaac took his pack seriously.

When I began noticing multiple New Testament stories in which Jesus gives the command "go," my thoughts gravitated to Isaac's go-pack. *Go* is a two-letter word with feet. It can be uttered in rejection—Jesus uses it this way once—but primarily it is His call to forward action. His "go" means transformation is on the way—and I don't want to miss it.

How did first-century people need to be equipped—and how do I need to be listening and ready—when Jesus says, "Go"?

A nine-year-old's go-pack might hold some clues.

**Lord, transform my go-pack into a "God-pack,"
filled with Your essentials for living.**
—Carol Knapp

**Digging Deeper:** Exodus 12:33–35;
Ephesians 6:10–17; 2 Timothy 3:16–17

---

# Sunday, March 16

. . . that my heart may sing your praises and not be silent. —Psalm 30:12 (NIV)

My friend and I laid our trumpets across our laps as the church piano sounded the next hymn's opening notes. We weren't playing with this one, but we had our hymnals open, ready to join in singing with the congregation.

I took a deep breath as the vocal entrance approached ... and then passed, with ... nothing. Nobody else came in. *Yikes—that'd been a narrow miss.* I'd almost been the guest musician who opened her big mouth when she shouldn't have. How mortifying would that've been?

I'd no sooner thought this, though, when my friend's voice rang out across the sanctuary, clear, confident, and—except for the piano—utterly alone.

I froze. *What was he doing? Nobody else was singing!* We were guests—it wasn't our place to call the shots!

But then, another voice joined his. And another, and another, until the sanctuary brimmed with song.

*Wow*, I thought. While I had been congratulating myself on avoiding a mistake, my friend had heard silence where he'd expected song, and solved the problem by just ... singing. If my fear had had its way, it would've silenced not only me but him too. We'd have still been listening to only the piano, trundling awkwardly along without its accompaniment.

As I added my own voice to the happy chorus, I said a quick prayer of thanks for brave friends and for the joyful noise that's possible when—free from fear—we open our mouths, lift our voices, and sing!

**Fear sneaks in so easily, God, and I often struggle to find my voice. Please grant me the courage to speak up, and sing out, for those who cannot—as You've asked us to do.** —Erin Janoso

**Digging Deeper:** 2 Chronicles 5:13–14; Psalm 98:4–6; Proverbs 31:8

---

## Monday, March 17

## SEEMINGLY INSIGNIFICANT:
### Seeking God's Will in Scripture
**Come now, let us reason together, says the LORD ... — Isaiah 1:18 (ESV)**

My husband, Kris, and I have always had farm dogs who live outdoors and spend happy lives roaming our farm and chasing each other and napping together in the sun. Our current farm dog, Karl—a boisterous, Weimaraner-like mutt—recently lost his elderly beagle companion. We're considering adopting another dog but worry Karl will resent a competitor for our affections.

So, when a friend an hour away asked us to keep his dog while his family attended a funeral, we said yes, eager to help him and also try out a short-term companion for Karl. Our friend wanted their dog kept inside, though, and Kris insisted, "Dogs live outside." So, in an awkward text, I reneged, and our friend hired a neighbor kid to pet-sit instead.

Our guilty feelings outlived that simple solution in the form of a lingering contentiousness between

Kris and me. After my Bible reading one morning, I pointedly praised Saul's son Jonathan's friendship with David, the object of Saul's jealous hatred. Jonathan jeopardized his relationship with his dad, his claim to kingship, even his life for David.

"We're supposed to sacrifice for our friends," I concluded. "Jesus said we're even supposed to be willing to lay down our lives for them."

Our ensuing discussion exposed my absurd logic. Kris wasn't murderous like Saul. Dog-sitting is hardly comparable to laying down one's life for a friend. And Jesus's instruction on loving one another applies not just to our friends but us too. It's tempting, but wrongheaded, to wield out-of-context lines from Scripture to bolster arguments. Better, in any relationship, is to jointly seek loving, God-honoring, rational accord.

**Lord, keep me from using—and thus abusing—
Your words out of context to win arguments.**
—Patty Kirk

**Digging Deeper:** John 15:9–17

---

# Tuesday, March 18

**Even to your old age and gray hairs I am he, I am he who will sustain you. —Isaiah 46:4 (NIV)**

Very few people reach old age without experiencing loss. Death has claimed all family members in the two generations before me. I've lost my precious husband of more than fifty years; my only female cousin; several good friends; and multiple beloved dogs and cats—especially my golden chow Tarby, a companion for thirteen years.

For the first time in five decades, I'm not in the musician rotation for my church: my arthritic hands can't span an octave on the keyboard. I need prescription glasses for reading and driving. My mind is sometimes . . . missing. I occasionally forget names, and I got hopelessly lost traveling in Colorado recently. I can't replace lightbulbs that require balancing on a ladder.

But for almost every loss, there are blessings. I have photos, diaries, and fond memories of departed loved ones, plus the joy of welcoming new generations. (Great-granddaughter Talyn is delightful!) My dog Pepper may never replace Tarby, but she's good company and is learning not to knock me down.

I enjoy playing hymns on my home piano, and our church musicians delight my ears and soul. I'm a safe driver—no tickets. When I was lost, some friendly firefighters gave me coffee, printed a current map, and headed me in the right direction. My son, Patrick, and his wife, Patricia, do "ladder work" and make repairs.

So morning and evening, I thank God for my blessings, especially for the faith-building lessons I'm learning from loss.

**Lord Jesus, thank You for being my strength and shield from childhood into old age.** —Penney Schwab

---

# Wednesday, March 19

**I kept quiet, not saying a word, not even about anything good! But my suffering only grew worse. —Psalm 39:2 (GNT)**

Learning to keep my mouth shut has been a hard discipline. Not that I'm a blustery, loudmouth extrovert, because I am not. I am a rather quiet man. Without my glib Irish wife around here to stir things up, our house might be as quiet "as an undiscovered tomb," as Henry Higgins put it in *My Fair Lady*.

But it's hard for me to bite my tongue when someone says something that's not true. If I had a college student in Proverbs class who said something that was doctrinally wrong, I wanted to jump on him with both feet and set him straight, right now.

One day I was watching a fellow professor teach his class. He is a gentle, harmless man. When a student said something in error, he would simply respond with questions: "I can see why you might think that, but what would you do with verse 3 in chapter 4? Does that shed any light?"

It has been said that Jesus used more than three hundred questions in the Gospels, and He knew the answer to all of them! But he wanted people to experience the joy of learning something for themselves. I like that approach.

So, if my friends and I are having a political conversation or just shooting the bull, and someone says something that's not true, I am learning to "ask, not tell."

**Lord, make me a gentle man, with the wisdom to know when to speak and when to be still.** —Daniel Schantz

**Digging Deeper:** Proverbs 11:12, 17:28

---

# Thursday, March 20

**Ask the LORD your God for a sign, whether in the deepest depths or in the highest heights. —Isaiah 7:11 (NIV)**

The sun was just rising as traffic swelled for the hour's drive into the city. I worried about the meeting. Colleagues were flying in for an entire day of discussion and decisions. I went over the agenda in my mind.

I was feeling melancholy. The anniversary of my sister's death was approaching, and the car ride, alone with my thoughts, made me miss her. I asked God for a sign of assurance that she was well and that she still hears me when I talk to her.

"I would love a heart," I said. "Please, if You can, show me a heart today. Thank You."

I turned on the radio and sang along to the song. My coffee had grown cold, and I was on edge in the bumper-to-bumper traffic. Roadwork had caused merging lanes that bottlenecked.

By the time I pulled into the parking garage, I was a wreck of nerves. The day hadn't even started yet, and I was already exhausted. I collected my things and walked toward the entryway.

Something red caught my eye. A car parked right by the door had a helium balloon tied to the driver's side handle, and a bright-red heart bobbed in the wind. And just like that, my heart filled with love in return.

**Thank You, thank You, thank You, Lord, for magical, beautiful moments in this world that connect me to the next one.** —Sabra Ciancanelli

**Digging Deeper:** John 5:24; 1 John 5:11

---

# Friday, March 21

**If you, then, though you are evil, know how to give good gifts to your children, how much more will your Father in heaven give good gifts to those who ask him!** —Matthew 7:11 (NIV)

The days are long, but the years are short. That's what they always told me. But it's hard to appreciate the wisdom of older parents when you're rocking a whiny newborn, trying to entertain a bored five-year-old, and attempting to calm a rowdy seven-year-old who wants to do anything but sit still.

Then I blinked, and now I'm standing months away from my oldest child's high-school graduation. This is the beginning of my empty nest. I've told God that I'm not prepared and wonder if my children will be. I've questioned if I've adequately taught them the basic life skills they need. Can they manage their finances, cook a decent meal, make wise choices when it comes to friendships? Will they always choose to walk in His precepts or will they veer off and try things that I'd rather they not? *Lord*, I pray. *Let my children stay in the light. Don't let them be consumed by this dark world.*

I know I'm not the only parent who wakes in the middle of the night with rushing thoughts and calming prayers. In those late hours, God speaks to me. Four words quietly rise in my spirit that encompass the depth of His love for all of us: *I love them more.* I'm reminded that my children have the same access to the Father's love, mercy, grace, wisdom, and protection.

**Thank You, Lord, that Your plans for my children's lives supersede my imperfect parenting. You are the omniscient and omnipotent Father of my children. I place their lives in Your hands.**
—Tia McCollors

**Digging Deeper:** Deuteronomy 6:6–9; Isaiah 48:17, 21; 2 Timothy 3:15; 1 John 2:15–17

---

# Saturday, March 22

**But if someone who is supposed to be a Christian has money enough to live well, and sees a brother in need, and won't help him—how can God's love be within him? —1 John 3:17 (TLB)**

I ran to my little grocery store in rural Wisconsin late yesterday. It was a Hon-I'm-baking-a-pie-but-we're-out-of-butter moment. In front of me was a mother with three small children; behind me was an older man all by himself.

When the man put his four items before the teenage clerk, he also pulled out his food stamps. "You're about five dollars short," the clerk said. I heard it as I was walking away.

I turned around and quickly saw two things: the old man turning to put items back on a shelf, and the young clerk looking directly at him. I was about to speak when the teenager said, "No," and then, "Don't do that. I have it here." He was reaching for his wallet in a back pocket. He pulled out a five-dollar bill. "Have a good weekend," the boy said.

A kid did that. A kid working a job on the weekend in rural Wisconsin.

I wish I would have reacted quicker, more instinctively, to give. But I am grateful to have witnessed one of my neighbors doing just that.

**Lord, may my path be filled with simple ways of being not only kind but generous today, without fanfare.** —Jon M. Sweeney

**Digging Deeper:** Ephesians 3:18–21

---

# Sunday, March 23

**And he said to him, "Teacher, all these I have kept from my youth." —Mark 10:20 (ESV)**

After a busy Sunday morning of classes and worship, I took great solace in a quiet Sunday afternoon. Since my eight-year-old, Jacques, was quietly drawing in the kitchen, it seemed like the absolute perfect time for a little nap. All snug on the sofa, I closed my eyes, thanking God for this respite.

I was almost asleep when I heard Jacques talking from the kitchen. No one else was home, so I was quite curious as to whom he was conversing. I got off the couch and quietly treaded to the kitchen with Jacques still chatting away. As I got closer, I realized Jacques's rhythm and words were The Lord's Prayer. Jacques's soft, sweet voice spoke to God, and I felt my heart gently turn toward the Lord.

Stepping into the kitchen, I asked, "What are you doing?" Jacques replied, "I'm praying, Mommy. We learned this in class today." I gave him a kiss and stepped out. I immediately recognized a note of gratitude was due to two special ladies.

Parenting and raising my children in a faith community means I am not alone. I texted Jacques's religious education teachers and thanked them for walking alongside my son in faith. The Lord inspired Jacques to pray out loud that afternoon, and I was able to bear witness to His movement within my son's life. I took the gift of witnessing Jacques's living faith over a nap this day and every day!

Lord God, may Your light shine in the lives of others and bear witness to the gift of salvation to us all. —Jolynda Strandberg

**Digging Deeper:** Matthew 19:16–30; Luke 18:9–17

---

# Monday, March 24

**"For I know the plans I have for you," declares the LORD, "plans to prosper you and not to harm you, plans to give you hope and a future." —Jeremiah 29:11 (NIV)**

I had struggled to say "no" most of my life. If someone needed help, I was there. Because of it, I was the chair of several committees, the coordinator of a moms' group, and a member of many community and church boards—all while working full time and trying to raise two little girls. It was good work, but it was stopping me from doing what I really wanted to do: write. I didn't have time to follow my dream to be a published author, because I was too busy.

All of that changed when I found out I was pregnant with twins. Suddenly, I didn't have time for all the commitments. My world became very small as I took care of my young family. It was hard to not be involved. I felt like I was missing out on so much. But it didn't take long to realize that this season of life was a gift from God. As my boys got a little older, I had a choice to make. Get busy doing all the volunteer work again—which was good and helpful—or focus on the ministry God had created me to do.

Now, ten years later, with thirty books under my belt and dozens of emails from people who have been blessed through my writing, I realize that the busyness was hindering my true ministry. It's not wrong to be busy or to do good work, but it had prevented me from pursuing the thing God has called me to do.

**Lord, when my busyness keeps me from pursuing Your purpose for me, remind me why You have created me.** —Gabrielle Meyer

**Digging Deeper:** Psalm 33:11; Proverbs 16:9; Ecclesiastes 3:1–22

---

## Tuesday, March 25

**Now faith is the substance of things hoped for, the evidence of things not seen. —Hebrews 11:1 (KJV)**

Visiting my mother in the hospital recently brought to mind a long-ago memory of a time just after I'd given birth to my son, Brock. My big extended family gathered at my parents' home to welcome the three-day-old new arrival. Though I tried visiting, I felt awful. Ushered to a guest room, I fell into bed. No one missed me for a while, Brock being the main attraction.

When my brother, Davey, came to ask how I was, I couldn't answer. I was trapped in a sort of deep dream. I could hear but I couldn't respond. Davey worriedly put a thermometer in my mouth. My temperature was a deathly 106 degrees.

My doctor said being transported to the hospital was too dangerous until my temperature fell, hence I was to be literally packed in ice on the spot. The men rushed out to area ice machines as the women, led by Aunt Zola, a "sort of" nurse, packed ice around my body.

Freezing, I concentrated on my socks, the only area the ice missed, and listened to the love that surrounded me. A "deep coma," my doctor said, yet I was conscious of everything.

Can a comatose person be as aware as I was? God gave me that possibility. So ever since then, when I visit critically ill people, I ignore the coma. I chat, read Bible passages, express love.

Which brings me to my mother's side in the ICU. "Comatose," the doctor says. But I talk to her, share memories, express love.

"Oh, Bebe," I say, "if only you could kiss me one more time."

I bend down to kiss her, and then comes my mother's last gesture on this earth. She purses her lips and offers me a final kiss.

**Father, so long ago, Your gift opened the way for my mother's final kiss. Thank You.**
—Pam Kidd

---

# Wednesday, March 26

**The fear of the LORD is the beginning of knowledge, but fools despise wisdom and instruction. —Proverbs 1:7 (NIV)**

When our grandson Logan lived with us, we'd often ask him what he learned that day when he came home from school. Sometimes he'd say, "Nothing" or "I don't know," but we'd usually ask enough questions to find out that he did indeed learn something new.

I decided to take that question along with me on my next vacation and play the "What did I learn today?" game. I kept a journal noting historical facts, important people, natural phenomena, etc., jotting down interesting information. The game changed the way I perceived things as I looked for something new, something I had not known before. I began to look forward to what I'd discover each day.

We often joke about our memory lapses, saying that old age has its benefits because you meet "new" people every day and learn "new" things! Research has shown that the brain has a greater capacity for memory than any device we've invented so far. Some experts define learning as the "voluntary and self-motivated search for knowledge," meaning you intentionally and continually seek to learn new things for your own benefit. But our attitude can stifle our learning. If we think we can't learn anything else, we won't try or pay attention to ways we can learn.

On the other hand, looking for the new in each day can give you a reason to look forward to tomorrow. God has given us the ability to learn and has provided us with an unlimited amount of information to acquire. What new thing did you learn today?

**Lord, thank You for giving us this wonderful world to discover and the ability to learn about it.**
—Marilyn Turk

**Digging Deeper:** Psalm 25:4; Proverbs 9:9, 18:15; Philippians 4:9

---

# Thursday, March 27

**But he said unto them, I have meat to eat that ye know not of. —John 4:32 (KJV)**

As I write this, my dear friend Mark's mother is dying. In all the years Mark and I have been friends, I never met his mom, but I know she was a woman of great faith.

I can't help but think back to my Aunt Faye's passing some months ago. Like Mark's mother, Aunt Faye was well into her eighth decade on this planet, and she slipped away gradually. I remember my cousin telling me that Aunt Faye began eating less and less until, finally, she would eat nothing at all.

I've learned this is not uncommon for those near death. As they make peace with their mortality, they no longer seek to fuel their earthly bodies. For people like my aunt, their lifelong faith and trust in God feed their souls. They have the spiritual nourishment Jesus spoke of to His disciples.

Aunt Faye was ready to meet the Lord. For her, it wouldn't be a big change, really: she'd spent nearly every day of her life getting to know Him. Although it hurt to lose my beloved aunt, I loved thinking about how wonderful it would soon be for her to finally behold the Great Love of her life and feel His embrace.

No need for food. She would soon be full.

**Father, thank You for the comfort of knowing that the death of Your saints is precious in Your sight.**
—Ginger Rue

**Digging Deeper:** Psalm 116:15; Matthew 5:4; Revelation 21:4

---

# Friday, March 28

**Be joyful in hope, patient in affliction, faithful in prayer. —Romans 12:12 (NIV)**

As I sat in the doctor's waiting room, I checked my watch for the tenth time in as many minutes.

He was already an hour behind schedule, and I had other appointments that day. My patience was wearing thin. The receptionist appeared, and I looked up expectantly, only to hear her call someone else for another doctor. It demanded every restraint I had not to tap my foot and point to my watch. Being goal-driven, there are few things in life that bother me more than wasting time.

Instead of focusing on how late the doctor was running, I closed my eyes and prayed. Almost immediately, God brought to mind Abraham, Sarah, and Joseph from the Old Testament. They, too, had spent time in a waiting room. And it was a whole lot longer than an hour. It was during those long years that God worked on their hearts, shaping them for the promises He had yet to fulfill.

The waiting room God placed me in when I decided to become a novelist lasted five frustrating years. In those years, God worked on my heart, humbling me, teaching me discipline and trust. Those years helped hone my writing skills and built in me the ability to look objectively at rejections so that when the time came, I was emotionally ready for the success that followed.

Over the years I've been stuck in several waiting rooms. Finishing my prayer, I opened my eyes just as the receptionist stepped back into the room, called out my name, and apologized for the long wait. I smiled and told her it hadn't been a problem; I'd used the time effectively.

> Waiting rooms are difficult; help me, Father, to recognize that they are also growing rooms.
> —Debbie Macomber

**Digging Deeper:** Isaiah 40:31;
2 Corinthians 1:20

---

## Saturday, March 29

**But one thing I do: Forgetting what is behind and straining toward what is ahead, I press on toward the goal to win the prize for which God has called me heavenward in Christ Jesus.**
—**Philippians 3:13–14 (NIV)**

My friend and I carried my trusty firepit carefully through the doorway of my new house to place it outside in the backyard. I was sentimental about this fireplace—lots of good conversation, laughs, and heartfelt exchanges had happened around its warm glow. Due to my divorce, I had to let go of old dreams and move out of a home I'd hoped to share with my family.

We had a little ways to go when my friend's grasp slipped. The firepit fell, shattering ceramic tiles that lined its tabletop as it hit the floor. I blinked back tears—jagged pieces of tile and dust lay spread out, in apparent ruin. I couldn't help but feel like it was a metaphor for the current state of my life. I gathered the pieces one by one. I hoped that if I was diligent enough, I could somehow completely restore the tiles to their prior places, the firepit to its former glory. I wished I could do the same in my own life.

The next day another friend came and saw what had happened. That person had a brilliant suggestion: that I measure the empty spaces and fill them with something new. Brand-new tiles, in any color and texture, that would suit me in this season of my life.

I had been sifting through my own broken pieces, mourning my marriage. God showed me that maybe not all my broken pieces had to fit into the mold of my past.

**Thank You, Father, that You redeem us and give us hope.** —Nicole Garcia

**Digging Deeper:** Ezra 4:12; Jeremiah 17:14; Hosea 6:1–2

---

## Sunday, March 30

**Always be humble and gentle. Be patient with each other, making allowance for each other's faults because of your love. —Ephesians 4:2 (NLT)**

I scanned the sanctuary. It was my first Sunday at this church. I hoped I could find belonging here, but, this morning, I'd settle for a place to sit. The sanctuary was fairly full.

Near the front of the sanctuary, I noticed a middle-aged man sitting alone in a pew. I joined him, setting my Bible on the pew, then shucking off my winter coat.

I turned to introduce myself. But the man cut me off.

"I'm saving this row," he said. He gestured to the pew in its entirety. Both his voice and indication were gruff.

My face turned red with embarrassment.

"I'm sorry," I said. "I didn't know . . . "

Before I could finish, the man turned away and shuffled down the pew.

My face burning, I collected my things and moved to an empty seat several rows back. The lights dimmed, and the worship team began to play.

In the darkness, my embarrassment gave way to anger. I watched the man raise his hands as the chorus began. How could he treat me poorly, then immediately begin praising the Lord? And what gave him the right to save seats in God's house?

As the worship music played, my anger bristled. Then the irony struck me. I myself was sinning in God's house. I was harboring anger and resentment toward a brother-in-Christ. Rather than forgiving, I was passing judgment.

So, as the music continued, I bowed my head in prayer.

**Spirit, help me to honor You in every action and thought. And help me to love others unconditionally.** —Logan Eliasen

**Digging Deeper:** 1 Peter 4:8;
1 John 4:21

**"I will be a Father to you, and you shall be My sons and daughters, says the LORD Almighty."**
**—2 Corinthians 6:18 (NKJV)**

I groaned when our Bible study leader presented that week's icebreaker question: *How did you get your name? What does it mean? Rename yourself with the meaning.* My reluctance to share the origins of my first name was not because I disliked it, but rather because of the ordinary and uneventful way my parents chose it.

"I didn't know anyone named 'Stephanie,'" said my mother with a shrug when I asked her decades ago. "I found it in a book of baby names and liked it." I later discovered the Greek origins of my name and its meaning: "crowned." That didn't fit either. There was nothing royal, or even special, about my heritage or the person I'd become.

When it was my turn during Bible study that morning, I quickly shared my common name and the way I had acquired it. I added I was far from a noble birth, lifting my hands over my head and making a crown in an effort to lighten the mood.

"So it suits me, I guess," I said with a laugh.

The Bible study ladies giggled.

Our leader turned solemn. "Since God is your heavenly Father, you are a child of God," she reminded me. "That makes you the daughter of the Most High King."

Her words warmed my heart. The origins of my name might be ordinary, but because I've been adopted into the family of God, I am *crowned* with a very special heritage indeed.

**Dear Father, thank You for adopting me into Your family. When I begin to doubt my worth, help me to remember that I am the daughter of the King.**
—Stephanie Thompson

**Digging Deeper:** 2 Samuel 7:14; Romans 8:15–17; Galatians 3:26

## WITH AN EVERLASTING LOVE

1 _____

2 _____

3 _____

4 _____

5 _____

6 _____

7 _____

8 _____

9 _____

10 _____

11 _____

12 _____

13 _____

14 _____

15 _____

16 _____

17 _____

18 _____

19 _____

20 _____

21 _____

22 _____

23 _____

24 _____

25 _____

26 _____

27 _____

28 _____

29 _____

30 _____

31 _____

# April

Let love and faithfulness never leave you; bind them around your neck, write them on the tablet of your heart.

—Proverbs 3:3 (NIV)

**For nothing will be impossible with God.**
**—Luke 1:37 (NASB)**

Today was the day! I logged on to the computer with a mix of excitement and nausea. Would my son get closer to his dream?

Brandon was six when he announced, "I'm going to be a marine biologist when I grow up." We'd just watched *Dolphin Tale 2*, so I understood his excitement. However, I couldn't picture my little city kid finding his calling in the ocean.

As my sons grew, Brandon's younger brother changed his future career each time he was asked. Brandon, however, confidently remained a "marine biologist." I wished I could share his certainty. With his struggles in school and newly diagnosed ADHD, I'd be happy if he simply graduated with his class.

My faith in him wavered, but his never did. I watched in amazement as he went from the possibility of being left back to graduating middle school at the top of his class. Now we were waiting to hear back from a high school on a little island off Manhattan that specialized in maritime studies. This dream I deemed impossible might actually come true!

I took a breath and pressed the button.

"He got in!" I screamed like a maniac, jumping up and down. I quickly made a sign with the school's name before he came home and showered him with confetti when he walked through the door. He didn't scream in celebration like I did. He simply smiled as if he'd known the outcome for years. Because the truth is, he absolutely did.

**Lord, help me to listen to the callings You speak into my life and to focus on Your voice alone.**
—Karen Valentin

**Digging Deeper:** Luke 21:19; Philippians 4:13

---

# Wednesday, April 2

**For the eyes of the Lord run to and fro throughout the whole earth . . .** —2 Chronicles 16:9 (KJV)

I still miss my grandfather, who passed away years ago. One of my favorite memories of "Pa" is from when I was a young boy. Pa was visiting that evening and I was beyond excited because I had something exciting to tell him: "Pa! I saw the most gigantic-ist dandelion when Mom was driving me home from school today!"

His barrel chest bounced up and down with a deep laugh. "I would've liked to see that, Lad."

The next morning, I popped out of bed to watch morning cartoons with Pa. When I got to the kitchen, there he was, sipping on a hot cup of coffee and standing over the huge dandelion. He had put it in one of Mom's vases. Seeing the Loch Ness monster or Bigfoot couldn't have thrilled me more.

He laughed his wonderful laugh again, taking pleasure in the wonder I was beaming out. So many years have flown by since then, and I still think about how he must have gotten up at sunrise and driven up and down the road until he spotted that dandelion. Nothing matches the pleasure of that memory.

Some people seem sent to Earth to remind us how much God cares for us ... my Pa was one of those people. In my life there have been moments of wishing and hoping and praying for things beyond my reach. And then when some longing is unexpectedly fulfilled, I can't help thinking of my Pa driving up and down the road in the dawning light, and of my Father God, His all-seeing eyes running across His creation searching for just the right answers for His children: for you and for me.

**Father, I know You are watching. Thank You.**
—Brock Kidd

**Digging Deeper:** Psalm 91:11; Haggai 1:13

---

# Thursday, April 3

**Look at the birds of the air: they neither sow nor reap nor gather into barns, and yet your heavenly Father feeds them. Are you not of more value than they? —Matthew 6:26 (ESV)**

I've mentioned this before, so I'm not letting the cat out of the bag when I say we *Walking in Grace* contributors submit our devotions well in advance of publication due to the "old media" realities of book publishing. I can't help but wonder what the world will be like when you read this. What will I be like?

Prodding my friends the other day for ideas for my 2025 devotions (I regularly harass my friends for inspiration), one suggested I mention my sober anniversary on April 3. "You'll have, what, twenty-nine years, if I'm not mistaken."

*Good idea.* There were so many people to thank—my brothers and sisters in Twelve Step, my family and friends, even the readers of *Guideposts*. I started to write: "A day at a time and with the grace of God, I have been blessed to be sober for ... "

But that famous phrase *a day at a time* stopped me. I'd struggled with addiction a day at a time for sure, with little regard for the future. When I finally found sobriety, it was a day at a time as well. Each day was a recommitment to God, myself, and others who struggled. It was the only way this alcoholic could have gotten and stayed sober. That bite-sized spirituality was all I could manage, yet it eventually led to a far more encompassing faith ... a day at a time.

So maybe I should back off announcing a sober anniversary in years when it is only today that counts. Each day a gift to be freshly embraced and thankful for.

**Lord, You care for me a day at a time. Let me live in the gift of this day. The years will take care of themselves.** —Edward Grinnan

---

## Friday, April 4

**For every house is built by someone, but God is the builder of everything. —Hebrews 3:4 (NIV)**

After the melting of winter snows, my husband, Kevin, and I returned to our cabin in northern Arizona to clean up the debris from a tree-thinning project, a necessary task to decrease the danger of destructive wildfires. I welcomed the time away after a work proposal had received a big "no," stirring up insecurity about the future.

As we stacked the lengths of pine, we wondered what the thinning project would mean to the wildlife in the area. What about our favorite gray squirrel, who often visited the bird feeder to grab a peanut or two?

The stellar jays returned first, five of them, scolding us as we raked pine needles and gathered broken branches for fires in our fireplace. Next, a rounded junco grabbed a few seeds before flying off to a safe distance. With a loud *waka waka,* an acorn woodpecker—flashing his red cap—swept down to chase off a curious mountain chickadee. A few minutes later, the howl of coyotes echoed across the lake bed.

For three days we enjoyed the evidence of creation's resilience for life, with one noticeable exception. No gray squirrel.

As I packed the car to head home, Kevin called me to the back porch.

"Look," he said, pointing above our heads.

The gray squirrel peered down from his pine bough highway, a peanut in his mouth. He leapt from branch to branch until he arrived at a dead tree, where he disappeared into a cavity in the trunk. Safely home.

**Jesus, in the thinning places of my life, where I receive a "no" instead of a "yes," may I still discover safe places to call home.** —Lynne Hartke

**Digging Deeper:** Deuteronomy 28:6; Psalm 121:8

---

# Saturday, April 5

**Brothers and sisters, we do not want you to be uninformed about those who sleep in death, so that you do not grieve like the rest of mankind, who have no hope. —1 Thessalonians 4:13 (NIV)**

The news hit my community hard. My son's former high-school football teammate Alex had passed away after a tragic motorcycle accident. The twenty-one-year-old college student's future had held so much promise. My husband and I had sat with Alex's parents at football games. I saw his mom at "Mom Potlucks" on evenings preceding game nights. We'd chat with his parents at the local grocery store. I never saw Alex without a huge smile, and I called him "Sweet Alex."

On the day of his funeral, an overcast sky released scattered showers. Even the heavens appeared to mourn the loss of this kind young man. My black heels sank into the soggy earth as I walked across the funeral home lawn-turned-parking lot. During the service, many spoke of Alex's love of adventure, his faithful friendship, and, of course, that big smile. We chuckled and wiped tears together. Yet I knew no one would feel the loss as deeply as his parents, who would soon bury their only child.

Feeling the weight of Sweet Alex's loss while driving home, I looked up and could hardly believe my eyes. The sky revealed a spectacular double rainbow. I believe God was speaking to me and our community, showing us that even in death there is hope. The Lord had not forgotten Alex's family and friends. Death is not the end of the road, and He had and would always keep His promises to His children.

**Lord, may we cling to hope in grief, because You are a Promise-keeper.** —Carla Hendricks

**Digging Deeper:** 1 Thessalonians 4:13–18; Revelation 21:1–7

---

# Sunday, April 6

**But I saw no temple in it, for the Lord God Almighty and the Lamb are its temple.
—Revelation 21:22 (NKJV)**

I can worship God everywhere except in church.

Well, it seems that way at times. Worship is somewhat instinctive with me. I awoke this morning with a children's chorus playing in my mind: "All through the day, all through the night, my Savior has been watching over me . . . " I will sing it softly to myself throughout the day.

But when I go to church, I clutch up. Church seems to have been designed by extroverts and for extroverts, but I am a sensitive introvert, like 30 to 40 percent of the population. The worship team, armed with multiple amplified guitars, drums, and keyboards, overwhelms my nervous system with their ear-splitting performance, leaving me irritable and exhausted.

I can't change what the church offers me. Instead, I focus on the sermon, the Lord's Supper, and the prayers, and I just grit my teeth through the music.

So, when I read in Revelation 21 that there is no temple in heaven, I am thrilled. Worship there will not be a performance by a team of rock stars, but something we all do, as naturally as breathing.

Meanwhile, I praise God wherever I am, from sunrise to starlight, with a special prayer of thanks for the soft pillow that takes away my daily cares. You might say that I am "practicing for heaven."

**I thank You, Lord, that I can worship You wherever I am.** —Daniel Schantz

**Digging Deeper:** Mark 5:6; John 4:21–24

**For God has not given us a spirit of fearfulness, but one of power, love, and sound judgement. —2 Timothy 1:7 (HCSB)**

"Come on, guys, we're going to the church," Mom calls, ushering us from the house into the blustering night. A storm's coming, along with the threat of tornadoes—my greatest fear.

Soon we're at church, speed-walking down the thinly carpeted stairs to the basement. A safe haven. Some friends are here—college-age, like me, among the younger kids in the room—and soon everyone else is relaxed as they talk, turn on *VeggieTales*, or start a game of air hockey. But I can't relax, or play, or talk. I'm storm-sick.

Shaking, I creep onto the ancient tan couch next to Mom. My stomach feels like a tornado's raging through it. My worry has decided to go rogue and take control of my body. Soothingly, Mom strokes my hair and tells me that everything will be all right.

"Rachel, what does worrying do for you?" she asks. A simple question, but not one I'd considered before. "If you're so worried that you're making yourself sick, how does that help you? Does it keep the storm away? Or get you somewhere safe faster?" I don't know how to respond. "Remember, sweetie, God is in control. You don't have to worry."

I still feel sick, but I focus on her words. I remind myself that I'm OK, that worrying won't change anything, and that the God of all creation is watching over me. Now, a few storms later, I'm not becoming storm-sick. I can watch the lightning and rain through the windows and take joy in their display as I remember Mom's words.

**Dear God, thank You for a wise mother, and for always being with me so I don't have to worry.**
—Rachel Thompson

**Digging Deeper:** Psalm 55:22; Matthew 6:25–34

---

# Tuesday, April 8

**. . . he saved us, not because of righteous things we had done, but because of his mercy.**
**—Titus 3:5 (NIV)**

I remember the sickening moment I realized I'd really messed up. The situation was already beyond rescue. I wouldn't be able to contain my time management fail this time. The importance of the commitments made didn't matter. There were too many of them, and there just wasn't enough time. I was going to let people down. And I hated it.

I didn't know what to tell everyone. Excuses felt silly and hollow. I ended up being honest, mostly because I couldn't figure out what to say otherwise. No matter what I said, though, the shame of it still burned.

But that's when something surprising started happening. The professor whose assignments I'd blown? She told our Friday class she wasn't assigning weekend homework "to give some of y'all a chance to catch up." The friend whose meeting I'd slept through because I'd been up until 3 a.m.? They walked across campus to bring me coffee. Over and over, where I'd expected judgment and condemnation, I was offered understanding and compassion instead.

It blew my mind. I'd messed up. I'd let people down. But instead of being excruciating and shame-filled, as I'd expected, the weeks that followed taught me again and again what it feels like to be on the receiving end of acceptance, patience, kindness, grace. In a word, love. "Love one another, as I've loved you," Jesus says. Love like that really does carry within it the power to change hearts, and change worlds—I know now—because it changed mine.

**I know it is because of Your grace, God, that I am worthy of love even when my own works fall far short. Thank You.** —Erin Janoso

**Digging Deeper:** 1 Corinthians 13:13; 2 Timothy 1:9

---

# Wednesday, April 9

**Therefore, my dear brothers and sisters, stand firm. Let nothing move you. Always give yourselves fully to the work of the Lord, because you know that your labor in the Lord is not in vain. —1 Corinthians 15:58 (NIV)**

As I walked our dog down the big hill and up the next one, as I've done hundreds of times, I rehashed a problem at work. I grew up on this very road and have many memories of walking exactly this path to make sense of my thoughts. As I went over a contentious discussion, my work angst wasn't leaving me. In fact, it seemed to be simmering and condensing into something worse.

A bird flew off a nearby oak. I looked up and, in the distance, I could see that the town road crew had been working, trimming trees and collecting debris from a harsh winter.

Piles of brush and limbs waited to be picked up. The workers had cut down trees that had perished, and I passed a few newly cut stumps. Ahead, something strange caught my eye. A worker had cut a dead tree at a sharp diagonal and then chainsawed a smiling happy face.

I walked up close to it and smiled back. Whoever had done it had a little fun on the job and, in return, passed that silly fun right back into the world— to me.

Something switched, and for the rest of the walk, instead of being fixated on who was right or wrong or how I might prove a point, I wondered how I might add a little joy to my job.

**Lord, help me to bring a happy face to the work I do and approach everything I do with a smile.**
—Sabra Ciancanelli

**Digging Deeper:** Psalm 1:1–3; Colossians 3:23–4:6

**Bless the Lord, O you his angels, you mighty ones who do his bidding, obedient to his spoken word. —Psalm 103:20 (NRSVUE)**

I had to make angel wings. It's sort of like making snow angels in the new-fallen snow, but in this case, doing it against a wall. Flap my wings and fly. Although this was a little more mundane—it was an exercise my physical therapist recommended.

It all made plenty of sense in her office. Standing against a wall, I spread out my arms wide and then extended them overhead, keeping them against the wall. Repeat fifteen times. Rest, and do it again. In my mind's eye, I looked a little like that male figure Leonardo da Vinci drew, a man in a circle with his arms extended.

But when I came home and tried to do the exercise the next day, I realized we didn't have enough empty wall space to do it. I walked around the house. Nothing. Too many pictures on all our walls. None of them da Vinci's, mostly things we got from family and friends.

I'd have to take something down to make room. I looked at various options and finally settled on a wall that had a stone carving of two cupids framing a mirror. Easy enough to remove it. I put my head in its place and flapped my wings.

And then I realized that the angels had been replaced by their human counterpart, though maybe not as elegant as them or as dexterous.

Somehow what was mundane had taken on spiritual resonance. How often do we get to imitate angels? For me, it happens at least twice a day, flapping my wings fifteen times.

**Lord, let me be an ally with Your angels, just as they look after me.** —Rick Hamlin

**Digging Deeper:** Matthew 24:31; Luke 4:10

---

# Friday, April 11

### He heals the brokenhearted and binds up their wounds. —Psalm 147:3 (NIV)

"TELL. THEM. TO. COME. BACK. AND. GET. ME," Beau, my five-year-old son, hollered.

His dad and big brother had headed out on an overnight baseball trip. Beau had decided, after great deliberation, to stay home with me. But now that night had fallen, he wasn't so sure he'd made the right choice.

As I snuggled him, he looked up at me with swollen eyes, red from crying, and said, "Mom, you know when you just love someone so much that you can't stand to be away from them for even one night? That's how I feel about Dad and James."

I gathered him closer, hoping to calm his heart. How hard it is to be away from those you love, even for a moment! When the Bible states that a day can be as a thousand years, I knew that was what Beau was feeling right then—one night may as well be forever.

I reminded him that one of the best things about being God's child is that one day, we'll never be away from each other ever again. There are no goodbyes in heaven. And while I don't want to rush through a day of my time on this earth, I'll welcome the day that I have everyone I love dearly in one place forever.

"Daddy and James miss you too," I told him. "Let's say a prayer for them for a safe drive, and a prayer for you for a good night's sleep."

**Lord, be with those who are far away but dear to our hearts. Help them to know they are loved and missed, even when we can't see them for long stretches.** —Ashley Kappel

**Digging Deeper:** Psalm 34:18–20; Proverbs 12:25

---

# Saturday, April 12

**He causes his sun to rise on the evil and the good, and sends rain on the righteous and the unrighteous. —Matthew 5:45 (NIV)**

I'd been waiting three years to start the basement renovation. I had an abundance of design and décor ideas, but some of the excitement dissipated when I realized how much prep work was involved.

The basement had become a dumping ground for a number of little-used items, but amid the junk was my well-organized emergency stash of food. I value being prepared, and it quickly became clear that the stash could use some cleaning out and updating. So, while my husband prepped for contractors, I rifled through canned goods with a box nearby to toss anything that had expired.

God often speaks to me when I'm doing the most mundane tasks. And He spoke to me there sitting in the middle of canned corn, green beans, and fruit cocktail. Life's troubles will inevitably arise in our lives. While some things may be a surprise to us, they are never a surprise to God.

Had I spiritually prepared myself for emergencies and times of personal crisis? Did I have an overstock of prayers, memorized scriptures, and wise counsel for when my time to dance turned into a time to mourn? When my season of laughter turned into a season of tears? His direction was clear. Seek first to store up treasures in heaven, so that my heart will be there also, because God's treasures have no expiration date.

**God, thank You for the well of Your Word.**
—Tia McCollors

**Digging Deeper:** Joshua 1:9; Psalm 46:1–3; Isaiah 12:2

---

# Palm Sunday, Sunday, April 13

## SHELTERED IN GRACE: Remembering God's Provision
**I watch, and am as a sparrow alone upon the house top. —Psalm 102:7 (KJV)**

Kiddos trundle down the church aisle swishing green fronds this glorious Palm Sunday. How they've grown! Some were just babes in arms when I last saw them—before the pandemic isolated us all and silenced our Hosannas.

The lockdown of 2020 had begun the very day I had arrived in Baltimore to care for my three-year-old grandson, whose daycare had temporarily closed. His parents, both professors, needed help for a week or so until a "corona bug" going around disappeared and normal life resumed. Little did we know that my two-week visit would become two months, or that the lethal virus would set off a pandemic. Little did we know how much the world would change, including my worship practices.

That Palm Sunday, I logged on to an online service led by my bishop, who spoke outdoors from Church of the Woods in Canterbury, New Hampshire. He stood alone wearing a winter jacket over his clerical collar. Behind him, a muddy trail with residual snow led into a spruce forest. Instead of palms, he held a fir branch. He had walked the labyrinth there, a fitting symbol of the uncertain path through the pandemic. The ancient puzzle eventually leads us to a center, a place of rest before we find our way out.

Now, on this joyful Sunday, antic youngsters remind me that we have, indeed, found our way out of the pandemic. I am grateful. This coming Holy Week, I will revisit that time fraught with fear and unknowing. I will reflect on the ways that God showered us with constancy and care, the Holy Week God sheltered us in place—and in grace.

**You who keep Your eye on the sparrow guided me through the pandemic. You are my shelter always.**
—Gail Thorell Schilling

**Digging Deeper:** 1 Samuel 21:6; Lamentations 3:28; Daniel 10:8; John 16:32

---

## Monday, April 14

**Therefore put on the full armor of God, so that when the day of evil comes, you may be able to stand your ground, and after you have done everything, to stand. —Ephesians 6:13 (NIV)**

I had successfully navigated a day pocked with disappointing incidents. But the day was not through with me yet, as in early evening I learned that severe weather was headed straight toward the motel where I resided.

"Lord, wasn't what I just went through enough for one twenty-four-hour period? Could you not have spread things out a little?"

A laughable prayer, perhaps. But in truth, when I heard about the hurricane, my first reaction was of the last-straw ilk. I felt a bit like the celebrated biblical prophet Elijah, who, after triumphantly withstanding 450 false prophets, instantly became a wanted man who was so tired that he could not even continue standing. One would think he would

146

have been strengthened by the spectacular miracle God had just wrought, in which Elijah had called down fire from heaven.

Instead, Israel's hero hid under a tree hoping to sleep through (or die in the midst of) the threat upon his life.

It is sometimes easier to be courageous in the heat of intense battle—such as the onslaught of a particularly bad day—than when we are called to continue standing through the day-to-day, seemingly never-ending vicissitudes of life. But in the verse above, Paul doesn't just admonish us to keep standing without a rallying cry. He lovingly reminds us that if our armor of truth, righteousness, peace, faith, salvation, and Spirit is consistently maintained, we as believers are equipped to continue to stand even when the downpour of battle settles into the drip of life's uncontrollable problems.

**Help me, Jesus, to remain battle-ready but also settled upon Your day-to-day love.**
—Jacqueline F. Wheelock

**Digging Deeper:** 1 Kings 18:16–19:9; Galatians 6:9

---

# Tuesday, April 15

**Jesus answered him, "You would have no power over me unless it had been given you from above; therefore the one who handed me over to you is guilty of a greater sin." —John 19:11 (NRSVUE)**

"We pray for all leaders, Lord, that they may know and do Your will for justice, peace, and joy on earth."

I pray these words with my husband daily. Do I mean them? Yes. Do I believe they will happen? Not really. I have little hope left in leaders and institutions. Sure, I know there are good leaders, but they seem to get swallowed up by the chaos, anger, and ineptitude that swirls through the world today.

"Where are our prophets?" I complained to my friend Sylvia. "Where are our Apostles? Where are those seeking the Spirit of God instead of their opponent's downfall?"

"We have to be those people," she answered without hesitating.

That brought me up short. A native of Sierra Leone, Sylvia has witnessed firsthand the failure of institutions in her nation and ours, yet she believes *we* can be prophets and disciples?

I realized how hypocritical it was for me to pray for leaders without trying to help in my own small way. Why should politicians assist the poor if I duck into another door to avoid the Salvation Army Santa at the store's main entrance? Why should leaders seek common ground while I avoid a friend because we disagree? Why should officials do God's will and work when I resent another request for help from my church?

Sylvia is right: It is easy to be a prophet and disciple. And yet so difficult!

Jesus, instead of waiting for the world's leaders to take up Your mantle, You gave it to the men and women around You. And to us. —Marci Alborghetti

**Digging Deeper:** Matthew 5:1–20; Luke 12:1–3, 35–38

---

# Wednesday, April 16

## JOURNEYING WITH JESUS: Binoculars

**Go, therefore, and make disciples of all the nations, baptizing them in the name of the Father and the Son and the Holy Spirit, teaching them to follow all that I commanded you. —Matthew 28:19–20 (NASB)**

This directive from a mountain in Galilee was a global "go" from Jesus to His eleven disciples. Because they didn't run from the "Great Commission"—deciding it was too risky or they had more practical things to do—I can know and follow Jesus two millennia later.

Our grandson Caleb, while in high school, agreed to a summer Teen Missions International short-term mission trip to Taiwan—completing work projects, sharing Christ, building friendships. An introvert, he told me, "I knew I didn't want to go the moment I signed up." But he braved it.

Caleb is now twenty-one; he is on staff with TMI, has been to Zambia, and is just returning from six weeks in Australia. He never imagined himself in these places—and neither did I!

My aunt traveled by ocean liner to China in 1931 to bring the Good News. And my great-grandfather was a circuit rider in the 1880s, trekking on horseback to preach in rural Missouri churches.

Me—I'm just the grandma, the niece, the great-granddaughter. But I have my place. I pull my binoculars from my spiritual go-pack and scope my family's trail behind and before. Waymarks for following Jesus were laid for me long ago so that I could also mark the trail for the ones to come. God opens my eyes to see how faith in His Son becomes a heritage that carries for generations.

And I feel invigorated for the path ahead. Ready to carry the Good News of Jesus into the future.

**Father, through my faith binoculars, let me clearly see how as I go You "enlarge my steps under me" (Psalm 18:36, NASB).** —Carol Knapp

**Digging Deeper:** Deuteronomy 4:9; Psalm 18:36; Acts 26:18; 2 Timothy 1:1–7

---

# Maundy Thursday, Thursday, April 17

## SHELTERED IN GRACE: Love in Action
**This is my commandment, that ye love one another, as I have loved you.** —John 15:12 (KJV)

The pandemic still darkens our church building this Holy Thursday evening. My thoughts drift to a Holy Thursday several years ago. Our pastor had invited the local rabbi and cantor to celebrate an instructional Seder meal, a teaching service to help us better understand Jewish tradition. The symbolism of the ritual fascinated me, but I still had more to learn this holy evening.

After the instruction and dinner, our pastor invited us to continue our Holy Thursday custom of washing each other's feet, remembering Jesus's humility toward His disciples. Following prayers, the basins, warm water, and towels appeared. People paired off. Except one distraught young woman, who quietly sobbed in a corner.

My friend Robin, a woman of deep faith and mother of eight, approached the young woman, who mumbled, "I'm off my meds . . . I'm off my meds . . ."

"Come, sit here," Robin invited her. The young woman complied. "Now, you don't need to wash my feet, but I'd like to wash yours, OK?" Sobs subsided and the woman nodded. Robin kneeled on the floor and gently washed and dried the young woman's feet. "Better now?" The woman nodded, then took her position at Robin's feet to wash and dry them.

Before the closing prayer, the woman rose and slipped out of the building. Perhaps, thanks to Robin's care, she felt a bit more loved and centered—I'll never know. But I do know that as much as any other Holy Week sermon or song or ritual, I had seen love in action. Jesus's love.

**Gracious Lord, may I always be quick to take on humble tasks.** —Gail Thorell Schilling

---

# Good Friday, Friday, April 18

## SHELTERED IN GRACE: Held by Faith

**Indeed the hour is coming, yes, has now come, that you will be scattered, each to his own, and will leave Me alone. And yet I am not alone, because the Father is with Me. —John 16:32 (NKJV)**

The solemnity of Good Friday coincides with the regular meeting of our Education for Ministry, a.k.a. Exploring Life Matters class, which I mentor. This week in 2020, separated as we were by the need to shelter in place, we met virtually to study Dietrich Bonhoeffer's book *Life Together*—an ironic title, scattered as we are in New Hampshire and Maryland. We soon discover that this Christian pastor, theologian, and martyr understood displacement very well indeed. In fact, he published the book in 1939 Germany as a guide for scattered seminarians when the Gestapo disbanded their Finkenwalde community.

The short text outlines how to build community: be Christ to each other, whether physically close or separated. Bonhoeffer advocates communal activities, especially meals, as well as prayerful time alone. He urges that the seminarians practice service, caring for each other daily. Most of all, he reminds the seminarians to pray several times a day for themselves, for each other. No matter where the community must flee, members can remain joined as a beloved community through prayer. Bonhoeffer's advice to seminarians, we learn, holds true even now for us in our COVID isolation.

Our online meeting ends with a communal prayer, then each member signs out. Faces disappear. My screen goes dark. Though miles separate the members of my beloved community on this dark day of agony on the cross, our faith still holds us together.

**Hold us close, Father, during this time of fear and separation. Comfort us.** —Gail Thorell Schilling

**Digging Deeper:** Exodus 5:12; Leviticus 26:33; Isaiah 24:1; Matthew 26:31; John 11:51–52

---

# Holy Saturday, Saturday, April 19

**SHELTERED IN GRACE: Light of Christ**
**The people who walked in darkness have seen a great light; those who dwelt in the land of the shadow of death, upon them a light has shined.**
**—Isaiah 9:2 (NKJV)**

Any other year, the Easter vigil service on Holy Saturday would be packed with worshippers, who gather in darkness just outside the church entrance. Here the celebrant would ignite a small fire easily contained in a cake pan. The dainty, flickering flames would symbolize that Christ is

153

alive. From this we would light each other's candles until the sanctuary glowed.

But not this year.

Instead, I hover over my laptop to watch the shadowy figure of Bishop Rob in his backyard garden as dusk deepens. In flowing white vestments, he glides about a pile of branches, prays, then sets it ablaze. Smoke and his pristine vestments swirl in the rising wind. Even with the handheld electronics, I hear the twigs crackle and spit. Orange embers fly into the night sky. This is no timid fire in a cake pan. This is the roar and rush of New Life. This is *real*. My goosebumps tell me so.

The bishop lights the Paschal candle from the blaze and, with family on hand to contain the bonfire, he moves to the basement to continue the sacred liturgy. Only a banner, a cross, and now this candle adorn his space. The liturgical particulars differ this year, but the message never changes: our Light has come.

**Lumen Christi! Deo Gratias. Light of Christ. Thanks be to God!** —Gail Thorell Schilling

**Digging Deeper:** Isaiah 60:1; John 8:12, 12:46; Ephesians 5:8–14

---

# Easter Sunday, Sunday, April 20

## SHELTERED IN GRACE: Rejoicing Together
He is not here, but is risen! —Luke 24:6 (NKJV)

Though my son and his wife don't share my religious beliefs, we do share a few childhood Easter traditions. This locked-down, rainy Easter together, we have surprised my grandson with colorful plastic eggs hanging from the crepe myrtle. My son has requested my bread with bright, hard-boiled Easter eggs woven into the top, a family staple for forty years. This year, however, the only eggs we can find are brown. Instead of neon colors, the dyed eggs look dredged from the bottom of a pond.

Hardly festive.

Churches remain shuttered. Online worship is my only option. This joyful morning, I ditch my bathrobe for a Zoom-worthy sweater and scarf, add earrings and a touch of makeup. Alone in my room, seated in a rocker with my laptop, I find the service conducted by our bishop, who, fully vested in white and gold, presides in his home basement, alone. (Much later we would learn that lumber and paint cans were hidden just out of view.)

I keep thinking about early Christians hiding in the catacombs to avoid persecution. Now we hide to avoid pestilence. Yet, thanks to the wonders of modern technology, our dispersed church community can meet virtually. We can see and hear each other. Without the thundering organ, banks of lilies, new spring clothes; without brass fanfare and "Christ the Lord Is Risen Today," together we celebrate the mystery of our faith. Alleluia!

Lord of all hopefulness, even in isolation,
we trust in Your promises and rejoice!
—Gail Thorell Schilling

**Digging Deeper:** John 11:25; Acts 5:20;
Romans 6:4–5

---

# Easter Monday, Monday, April 21

## SHELTERED IN GRACE: Resurrection Life
**For if we have been planted together in the likeness of his death, we shall be also in the likeness of his resurrection. —Romans 6:5 (KJV)**

By Monday morning, only a chunk of Easter bread remains. Rain drips on the orange, pink, and purple plastic eggs dangling from bare branches by the back stairs. I no longer wear pretty Easter clothes around the house. My scant festivities are over. Now the seriousness of the pandemic closes preschool indefinitely. I agree to care for my grandson while his parents wrap up their semesters by teaching online in their bedroom.

When the rain lets up, my three-year-old pal and I don rubber boots and stroll the gardens that abut his rowhouse home. I teach him to name what he sees: periwinkles, tulips, daffodils. Each day we check the tightly budded azaleas to see if they have bloomed. We sprinkle lettuce seeds in the backyard. We plant beans in eggshells filled with garden soil. Over the next few weeks, we will watch the dead-looking seeds erupt from the soil, full of life. New life! Even a three-year-old grasps the miracle. These simple plants remind me of the Resurrection. My wonderment transcends my understanding.

Outwardly, nothing seems to have changed. Yet for me, everything has changed. Easter has renewed my hope. Even here, separated from my beloved community, hope and new life rise again.

**Lord of Creation, only You could remind us of the promise of New Life in such beautiful ways. Thank You.** —Gail Thorell Schilling

**Digging Deeper:** Luke 24:1–8, 33–34; John 11:25–26; Colossians 3:1–4

---

# Tuesday, April 22

**Let us not become weary in doing good, for at the proper time we will reap a harvest if we do not give up. —Galatians 6:9 (NIV)**

My friend, a young mother who is struggling to juggle her responsibilities, called to bemoan her guilt over a meltdown she'd had the previous evening. Her two-year-old had been disobedient, provoking an argument between her and her husband. She was frustrated for not being a better wife and mother while trying to work from home so she could be with her child.

"I feel like a failure," she said. "Maybe I'm not cut out for this."

I could relate, having experienced the same feelings when I was raising my children and working full time. But I've had feelings of doubt and frustration at other times too, especially when life gets hard, making me question whether I was doing what I was supposed to be doing or if God had other plans for me.

After the conversation with my friend, I walked into my kitchen and peered out the window. Just feet away, I spotted a mother finch sitting on a nest partially hidden among the fronds of a hanging fern. Every day, she sat there. One day, her eggs would hatch and her job would change; then she'd be busy feeding her young before they left the nest. However, for now, she was where she was supposed to be, doing what God planned for her to do.

I called my friend back and told her about the finch, and how she, too, was right where God wanted her to be.

**Lord, we often get tired of our everyday lives, not seeing the fruit of our labor. Help us to appreciate that we're where You want us to be and that our efforts will be rewarded.** —Marilyn Turk

**Digging Deeper:** 2 Chronicles 15:7; Titus 2:7

---

# Wednesday, April 23

**...you will protect me from trouble and surround me with songs of deliverance. —Psalm 32:7 (NIV)**

My horse hates his blanket. Pinned ears, stomping feet, a pop at me with his nose, Jack makes it clear that, although he is in his upper twenties, he is not cowardly. Normally an easygoing horse, blanketing him is one of the few activities in which I have to halter him. "Can't you see I'm trying to help you?" I tell him. Fortunately, there are usually only a few days a year in which I need to give him extra protection from the weather.

Jack had already shed out his winter coat when a late-season storm hit. Temperatures dropped into the teens with high winds and relentless snow that hurt when it hit skin. I brought grain out to give Jack a boost of warmth. Snow was caked over his back and left side. He was shivering. This time, he didn't stomp when I hauled out his blanket. I rubbed the snow off his back and draped the blanket over him. I could almost hear him sigh, "Aaaah!"

I admonish him, but Jack is exactly like me. I tell myself I'm tough. I don't need help. I can handle anything. I can, that is, until the storm comes. Then I want God's protection. Then I embrace the security and help I've been too willful, foolish, and independent to accept. Just like I wish Jack would let me help him before the storm gets bad, I need to allow God to help me before I get in over my head—which means, every day.

**Father God, thank You for loving me even when I am too foolish to see when You are wrapping me in protection. —Erika Bentsen**

---

# Thursday, April 24

**Do not be anxious about anything . . .**
**—Philippians 4:6 (NIV)**

I was walking my dog at high noon when I looked up to see the moon fully visible. Not only that, a large flock of crows flew overhead, squawking and circling repeatedly.

It was a scene that could've established the setting for a fictional story—a tableau almost worthy of Shakespeare's *Macbeth*. Or one that perhaps an ancient soothsayer might have considered a disturbing portent, a sign predicting how an army would fare in an upcoming battle.

How wonderful that I could instead just casually muse on these things as I continued my walk! For unlike Macbeth or an oracle, I need not attempt to predict the future: I know what to expect.

Paul tells the church in 1 Thessalonians 4:13 that he does "not want you to be uninformed" about the things to come. Our minister explained to us recently that some of the church in Thessalonica were worried that those who died before Christ's return would miss out on His glorious Second Coming. Paul wrote to reassure them that, on the contrary, the "dead in Christ [would] rise first" (verse 16) when the trumpet of the Lord sounds. He tells them—and us—exactly what's in store for our eternal destiny, ending his explanation with the most beautiful of hopeful assurances: "And so we shall be with the Lord forever" (verse 17).

I never did find out what the crows were going on about that day, but the Scriptural teaching they reminded me of will stay with me for a long time.

**Father in Heaven, thank You for allowing me to rest in Your promises.** —Ginger Rue

**Digging Deeper:** Matthew 24:36; 2 Peter 3:10

---

# Friday, April 25

**He heals the brokenhearted and binds up their wounds. —Psalm 147:3 (ESV)**

We made the gutting decision to find a new home for our twenty-one-year-old horse. My daughter's riding ability outgrew Snow, and Snow became a very beautiful lawn ornament. She was such a good and useful girl, so we thought finding Snow a place where she could be used in teaching riding lessons would be ideal. We stumbled on the perfect home for her, and I ugly-cried for a week.

When we had Snow, I spent every Friday taking care of her needs—feeding, brushing, cleaning, giving her treats, and just general togetherness. It never occurred to me her absence would leave such a hole in my routine. Without me realizing it, caring for Snow had become a beloved Friday ritual: spending time with Snow nurtured my spirit and recharged my heart. And, yes, I met God there too. God was in the nature that surrounded us, in the knicker of the other horses, and the wisp of unexpected breezes.

My first Friday without Snow, I felt lost. Time slowed down on those Friday afternoons and I could connect with myself, with Snow, and with God. Perhaps when my tears cease at the thought of Snow, I may be ready to explore new Friday rituals. My afternoons with Snow showed me that everyday activities have the potential to become rituals, leading us back to our spiritual selves, leading us home.

**Dear Father, may my soul find a home in Your love, in Your grace, and in Your mercy.** —Jolynda Strandberg

**Digging Deeper:** Proverbs 3:5–6; John 14:25–31; Romans 8:18

---

# Saturday, April 26

**Now all we can see of God is like a cloudy picture in a mirror. Later we will see him face to face. We don't know everything, but then we will, just as God completely understands us.** **—1 Corinthians 13:12 (CEV)**

As the boat motored toward the airport, I felt a sense of loss leaving the Galapagos Islands behind. I'd had such a joyous journey exploring the Ecuadorian archipelago and its weirdly wonderful wildlife. But endings are an inevitable part of this life, and it was time to say farewell.

Suddenly, a short distance from the boat, a ray broke the surface of the water, jumping high into the air. As soon as it splashed down, it leapt up again. And again. And again. I lost count of how many times that ray soared and splashed, leaping like an aquatic ballerina across a saltwater stage. It seemed like it was saying, "Bye! Good to see you! Come again soon!"

Of course, I have no idea what—if anything—that ray was communicating. Even marine biologists are uncertain as to why rays jump. They theorize it could be to escape predators, shake off parasites, give birth, or just for fun. Personally, I lean toward the latter.

God's creation continues to hold so many mysteries. As does the Creator Himself. Although God communicates with us through Scripture, His Son Jesus, and the Holy Spirit, there's still so much room for misunderstanding—and questions—on my part. I do love this awe-inspiring world. But I look forward to the day when I'll step beyond its boundaries and meet God face to face. Maybe then I'll understand why rays jump . . . and oh, so much more.

**Father, may I hear Your voice, and understand what's true, with as much clarity as possible.**
—Vicki Kuyper

**Digging Deeper:** Proverbs 3:5–6; Isaiah 55:8–9; Romans 11:33, 12:2

# Sunday, April 27

**Your eyes light up your inward being. A pure eye lets sunshine into your soul. —Luke 11:34 (TLB)**

One Sunday morning I picked up my friend Suzanne, and the two of us headed for Mass under the big-top tent that my parish, St. Jerome's, puts up anytime they expect an overflow crowd.

The tent was filled with hundreds of people sitting on white plastic chairs. We sat toward the back, where I noticed a wiggly baby three rows ahead of me. As the bouncy five- or six-month-old jumped up and down on his mother's lap, I kept staring at him and grinning. Suddenly the baby locked eyes with me.

I grinned. He grinned. He kept staring right into my eyes. Suddenly I felt as if that is exactly how Jesus sees me. Directly. Right into my heart, soul, and mind.

That squirmy, funny baby never met a stranger. Jesus never met a stranger either. That was the moment I was certain that Jesus sees me as that baby did. He sees me. Really sees me. The only difference is that Jesus sees me, knows me, forgives me, puts up with my bad choices, and loves me unconditionally in spite of myself.

Thanks to that staring, smiling baby, it was a joyous Easter season, because I truly felt the eyes of the risen Lord looking directly into mine.

**Jesus, thank You for looking into my eyes, heart, soul, and mind with such love, and for inspiring**

me to look at others the way You look at me.
—Patricia Lorenz

**Digging Deeper:** Psalm 11:4–7; Luke 11:35–36;
1 Peter 3:10–12

---

# Monday, April 28

**He injures, but He binds up; He wounds, but His hands heal. —Job 5:18 (JPS)**

While my house is surrounded by tall evergreens, there is only one tree inside our six-foot wooden fence. Our tame tree was a lilac, about my height when we moved in. Over the next fifteen years I watched it grow taller, and I was proud of its stature and strength, as well as its beauty and fragrance.

In year sixteen, I noticed that it had started leaning. I tried to prop it up by wedging a board between its trunk and the ground on the lower side, but soon we had one of our major windstorms, which knocked the board away, and I could never get it into place again. I was sure the trunk would snap off at the base.

The morning in year eighteen when I woke to find the entire crown of the tree had finally hit the ground, I figured it was done for at last, the strength and stature I loved about it absolutely gone. I couldn't afford a tree service to come cut it up and haul it away, so I just left it alone.

Soon I discovered that wild bunnies were using the downed branches as a thicket, which made the dog ecstatic because she got to chase them. A few weeks later, I saw that new shoots were growing from the earth around the roots. Then some of the branches began sprouting leaves and buds. The tree, it seemed, might have no longer had the stature, but it certainly still had its strength.

**God, You found a wonderful way to show me that even if something or someone looks broken, it can still be beautiful and full of life.** —Rhoda Blecker

**Digging Deeper:** Isaiah 58:8; Hosea 6:2

---

# Tuesday, April 29

**I no longer call you servants, because a servant does not know his master's business. Instead, I have called you friends, for everything that I learned from my Father I have made known to you. —John 15:15 (NIV)**

I sat on the edge of my seat as a retreat speaker shared her quiet-time ritual. Each morning, she poured two cups of coffee. She placed one in front of the empty chair at the head of her kitchen table. She sat down in a chair to the right, the other cup in hand. Sipping the warm brew, she envisioned Christ seated beside her. Chatting with Jesus like she would a trusted friend, she visualized Him in a relaxed pair of jeans, a comfy sweatshirt, and running shoes as she talked about her worries and her hopes. Like any companion offering sage advice, she listened too.

I couldn't help but giggle at her unorthodox habit. My relationship with Jesus has always been more formal and reverent. I see Jesus as my Savior. He is Emmanuel, Redeemer, Messiah, Lord, and Master to me.

A few days later I had trouble focusing on my Bible text. After I finished reading and got ready to pray, I thought of the retreat speaker. The Jesus I see in my mind wears a tan robe and sandals, like He did in biblical times. But isn't Jesus also here in the twenty-first century?

Today, I imagined Jesus sitting beside me wearing modern-day clothing. I tried talking to Him casually, like He was my best friend. I may have poured an extra cup of coffee too.

**Dear Jesus, my Savior, You are Emmanuel, Redeemer, Messiah, Lord, and Master. Help me to also embrace You as my intimate Friend. Amen.** —Stephanie Thompson

**Digging Deeper:** John 15:12–14; James 2:23, 4:4

---

# Wednesday, April 30

**Therefore, as we have opportunity, let us do good to all people, especially to those who belong to the family of believers. —Galatians 6:10 (NIV)**

When my eighty-eight-year-old mother lamented that she missed receiving mail from her family and friends—most of whom were quite elderly or deceased—I knew exactly what I would do for her birthday. I called, texted, and emailed everyone I thought might be willing to take the time to send Mom a birthday card. I asked my sister to do the same. Most were more than willing to perform this small act of kindness. As a result, Mom received seventy-seven birthday cards in one week! She happily displayed those cards throughout her small apartment. I felt gratified.

One day shortly afterward, the mail carrier knocked on Mom's door to inquire if she was all right. She'd noted that Mom had received more mail than she'd ever received before. Luella feared Mom was sick or perhaps recovering from an injury or surgery. "I just want to make sure you're OK," she explained.

I was touched by the woman's kindness. So was Mom. Later I recalled a poster one of my elementary-school teachers had displayed in her classroom—a quote by Aesop: "No act of kindness, no matter how small, is ever wasted." There are many Bible verses, too, that urge believers to be kind and do good. In Paul's letter to the Galatians, he reminds us that kindness is one of the fruits of the Holy Spirit. And it was the kind gestures—all of them—Mom treasured the most for her birthday.

**Dear Heavenly Father, help me be as kind and compassionate to others as You have been to me.**
—Shirley Raye Redmond

**Digging Deeper:** Acts 28:2; 1 Corinthians 13:4; Galatians 5:22

## WITH AN EVERLASTING LOVE

1 _____

2 _____

3 _____

4 _____

5 _____

6 _____

7 _____

8 _____

9 _____

10 _____

11 _____

12 _____

13 _____

**14** _____

**15** _____

**16** _____

**17** _____

**18** _____

**19** _____

**20** _____

**21** _____

**22** _____

**23** _____

**24** _____

**25** _____

**26** _____

**27** _____

**28** _____

**29** _____

**30** _____

# May

We love because
he first loved us.

—1 John 4:19 (ESV)

# Thursday, May 1

**To answer before listening—that is folly and shame. —Proverbs 18:13 (NIV)**

I signed up for a coaching course. My goal was to develop a mentoring mindset and acquire the skills to help others. On day one the instructor said, "Listening and asking good questions are two key tools of an effective coach."

I knew that would be a challenging skill for me. After forty-plus years of ministry and marriage, listening should come easily to me, but it doesn't. Many times, I find myself listening with the intent to reply, thereby missing out on what the person is saying. In Scripture, James advises us to be quick to listen and slow to speak (1:19). Much harder to do than to say.

Listening is not just an important skill for coaching. It's a skill that applies to my other roles: husband, father, brother, friend, pastor, and follower of Jesus. I am still learning to listen to God, who speaks in many different ways to me. Some days I'm quick to speak and slow to listen.

The course reminded me that listening to others and God is a work in progress. I'm glad the Lord is my coach, who listens like no one else and whose questions guide me along His path ... and who doesn't give up on me when I don't listen or follow His ways.

**Lord, teach me to be quick to listen and slow to speak; help me follow Your guidance. —Pablo Diaz**

---

# Friday, May 2

**Two are better than one, because they have a good reward for their toil. —Ecclesiastes 4:9 (ESV)**

I was in New York and promised Gracie a long walk through our Chelsea neighborhood. My golden loves the bustle of the city as a change from the country. We stopped at a few old haunts we hadn't visited since before the pandemic. Amazing how Gracie still remembers all the business owners who have a treat behind the counter for her. "Hey, it's Gracie! Welcome back!"

We ended up at the Chelsea Waterside Park dog run. The run had undergone a big reno since our last visit some four years ago. A nice spongy surface, some colorful artificial hillocks, a little plastic stream.

Gracie politely greeted the few dogs that were present. I wondered if any of her old friends were around, the ones she had bonded with as a puppy. Things had changed so much in the last few years.

The dog run gate clattered as a new dog and owner entered. Gracie sprang up. Across the space the two dogs' eyes met. Was this Jazz, a Great Pyrenees Gracie had grown up with? Her old dog run pal?

They ran to each other and met atop a hillock, bumping and wrestling, then they were off, running and barking. A friendship renewed.

I thought of my own friendships, so many of them disrupted by time and distance and the years of isolation. God brings people into my life for a reason. They are gifts. Wouldn't it be good for my soul to renew these blessings that had fallen by the wayside? Today I would start.

**Life is full of Your gifts, Father. The blessing of friendship is one of the greatest. When I tend to my friendships, I tend to my soul.** —Edward Grinnan

**Digging Deeper:** 1 Thessalonians 5:11; 1 Peter 4:8–10

---

# Saturday, May 3

**I will turn their mourning into gladness; I will give them comfort and joy instead of sorrow. —Jeremiah 31:13 (NIV)**

Helping my daughter Emily move into her condo reminded me of earlier moves.

After college, I moved into my first apartment. Dad gave me a round metal box with miscellaneous screws and nails, along with my first tool kit. When Emily's sister moved into her first apartment, I gave her Dad's tool kit and the metal box.

When my husband and I bought our first house, Dad helped Dave improve our kitchen. I cherish the photo of them shaking hands through our new window. Emily moved into her first apartment the same year Mom moved from her house into assisted living. Mom gave Emily many of her plates, bowls, glasses, and utensils.

Now Dad is in heaven and Mom is in memory care. This move felt sad without them.

On moving day, I emptied Emily's apartment kitchen, packed it up, then put things away in her condo kitchen. I smiled at Mom's familiar kitchenware. Then I recognized a magnet from Mom's refrigerator: "Life Is Full of Questions ... Chocolate Is the Answer!"

Emily's friends driving the truck needed a blanket to protect her furniture. I reached into my car and handed them Dad's army blanket. When I unpacked Emily's desk drawer, I found Dad's fifty-year-old General Electric pencil! We looked at each other. *How did that get there?*

Emily's sister gave her a gently used drill and Dad's round metal box of miscellaneous screws and nails.

Mom and Dad were nearby that day, after all.

**Dear Lord, I know they're just things, but they're familiar—like family. Thank You for turning my sadness into comfort and joy.** —Leanne Jackson

**Digging Deeper:** Psalm 119:76; Matthew 5:4

---

## Sunday, May 4

# WHEN CHANGE COMES:
## Leaning on the Lord's Strength
**Finally, be strong in the Lord and in the strength of his might.** —Ephesians 6:10 (ESV)

My family asked for BLTs for dinner, so I stopped by a roadside stand for tomatoes. Normally I'd have taken the interstate, but I needed the calm of the country. I regretted the route when my pocketbook brought forth twenty cents.

"I have it," came a kind voice from behind. A hand stretched forward to poke bills into the honor-system cash box.

I was relieved, though the help didn't alleviate my underlying stress. The next day, after twenty-two years of home teaching, I'd be a phlebotomy student. My boys had grown, and now it was my turn. I was terrified. Helping others drew me, but blood made me queasy. I knew I was a good teacher, but how would I do when the tables were turned? "Help me, Lord," was my plea.

"Shawnelle?" the lady behind me asked when I turned to say thank you. I recognized her as a long-ago friend from church, Andrea. We'd never gotten close, but respect for her ran deep.

"Does your family like cucumbers?" she asked after we visited. "Follow me home. I'll share."

Andrea's home was sweet salve. She and I sat in the sunroom, and my heart spilled free as the morning rays. Andrea was a retired nurse and woman whose faith had taken her through fire. Now, she met each of my fears with truth of God's presence and power. And when I left, I stood strong, knowing the Lord would be with me—no matter what.

After all, He'd ordered every detail of an unexpected encounter to remind me.

Oh Lord, when I'm weak and uncertain,
I'll count on Your strength. Amen.
—Shawnelle Eliasen

**Digging Deeper:** 1 Chronicles 16:11;
Psalm 28:7; Isaiah 40:29

---

# WHEN CHANGE COMES: Trusting Him
**May the favor of the Lord our God rest on us;
establish the work of our hands for us—yes,
establish the work of our hands. —Psalm 90:17 (NIV)**

"I'll drive you to school tomorrow," seventeen-year-old Gabriel said. "On your first day." His expression spoke deep love. And the next day, there he was. Waiting in his car as I shoved crisp new notebooks into the floral-print backpack he'd given me for Mother's Day. "You'll do great," he said when I opened the door and sat beside him. My throat was thick with emotion. I nodded and swallowed hard.

The road to school ran along the river, and a thousand memories came crisp and clear. Boating in the summer sun. Bike rides with the boys. Read-aloud books on a blanket. Home teaching had been so sweet. It was hard to let go.

Rain began as downtown came closer, and by the time Gabe parked in front of the tall brick building, the pelts were fast and hard. I looked at the door and at my son, and he nodded. "You taught us to move forward," he said. "But let's sit

177

just a minute more." When I left the car a moment later and glimpsed back, I saw him wipe a tear.

Moving forward means letting go, and it's the ultimate trust in God. Looking at this strong, solid boy, his heart rich with mercy, reminded me that the Lord had shown me favor and had ordered my work. He'd blessed it—and this beating-heart boy was flesh and fruit. The Lord would establish my next steps and relationships too.

**Oh Father, thank You for the blessing of yesterday. Help me to be brave, confident, and expectant as we walk forward together. I trust You. Amen.**
—Shawnelle Eliasen

**Digging Deeper:** Psalm 143:8; Proverbs 16:3

---

# Tuesday, May 6

# WHEN CHANGE COMES:
## Leaning into the Lord's Intimacy
**But now thus says the Lord, he who created you, O Jacob, he who formed you, O Israel: "Fear not, for I have redeemed you; I have called you by name, you are mine." —Isaiah 43:1 (ESV)**

For twenty-two years, I home-taught our five boys. Decades of classic books and flashcards. Art supplies and field trips. Posters of alphabet letters, U.S. presidents, and the periodic elements stretched like garland on our schoolroom wall. Teaching and training fulfilled me. But that was no longer.

Isaiah, our youngest, had started public high school.

"Hey, Mom, I made something for you in wood class," he said one afternoon. We'd both just gotten home from school. We were months into our new lifestyles, but my heart still ached for our days-of-old. When a cutting board tied with a brown bow came from behind my son's back, I stopped still. I couldn't believe the blessing.

Thick stripes of oak, walnut, and cherry sanded smooth.

I'd seen one in an Amish shop years before, and I'd longed for it. But this one, on the backside, bore our names. "To Mom. With love, from Zay."

Emotion swelled in my soul. The etching of a name speaks love. Sweethearts carve initials on trees. Jewelry is engraved to encapsulate devotion. The Lord Most High inscribes the names of the saved on the inside of His hand.

"Oh, Isaiah," I said. "It's beautiful. I can't believe you've done this for me."

"I love you, Mom," he said.

This gift will remind me that change comes as a constant, and even beloved days cannot remain. But the Lord is with us always.

We are His. And He calls us by name.

**Lord, thank You for reminders of Your intimate love.** —Shawnelle Eliasen

**Digging Deeper:** Isaiah 45:3, 49:16; John 10:3

# Wednesday, May 7

## WHEN CHANGE COMES: Leaning into the Lord's Care

**Look at the birds of the air, they do not sow or reap or store away in barns, and yet your heavenly Father feeds them. Are you not much more valuable than they? —Matthew 6:26 (NIV)**

I'd knowingly chosen to study phlebotomy because I wanted to help people who, like me, were terrified of the process of drawing blood. But when the bookwork paused at school and it was time to work on practical skills, my own stomach turned. We raised our sons in an 1864 home—blood tests for lead were frequent. Little-boy Samuel had been terrified. However, his fear of being poked paled compared to my fear of poking. I passed when my turn came to draw blood. I wanted to quit class and never return, but I'd taught my sons perseverance.

"Are you OK?" a classmate asked as I walked in the next day. "You didn't look well yesterday." I thought about bluffing, keeping my cool. Yet I'd prayed for the Lord's care, and this seemed time to come clean. I shared how I wanted to help others but had gotten sick when my boys had gotten hurt. Of how I was afraid of blood.

When I looked up, I expected to see disapproval. But what I saw was the opposite.

"When you draw today," my classmate Rinkal said, her voice kind and warm as her brown eyes, "we will stand beside you. This way, you will know that you are not alone." And that's what happened. When it was my turn, these ladies left their stations. A classmate sat in my chair and extended her arm. Rinkal and the others curved close. My hands trembled. I missed the vein by a long shot.

But it was OK. The Lord had cared for me by providing a circle of compassion, help, and love.

**Jesus, You spoke of lesser creation to share Your care for me. And You never let me down.**
—Shawnelle Eliasen

**Digging Deeper:** Psalm 55:22; Isaiah 43:2; Lamentations 3:25

---

# Thursday, May 8

## WHEN CHANGE COMES: Leaning into the Lord's Provision

**You gave your good Spirit to instruct them. You did not withhold your manna from their mouths, and you gave them water for their thirst. —Nehemiah 9:20 (NIV)**

"Shawnelle, I'm going to the processing lab. I'll be back soon," our lead phlebotomist said. I'd been hired to work in the outpatient lab of a large hospital. Though I'd passed my written exam with a high score, I was slow to master skill.

It wasn't long before a patient came in. I registered her and showed her to the draw chair. When my needle tip hovered above her arm, she noticed my uncertainty. "I'm outside of my comfort zone a lot too," she said. "I breathe deep. I breathe deep and pray."

I clipped the cap over the needle.

The woman and I began to share, and it didn't take long for us to learn that we were both believers. "My husband recently passed away," she said. "I'm left to raise our daughter."

Oh, the timing of that visit—rich in the goodness of our gracious God.

The lab usually overflowed with patients, and phlebotomists ran at breakneck speed. But the cadence of the day had been slow, and the Lord had carved time for Cathy. I listened to her story with my whole heart, and when Cathy finished sharing, she and I prayed. I then drew her blood with hands that were steady and strong.

"How did it go while I was away?" my lead asked when she returned.

"Things happened just as they needed to," I said.

I understood that God's provision is always perfect, and although His children may walk different wildernesses, manna from the Almighty is always enough.

**Lord, help me to trust in Your provision. Amen.**
—Shawnelle Eliasen

**Digging Deeper:** Deuteronomy 29:5; Psalm 81:10; Philippians 4:19

## WHEN CHANGE COMES: Leaning into the Lord for Courage
**Be strong and courageous.**
—Deuteronomy 31:6 (NIV)

Dawn stretched over the cold winter horizon. I could see it in the rearview mirror of my car. I needed to press on—the hospital time clock awaited. But inside I felt frozen, and I turned my car around and watched and waited for the sun.

My home, outside my window, was quiet. My teenage boys would be up for an early swim soon. I remembered them as little boys in a different house. I'd wake in the morning and have quiet time with the Lord in my soft, worn rocking chair. By the time the boys tumbled from bed, rumple-headed and sweet-smelling from sleep, I'd be waiting by the fire in our schoolroom. From the window at the back of the house, we'd watch the sky color as the sun would rise.

I sat in my car, so full of missing that I could hardly breathe. I wished I could drive to that century-old home that sat on the hill. Maybe I'd find that time loop and I could park my car and walk inside. Lonny would be sleeping softly. The house would smell of coffee and candles, and soon the stairs would creak with the footfalls of family.

But the Lord tells us to be strong and courageous, and courage means moving forward even when we'd rather look back.

So, I headed toward the hospital, where I knew the Lord would meet me. His presence would give me courage, beautiful as the birth of a new day.

**Lord, in You I can find the courage to walk the present when I want to cling to the past. Amen.**
—Shawnelle Eliasen

**Digging Deeper:** Psalm 27:1; Isaiah 41:10–13; Ephesians 6:10

---

# Saturday, May 10

**Truly I tell you, whoever does not receive the kingdom of God as a little child will never enter it. —Mark 10:15 (NRSVUE)**

Have you ever prayed with a kid? I don't mean just saying bedtime prayers or grace at dinner, but finding yourself in the prayerful presence of a child.

We'd flown out to San Francisco to look after Baby Ricky while his hardworking parents flew to a wedding, a well-deserved break for them. Even so, I wasn't sure I was up to caring for an eleven-month-old. It had been so long since our own two boys were that age.

Ricky is wonderfully good-natured and loves to eat. He watched me cooking my oatmeal and raised his hands up. He wanted some too. Indeed, as I sat with him, I shoved as many spoonfuls into his mouth as into my own, especially the ones with blueberries.

Later, we sat on the floor, amidst the array of balls, books, and toys, not to mention the pumpkin he pulled off the coffee table. We rolled a ball back and forth, turned the pages in a book, pushed blocks along the floor, spun around and sang. Normally in the mornings, I'm looking at my watch, checking my phone, logging on, calculating what I need to get done during the day. No time for that now. I had to be fully present. Didn't even have time to read my usual psalms for the day.

Then it occurred to me that, this, too, was a way to pray. Being fully present in the moment. Savoring it. Singing along with "The wheels on the bus go round and round . . ."

I'd look at the psalms later. For now, I had Ricky.

**Lord, may I be open to Your blessings like a child.**
—Rick Hamlin

**Digging Deeper:** Psalm 127:3; Proverbs 17:6; Isaiah 54:13

---

# Mother's Day, Sunday, May 11

**We love each other because he loved us first.**
**—1 John 4:19 (NLT)**

I'd just left the podium and returned to my seat. Everyone around me was standing, applauding. I couldn't look up, for fear that those around me would see the tears in my eyes. The fact that the applause was directed at me was a totally unexpected Mother's Day gift. I was happy, but humbled. This was certainly the only time I'd received a standing ovation for being a parent.

Though my two children had grown to have families of their own, my role as their mother continued—and continued teaching me about my heavenly Father's ongoing love and care for me as I matured. That lesson was the heart of the message I'd just shared with my church's congregation.

I'm sure much of the applause was simply my fellow mothers' way of shouting, "Amen, Sister!" We shared the knowledge that although being a mother is an incomparable blessing, the pressure to be a good one can be a weight we struggle to carry at times. No one claps when we calm an out-of-control child or grandchild, when we spend more time cleaning up after a family meal than cooking it, or when we continue working hard to "raise" those we care for even on the days we can hardly raise ourselves out of bed. Yet we persevere. Love is a choice we make minute by minute, day after day, year after year. It's a God-given gift that increases in size every time we give it away.

**Father, Your unfailing love is not only my example, but a seed You've planted in my life. May it never cease to bear fruit.** —Vicki Kuyper

**Digging Deeper:** Proverbs 1:8–9, 31:28–31; Isaiah 49:15; Galatians 6:9; 1 Peter 4:8; 1 John 4:7–21

## The heart of the wise teacheth . . .
—Proverbs 16:23 (KJV)

They rarely live on great estates, hold high offices, or get their names written across building fronts. Seldom do they receive monetary rewards. They are God's real stars, though their faces never make magazine covers. They are the real "influencers" of our lives, yours and mine.

We call them *teachers*.

At this moment, one floats across your memory. "Yes," you say. "Yes."

My sixth-grade teacher, Mrs. Setzer, once wrote me a letter that I wouldn't trade for a bar of pure gold. It is my reminder of that "best person" my teacher believed me to be. I truly thank God that I wrote back before she moved to heaven.

Our granddaughter Abby calls from college. "I have something to tell you."

David and I anguish. Is it fallen grades, financial problems? She has been on a great path, loves school, has good friends, stays close to family. She talks of following her Uncle Brock in the investment business and of the fun she'll have with all that money.

At lunch, she looks across the table at us. "I hope you won't be disappointed," she says. "I'm changing my major. I want to be a teacher."

I feel like springing up and doing a dance. How perfect! Abby has always been a natural lifter-upper.

But I stay calm. She needs room to work out her decisions without my painting her in a corner. So, calmly, I ask, "Why do you want to be a teacher?"

The answer of dreams comes then: "Because they are the happiest people I know."

**Father, hold Abby and all our children close. Lead them toward the happiness that comes from serving others.** —Pam Kidd

**Digging Deeper:** John 21:15; 1 Peter 4:10

---

# Tuesday, May 13

**For whoever finds me finds life and wins approval from the Lord. —Proverbs 8:35 (TLB)**

One year for Mother's Day, I received a blank journal in the mail. In large, bold letters the title of the book was, "Sorry about your other children. At least you have me."

The card inside was typed, leaving no clue as to the identity of the sender. "Happy Mother's Day from your favorite child."

The thing is, I have four children, all of whom I love, admire, and cherish equally, and all four have a great sense of humor. So my dilemma was who to thank.

I figured it out a few days later when my son Michael asked if I'd received a package in the mail. We had a good laugh over that book.

But during those days of wondering which one of my kids thought he or she was my favorite, I started wondering if I was anybody's favorite sister, aunt, grandma, or friend. Then I asked myself the important question, "Am I on God's list of favorite people?" I could almost hear the good Lord say to me, "Sorry about the rest of the world. At least you have me."

Next time I was fearful during a storm, or driving home late at night, or wondering if my GPS would get me there safely, or how I would cope with living and traveling alone for the rest of my life, I remembered those words. "Sorry about the rest of the world. At least you have me."

Isn't it amazing that every human's name on earth is written in the book of God's favorite people? Wow.

**God, thank You for loving me, cherishing me, encouraging me. Never let me take Your grace for granted.** —Patricia Lorenz

**Digging Deeper:** Psalm 35:27–28; Acts 2:47; 1 Timothy 5:21

---

# Wednesday, May 14

**I seek you with all my heart; do not let me stray from your commands. —Psalm 119:10 (NIV)**

Our golden retriever, Dolly, loves to go for walks. However, it takes some effort to control her seventy-pound energy when we go out. She bolts when she spots a squirrel, almost jerking us off our feet.

Obedience classes helped her learn commands such as "sit" and "stay," although sometimes her enthusiasm overrides her desire to obey. We keep the leash taut when other people or dogs approach because Dolly is very friendly, wanting to greet everyone and play.

As she's gotten older, my husband has taken her to more open areas, where he unleashes her and lets her run free. At first, I worried about her running off, but she enjoys coming back to whiz past us as if to say, "*Whee*, this is fun!"

One day, we took Dolly for a walk in the woods. Chuck unleashed her and she took off. She raced through the woods, her tail waving high like a flag. Finally, she returned to trot on the trail ahead of us while we followed dutifully behind. To test her, I told Chuck to stop and see how long it would be before she noticed we weren't behind her anymore. As expected, she continued on, oblivious to the fact that we no longer followed. Suddenly she stopped and looked around. Spotting us some distance behind, she raced back to us. She knew she needed to be near her masters and returned to us.

Like Dolly, we can stray from God and go our own way without Him, sometimes with dire consequences. How reassuring it is to know we can run back to Him.

Lord, forgive me when I've strayed from Your side.
Thank You for welcoming me back.
—Marilyn Turk

**Digging Deeper:** Isaiah 53:6; Acts 3:19

---

# Thursday, May 15

**If any of you lacks wisdom, you should ask God, who gives generously to all without finding fault, and it will be given to you. —James 1:5 (NIV)**

Our church was facing an issue. I was asked to share my position in an upcoming congregational meeting along with several others offering their position. Whenever I seek discernment, I'm always concerned that I don't mistake my own biases or emotions for God's guidance. "I wish I could talk about this face-to-face with Jesus over coffee," I said to our pastor. He just smiled.

I asked for God's wisdom to guide me. I studied the issue and read the related scriptures. I found insight from one of Jesus's parables, which led to the position I took. I drafted a few talking points and shared them with a faith friend. Even after revising the draft with the suggestions I received and further refining it, I wasn't yet satisfied.

A few days before the congregational meeting, my morning coffee and prayer time was interrupted by new ideas filling my mind so quickly that I paused my quiet time—something I rarely do—to capture them on paper. After reworking the script using the ideas, I was finally ready for the talk.

The morning after giving the talk, I reread the script. There was nothing I would have changed. Never had I given a talk that there wasn't something I would have changed afterward. I believe Jesus provided, through the Spirit, the words and content flow I needed.

**Dear Lord, I longed to talk with You about the issue at hand. Thank You for helping me—not in a coffee shop, but during our regular morning meeting instead!** —John Dilworth

**Digging Deeper:** Psalm 119:125; Proverbs 5:1–2; Mark 11:24

---

# Friday, May 16

## JOURNEYING WITH JESUS: Rope
**And Jesus said, "I do not condemn you, either. Go. From now on do not sin any longer."** —John 8:11 (NASB)

My pack is feeling heavy—pressing me down so I'm nearly doubled over my feet. I have added the weight of sin. Deliberate sin—choosing a relationship outside my marriage covenant. I've raised the veil between God and me (2 Corinthians 3:13–15). I cannot participate in this sin unless I hide His face.

Remembering the internal struggle of that time, the parable of the adulterous woman in John 8:1–11 hits me anew. Little is known of the woman dragged before Jesus. Her accusers boast they have caught her in "the very act." She is in danger of being stoned for adultery.

What will Jesus say? Will He follow the Law of Moses? They want to catch Him out too—in "the very act" of being an imposter—claiming to be the infallible Son of God. Jesus is ready for these heartless religious leaders. Whoever among them is without sin can throw the first stone. Silently they leave the temple court. The nameless woman is utterly humiliated. But Jesus is gentle with her—asking if no one has condemned her.

"No one, Lord," she chokes out, her eyes cast to the ground. She calls Him Lord, acknowledging His authority. She hears His pardon. And then she hears, "Go." Go back to her life—maybe to a marriage needing repair. But go—break free from intentional wrongdoing.

I grab for the rope near the bottom of my spiritual go-pack, hand one end to Jesus. I keep the other. The allure is strong. Only He can pull me away. I'm holding on tight. I won't let go this time. I want His forgiveness—I want to "look full in His wonderful face"—and see the love that is there for me.

**Jesus—You are my Savior in all things—my lifeline, if I will only hold on.** —Carol Knapp

**Digging Deeper:** 2 Corinthians 3:15–18; Galatians 6:1; James 2:10–13

# Saturday, May 17

**Behold, the former things have come to pass, and new things I now declare; before they spring forth I tell you of them. —Isaiah 42:9 (ESV)**

I have never liked pancakes. Even as a kid, I thought they were too heavy and overwhelming to eat, especially in the morning, so when a short stack appealed to me on the diner menu, strangely, I gave in to my unusual craving.

As the waitress took our order, my husband looked at me quizzically.

"Honey, you hate pancakes," he said.

"I know. I just felt like having them." I shrugged.

The pancakes came with a fancy tray of cute little tubs of jelly, butter, and syrup, and I felt like a kid—a kid who likes pancakes. They were amazing, and I ate every bit.

"I don't even know what to say," my husband said.

As the waitress cleared the table, she asked, "Everything OK? You folks good?" Taking my empty plate, she remarked, "You did good!"

"Best pancakes of my life," I said.

On the drive home, my husband joked, "I don't know who you are."

And I thought about other things I might be missing. Things I may have misjudged long ago. Foods like Nutella or bananas, and hobbies like crosswords, sports like baseball and football, and who knows what other treasures I have grouped into a bucket of dislikes that, with time, I may have grown to love.

**Lord, lead me to discover some of Your blessings that, out of habit, I've shunned. Open me up to experience new blessings.** —Sabra Ciancanelli

**Digging Deeper:** Ezekiel 36:26; 2 Corinthians 5:17

---

# Sunday, May 18

**... whatever is true, whatever is honorable, whatever is just, whatever is pure, whatever is lovely, whatever is gracious, if there is any excellence, if there is anything worthy of praise, think about these things. —Philippians 4:8 (RSV)**

My neighbor Oliver loves dogs and border collies in particular. He loves them so much, in fact, that he intends to start a rescue program at his home for the breed as soon as he retires from his job as a college professor two years from now. He is already building their crates and forming a "run" for them through his big backyard.

Oliver says he believes that a border collie running through a field of grass must be the most perfect and beautiful example of a creature fulfilling its destiny there ever was. "The ears! The jowls! Their smile," Oliver tried to explain to me the other day. I had to see it for myself, and then I did. If it didn't sound crazy, I'd say that Oliver's border collies look like they feel the joy of their creation as they bound through that tall grass with what looks like smiles broad on their happy faces.

Now, whenever I see a happy dog, I think of Oliver's border collies, and not only them, but every creature made by our beneficent Creator.

If we could only see ourselves in a similar light. Whether it's first thing in the morning, looking at ourselves in the mirror, on our bicycles, or just walking around the block, feeling the sun and wind on our skin, in our hair—we are just as we were made to be! Consider your own beauty, what it means, and where it comes from.

**Lord, help me shine for You today. Help me to see everyone else and how they shine too.**
—Jon M. Sweeney

**Digging Deeper:** Psalm 139:13–16; 1 Peter 3:3–4

---

# Monday, May 19

**He was teaching and saying, "Is it not written, 'My house shall be called a house of prayer for all the nations'?" —Mark 11:17 (NRSVUE)**

"You should join our prayer circle," Grace chuckled. "It's right up your alley!"

She was not complimenting my stellar prayer skills. My friend was gently teasing, knowing that I'm not a joiner. The St. James Prayer Circle folks pray daily for those struggling with illness, grief, finances, or any trouble imaginable, as I would soon learn. An email list circulates, with names added as needed. Everyone prays in their own way and space. No committees, meetings, agendas. Grace was right—it was perfect for me, so I joined, thinking I could include the names in my daily solitary prayer time.

Months later, I feel anything but solitary in this venture. We may not gather, but we send each other encouraging notes, especially when one of us ends up on the list. Some ask for prayers during natural disasters or world conflicts, others focus on individuals. I had not imagined being open to so many people and needs.

While I know my prayer partners, I often don't recognize names on the list. By praying, I come to know them. I may start by lifting a name to God, but soon find myself lifting a real person, along with family, doctors, and even communities. Sometimes a name reminds me of someone I know who needs prayer, and I add that person. Other times I pray for all who share a person's name or problem.

Though I joined the Prayer Circle as a solitary pray-er, this partnering prayer has brought the world into my little space, and, to my surprise, there's plenty of room!

**Listening Lord, thank You for welcoming me into the world of prayer.** —Marci Alborghetti

**Digging Deeper:** Psalm 31:1–5;
Daniel 3

# Tuesday, May 20

**Nevertheless, God's solid foundation stands firm . . .** —2 Timothy 2:19 (NIV)

"I hope you and Rebecca can come for Mom's birthday," my nephew Jeff texted. "Dad has a special surprise planned." It sounded intriguing, so my daughter and I went to Oklahoma for the weekend.

Saturday morning, my brother-in-law Tim drove us over a familiar route toward the house where my sister, brother, and I grew up and Rebecca used to spend time each summer. Although we'd sold the house years earlier, the surrounding area was much the same: wheat ground to the east and a tiny creek running across the south edge. But the house was completely transformed! Instead of plain cinder block, the outside was ivory-colored stone. The front porch was enclosed and sported five windows. There were two additions and a beautifully landscaped yard.

Kathy, the owner, welcomed us inside. *The southwest décor is perfect,* I thought, as we toured the cozy kitchen, spacious living room, and master bedroom with en-suite bath.

"The house was in terrible shape when we bought it at a bankruptcy sale," Kathy said, "but the foundation was firm." She and her husband, a builder, were able to complete work on the house during the COVID lockdown.

The tour was the perfect birthday gift for my sister, Amanda. It was a gift for Rebecca and me too. We appreciated the time and talent that transformed the house. And we remembered and gave thanks for the foundation of faith in Christ that was provided through all the years the house was ours.

**Thank You, Jesus, for a house and people transformed by the sure foundation of Your love.**
—Penney Schwab

**Digging Deeper:** Isaiah 28:16; Luke 6:46–49; 1 Corinthians 3:10–12

---

# Wednesday, May 21

*Can any one of you by worrying add a single hour to your life?* —Matthew 6:27 (NIV)

"Mom, I'm really nervous about the second-grade musical," James, eight, said. "What if I mess up and everyone laughs?" Tears welled up in his eyes.

Just the week before, we had been to his sister's show choir performance. I reminded him how a few kids forgot their words, and some didn't sing loud enough to be heard even with the microphone.

"Did we laugh?" I asked.

"No!" he said, his eyes huge. "We would never laugh at them! They were doing their best!"

Over the next few minutes, James and I talked about how standing up and trying something new is a brave thing for anyone, that it was OK to be scared, and that he is never alone up on stage.

"I know, Mom. There are, like, a hundred of us," he said.

I laughed. "No, buddy! I mean you've got God up there with you too. And even if you mess up, He sees your heart and your hard work and is incredibly proud of you, and so am I!"

How easy it is to focus on what others will think about what we say or do and forget that it is God and ourselves we have to answer to. At the end of the day, have you done your best? Given your best effort? Tried to show His love in all you do? If so, I truly believe He will bless your efforts and you will feel rewarded, whether on that stage or up in heaven.

**Lord, help me bring all my worries to You and lay them at Your feet so I may focus on doing my best in Your name.** —Ashley Kappel

**Digging Deeper:** Luke 12:22; 1 Peter 5:10

## Thursday, May 22

**The threshing floors shall be full of wheat, and the vats shall overflow with new wine and oil. —Joel 2:24 (NKJV)**

Sometimes our to-do lists can carry us down the stairs and out the door toward a myriad of tasks before we even get out of bed. No matter how balmy the day, we check off in our heads the things that need doing and come to one conclusion: Life is overwhelming.

But what of the blessings that overflow the banks of our daily lives? What might it be like to keep a list of, and closely examine, those?

What of that grandchild you thought you would never have and now absolutely adore? Or the meal you tasted recently that satisfied taste buds you didn't know you had? Or the roses on your birthday? Or the misdiagnosis of a friend who is now thriving?

Or simply each glorious breath.

The question looms: Is life dedicated to overwhelming us with stresses? Or are our days just as easily overflowing with blessings? Sadly, too often it's a matter of relegating the blessings to "What has God done for me lately?" The likelihood is there is always a blessed overflow. We simply have to put our awareness to the test.

The prophet Joel speaks of floors full of wheat and vats overflowing with oil—clearly a bent toward overflow. Yet all too often many of us— myself included—can only see what a "stressful" day it has been.

In the end, I am a firm believer that if we dare to fix upon the blessings our heavenly Father extends each day, they will so far outstrip the stresses that comparison won't be an option.

**Lord Jesus, when life presses in like a flood, help me to not only count my blessings but to relish the abundance.** —Jacqueline F. Wheelock

**Digging Deeper:** Deuteronomy 28:2; James 1:17

# Friday, May 23

**But the goal of our instruction is love from a pure heart, from a good conscience, and from a sincere faith. —1 Timothy 1:5 (NASB)**

Screams and laughter of more than a hundred teens drifted through the dark night. Spotlights illuminated a basketball court and an area where the kids were playing kickball and tug-of-war. Each year my church hosted "Rep Your School," where high-school students throughout the valley would come together to compete—school against school—to see which would win. This year, Willow, my German shepherd, and I offered to walk the shadows of the co-ed event, just to keep an eye on things. But my deepest desire was to share God's love. Would it work to have Willow as the bait to draw them to me?

The first few laps around the property, the kids backed up when they saw seventy-five-pound Willow. But soon they clustered around us, asking questions and sharing stories about their dogs. The girls made Willow a glow-stick necklace—orange, purple, and neon green. And while they loved on her, I shared how much God loved them.

My greatest surprise of the evening came when Willow and I patrolled into the shadows. A voice behind me shouted, "Ma'am." I turned and looked to see a steely-faced giant of a teen, who was nearly as wide as he was tall. "Would it be OK if I pet your dog?" I nodded. The teen dropped to the ground next to Willow and wrapped his arms around her.

For a couple of minutes the tough-guy melted into a little boy. When he stood up, he had tears in his eyes. "Thanks."

**Lord, it amazes me how simple it is to share Your love. Thank You for opportunities all around me. Amen.** —Rebecca Ondov

**Digging Deeper:** Philippians 2:1–4; 1 Peter 1:22–23

---

# Saturday, May 24

**And what does the LORD require of you but to do justice, and to love kindness, and to walk humbly with your God?** —Micah 6:8 (RSV)

Sometimes my neighbor, a teen with developmental delays, catches me off guard with oddball "this or that?" questions. When my brother was visiting, he excused himself to go work on the computer. She asked, "Is he going to make words or find words?"

Her questions remind me of a lifetime of either-or options. Some were trivial and arbitrary: in childhood, we could make a sandwich of bologna or cheese, not both. Some were spiritual and significant: the biblical challenge to choose faith over fear.

But if I take some advice from Joni Mitchell and "look at life from both sides now," I appreciate abounding graces in "both-and" opportunities and assessments. I'm grateful that last night

I didn't have to choose ice cream or peaches for dessert—I could enjoy both. My career has involved both editing and writing. When my parents died, a friend reminded me that I was more than a daughter—I was and am a sister, neighbor, colleague, and confidante.

As for asking questions, I repeat and commend the prophet's memorable list: "And what does the Lord require of you but to do justice, and to love kindness, and to walk humbly with your God?" (Micah 6:8).

**Lord, thank You for the ands that distinguish my life and service.** —Evelyn Bence

**Digging Deeper:** Micah 6:3–8; Acts 2:42, 46–47

---

# Sunday, May 25

**May he send you help from the sanctuary and grant you support from Zion. —Psalm 20:2 (NIV)**

"Are you OK?" Cathy mouthed the question from across the church sanctuary after the final hymn. I nodded and assumed that she had noticed my limping gait.

In the church parking lot, I saw Cathy again and requested prayers for speedy healing. My injury had happened a week earlier while wearing my slippers in our cluttered basement. Stepping over a rolled-up carpet, my left foot had twisted awkwardly and I heard a faint snap accompanied by shooting pain. Limping upstairs, I quickly swallowed some Advil and elevated my foot, applying ice to minimize any swelling and promote healing. But a break is a break, no matter how small, and the podiatrist's X-ray confirmed that one of my twenty-six foot bones was fractured.

I said to Cathy, "Bones take six weeks to fully heal and I'm flying overseas in a few days to visit my grandchildren." She assured me of her prayers and offered a fold-up cane to aid me in traversing the lengthy concourses at London's airport.

"Or perhaps, you can get a ride," she suggested eagerly. I pictured the electric carts that whiz about at airports, transporting those unable to walk.

No, I'd be fine, I assured Cathy, but was grateful for her prayers. Later, I pondered the ride idea—perhaps I should arrange for a wheelchair or cart, or maybe I should consider using Cathy's fold-up cane. Either way, the loving care expressed by someone in my church family supplied a deep sense of support and healing.

**Lord, thank You for Christian friends whose spontaneous and sincere offers help us both emotionally and physically.** —Lisa Livezey

**Digging Deeper:** Romans 14:19, 15:2; Philippians 2:4

---

# Memorial Day, Monday, May 26

**Commit to the LORD whatever you do, and he will establish your plans. —Proverbs 16:3 (NIV)**

I wonder if Yeoman First Class Laun Storm heard the planes coming on December 7, 1941, the day that Pearl Harbor was bombed. I wonder what he thought as the first explosion ripped into the forward gun turret. Did he look down at the photograph of his smiling wife and little boy? Did he have any idea this would be the last time he'd see their faces this side of heaven?

*"General quarters, all hands man your battle stations!"* The smell of oil and sweat and fear. The sound of a thousand feet pounding across steel.

Then the next explosion and the next. The final bomb penetrating deep into the bowels of the battleship, igniting the gunpowder stores below with an enormous blast.

Did terror turn Laun's muscles to water? Did he shout? Did he pray? Did he have time to do either? It all must have happened so fast. How could he know the cacophony raging around him would change the world? He couldn't.

Like he couldn't know that almost eighty years after Laun Storm lost his life in service to his country, a very humbled writer would stand on the deck of the USS Arizona Memorial, stunned to see his own last name on that venerated wall of Gold Star heroes. I'll never forget that day, or the realization that my own family blood rested in the deep beneath my feet. In that moment, Memorial Day became so much more personal. Laun Storm had hopes and dreams. And he, like so many others, relinquished them so that we might live out ours.

And I am grateful.

Dear God, thank You for the freedoms I too often take for granted. Freedoms our heroes, our family, fought and died for. Help me to remember, Lord, not only on this day, but every day. —Buck Storm

**Digging Deeper:** Psalm 145:14–15; Romans 13:7

---

# Tuesday, May 27

**Greater love has no one than this, that someone lay down his life for his friends. —John 15:13 (ESV)**

My office is nested in a busy military chapel. The busyness of the chapel often hums with energy. A bevy of activity is common, but when dozens of soldiers were waiting to get in the building as I drove up this warm summer morning, it meant there was an upcoming ceremony—a memorial ceremony. These solemn occasions remind me of the high stakes and seriousness of military service.

As I unlocked the doors for the waiting soldiers, they thanked me and rushed into the building with purpose. I've watched this meticulous process of cleaning and setting up for memorial ceremonies over the years, and this day I paid a little more attention. I watched them set up a family room to ensure privacy for the soldier's family; I watched them make windows sparkle; I watched the soldiers vacuum each nook and cranny. I'm embarrassed to say I never realized how hard soldiers worked ensuring the ceremony justly honored the soldier. I spontaneously prayed for these hardworking soldiers and their fallen soldier in arms.

Once I prayed, my perspective changed. I realized the soldiers' activity wasn't just about hard work or meticulous attention to detail, but about love. How do you honor a soldier's ultimate sacrifice? Love their family, love their memory, and celebrate their selflessness. This is exactly what those soldiers accomplished. On this summer day, a soldier's sacrifice was honored, his family was loved, and his fellow soldiers grieved. May his soul rest easy in the Lord's love.

**Father, may we all strive to follow Your example and love others as You have loved us.** —Jolynda Strandberg

**Digging Deeper:** Psalms 23, 82:3–4;
1 Thessalonians 5:9–11

---

# Wednesday, May 28

## SEEMINGLY INSIGNIFICANT:
## Caring for Widows
**Pure and genuine religion in the sight of God the Father means caring for orphans and widows in their distress . . .** — James 1:27 (NLT)

My sister Sharon has a ministry to widows, and often updates me on her various "ladies" in our regular phone calls. Since women live longer than men and are less likely than men to remarry after being widowed, her list is constantly growing.

That is, I think, the lamentable plight of widows. Despite the Bible's commands to look after widows, despite Jesus's modeling these commands by looking after his mother's needs even as he was dying on the cross, despite the loneliness and need of widows documented by sociologists, they often go unnoticed.

That's what occurred to me when I read Luke's account of the widow Anna this past Advent. She met Jesus as a baby when his parents presented him in the temple. At eighty-four, having lost her husband seven years into their marriage, she'd been a widow for half a century and lived all alone in the temple, a public and inhospitable space, as places to live go. No kitchen or bathroom. No cushy couch. No next-door neighbors for companionship. Anna never left this chilly, dark, echoey space built of stones, but spent her days and nights there worshipping and praying. Had she no children? No siblings? No friends? Luke doesn't say. In our time, she'd be considered homeless.

Jesus's perhaps earliest ministry—assisted by devout parents who didn't disdain an elderly stranger lurking there—was to this elderly, surely lonely widow. Anna, though a prophet, needed love and attention as much as anyone else, as her thanks and hope reveal. I want to be like baby Jesus.

**Jesus, help me notice and love the widows around me.** —Patty Kirk

**Digging Deeper:** Luke 2:36–38

# Thursday, May 29

**You will keep in perfect peace all who trust in you, all whose thoughts are fixed on you!**
—Isaiah 26:3 (NLT)

My mind and body were feeling the impact of world events and life stressors. Looking for a better way of handling them, I decided to try meditation. Adjusting my earbuds as I settled into a comfy chair, I listened to instructor Jeff Warren saying, "Take a few deep breaths, then focus on your homebase. Meditation is about...choosing what to focus on." Part of this meditation practice was to select what Warren called a homebase, something to pay attention to and come back to when distracted. Many choose their breath, but a homebase can be anything.

What would my homebase be? I tried my breath. That worked only to an extent. I tried the sensation of my body on the chair. That wasn't wildly successful. The warmth of my hands? Nope, just didn't feel right.

What did I hope to achieve through meditation? I wanted that Philippians 4:7 peace that passes all understanding, that Hebrews 6:19 anchor for my soul. So, what should I pick as my homebase? Suddenly the answer came to me. Jesus. He should always be my homebase, that to which my thoughts, my heart, my focus immediately and gently return whenever my mind is pulled toward the anxieties and challenges of this world.

I took a few deep breaths, then focused on Jesus. I deliberately chose to fix my thoughts upon Him. He is my homebase. Not just for ten to twenty minutes of meditation time, but all the time, every day. For each time I return to my homebase, I receive His peace, the anchor for my soul.

**Lord Jesus, You are the homebase we all need. Thank You for being my rock, my shield, my shelter from the storm.** —Kim Taylor Henry

**Digging Deeper:** Colossians 3:1–2; Hebrews 3:1, 12:1–2

---

# Friday, May 30

**Joy comes in the morning.** —**Psalm 30:5** (NASB)

At 4:26 a.m., BlueDog yawned loudly, stretched, and gave me a soft, short "woof." I peered at the clock with one squinted eye and flipped the blanket over my head. "One more hour," I mumbled. Cattle dogs thrive on routine. For several weeks following my husband, Randy's, knee surgery, he needed to be driven to physical therapy in town, so I had to hustle in order to feed all of the animals before we left for his 8 a.m. appointments. BlueDog went out with me faithfully each morning to help with chores. Now that Randy's knee was healed, I didn't need to get up this early anymore.

For a week, I tried ignoring BlueDog. I tried grumbling. I even threw pillows. It didn't faze him.

He not only persisted, but he upped his game. He marched across the bed to stand on me, his nose millimeters from mine, which I sensed through the blanket. His stub of a tail wiggled so fast it shook his whole body, which shook my whole body. Joy cometh in the morning; mine cometh wrapped in fur. The second I giggled, BlueDog fell on me in a wriggling mass of sheer happiness. He knew he'd won.

How could I really get mad at his boundless enthusiasm? Wasn't I complaining to myself just the other day that I didn't have enough time to do my daily Bible study and devotions? Maybe my "canine alarm clock" was right on time.

**Dearest God, I praise You for wet noses in the morning and this extra special time with You.**
—Erika Bentsen

**Digging Deeper:** Nehemiah 8:10; Romans 15:13

---

## Saturday, May 31

**A man with leprosy came and knelt before him and said, "Lord, if you are willing, you can make me clean." —Matthew 8:2 (NIV)**

In 1971, I was a member of my Okinawan high school's service league. Our spring project involved collecting soap, toiletries, cases of soda, and other treats to be delivered to the seven hundred leper patients living at the Airakuen Sanatorium. On the short boat ride over to the small island where the colony was located, my classmates and I discussed our anxieties about what we might see. I didn't know much about leprosy—a contagious disease that causes seeping lesions; loss of feeling; and, if not treated, disfigurement of the hands, feet, and facial features, and eventual death.

We were met by a doctor in a long, white coat who gave us a brief tour of the tidy facilities while sharing the colony's history. He explained that leprosy, now called Hansen's disease, was common on Okinawa and greatly feared. Sadly, when most patients came to the island, they rarely saw their friends or families again. *How did these people keep hope alive,* I wondered.

I was moved to learn there were also people living here who'd given up everything to remain with their infected daughter, mother, sister, or husband. They risked contracting the disease themselves while caring for their loved ones. That's the kind of self-sacrificing love Jesus demonstrated for us and why I accepted Him as my Lord and Savior a year later. I marvel at that love. It's the kind that keeps hope alive. I remind myself each day that Christ's love is an action verb, not merely an emotion.

**Dear Lord, help me to love You and others in a more sacrificial way.** —Shirley Raye Redmond

**Digging Deeper:** Luke 17:12–15; John 15:13–14; 1 Corinthians 13:4–8

# WITH AN EVERLASTING LOVE

1 _____

2 _____

3 _____

4 _____

5 _____

6 _____

7 _____

8 _____

9 _____

10 _____

11 _____

12 _____

13 _____

14 _____

15 _____

**16** _____

**17** _____

**18** _____

**19** _____

**20** _____

**21** _____

**22** _____

**23** _____

**24** _____

**25** _____

**26** _____

**27** _____

**28** _____

**29** _____

**30** _____

**31** _____

# June

But You, Lord, are a compassionate and gracious God, slow to anger and abundant in mercy and truth.

—Psalm 86:15 (NASB)

**. . . God had finished the work he had been doing; so on the seventh day he rested from all his work. Then God blessed the seventh day and made it holy." —Genesis 2:2–3 (NIV)**

When I learned our church was starting a sermon series on the concept of Sabbath, inviting us not only to learn about it but to try practicing it, I was both curious and a bit resistant. Curious because I knew so little about Sabbath and resistant because I assumed it was shaped by rules. And giving up a chunk of Sunday reminded me of how I used to feel about doing homework on Sunday.

"Jesus celebrated the Sabbath," our pastor began, "and if we want to be more like Jesus, shouldn't we do what He did?"

*Sure,* I thought. *But I like to get things done on Sundays.*

The pastor read my mind. "We get our significance from what we accomplish. Celebrating Sabbath is countercultural because it is a day to stop working and experience life-giving rest for our souls." My soul is a mystery to me. God created us with a physical body that is visibly responsive to our care. But He also created us with a soul, the invisible place within each of us that longs for intimacy with God.

"Practicing Sabbath can start slowly. Try it for a few hours," the pastor encouraged in closing.

When we got home, my husband said he was Sabbath-ing and quickly fell asleep on the couch.

I disappeared into our bedroom, got in my comfy spot to read, then fell asleep. When I woke, I took our dog for a long walk. My soul felt peaceful and energetic.

**Lord, after You worked creating the Universe, You rested and blessed the seventh day as a gift for us to do the same. Thank You.** —Carol Kuykendall

**Digging Deeper:** Deuteronomy 5:12; Psalm 23:1–3

---

# Monday, June 2

**Do not be anxious about anything . . .**
**—Philippians 4:6 (NIV)**

My job involves managing volunteers who serve children in state custody and their families. Like most social work, my job tends to be status quo on good days, heartbreaking on bad ones. I sometimes witness happy endings, like reunifications, adoptions, and teenagers transitioning to college. Yet most days I respond to tragedy: children experiencing abuse and neglect, families being torn apart, and parents permanently losing their parental rights.

After a four-day weekend visiting with family in Maryland, I sat on a half-empty plane, in a row alone, contemplating my transition back to work the next day. I felt my shoulders tense as I thought about the busy week ahead of me. There were all-staff meetings to participate in, a volunteer training to co-facilitate, and juvenile court hearings to attend. I worried that I'd struggle to get it all done.

Shortly after the flight began, we experienced some turbulence. The captain directed us to remain seated with our seatbelts fastened. I complied and prayed the turbulence would calm. I peered through my window, noticing roads, houses, and rivers appearing smaller and smaller.

Once we'd reached over 30,000 feet of altitude, our captain returned to the mic, assuring us more stability. Another peek out my window revealed cotton-like clouds as far as I could see. We had flown above the turbulence, and the rest of the flight was peaceful and smooth.

I wondered ... maybe if I "flew above the turbulence," focusing more on God, life wouldn't feel so shaky and uncertain. Maybe I wouldn't be anxious about things I cannot change. Maybe my heart would be more peaceful, just like the flight that day.

**Lord, may I stay focused on You, so I, too, can fly above the turbulence.** —Carla Hendricks

**Digging Deeper:** Isaiah 40:28–31; Philippians 4:4–9

---

# Tuesday, June 3

**The LORD is my rock, my fortress and my deliverer; my God is my rock, in whom I take refuge, my shield and the horn of my salvation, my stronghold.** —Psalm 18:2 (NIV)

My husband, Wayne, and I were on a Mediterranean cruise, and we stopped at the Rock of Gibraltar. I was fascinated to learn that during World War II, the British found it vital to hold on to this tiny sliver of land. Whoever held the rock, which is located at the narrow passage from the Atlantic Ocean to the Mediterranean Sea, would control the entire Mediterranean area. In preparation for defending their position, a thirty-four-mile tunnel was carved into the rock and filled with fortifications. Inside the rock was a hospital, barracks for fifteen thousand men, and a six-month food supply for the armed forces, plus every citizen of Gibraltar. To what could only have been God's hand, the Germans never attacked the Rock.

Amazed by all we'd learned, Wayne and I returned to the ship. Once on board, I checked my phone and found an urgent prayer request from my friend Mary Lou. With only a few words I could feel the urgency of her fears. Her nephew, Lewis, was seriously ill, and the physicians didn't hold much hope of him overcoming the multitude of serious medical issues.

I'd prayed for Lewis several times over the years. I immediately closed my eyes and prayed, realizing how desperate the situation was. As I opened my eyes, my gaze fell upon the Rock, one of many miracles from World War II. In that moment, I felt God was ready to grant another miracle for Lewis. And He did. To the shock and amazement of the medical staff, Lewis recovered enough to eventually leave the hospital. The Lord is indeed our Rock, in the past, now, and forever.

**Lord, thank You for the miracle You performed for Lewis. Help me to recognize the ones You perform every single day.** —Debbie Macomber

**Digging Deeper:** Psalm 61:2; Isaiah 26:4

---

# Wednesday, June 4

**But whoever looks intently into the perfect law that gives freedom, and continues in it—not forgetting what they have heard, but doing it—they will be blessed in what they do.** —James 1:25 (NIV)

The Bible app that I read most often commended me daily for my participation, and after a string of engaging with it for a consecutive 164 days—a record for me—on day 165, I forgot to log in. I initially brooded and chastised myself, as if missing a day meant that I failed in my mission to connect daily with the Lord.

But on the day that I neglected to log in, I realized that I had spent more time speaking with God directly in prayer. I took time to pour my heart out to God, starting with words of thanks and praise, progressing through to a full conversation, confession, and request for forgiveness. The conversation was deeper, more powerful, and more comforting than many I had during my 164-day streak of readings.

Still, I was disappointed in myself and what I perceived to be a lack of commitment to the Lord.

A few days later, a prayer popped up in the newsfeed of the Bible app that reminded me that being obedient to God is so important to living the life He creates us to live. And obedience isn't measured solely by the number of days spent in an app, but by having a sincere relationship with Christ.

**Thank You, God, that I don't have to depend upon my own selfish ambition. You are always there for me to depend upon.** —Gayle T. Williams

**Digging Deeper:** 1 Corinthians 15:58; Ephesians 5:19

---

## Thursday, June 5

**The LORD is my strength and my shield; in him my heart trusts, and I am helped ...** —Psalm 28:7 (ESV)

It was midnight when I let Gracie out. Instead of sleepily doing her business, she bolted, streaking into the yard toward the apple tree, barking her head off. Immediately I knew. This degree of bravado she reserves for bears. Gracie hates bears.

*Dear Lord*, I prayed. I grabbed a high-beam flashlight and a can of bear spray and tore after her in my robe and slippers. She was circling the tree, jumping and barking like a lunatic.

"Gracie!" I yelled. "Gracie, come!"

But she was in a frenzy. Her blood was up.

The apple tree is sturdy but not large. The bear's hindquarters were hanging down. He was snarling and snapping his jaws.

I caught Gracie by her collar and dragged her back toward the house. She kept looking over her shoulder and barking defiantly. I tightened my grip. "C'mon, Cujo."

I saw the bear descend and lope off into the woods. I wrestled Gracie inside and slammed the door.

"What were you thinking?" I cried.

But Gracie was back to her cheerful self, gazing expectantly at her treat jar, which, ironically, is shaped like a bear.

"You are never going outside again," I said. And in the moment, I almost meant it.

We treat our animals like family, and Gracie is surely part of mine. She is a fierce protector. In the end, though, nothing protects like prayer. And when I finally calmed down that night, I said a prayer of profound thanks to the Great Protector who guards me and all those I love.

**Father, even in the dark of night with a prowling bear and a brave dog on the loose, You are there to keep us safe.** —Edward Grinnan

**Digging Deeper:** Psalm 91

---

# Friday, June 6

**For I consider that the sufferings of this present time are not worth comparing with the glory that is to be revealed to us. —Romans 8:18 (ESV)**

It wasn't a serious ride, just an evening pedaling around with friends on beach cruisers.

I didn't see the crash, but I heard metal clatter and someone shout. My heart sped. "God, not my wife, please." Seconds later, I saw the tangle of legs and bike. It was her.

The world blurred as we got her up. Blood from her split chin dotted the sidewalk. She held her face.

At the emergency room, the news wasn't as bad as it could have been, but it wasn't great either. A broken jaw. So began our "through-a-straw" phase. One that lasted for nearly two months.

I can fix a lot of things. Plumbing. Electrical. I can patch up my granddaughter's bloody knee. But I can't fix a broken jaw. I hated it and I would have done anything to trade places with her.

I don't know why suffering comes hand in hand with this life. But I know there is a reason. And the reason must be good because God is good. And how Jesus must suffer with us because He is love.

I'm sure many reading this are going through hardships you never expected. Life hurts, both physically and emotionally. Maybe, like I did, you're watching a loved one suffer. But know this: There is a plan and that plan is *glory*. Jesus offers peace even on the darkest parts of the road. I don't understand broken jaws and too much soup now, but one day I will. And we will all rejoice in love and life eternal.

**God, I don't always understand, but You do. And I will trust.** —Buck Storm

**Digging Deeper:** Psalm 37:23–24; Romans 8:28

**Though your sins are like scarlet, they shall be as white as snow; though they are red as crimson, they shall be like wool. —Isaiah 1:18 (NIV)**

When my husband's grandmother moved in with us, she suggested we hire a house cleaner to come every two weeks, not just to tidy her areas but to clean the whole house. And Mam Ma insisted on paying for it. She wanted to do it as a convenience for me, as she didn't want me to have extra chores on her account.

I'll be the first to admit that I have never been a meticulous housekeeper. The idea of having someone else to do my dirty work was exciting. I couldn't wait!

The evening before the cleaning crew was scheduled to arrive, I looked around. Books were stacked on top of the book shelves, unopened mail piled on the entry table, my side of the lavatory was littered with makeup and other beauty supplies, folded laundry on top of my dresser, spices and dishes I'd used the day before still were on the kitchen counter—I was a slob! I spent more than an hour scurrying around to tidy up before the housekeepers arrived.

As I watched the experts haul in their supplies, I realized there have been times in my life that I felt like I needed to clean up my act before coming to God too. But that just wasn't necessary. Jesus has done all the work to pay for my sins. Nothing I do will add to what He has done on the cross. And it's only through Him that I can be made fully clean.

**Dear Jesus, I'm grateful I can come as I am to You (no pre-cleaning necessary). Thank You for making me clean. Amen.** —Stephanie Thompson

**Digging Deeper:** Psalm 51:2–10; Hebrews 9:14; 1 John 1:9

---

# Sunday, June 8

**Is anyone among you in trouble? Let them pray. —James 5:13 (NIV)**

Three weeks after giving birth to my first child, I admitted my mom into the hospital. She'd suffered with rheumatoid arthritis for twenty-one years, and now something was very wrong. My mom suffered in pain and became paralyzed. After two weeks, she received a diagnosis of vasculitis and began treatment.

I was one of her primary caregivers for the first six months—but I was also caring for my infant. As I pushed my mom in her wheelchair, and watched her suffer deep depression, I felt helpless. We were all up against a disease we couldn't control. My biggest fear was that she wouldn't be there to watch my daughter grow, just like my grandma hadn't been there for me. In my helplessness, I did the only thing I could. I turned to prayer.

I learned a lot of lessons during that time, but the greatest was the power of prayer. Hundreds of people prayed for my mom—and our prayers were answered. One year later, my mom was on a bike ride in the Black Hills of South Dakota. Two years later, she was elected mayor of our town. And, eighteen years later, she is here to cheer my daughter on at graduation. She still suffers long-term symptoms, but she is the first to give thanks for her recovery.

Whenever I feel helpless, I'm reminded that prayer works. God listens to the prayers of His people, and though sometimes we do not get the answer we want, He is always faithful to give us the answers we need.

**Lord, help me to turn from the impossible situations before me and lay them at Your feet. Thank You for Your love and faithfulness.** —Gabrielle Meyer

**Digging Deeper:** Psalms 17:6, 102:17; Mark 11:24; 1 John 5:14

---

# Monday, June 9

**. . . set food and drink before them . . .**
**—2 Kings 6:22 (JPS)**

Every so often I treat myself to a coffee from one of the kiosks that sit on almost every third block in Bellingham. After all, it's the Pacific Northwest, and just about the first thing someone told me after we moved here was, "If you don't drink coffee, we'll have to ask you to move away."

Often there are lines of vehicles for the drive-up window, which were especially long when coffee shops were closed in the months of the pandemic. Since I don't have a nine-to-five job, I was never in a hurry. So when a pickup truck driven by a woman with at least one child beside her arrived at the end of the line at the same time I did, I braked and gestured for her to go first.

When I reached the window and held out my card, the server said, "You've been paid for. The woman in front of you wanted to thank you for letting her in."

I immediately said I would pay for the person behind me and drove away feeling warmed by someone's generosity. The following week, it happened again, but without any need for courtesy on my part. The server said, "The man in front of you had a free coffee coming, and he told me to use it for you."

In the enforced isolation of COVID-19, finding places where strangers could be kind to one another seemed like an incredible gift.

**Dear God, I will always remember how You moved us to give each other the coffee of human kindness when we might have seen social distancing as really keeping us apart.** —Rhoda Blecker

**Digging Deeper:** Exodus 35:29; Proverbs 18:16

**Do not forget to show hospitality to strangers...**
—Hebrews 13:2 (NIV)

I first met the gray-striped cat late one spring night when I was sitting in a wicker chair on our front porch staring at a beautiful moon. Scattered luminous clouds were whisking by the shining orb when something also whisked by the cuff of my blue jeans. Glancing down, I saw a cat quietly perched by my feet. She was obviously tame, so I slowly reached down and carefully rubbed her neck and back. Not wanting stray cat bites or scratches, I was cautious. Soon, this new friend was sitting in my lap purring.

It did not take a veterinarian to soon surmise that she was pregnant—bursting at the seams. And she was looking for a place to nest. I went inside, found a cardboard box, filled it with a few towels, and then placed it under the porch table. She crawled in the box and curled up. Momma Cat had found "a crib in the manger." I fed her some cat food and milk and went inside to find my bed as well.

The next morning she was still there, quite content with her new accommodations. Several days later, eight kittens were born. Within two months, homes had been found for all of the kittens and an odyssey completed. My wife, Beth, and I had been blessed by a grand adventure.

Strangers come into our midst at the most unexpected times. And sometimes in so doing, God brings to us a great gift of surprise and wonder. I am glad that a gray-striped cat had the courage to "rub across" my life and give me one more reason for living.

**Lord, thanks for the unexpected gifts that come our way. May we do what we can whenever we are able to. Amen.** —Scott Walker

**Digging Deeper:** Psalm 147:9; Proverbs 12:10

---

# Wednesday, June 11

**Love the LORD your God with all your heart and with all your soul and with all your strength. These commandments that I give you today are to be on your hearts. Impress them on your children. Talk about them . . . when you walk along the road . . . —Deuteronomy 6:5–7 (NIV)**

I'd always longed to pass on my faith to a kid of my own. *Didn't You hear those prayers, Lord?* I often wondered.

When God delivered me from prescription opioids, I was asked to share my journey at the university and community gatherings. At the office supply counter, a pretty young lady with dark, soulful eyes printed my handouts for a presentation. Studying the content, she read the title out loud: *What I Wish People Knew About Opioid Addiction.* "What exactly are you, a professor?" she asked. As I steeled myself for an answer, she added: "My best friend just died from an overdose. Got started on pills from her mom's medicine cabinet." Her eyes searched mine. "There's others at school on drugs. We're dying inside."

I tugged on my navy blazer. *You cleaned up real good today, Roberta. If you tell her your story, she'll Google you to find out if it's true. And the next time you come in here, she'll see an addict, not a professor.* I straightened the gold chain around my neck. The chains that had held me captive spoke louder.

I reached for her hand. Pointed to links on the handout that told it all. The pain. The shame. How I'd lost nearly everything. How God had restored it all and given me more.

**That kid I asked You for, Lord? I never expected this one.** —Roberta Messner

**Digging Deeper:** Psalm 78:4; Joel 1:3

---

# Thursday, June 12

**... and endurance produces character, and character produces hope ...** —Romans 5:4 (ESV)

Our family anticipated an exciting time full of possibility as we searched for a new horse for my daughter. We found a sweet lady for JoElla, whom she renamed Hope. When we had the veterinarian exam and complete X-rays on Hope's legs, we found she had bone disease. We had some decisions to make. We decided to take Hope home with us on "trial" while we decided.

For two weeks Hope was an absolute angel—kind, gentle, and sweet. Our entire family loved caring for her. As the time came to re-examine Hope for purchase, I prayed intently, and the words of the Lord's Prayer, "Thy will be done," seemed to be etched in my heart. I prayed not for Hope, but for the Lord's will. The re-examination did not bear good news. Hope's bone disease was aggressive; it couldn't be cured or slowed. I really liked her and still wanted to purchase her—an emotional decision. My sweet husband was the voice of reason. He helped me realize Hope's longevity didn't match our daughter's needs.

"Thy will be done" meant trusting the Lord had a plan for us even though we couldn't see it just yet. We returned Hope, and as she trotted through the pasture, I thought about the name my daughter gave her. Hope indeed. The Lord's plan for us is always better than we have imagined for ourselves—our family is trusting this truth.

**Lord, may I always have hope in Your will and assuredly trust in Your plan for my life.**
—Jolynda Strandberg

**Digging Deeper:** Psalm 42:10–11; Jeremiah 29:10–12

---

# Friday, June 13

**You will live in joy and peace. The mountains and hills, the trees of the field—all the world around you—will rejoice. —Isaiah 55:12 (TLB)**

My medical insurance company gives seniors gift cards if we've completed our annual wellness visits and if we've exercised, volunteered, and socialized regularly.

My favorite is the socializing. My pool time every morning includes at least an hour of gabbing after the water aerobics class while flinging my arms and legs in the water for even more exercise. Plus, I play cards regularly, take my senior friends to the movies, and attend all sorts of fun, healthy social events. I'm on the "I-want-to-live-to-110" plan.

One of my favorite social events is "hot-fudge-sundae night" at my condo. Nothing brings out more stories and laughter than a group of women eating hot fudge sundaes.

As I looked around the room I saw Mandy, sporting a cast on her arm, broken in three places after tripping over her grandson's foot at the ballpark. Vicki was sharing stories about her cranky ninety-three-year-old mother who lives across the street from her. Candi shared that she was working overtime at the sheriff's department to make ends meet. Hilda was worried about her ninety-six-year-old mother living in New York. Mary Lou, age eighty-five, had just graduated from walker to cane after hip surgery. Shirley, age eighty-eight, was starting to notice vision and hearing loss.

All of us were dealing with aging in our own way and yet we women have each other's backs, navigating old age with faith in God, medical science, and each other. An occasional hot fudge sundae is a big help, I might add.

**Father, give me the grace to age well and long and to stay on the path to Your kingdom.** —Patricia Lorenz

**Digging Deeper:** Psalm 113:5–9; Isaiah 52:7–10

---

# Saturday, June 14

**Before I formed you in the womb I knew you.
—Jeremiah 1:5 (NIV)**

It was my first experience with death as a volunteer Emergency Medical Responder. Our ambulance was dispatched to a lake where a youth had been swimming with friends and had gone missing underwater.

On the way, our medic, a veteran of the Afghanistan war, prepped us for what we'd likely face. "He's been underwater over forty-five minutes. Odds are he won't revive, but we're going to do everything we can to try. The helicopter cannot transport patients without a pulse, so it's on us."

Fire arrived on scene, located the youth, and began CPR. We rolled up and loaded him. I started chest compressions as the paramedic readied the mechanical CPR device. During our one-and-a-half-hour transport to the hospital, the medic administered medication to stimulate heart function as I sat by his head and systematically breathed for him. He was so young. What were his life's ambitions? Was he a believer? I didn't even know his name.

At the hospital, the ER team took over and fought for another two hours. The youth's pastor pushed by me and began to pray. At that moment, I knew this lost youth was with the One who knew him completely, from before he was formed in his mother's womb. He was already in heaven, experiencing more love and joy than we can possibly imagine. The end really isn't the end for those who believe.

**Lord, we view tragedy through human terms, yet You know infinitely more about us. Please ease the hurt of broken families with the assurance that they will be reunited for eternity.** —Erika Bentsen

**Digging Deeper:** Job 14:5; Psalm 139:16; Hebrews 12:1–3

---

# Father's Day, Sunday, June 15

**If any of you lacks wisdom, you should ask God, who gives generously to all without finding fault, and it will be given to you. —James 1:5 (NIV)**

As I help care for my ailing ninety-four-year-old father, I often find myself in a fit of worries: Will his home health aides show up? Will they be responsible and kind? Am I taking the right steps to seek the best care for him? And my most pressing question: Why don't I maintain the same level of faith in my Almighty Father that my wise dad holds?

When my father notices my anxiety rising about his care, he simply says, "God has me!" And when I take a moment to truly adhere to the wisdom that

Dad has showered upon me for my whole life, I realize that he's right.

I see God's love in so many small places, like in the warm, purposeful "hello" from a kind stranger as I waited for the results of my daily COVID-19 test before visiting my father at the rehabilitation center where he temporarily resided; or in the daily messages of encouragement from my sister-friend Cynthia, who was in this exact predicament a year earlier with her hundred-year-old grandmother.

As Dad reminds me often, there are so many reasons to praise the Lord: for being able to observe the rising of the sun to its glorious setting; for health, breath, and life itself. On all days and in all ways, Dad says, the Lord is great. I pray that not only do I hear my father's sage advice, but that I also *listen* to it.

**Dear God, I am so very grateful for the wisdom of a praying father here on Earth, especially one who follows Your Word and Your teachings.**
—Gayle T. Williams

**Digging Deeper:** Psalm 90:12; Proverbs 4:1

---

# Monday, June 16

**He replied, "Because you have so little faith. Truly I tell you, if you have faith as small as a mustard seed, you can say to this mountain, 'Move from here to there,' and it will move. Nothing will be impossible for you." —Matthew 17:20–21 (NIV)**

I hadn't noticed that it was past my bedtime. I was working late when I heard the unmistakable sound of my dog's tags jingling outside my home office door. Only Soda is blind, and we keep a safety gate at the bottom of the stairs to stop him from climbing them alone, so I must be imagining it.

But then, it happened again. The tags jingled, so I got up and opened the door. Soda, our little blind dog, was at the tippy top of the stairs. Three cats surrounded him—all wide-eyed.

I scooped up Soda and looked down the stairs. The gate was still up! Somehow, Soda had jumped the gate and climbed the stairs to come to bed with me. I gave him a huge hug, thankful for his safety.

When he first lost his sight two years ago, we put up the gate. It never occurred to me that, maybe, he didn't need it anymore. As I lay in bed, I thought about the limitations I place on myself and others out of habit. What gates do I keep up even though I've grown enough to leap over them and climb to the next level?

**Lord, thank You for Soda, who teaches me new things every day, and for showing me that sometimes You don't move mountains for us. Instead, You give us the courage to blindly jump over them.** —Sabra Ciancanelli

**Digging Deeper:** Mark 9:23;
Ephesians 3:20

# Tuesday, June 17

**I am reminded of your sincere faith, which first lived in your grandmother Lois and in your mother Eunice and, I am persuaded, now lives in you also. —2 Timothy 1:5 (NIV)**

"What do you want to sew?" I asked Madelyn when she came to my house, along with her brothers, Micah and Benjamin, for a week of Grandma Camp in June. Her mom, Rachel, had informed me of Madelyn's desire after being inspired by Laura Ingalls Wilder's frontier stitching skills in the *Little House on the Prairie* books my granddaughter had been reading.

"I want to sew a dress."

I gazed at my granddaughter, her straight brown hair framing her earnest face. At age eight, I worried she was too young to learn. "How about we start with something simpler?"

After tightening the fabric on an embroidery hoop on her chosen project—an owl sampler pattern—Madelyn began outlining the bird in purple embroidery floss. Up and down, she wove the needle, around the head and both wings, while her boisterous brothers wrestled in the other room, their laughter filling the house.

"I remember my mom teaching me to sew," I said as Madelyn added French knots for the owl's eyes.

"Great-Grandma Lois?" Madelyn asked, naming the woman who had died when Madelyn had been a baby. While we added new colors, Madelyn asked questions about her great-grandmother, figuring out her relationship in the collective family memories.

When the final herringbone stitch was knotted in place, I gave thanks for an afternoon with my granddaughter as she threaded her place of belonging in the fabric of our family's stories, something none of us is too young to learn.

**Thank You, Jesus, that no matter my heritage, I belong in Your story.** —Lynne Hartke

**Digging Deeper:** Deuteronomy 4:9; Psalm 100:5

---

## Wednesday, June 18

# JOURNEYING WITH JESUS: First Aid
**Then Jesus said to him, "Go and do the same."** —Luke 10:37 (NASB)

In my go-pack is a first aid kit. That's not something I generally carry around. My medical knowledge is limited. You'd never know I am a registered nurse's daughter. But I could manage applying antiseptic and basic bandaging.

The Samaritan who found the beaten man along the roadside must have been prepared. In those days of exposed travel, one had to anticipate anything—especially when alone. He was able to do some immediate doctoring—pouring oil and wine on the man's wounds to clean and soothe them, and wrapping them in bandages.

This man shared his own animal to get the injured man to an inn—and then cared for him overnight. Not long enough for the man to heal, so his rescuer gave money to the innkeeper to continue the care.

It's an inspiring story of how to be a neighbor. And that's just what Jesus was emphasizing to the lawyer who questioned, "Who is my neighbor?" After teaching the parable Jesus told him, "Go and do the same." I wonder if he did.

I still regret a time I could have exhibited caring and kindness—been a "first aid" friend—and failed. A neighbor, Carolyn, who is older and lives alone, had hip replacement surgery and no one to help her while she recovered. I could have stayed with her.

I didn't because she had mousetraps in her house—and I have a phobia. I let that keep me from going. The unvarnished, embarrassing truth. Since then, I've had many successful opportunities to aid her.

**Jesus—I fail to act because of my own flimsiness. And then Your mercy grants me "next times."** —
Carol Knapp

**Digging Deeper:** Leviticus 19:33–34;
Luke 6:32–36, 10:25–37; Romans 13:8–10

---

# Juneteenth, Thursday, June 19

**For he says, "In the time of my favor I heard you" . . . now is the time of God's favor . . .**
**—2 Corinthians 6:2 (NIV)**

The recently enacted federal holiday Juneteenth marks the official day on which the slaves of Galveston, Texas, in 1865, joined millions of other formerly enslaved persons in America in the knowledge that they, too, were finally free. Unbeknownst to these and other Texas slaves, President Lincoln had declared them free more than two years prior.

But isn't it possible that some beleaguered slaves in Galveston, though not formally told of their freedom, were already secretly praying for it?

2 Corinthians 6:2 says, "In the *time* of my favor [emphasis mine] I heard you." And while twenty-first-century people, including me, might struggle with the idea of a people forced to live a critical untruth for more than two years, the National Museum of African American History and Culture addresses the issue adeptly: "The historical legacy of Juneteenth shows the value of never giving up hope in uncertain times."

We may never know whether the praying slaves had received a tip about Lincoln's Emancipation Proclamation or whether whispers of the recent surrender by General Lee had reached their ears. But given the history of African Americans and how they have clung to the knowledge of the Lord Christ through the centuries, I choose to believe someone among them was seeking "the time of [His] favor."

There will always be outpourings of God's grace that astound mortals and afford glorious results, but there is a timing also. As we celebrate June 19,

I submit that God's blessings are always perfectly timed, even when they challenge our understanding.

**Holy Spirit, help me to remember to consistently consider Your timing in my daily walk with You.**
—Jacqueline F. Wheelock

**Digging Deeper:** Ecclesiastes 3:11; Lamentations 3:25–26; Habakkuk 2:3

---

# Friday, June 20

### A faithful man will abound with blessings . . .
**—Proverbs 28:20 (NKJV)**

I was very discouraged and down on myself, complaining to my redheaded wife.

"You know, Hon, I have never done one outstanding thing in all my life. I have always just been so-so at several things—a fairly good father, a pretty good teacher, an ordinary gardener . . . "

She glared at me. "Well, there's one thing you do really well—you stick with things. You are not a quitter. Like, you have been married to me for sixty-three years, and we both know that redheads are not the easiest people to live with. You have been a faithful Christian since you were just a boy. We have stayed in Moberly for sixty years, and we have a lot of friends because of that. And even though college teaching was especially hard for an introvert like you, you stayed with it for forty-three years. That's amazing!"

"Well, I was just too dumb to quit."

"It's not dumb to be faithful. It's the smartest thing of all, and very hard to do. A lot of hotshots out there have messed up their family, health, and reputation trying to be superstars. I'm thankful that you have been a steady-Eddie. You have been a blessing to all of us."

Now I remember why I married this woman. She always has perspective. Finding her was the one outstanding thing I have done, and that only with the help of God.

**I am relieved to know, Father, that it's OK to be ordinary, as long as I am faithful.** —Daniel Schantz

**Digging Deeper:** 1 Corinthians 4:2; 1 Timothy 1:12

# Saturday, June 21

**You're blessed when you stay on course, walking steadily on the road revealed by GOD. —Psalm 119:1 (MSG)**

I hoisted the steel tube post pounder over the metal fence post, then let it drop. The sound of metal slamming metal rang through the air. The post sunk a couple of inches into the ground. It was a Saturday in June and I was hurrying to finish up fencing some new garden spots. *How will I get everything done?*

When I finished setting that post, I looked at another garden. *I've got to plant those seeds today.* But before I got them planted, I remembered I needed to water the fruit trees, so I dragged hundreds of feet of hose across my little farm to the trees, then set the timer. On my way back to the garden I spotted the canoe against the fence. *I've got to move that out of the way.*

Grabbing the ropes on the bow of the canoe, I grunted and dragged it across the grass. A memory surfaced of the time I took a friend canoeing. She wanted the stern, to be the person who steers. But with every stroke, the canoe pointed in a different direction. *How frustrating!*

I stopped to take a breather and looked at the mess in the yard. I was doing the same thing she had. Normally I set the course for my day in prayer, but today I hadn't. Instead, I insisted on being in the stern. *Lord, help me to make sense of this day.* He led me to finish—one thing at a time.

**Lord, thank You for reminding me that You always have the perfect course for my day. Amen.** —Rebecca Ondov

**Digging Deeper:** Psalm 119:5, 32–35

# Sunday, June 22

**For where two or three are gathered in my name, I am there among them. —Matthew 18:20 (NRSVUE)**

I've always been a big fan of church coffee hours, even though I don't drink coffee. Just that chance to talk to your fellow parishioners, meet people, and welcome newcomers. You never know what you'll find.

Years ago, when I'd just graduated from college, I didn't have a clue what I'd do with my life. I'd studied Italian and wanted to live in Italy for a while. I painted my sister's house that summer and with the money I earned I flew to Europe, took the train to Florence, and figured the travelers' checks might last for a couple of weeks. If I was lucky.

That first Sunday I dropped by the American Church—one of my professors had recommended it—and lingered afterward at coffee hour. I stood there chatting with an American woman, a stranger, who politely asked what I was doing in Florence. I told her I was a recent graduate and hoped to stay for as long as I could.

"What was your major?" she asked.

"English," I said.

"I run a school here where we teach English. Would you be interested in that?"

Would I ever! I went for an interview, got hired, and the rest is history. I found other work, teaching, tutoring, even got a gig housesitting at a palazzo. I studied voice, sang in the Duomo choir and at the American Church, and made lifelong friends. After two years I returned to the States, ready to move forward in my life.

Church coffee hour? Fellowship like that can change your life. It did mine.

**Lord, I give thanks for all those opportunities of fellowship. Help me give them to others.**
—Rick Hamlin

---

## Monday, June 23

**Wolves will live with lambs. Leopards will lie down with goats. Calves and lions will eat together. And little children will lead them around. —Isaiah 11:6 (NIRV)**

It was teatime. We'd been up since dawn, viewing wildlife in Zambia's South Luangwa National Park. After three hours of bouncing our way through the underbrush, our safari guide parked our open-air jeep at the Starbucks of the savannah, a.k.a. the watering hole.

All the locals were there. Hippos lolled in the water. Malachite kingfishers searched for insects along the muddy banks. A family of elephants gathered nearby, a calf playfully spraying water from its trunk. A giraffe eyed me as he sipped from the water's edge, while I eyed him as I sipped tea from a warm tin cup. I was enchanted by the novelty of the moment.

Being in the presence of such a variety of animals, all congenially enjoying "teatime" together, brought to mind Isaiah 11:6, a prophetic picture of how all creatures would one day live together in peace. But I was fully aware that day hadn't yet arrived. Earlier that week, I'd seen wild dogs feast on an impala and a leopard munch on a baboon. One morning, three lionesses had sauntered past our jeep, so close I could have reached out and petted them. But I knew better than to act on that impulse.

Heaven is still a distant shore. But my glimpse of heaven on earth around the watering hole that morning left me longing for that "someday" home, a place of harmony and serenity, where animals—and people from every walk of life—will coexist in peace.

**Father, please show me how I can help foster peace in this world, as I wait for Your Kingdom to come.** —Vicki Kuyper

**Digging Deeper:** Psalm 145:9; Matthew 6:9–13; Romans 12:18

---

# Tuesday, June 24

**If God is for us, who can be against us? —Romans 8:31 (ESV)**

I've never felt emotionally invested in a sports team, though my interest gravitates toward baseball. Growing up, we attended an occasional minor-league kids' night. And I'd overhear my dad listening to the World Series radio broadcast while he painted the house.

My attitude changed last fall when I discovered a Washington Nationals game on the radio. The announcers' running dialogue captured my imagination. Something clicked between me and my home team, and now I hardly miss a game. I occasionally, uncharacteristically, pump my fist at a critical "safe!" It doesn't matter if my team sits at the bottom of the standings. I root for them, expect the best of them. If they don't win, I anticipate the next night's play. I'm always hopeful for the next yes!

When I read Romans 8, I can envision God as being emotionally invested in His team, as I now am in the Nats, as I more personally am in the life of a neighbor girl I've mentored for a decade now. I've walked alongside her through disappointing strikeouts and errors as well as base hits and runs to home plate. I recently went to her high-school graduation. From my vantage point, sitting on sports bleachers, I cheered my student on the field below and appreciated other families as they hailed their graduates.

I can see that our human bolstering efforts pale in comparison to that described in Romans 8, which names both the Son and the Spirit as heavenly intercessors. The ultimate support. The best yes.

**God, today help me see evidence of Your support and encouragement.** —Evelyn Bence

**Digging Deeper:** Romans 8:18–39

---

# Wednesday, June 25

**Clothe yourselves, all of you, with humility toward one another, for "God opposes the proud, but gives grace to the humble."** —1 Peter 5:5 (RSV)

I picked up the package on our front porch and tried to decipher the return address. It took a second before I realized it was from Raem.

Remembering my former student Raem sent me into "The Dance," as my kids call it. When I encounter bad news—a blown gasket, a burst pipe, a notice from the IRS—I rub my neck, rhythmically shift my weight from one foot to the other, and commence a string of invectives that all begin with the word *awww*.

I first met Raem when she was a senior in her sixth year and counting. She had exhausted her student loans and her advisor's patience (that would be me). Her grades were below C level, and Raem herself was below sea level—she was drowning. Countless emails and meetings proved ineffectual. She took off a semester to regroup, then another. Eventually, I left my job at Pitt and lost contact with her.

So you can imagine my trepidation in opening her package. Inside was a delicious fruit basket and the following note:

*Professor Collins, Thank you for all your work on my behalf. It took a while, but I was finally able to graduate last year, and wanted to thank everyone who helped me on my journey.*

I'm hoping the neighbors didn't see me that day—a grown man standing on his porch softly weeping into a fruit basket. If they were listening close, they would've heard that man utter a single word: *awww*... only this time he meant *awe*. In the words of *The Book of Common Prayer*,

---

## Thursday, June 26

**But I am like an olive tree flourishing in the house of God; I trust in God's unfailing love for ever and ever. —Psalm 52:8 (NIV)**

My grandmother's yard is a picturesque country landscape. Her small brick home sits on a lush carpet of the greenest grass I've ever seen, and evergreen trees, bushes, and flowers flourish without effort. The walnut tree I used to climb still sits at the top of the driveway and the apple tree in the backyard still produces fruit. Most of the trees have a family story, like the one that was planted by my grandparents' window when they built the home in 1969. Then there's the towering tree that was first planted from a seedling my brother brought from school in a Styrofoam cup more than thirty years ago.

But my favorite is the umbrella tree. That's not the common or scientific name for the tree that grows outside her back door, but its shape lends itself to the nickname. Growing up it provided me with shade from blazing North Carolina summers. I'd taken shelter under it when I had to adjust the chain that had slipped off the crankset of my bicycle. It was the place where we shucked corn on the cob, shelled peas, and snapped green beans. And as the sun set, it was the most remarkable area to catch lightning bugs.

Our family trees are planted in the same way as our family's faith. Over the years, our lineage has been watered with God's Word; it's been pruned by affliction, but grown back thriving and still able to offer hope to others. Faith that is deeply rooted can't easily be destroyed.

**Lord, show me the good ground to plant seeds that will last for future generations.** —Tia McCollors

**Digging Deeper:** Micah 4:4; John 15:1

---

# Friday, June 27

**This is the day that the LORD has made; let us rejoice and be glad in it. —Psalm 118:24 (ESV)**

"Don't save it for the hospital," I always tell my daughters when I give them a gift. It's a reference to a story about my hard-working, practical grandmother.

A young bride in 1926, "Mema" brought nine children into a family poor in material things but rich in love. When my grandfather passed, it was up to her to provide for the children.

Stretching the budget meant that she herself often did without. Maybe over time, she forgot how to enjoy beautiful things. "I'll save this in case I get put in the hospital," Mema would explain when we gave her a new robe or nightgown.

After Mema could no longer live without assistance, we found dozens of fine garments tucked away in drawers—years' worth of gifts she'd never enjoyed.

It's a lesson I've never forgotten. All these years later, when I'm at home, doing nothing special, I often wrap up in my soft robe, the one I feel almost guilty for wearing because it feels so self-indulgent. And I remind my daughters that they don't have to wait for a special occasion—or a trip to the hospital—to enjoy wearing something pretty.

I'm practical too, but when I think of my self-sacrificing grandmother, I'm reminded that today is the best day to enjoy life.

**Father, help me remember that we are not promised tomorrow and to make the most of today.** —Ginger Rue

**Digging Deeper:** Matthew 6:34; James 4:14

---

# Saturday, June 28

**As they talked and discussed these things, Jesus himself suddenly came and began walking with them. —Luke 24:15 (NLT)**

While visiting my dad, who is in his mid-eighties, I decided to take him to a restaurant for dinner. He loves to walk, so I planned for us to stroll to the restaurant. It wasn't long before I realized that his pace is much slower than I had remembered. My siblings warned me that it takes him much longer to go from one city block to another. Because I live in Florida and don't see him as often due to the distance, I was surprised.

It took some adjusting as my body and mind wanted to walk at my speed. When I did slow down, my dad and I were at the same tempo. With each step, we took in the city and enjoyed each other's company. He could be himself and walk at his pace. And I was in the moment with him.

This experience got me thinking about how important it is to walk along with our brothers and sisters of the faith at their pace. Some are strong; others are struggling to keep their faith. Each person is at a different place, and at a different pace, of the faith walk. It's my task to meet them where they are in the journey. It might mean to slow down, stop, or maybe speed up. This is what Jesus does for us ... meets us where we are in the walk of life.

**Lord, teach me to walk alongside people who are at a different place and pace in their faith journey than mine.** —Pablo Diaz

**Digging Deeper:** Luke 24:28–31; 1 Corinthians 9:22

---

# Sunday, June 29

**But I trust in your unfailing love; my heart rejoices in your salvation. —Psalm 13:5 (NIV)**

I went to high school in Belgium. My best friend was a great guy named Charlie whose dad was pastor of a Baptist church. Charlie used to invite me to services even though I was Roman Catholic. Charlie's church was very different than my church: in his, there was laughter and talking, Bible study, "fellowship," and even ice cream socials.

That summer, along with Charlie and other high-school friends, I attended the European Baptist Convention in Switzerland.

On the last evening of the convention, there was an altar call—something unfamiliar to me. "Just as I Am" was sung for what seemed like hours. I wanted to walk down, but I was hesitant. What would the people at my Catholic church say? But I told myself, "If they sing another verse, I will go." And they'd sing another, but I wouldn't budge. Time passed and I thought I had waited too long. My desire to respond to the altar call was rewarded when another verse was sung.

As I neared the front of the stage, I saw a high-school friend, Brenda, smiling brightly at me from the choir. Her smile made me feel as though I had made the right decision. Soon, I saw Charlie's dad and went to him. We knelt. His hands covered both of mine and there were tears in his eyes. "Oh, Adam, I was praying that you'd accept the invitation." He then prayed a beautiful prayer, a prayer that was gentle and glorious and wonderful. Tears flowed down my face.

That night, I was invited *just as I am*, and accepted the invitation. And life has never been the same.

**Lead us on the right path, Lord. Amen.** —Adam Ruiz

---

## Monday, June 30

### LIFE LESSONS FROM THE BEACH: Truth

**Your way is perfect, Lord, and your word is correct. You are a shield for those who run to you for help. —2 Samuel 22:31 (CEV)**

Early-morning walks on the beach generate many rewards—sunrises, few people, and abundant wildlife, to name a few.

One of my favorite birds to watch along Hilton Head Island in South Carolina is sandpipers. On skinny legs they rush to the water's edge, probe in the wet sand for food, and race away before the next wave arrives. Adults repeat the process until their tummies are full, using their short bills to pry open small, hard-shelled creatures and pick out the meat. Baby sandpipers join their parents and feed themselves by hunting for worms and insects, a rare trait in the bird world. Unlike noisy and competitive seagulls and pelicans, each sandpiper claims a patch of wet sand and focuses on its mission.

One morning my daily devotion highlighted this verse and connected to my beach walk the instant I saw a group of sandpipers exploring the shoreline for breakfast. The birds found food by digging the same way reading God's Word nourished my soul.

As I search His truth, I find meat to grow stronger in Him. The more I dig, the more I learn, the more I mature spiritually, which pleases Him. In marvelous ways our heavenly Father provides food for all His creatures, and many times the best morsels are discovered by digging deeper.

**God, thank You for providing truth to a world searching for answers. Thank You for shining light in a world battling darkness. Help me to walk in Your light and seek Your truth daily.** —Jenny Lynn Keller

**Digging Deeper:** Isaiah 45:18–19; John 1:1–5, 14:6; Colossians 3:16; Hebrews 4:12–13

## WITH AN EVERLASTING LOVE

1 _____

2 _____

3 _____

4 _____

5 _____

6 _____

7 _____

8 _____

9 _____

10 _____

11 _____

12 _____

13 _____

14 _____

15 _____

16 _____

17 _____

18 _____

19 _____

20 _____

21 _____

22 _____

23 _____

24 _____

25 _____

26 _____

27 _____

28 _____

29 _____

30 _____

# July

For God so loved the world, that he gave his only begotten Son, that whosoever believeth in him should not perish, but have everlasting life.

—John 3:16 (KJV)

**The Lord himself goes before you and will be with you; he will never leave you nor forsake you. Do not be afraid; do not be discouraged. —Deuteronomy 31:8 (NIV)**

My Labrador, Sport, and I walk along the sidewalk. Darkness is just beginning to press down from the sky. The July evening is peaceful. Cicadas thrum in the background. Sport treads confidently beside me.

Suddenly, the calm is broken by a series of sharp whistles. The sky breaks into a display of light. Fireworks. Independence Day is less than a week away. My neighbors must be celebrating early.

Beside me, I hear a yelp. Sport hunkers down close to the grass. He is terrified. To Sport, this must seem to be a bombardment. He has no understanding of firecrackers or bottle rockets. As whistles and crackles continue to fill the air, I kneel next to my terrified dog. I cup his head in my hands and look him in the eyes.

"You're safe," I say. "I'm right here."

His dark eyes seem unconvinced. I understand.

I have been struggling to trust the Lord. It's been a difficult year. A close friend has broken my trust. My workload has increased exponentially. A relationship has gone unexpectedly awry.

I know that the Lord has promised that He will be with me always. But, lately, I've questioned both his presence and his providence.

Sport presses close to me. He is still scared by the cacophony around us. He does not understand the bright bursts of light. But he is trusting that we will get through this together.

And, amidst the noise, I silently pray for a similar faith.

**Jesus, help me to rely on Your promises and trust in Your goodness.** —Logan Eliasen

**Digging Deeper:** Joshua 1:9; 1 Chronicles 28:20

---

# Wednesday, July 2

## LIFE LESSONS FROM THE BEACH: Faith
**These trials are only to test your faith, to see whether or not it is strong and pure. It is being tested as fire tests gold and purifies it—and your faith is far more precious to God than mere gold. —1 Peter 1:7 (TLB)**

From our hilltop location on St. John in the Virgin Islands, we watched cruise ships sail from St. Thomas to St. Croix every night. Their festive lights and music traveled far across the water and darkness.

Not so pretty is the trash thrown overboard by other boats. To keep the island's beaches pristine, residents organize regular cleanup efforts and occasionally find highly prized sea glass in the debris.

As we observed a local craftsman create sea-glass jewelry, he explained the ocean's process of transforming trash into treasure. Waves break discarded bottles and glassware into many pieces. Decades of tossing and turning remove sharp edges and make the pieces smooth and frosted. Brown, green, and white are common sea-glass colors. Red, orange, and turquoise are rare.

Nowadays, when wearing my pink sea-glass earrings, I'm reminded how their journey from broken shard to lovely jewelry resembles my life. After years of tumbling in multiple directions, facing trials and being tested, I finally acknowledged God is more precious to me than anything the world offers. As my daily faith walk continues to smooth my rough edges, I'm thankful God is compassionate, gracious, slow to anger, and abounding in love and faithfulness.

**Lord, Your refining process is difficult and sometimes painful. Give me strength and perseverance to endure trials. Give me faith and wisdom to trust You for an outcome blessing others and glorifying You.** —Jenny Lynn Keller

**Digging Deeper:** Psalms 66:10, 86:15; Proverbs 3:3–4; James 1:2–6

---

# Thursday, July 3

**In the world you have tribulation, but take courage; I have overcome the world. —John 16:33 (NASB)**

My husband, Terry, is managing a disability—accompanied by chronic pain—neither of us planned on. Unable to balance and walk on his own, he needs Canadian crutches—crutches attached to your forearm by a plastic ring, where you lean on a waist-height handle. His "sticks," as he called them. He's spent ten years adjusting to "slow and awkward."

It hasn't stopped him from doing difficult things—like elk hunting with a friend in high-elevation, mountainous central Idaho. When he spilled on the ATV, negotiating a tricky washout, he sat in the trail saying, "I can't get up without my sticks." His friend retrieved them and they were off once again.

Certain things are beyond him. We quit going to fairgrounds for all the walking—until we purchased a battery-powered scooter.

A trio of young grandkids spent an eight-hour marathon with us at Spokane's Interstate Fair. The scooter battery was alarmingly low as we headed for the parking lot. They grinned over how slow Grandpa was. I quietly explained he was conserving battery.

When I brought it up on the drive home, Terry exclaimed, "I wasn't conserving battery. That's all the faster it would go. I had it wide open!" How we laughed.

Making the best of an unwanted hit: persevering, getting creative, finding humor. Terry is our family's embodiment of the verse, "I can do all things through Him who strengthens me" (Philippians 4:13).

**Jesus, You are a sustaining Savior—I can't do it without You.** —Carol Knapp

**Digging Deeper:** Psalm 3:3; Romans 12:12; 2 Corinthians 12:9–10; James 1:2–4

---

## Independence Day, Friday, July 4

**Be strong and courageous, because you will lead these people to inherit the land ... —Joshua 1:6 (NIV)**

I could hardly believe it. Gary was coming with his guitar. He was a fixture at our community Independence Day BBQ. A handlebar mustache, cowboy hat, jeans, and boots—everyday clothes for him—Gary sang cowboy ballads from a lifetime of firsthand experience. Recently he'd been in an accident that should have cost him his life.

It's every horseman's nightmare. While herding cattle, his galloping horse flipped end over end, and Gary's foot hung up in the stirrup when he was pitched from the saddle. The horse bolted, dragging him into a barbed wire fence. He was detached and flung into a heap. His riding partner thought he was dead. Bleeding and busted up badly, Gary rode in the bed of a pickup to the ER, after insisting they stop by his house first so he could change into sweats. He saw no sense in having the hospital cut off a brand-new pair of Wranglers.

Character is custom-built to order, shaped by circumstance and hard knocks, honed by deepest hope, polished by sheer will and determination, tested often by tribulation. When I asked Gary about the accident, he said, "Don't worry, my horse is just fine." He ended up with eight broken ribs, a broken leg, a broken ankle, a concussion, and a collapsed lung. "But the Good Lord must not be done with me yet." It seems to me that the independent spirit that shaped this country is alive and well today, and still riding for the brand.

**Lord, bless this land and the people in it. Revive our spirits to honor You.** —Erika Bentsen

**Digging Deeper:** Deuteronomy 28:1–14; Isaiah 41:9–10

---

# Saturday, July 5

**. . . being confident of this, that he who began a good work in you will carry it on to completion until the day of Christ Jesus. —Philippians 1:6 (NIV)**

Emily, age six, stood at the microphone with her head down. Her long hair covered her pale cheeks but could not hide her quivering terror at auditioning at a children's music camp where I was a teacher.

"What joke did you practice?" asked Dawn, the director, eyeing the dozens of children who still wanted to audition for a chance to tell a musical joke at the concert. "Start by saying your name."

Gathering her courage, Emily stated her name, as her peers cheered their support. "You can do it, Emily!"

Their encouragement had the opposite effect. Startled into remembering others were in the room, Emily began to wail, her sobs filling the auditorium as her dad carried her out. Her mom confided how

Emily had had a breakdown on stage at a dance recital three weeks earlier. Those teachers had not been sympathetic.

I understood the dilemma. As a teacher, with a stage filled with other children, when do you step in and rescue, and when do you say, *Enough*?

Five minutes later, I felt a tap on my arm. Emily, with red-rimmed eyes, whispered, "Can I have another chance?"

I glanced at Dawn. She nodded. "Once we audition all the other kids."

This time, Emily stood on her mark. She spoke her name into the mic. She began her joke, quietly, but clearly. "What type of music did the avocado like?" "What?" the other kids asked.

"Guac and roll."

Everyone applauded while Emily beamed.

**May I extend grace today, God of Second Chances, to others and to myself.** —Lynne Hartke

**Digging Deeper:** Psalm 138:8; Ephesians 4:2

---

# Sunday, July 6

**The King will reply, "Truly I tell you, whatever you did for one of the least of these brothers and sisters of mine, you did for me."**
**—Matthew 25:40 (NIV)**

Hi, everyone. Gracie speaking, with Edward's help, like I sometimes do. You remember me. Golden retriever. Eight years old. Very popular. I'm told I get lots of likes on Facebook and Instagram!

I love my morning walks in the city. So many smells and occasionally some bits of food that I try to snatch before Edward kicks them away. Today we walked east—I have a great sense of direction!—past St. Francis of Assisi Church. I'm told this human was good to animals, which makes me happy. More people should be like that, right?

There was a line of people waiting for donated clothing and food. Admittedly, I don't understand much about the clothes humans wear. So weird! But I understand the need for food. I'm an expert on being hungry.

Still, I know I'll always be fed. These people didn't know if they would eat. Honestly, I find that very hard to accept. Humans have so much food—how can some of them be without? Just walking along the street, my trusty nose tells me how much food you all throw out. So wasteful!

I heard a story about someone called Jesus who could produce bread and fish for all who were hungry. Now that's love. He's right up there with St. Francis, IMO. Why can't more people be like Him and make sure everyone gets fed? It is a terrible thing to be hungry and have no food.

I don't mean to sound judgmental. That's not my jam. I just think if everyone helped out a little bit there wouldn't be so many hungry people. Don't you think that would be a good thing?

**Lord, Gracie reminds me that today what I do for the least of us I do for You.** —Edward Grinnan

**Digging Deeper:** Proverbs 22:9; Matthew 15:29–39; Luke 12:33–34

---

# Monday, July 7

**So do not fear, for I am with you; do not be dismayed, for I am your God. I will strengthen you and help you; I will uphold you with my righteous right hand.** —Isaiah 41:10 (NIV)

As I am writing these words, it is late afternoon and I am exhausted. Late last night, my wife and I were jarred awake when a savage thunderstorm descended on middle Georgia. Wind slashed the windows and our pre-Civil War wooden house rocked and swayed like a boat adrift. We seemed to be in the "bull's-eye" of explosions and violent lightning.

As Beth and I groggily quaked in our bed and worried about adequate house insurance, our fierce, brave golden retriever jumped in the bed with us in a panic. When you and your dog can "smell" lightning in addition to being blinded by its brilliance, the primal instincts of fear and worry erupt! Even the television weatherman appeared shaken as I flicked on the Weather Channel hoping for reassurance and comfort.

An hour later, the storm had sped off to awaken another community, and Beth and I were asleep.

This was certainly not our first encounter with a storm or danger. But trauma never fails to arouse our primal instincts and fears. Even seasoned adults quake in terror from time to time. In these moments, we need to be reminded that the sustaining presence of God is with us.

**Father, in the midst of my anxiety and worry this day, may I feel Your presence with me. Amen.**
—Scott Walker

**Digging Deeper:** Mark 4:35–41; 1 Corinthians 10:13

---

# Tuesday, July 8

**He who made the Pleiades and Orion, who turns midnight into dawn and darkens day into night, who calls for the waters of the sea and pours them out over the face of the land—the Lord is his name. —Amos 5:8 (NIV)**

My son and I like to go on walks at night. Flashlights in our pockets, we trek down our country road and into the village. It's a ritual that started during the COVID-19 pandemic—a safe way to get out of the house and get some air—and has stayed.

Tonight, the weather is mild. A chorus of spring peepers serenades us. In our field, magical sparks of fireflies dance, and Solomon puts his arm over my shoulder and says, "This is the best part of today."

As we enter the long, lonely stretch with a canopy of trees that hug that road, I tell Solomon about the time, right on this very spot, a few days after my uncle went to heaven, a beautiful purple-and-black butterfly landed on my hand as I rode my bike and it stayed there for the longest time—and I felt it was a sign, that all was well, he was safe in heaven.

Solomon tells me about the classes he is taking in college. The professors he likes and the ones he is challenged by—and we opt to go for what we call the "big loop" because we both aren't tired, and it's too beautiful not to venture deeper into the night.

And I am happy, for this moment, that I am right here in this little town, with my son at my side, taking in the darkness and light of the journey.

**Lord, thank You for filling me with gratitude for every step I take on this amazing and wonderful life.**—Sabra Ciancanelli

**Digging Deeper:** Psalm 23:4; Ecclesiastes 3:11; Romans 15:13

---

# Wednesday, July 9

**This is the day that the LORD has made; let us rejoice and be glad in it. —Psalm 118:24 (ESV)**

Fifty. The number taunted me with its heaviness as my birthday approached.

"Oh, it's not so bad," my sister had said. "It's just a number."

She'd celebrated her fiftieth birthday two years before—a festive party organized by her husband.

*Who's going to organize my celebration?* I thought. No one. This birthday would be no different from the others. I had no husband, and my children were too young, my parents too elderly, and local friends too swamped with their own families to throw a party. For some time, birthdays had become a day of disappointment and a reminder of what I lacked in my life. What would my fiftieth birthday do to my mental state? A wave of defiance came over me as it consumed my thoughts.

*No,* I decided, *I'm going to make this the best birthday of my life!*

Months later, I woke up on a glorious July morning and welcomed "fifty" in Costa Rica. Accompanied by a friend, I celebrated in a rainforest surrounded by waterfalls. I jumped off a cliff into a pool of ancient water and felt reborn. That day, and the days that followed, I didn't feel old, sad, or filled with regret; instead, I watched sunsets, explored jungles, and delighted in a world of fish and coral beneath the ocean waves. I welcomed fifty, not dwelling on what was missing, but embracing what I had. With gratitude, I celebrated the gift of life God had given me all these years, and everything that is yet to come.

**Dear God, thank You for the gift of life. Help me to cherish every moment with positivity and gratitude.** —Karen Valentin

**Digging Deeper:** Ruth 4:15; Philippians 4:8

**But the tax collector, standing far off, would not even lift up his eyes to heaven but was beating his breast and saying, "God, be merciful to me, a sinner!" —Luke 18:13 (NRSVUE)**

The Jesus Prayer, as it's called, comes in different versions, but the one I like goes, "Jesus Christ, have mercy on me, a sinner."

It goes back to Jesus's parable of the Pharisee and the tax collector. The two are going up to the temple to pray. The Pharisee leads the way, praying, "God, I thank you that I am not like other people: thieves, rogues, adulterers, or even like this tax collector." He fasts, he tithes. By contrast, the tax collector stands at a distance, not even able to look up to heaven, but he beats his breast, saying, "God, be merciful to me, a sinner."

He is the one Jesus calls out as worthy of emulation.

I might have a dedicated time of prayer every morning, sitting on our lumpy sofa at home, my eyes closed, but often enough I fear I'm not very good at it. Unworthy.

That morning, I was distracted by a million worries, unable to concentrate. Then that ancient prayer came to mind: "Jesus Christ, be merciful to me, a sinner." I prayed it over and over.

I have friends who prefer to leave out the bit about being a sinner. I find it liberating and grounding. Indeed, isn't that who we all are? And in prayer, aren't we reaching out to the Source who can help us?

The rest of the day I held on to that prayer, and the worries receded, or at least spoke up in a manageable form.

And I moved forward, humbly.

**Thank You, Lord, for the gift of humility, where I seek You and find You.** —Rick Hamlin

**Digging Deeper:** Proverbs 22:4; James 4:10; 1 Peter 5:6

---

# Friday, July 11

**And let us consider how to provoke one another to love and good deeds, not neglecting to meet together . . .** —Hebrews 10:24–25 (NRSVUE)

Over several decades, I've received accolades for hosting guests at my table. When feeling urbane, I'd refer to them as dinner parties. My mother would have called them suppers. I anticipated the get-togethers, even wrote a book about hospitality. But I admit that as I aged, the evening gatherings more often than not depleted my energy reserves. *Is this worth the effort?* I'd wonder as I cleaned up. Then came the COVID-19 crisis. Understandably, my hostess heart shut down. For less obvious reasons, its doors didn't reopen in the subsequent seasons. "I'm never having a dinner party again. I'm tired,"

I told a confidante. Apparently, many in my circle felt a similar ennui.

But then, on short notice, a friend invited me and a few others to a July 4 backyard cookout. Yes, I responded—to the first sit-down home gathering I'd attended in, well, way too long. Hamburgers, salad, iced tea, watermelon. The table's simple fare satisfied the day's physical hunger. But the engaging conversation, the laughter, even the well wishes broke through my shell. Anticipation—*I want to invite people for a meal*—overpowered an underlying drag, *it's too much work*.

It's July 11. I've invited five women for a supper next week. I'm planning the menu; I've pressed and set aside a tablecloth; and I've disbursed a bag of corner clutter. God willing, the dinner is on—inspired by a friend who picked up the phone and fired up a grill.

**Lord, as I look to others for patterns to emulate, give me opportunity and energy to model good deeds for the benefit of my community.** —Evelyn Bence

**Digging Deeper:** John 21:9–12

---

# Saturday, July 12

**Our mouths were filled with laughter, our tongues with songs of joy. —Psalm 126:2 (NIV)**

Pushing aside a stand of grass, I sighed. It revealed just more tangled grass. My friends and I were searching for a metal T-post with a #7 welded to its top. Just a few short years ago, it'd been one of many numbered posts dotting Roundup, Montana's RiverWalk—a lovely Heritage Trail that wound its way along a stretch of the Musselshell River. The posts had corresponded with a brochure that described highlights along the walk's length.

But then a devastating flood ripped through, ravaging everything in its path—the RiverWalk included. The plan was to restore the posts to their places, but we had to find them first, and sometimes it seemed the only thing our searches turned up were reminders of how quickly destruction could be visited upon beautiful things.

"Look!" my friend shouted, excitedly. She was pointing to the elusive #7, which a large tree, felled by beavers, had driven straight into the ground as if it were a giant nail. No wonder it'd been hard to find.

"Get this!!" my other friend exclaimed. She'd pulled the brochure up on her phone. Number 7's entry was about—can you guess? Beavers. Its last sentence asked RiverWalkers if they could "see evidence of beaver from where they were standing?"

We erupted in laughter. What were the chances?

As we walked back to town with a fresh spring in our steps, I sent a prayer of gratitude heavenward for the restorative power of God's divine sense of humor.

**Thank You, God, for laughter. When shared lovingly with friends, it has the power to lift**

even the most flagging of spirits. It really is a
gift You gave the world. —Erin Janoso

**Digging Deeper:** Ecclesiastes 3:4; Luke 6:21

---

## Sunday, July 13

**And all the tithe of the land . . . is the Lord's.**
—Leviticus 27:30 (KJV)

When I was twelve, I had my first summer job, as
a hauler and fetch-it guy on a construction site.
Tough work for a kid struggling with wheelbarrows
of bricks and overflowing buckets of wet concrete.

On my first payday, I couldn't believe my eyes
when I opened my pay envelope. Ten crisp ten-
dollar bills. I was rich.

Already my mind was reeling with all the things
I could buy for myself. "Don't forget your tithe," my
mom said, crashing my lofty dreams.

*Ten percent,* I thought, *one of my ten-dollar bills.
No, I deserve it all.*

Back home that evening, my sister, Keri, was
playing with her Strawberry Shortcake dolls.

"Look, Brock, I have Angel Cake and Apricot, and
someday, I'm gonna get Purple Pie Man."

My dad grinned when I proudly showed him my
loot. "You should save part of your earnings . . . and
don't forget your tithe."

I went to bed that night with selfish thoughts. A
hundred dollars. It was all mine. The next morning,

I felt sad, somehow. I didn't know why. It was then that a card propped up on the kitchen counter—one that had been serving as a decoration for so long I'd almost forgotten about it—caught my eye. The front said: "Some people are so poor all they have is money."

In that very moment something broke free inside me. It was one of those times when a kid decides who they are going to be. I went upstairs and pulled out a bill for the next morning's collection plate. Later, I asked Mom, "Can you take me to the store? I want to get Keri a surprise."

And so it is today: My tithe is automatic and part of my hard-earned pay turns into surprises. I am free from being "poor."

**Father, make our lives rich in our giving.**
—Brock Kidd

**Digging Deeper:** Proverbs 3:9–10;
2 Corinthians 9:7

---

# Monday, July 14

## LIFE LESSONS FROM THE BEACH:
### Encouragement
**May our Lord Jesus Christ himself and God our Father, who loved us and in his grace gave us unfailing courage and a firm hope, encourage you and strengthen you to always do and say what is good. —2 Thessalonians 2:16–17 (GNT)**

When you're a three-year-old at the beach and can't go beyond the breakers with your older brother, you wade in the surf and pout.

To take my nephew's mind off what he couldn't do, I asked him to help me build a sandcastle. We constructed a fortress, dug a moat around it, and created an adjoining village. Hours later, we admired our work and accepted compliments from family and neighbors.

The next morning, he grabbed his sand bucket and announced we were building another castle. When his older brother joined us instead of swimming in the ocean, the smile on the little boy's face made my day.

As they designed and built their sand village, I moved to a chair under the beach umbrella and enjoyed watching them work together. By lunch, the castle stood taller than my chair, and the moat measured deeper than our bathtub. Mission accomplished.

A little encouragement led to larger achievements, reminding me how my parents helped me overcome a few obstacles along the way. While recalling several significant life moments, I remembered finding hope and encouragement in specific Bible verses, now my favorites, as if God wrote the words just for me and my situation. On second thought, He graciously did, knowing all my days before one of them came to be.

**Lord, thank You for providing specifically what each of us needs to serve You and others. Give us**

**encouragement and strength to share Your love.** —Jenny Lynn Keller

**Digging Deeper:** Psalm 139:13–16; Romans 15:4–6; Colossians 2:1–3; Hebrews 10:23–25

---

# Tuesday, July 15

**You shall not steal. You shall not bear false witness against your neighbor.** —Exodus 20:15–16 (NRSVUE)

I had just successfully avoided a juicy gossip session and was silently congratulating myself. While piously thanking God for helping me turn away from meanness, clear words came into my mind: *Don't condemn with your voice or your heart.* Suddenly, I didn't feel so proud.

I'd never liked the man my companions were discussing. I thought him loud, arrogant, and full of opinions—it didn't help that I disagreed with most of them. And avoiding gossip had not stopped me from telling my husband, Charlie, what I thought about the man more than once. Even worse, while I didn't participate in the comments, I did secretly enjoy hearing others agree with my assessment.

The words of warning in my mind reminded me of a friend, a church deacon, who said that mean gossip was one of the worst kinds of stealing because it robbed a person of his good name and reputation. *This is exactly what I was doing in my heart.* I didn't know much about this person, only that he rubbed me the wrong way. Just because I felt uncomfortable with him, was that a reason for me to rob him of his character?

Those words of warning were quickly becoming words of wisdom. It could very well be that this man's need to express opinions were born of his own strongly held convictions, or perhaps he was working through his own insecurities. In that way, we were not so different after all.

**Patient Father, give me just a sliver of Your true patience, tolerance, kindness, and love.** —Marci Alborghetti

**Digging Deeper:** Job 19; Acts 10:1–29

---

# Wednesday, July 16

**Trust in the LORD with all your heart and lean not on your own understanding. —Proverbs 3:5 (NIV)**

I cringed as I wrote the words on my calendar: "Zeke's Cancer Surgery." Zeke is our five-year-old golden retriever, our fourth golden. Of our first three, two died of cancer. One was my reward for finishing chemotherapy. Kemo was my faithful companion until he died at nine years old after a short battle with cancer. We vowed we'd never get another dog . . . until a couple of years later, when our empty nest felt too empty and we got Zeke, a newer breed of white goldens said to have less incidence of cancer.

Zeke entered our lives. We've loved him and all was well until his recent checkup, when the vet discovered a lump and was pretty sure it was cancer. "We need to surgically remove it and send it to the lab for more information." We set the surgery appointment and headed for the car. I was blinking back tears as Zeke jumped in, watching me.

One of the things I love about Zeke are his eyes. They look more like people-eyes than dog-eyes, and he tilts his head from side to side as he listens. We have our best heart-to-heart talks, eye-to-eye.

"Know what, Zeke? We're going to pray and wait and trust God!"

And that's what we did. Through the surgery and waiting for the lab results. Finally, the vet called: "Good news! It's the lowest grade of cancer and likely won't even come back. So, let's just wait and trust."

"And pray," I added. And that's what we're going to keep doing.

**Lord, I trust You, and that is where I find my strength.** —Carol Kuykendall

**Digging Deeper:** Psalm 27:14; Isaiah 30:18

# Thursday, July 17

**Now this is eternal life: that they know you, the only true God, and Jesus Christ, whom you have sent. I have brought you glory on earth by finishing the work you gave me to do.** —John 17:3–4 (NIV)

I felt overwhelmed as I struggled through a work training session about a new Excel sheet designed to organize company data. I was unfamiliar with the extent of the program, and I didn't see how I could possibly understand it all. I scrambled to take notes, fearing the day I would have to do this on my own.

The person training me was about to be changing departments, and it was important that I knew how to take on this new task independently within the next few days. The trainer kept telling me that I didn't have to worry. He reassured me that he had done the hardest part, so that the work would be easier for me when he left.

Although I didn't feel like the work left for me was easy, I did appreciate the gesture. I thought of how Jesus did the same for me. On the cross, He did the hardest part of all, because He cares for us so deeply. If we rely fully on Him, our workload is much lighter, even during troubled times.

And as for my computer troubles? After practicing the software alone, its framework and structure made sense to me. I was able to organize and present the data successfully.

**Thank You, Father, that You carry the weight of my sin and hardship for me, and I can rest in You when things seem too hard for me on my own.**
—Nicole Garcia

**Digging Deeper:** Ecclesiastes 7:8;
John 4:34, 19:30

# Friday, July 18

**The human mind may devise many plans, but it is the purpose of the LORD that will be established. —Proverbs 19:21 (NRSVUE)**

I was uneasy at our lake cabin one July afternoon. I knew rain was coming soon, but I was determined to get my child out of the house and onto the water in a kayak while it was still bright and sunny.

I fastened the life jacket around her shoulders and explained why it was necessary to wear one. I showed her how the paddle works, and how to hold it properly. Then we pushed off the shore and paddled all around the lake. There were turtles and fish in the water and birds of prey in the sky above our heads. It was beautiful. It would be one of those great dad moments, I said quietly to myself, a day my child would always remember.

As we approached the shore again, I explained the importance of getting up from the kayak slowly and steadily. "This is when people often fall in," I said, placing my feet carefully on either side of the bottom of the kayak, as I began to stand. "Do it like this," I said—and then, it's true, I tipped sideways and tumbled into the water.

Oh, yes, my daughter remembers that day—I've watched her tell friends all about it—as an example of her dad's overconfidence. We're always teaching with our lives in one way or another.

---

## Saturday, July 19

# JOURNEYING WITH JESUS: Garden Seeds

**But He said to them, "How many loaves do you have? Go look!" —Mark 6:38 (NASB)**

Jesus's disciples wanted Him to send the crowd into neighboring villages to get something to eat. Thousands had gathered for hours outdoors listening to Him teach. How shocked they must have been when He said, "You give them something to eat!"

They had no way to do that. But Jesus had something more in mind. He sent them among the people to search out loaves of bread. They returned with five loaves and two fish. A laughable amount for the size of the crowd. Raising His face to His heavenly Father, He blessed the food in His hands.

What happened next must have astounded the disciples. Jesus kept handing them bread and fish to pass to the people—generous servings until they were all full. There were even a dozen baskets of bread and fish left over.

The tiny garden seeds in my spiritual go-pack will produce a feast by God's design. They need time—not every increase happens instantly. But they remind me to give the little I have and watch what God can do.

So many occasions when I am discouraged or weary or afraid—like last night, when I was way too tired to cook dinner—Jesus says, "Go look!" I give Him my little joy, my little strength, my little faith. In His hands, beyond what I can explain, it grows into more than enough.

**Lord, when I place in You my smallest trust, You bless and increase it. The elk chili was delicious!**
—Carol Knapp

**Digging Deeper:** Isaiah 49:6; Matthew 13:31–32; Mark 12:41–44; 2 Corinthians 9:10

---

# Sunday, July 20

**I will say to the LORD, "My refuge and my fortress, my God, in whom I trust." For he will deliver you from the snare of the fowler and from the deadly pestilence. —Psalm 91:2–3 (ESV)**

I admit it: when golf ball-sized hail was flying at my windshield, I wasn't just *saying* the words of Psalm 91, I was screaming them.

My husband and I, two teenagers, a preteen, and two golden retrievers were driving back to Texas from Colorado. It was a beautiful day—blue skies, tumbleweeds sitting still on the plains, the sun baking overhead. We had our ice teas in the cup holders, our podcast on full volume, and we were rolling.

We had just hit that stretch of land where the plains of Texas seem to go on for a thousand miles in every direction when the sky got dark. Three minutes later, the rain started to fall. Five minutes after that, we were pulled over on the side of the road, hail pounding our car, teenagers ducking under pillows in the backseat.

There was literally nowhere to take cover—no gas station, no covered parking area, no tree. We were in the wide open.

So I started to chant. OK, yell. "The Lord is my refuge. He is my fortress. In Him I trust."

The kids followed suit.

The storm maybe took five minutes to pass, and then the sky was clear again, the air smelling sweet and clean. The windows were intact. Our car had a few dents, but it ran fine.

He *was* our fortress. He *did* protect us. And I learned that I can trust in Him. Even if I do it through screams of fear.

**Dear Father, when the storms of life come, please keep protecting me and help me to trust You even more.** —Erin MacPherson

**Digging Deeper:** Nahum 1:7; 2 Corinthians 12:9

---

# Monday, July 21

## LIFE LESSONS FROM THE BEACH: Love

The Lord is good; his love is eternal and his faithfulness lasts forever. —Psalm 100:5 (GNT)

My husband anchored the boat in shallow water, and we waded ashore to explore an uninhabited island in the Bahamas. Within moments of taking in the cloudless sky, sun-drenched beach, and crystal-clear ocean, we declared this patch of sand a tropical oasis.

The only sound we heard for hours equated to nature's version of a lullaby—gentle waves lapping against the beach. Under the shade of coconut palm trees, we ate a picnic lunch and listened to the waves roll in and out. The soothing melody lulling us into a brief nap. Not eager to end our visit in paradise, we meandered along the shore and explored the surf for shells on our way back to the boat.

When we reached the inlet, we discovered higher water and no boat. Yikes, were we stranded? A frantic search farther down the beach located the boat about twenty yards offshore in deeper water. After a short swim to reclaim our transportation, we motored home and acknowledged a valuable lesson learned the hard way.

While we enjoyed a day of leisure, the tide worked on schedule and with force, reminding us in many ways of God's love. Both are constant, dependable, always at work, and powerful—never growing tired or sleepy like the two of us.

**Lord, the beauty and complexity of Your creations overwhelm me. I cannot comprehend Your endless and unfailing love offered to all of us. Thank You for Your faithfulness and constant work in my life. Please forgive my shortcomings.** —Jenny Lynn Keller

---

# Tuesday, July 22

**Hear me, Lord! Listen to me! For I groan and weep beneath my burden of woe. —Psalm 55:2 (TLB)**

One summer day I was complaining to a friend about the heat and humidity here in Florida. She reminded me that the Tampa Bay area—where I've lived since 2004—is known for sun, sand, sea, sunsets, serenity, 361 days of sunshine per year, and thirty-five miles of white sand beaches along the Gulf of Mexico. I reminded her that we're also known for hurricanes, palmetto bugs (what Floridians politely call cockroaches that are bigger than your thumb), and hot, humid days that force you to stay indoors in the air conditioning most of the summer.

Then she reminded me that I had lived for twenty-four years in Wisconsin, where I had to contend with gray skies, super-cold weather six months a year, and hard-to-navigate driveways and streets when the snow began to fall. I reminded her that having four distinct seasons up north was nice and certainly broke the monotony.

Finally, I got the point. There's good and bad everywhere in the world. I just need to choose whether I'm going to be a happy optimist or a cranky pessimist. It's up to me to love where I am and to concentrate on the good, happy parts of every day.

Now, if I could just think of something nice to say about those giant palmetto bugs!

**Lord, don't let me be a complainer. Give me an attitude adjustment next time I grumble about the heat.** —Patricia Lorenz

**Digging Deeper:** Numbers 11:1–3; Job 23:2–7; Jude 16–20

---

# Wednesday, July 23

**God is our refuge and our strength, a very present help in trouble. —Psalm 46:1 (KJV)**

The photo of a beautiful baby pops up on my email. Abandoned and malnourished, she has been welcomed into our Village Hope family by directors Paddington and Alice. We are committed to lifting up the children of a rural Zimbabwean community. So, when an orphaned child appears at our gate, we say, "Yes."

From the beginning, I promised that every gift offered by others would go to Zimbabwe. Our family covers all outlying expenses, including hundreds of dollars a month for mailings and annual travel. My daughter, Keri, and I use our real estate earnings to provide daily school lunches to more than two thousand children.

Beyond this, a fair measure of our actual budget comes from *Walking in Grace* readers. Every penny funds sprawling projects headed by Paddington.

A fine school for the poorest children. Food for dozens of people living in mud huts. Plus, teaching women sewing, gardening, and raising animals.

All this started with a clear call from God, so I have a serious chat with Him. I remind Him that our family is stretched and our budget grows with new children, teachers, projects. "Don't forget us, Father."

He finds a clever way to answer back. A monthly check arrives from a generous woman with meager means. She writes, "I wanted to take time to thank you and remind you that your work is precious. I have written down every name of the beautiful children and laborers at Village Hope. I pray over them daily. God sees your work, and Keri's, and your family's. God knows and understands your efforts and sacrifices."

I am renewed.

**Father, God, Your reminder from Your daughter is clear. You haven't forgotten us. We move forward.**
—Pam Kidd

**Digging Deeper:** Ezekiel 36:27; Philippians 4:19

---

# Thursday, July 24

**. . . when you refused to help the least of these my brothers and sisters, you were refusing to help me. —Matthew 25:45 (NLT)**

Summer heat radiated off the asphalt. As I neared the door to the grocery store, I noticed a man and his dog, leaning against the building. His tattered clothes, dirty hair, and knapsack told the story—he was homeless. In the past I've shown compassion toward others, but just a couple of days ago a friend of mine uttered words that shook my world.

For years we'd prayed for her son, who had been raised in a middle-class working family, but due to mental illness had become one of the tattered-clothed homeless roaming the streets. As we were ending our prayer, she cried and shared how mean people were to her son—on a daily basis. "Don't people realize that he's somebody's son? How would they want someone to treat their son?"

As I approached the man, her words rang in my mind and I prayed. *Jesus, You never avoided the broken; instead You sought them out to share Your love. Give me wisdom on how to do that.* The man was beading a hat band, so I briefly chatted with him about the art he was creating. The next time I asked about his plans for life and encouraged him that God had great plans for him. The following time I bought him a meal. Over the dozens of times I've reached out in God's love, he's never recognized me, but I continue to pray for him—because he's somebody's son, who was created by God Himself.

**Lord, I lift up the homeless and their families. Show me how to pour out Your everlasting love on them. Amen.** —Rebecca Ondov

**Digging Deeper:** Matthew 8:2, 9:27–30; Mark 1:40–42

**So when the L**ORD** saw that he turned aside to look, God called to him from the midst of the bush and said, "Moses, Moses!" And he said, "Here I am."** —Exodus 3:4 (NKJV)

There have been a number of times when I've heard God speak into my life.

I remember the first time it happened. Wayne and I were driving through Glacier National Park and we slowly drove past the weeping wall. The rock is made up of basalt, and as the snow melts, it literally leaks through the rock. As I gazed upon the site, I mentally told the Lord how beautiful this was. Immediately His words flashed into my mind: *If you think this is beautiful, just wait until you get to heaven.* The words came so fast and sure, I knew they were from the Lord.

During my school-aged years, I often stopped off at my father's upholstery shop on my way home from school. While he worked, I'd tell him about my day. Because Jesus had been a carpenter, I decided I would put myself back in Dad's shop while I talked to Jesus. Like my dad had years earlier, I envisioned Jesus working on a piece of furniture as I told Him of my concerns. All at once, Jesus turned to me and said as plainly as if He had spoken the words aloud, *Debbie, My daughter, I have such wonderful stories for you to write in heaven.*

Of all the times I've heard God's voice and felt His presence, that day while in prayer remains one of the most profound. Just think, my friends, not only has God prepared a mansion for us, but we will also have the opportunity to do the very things we did in life that bring us joy.

**Father, heaven is closer than we think. I can hardly wait to plot with You.** —Debbie Macomber

**Digging Deeper:** Genesis 3:9; 1 Samuel 3:8

---

# Saturday, July 26

**I tell you, on the day of judgment people will give account for every careless word they speak, for by your words you will be justified, and by your words you will be condemned. —Matthew 12:36–37 (ESV)**

Commenting on a devotion I wrote on the power of words, a reader emailed me that there should be an app that tracks what we say. That idea got me thinking.

Back when I was a practicing litigation attorney, courtrooms had stenographers who took down every word spoken. We'd receive a printed copy of the proceeding that contained all that had been said. *What if, at the end of every day, I received a transcript of all I had uttered that day? Would I be happy, embarrassed, or even ashamed of its contents?* Unfortunately, it would too often include words I'd wished had been left unspoken, words I regretted.

It's so easy for me to let my words flow, to say whatever comes to mind, especially when I'm irritated or upset. I remembered Jesus's words in

Matthew 12:36–37. God hears all the words I speak. And I will be judged by them.

I resolved then and there to try to picture all my words being recorded, for somehow they are, not only in heaven, but in the hearts of those to whom I speak. When I'm tempted to say things I'll be sorry for later, I can imagine there is indeed an app, or a stenographer, documenting every word I speak, and that it will be played back to me in eternity.

**Dear God, thank You for that precious reader whose email reminded me how every word I say has ramifications, both now and eternally. Help me to think before I speak and to choose my words carefully. Amen.** —Kim Taylor Henry

**Digging Deeper:** Psalm 19:14; Proverbs 18:21; Ephesians 4:29; James 3:6

---

# Sunday, July 27

**Those who go out weeping, bearing the seed for sowing, shall come home with shouts of joy, carrying their sheaves. —Psalm 126:6 (NRSVUE)**

I've always emotionally connected flowers with worship. I grew up in a non-liturgical church. No frills except for the fresh bouquet—I remember especially roses and lilacs—set on the flower stands.

Now, in my more liturgical church, a florist and—since COVID, to save expenses—a volunteer always provided weekly arrangements for the altar.

But recently our flower lady "retired." The plan, I heard, was to hang a seasonal silk-flower wreath high on the chancel wall. I didn't object until I walked in one Sunday and saw the empty flower nooks. *Oh, my heart.*

I made a few "may I?" calls, bought red roses and baby's breath and early the next Sunday placed my two bouquets in their appointed spot. As I stepped back to inspect the bounty, I started to cry. I didn't know why.

On Monday I told my sister about the tears. She cut in. "Did you remember that yesterday was the anniversary of Dad's death?" No. Not consciously.

In *Whistling in the Dark*, Frederick Buechner urges readers to pay attention to "unexpected tears." Connecting the past to the future, he suggests, "More often than not God is speaking to you through them of the mystery of where you have come from and is summoning you to where . . . you should go to next."

Hmm. A call to service? I hear other parishioners have rallied, offering to arrange altar bouquets. I've put my name on the roster.

**Lord, You have so many ways—memory, emotion, beauty, to name a few—to nudge me toward health and wholeness and service. Speak to my heart today. —Evelyn Bence**

**Digging Deeper:** Psalm 126;
Ezekiel 17:22–24

# LIFE LESSONS FROM THE BEACH:
## Purpose

**They are my own people, and I created them to bring me glory. —Isaiah 43:7 (GNT)**

Located off the South Carolina coast and owned by the state university, Pritchards Island rewarded us with a day of fun and learning. The kids enjoyed the boat ride, and the adults appreciated the guided educational tour.

Along the wide beach, we observed loggerhead turtle nests, bobcat tracks, and an abundance of hermit crabs. Our student guide described how hermit crabs differ from other crustaceans in three ways—part of their body lacks a hard shell, they borrow shells from other animals for protection, and they must find a larger abandoned shell before outgrowing the current one. Since they can't make their own shells, the end of their abdomen is designed to wrap around and grip the coiled inside of snail shells. When a shell isn't available, they search debris on the beach until suitable protection is found. Our guide once saw a crab wearing a bottle cap.

Based on this information, I decided these resourceful critters qualified as originators of recycling. They did what they were created to do with the materials available, and the same principle applies to me. God created everyone and everything for the purpose of bringing Him glory, and He supplies our needs to accomplish His mission. The decisions I make not only impact me but also affect others. When I follow God's plan for my life, I find contentment, much like the crab delighted in wearing a bottle cap.

**Lord, thank You for making each of us unique, giving our lives purpose, and loving us the way You created us. Remind us to do everything as if we are working for You.** —Jenny Lynn Keller

**Digging Deeper:** Psalm 139:13–16; Proverbs 19:21; Colossians 3:23–24; 1 Thessalonians 5:16–18

---

# Tuesday, July 29

**There is no fear in love. But perfect love drives out fear. —1 John 4:18 (NIV)**

I've been a perfectionist all my life. Schools rewarded me with grades, and jobs with praise. But lately my projects don't give rewards. They seem too massive to ever finish, so I get discouraged before I begin. If I do get started, I see only the mountain that remains.

I prayed, *Would I still be me, Lord, if I were less of a perfectionist?*

I texted my daughter Katie. "Want to be a charter member of PA?"

Perfectionists Anonymous's dues are free, just like God's love. We send each other texts whenever we make progress on a project. Not finished. Not perfect. No schedule for completion. We celebrate our successes, especially the nearly invisible ones.

Katie texted me: "PA Report. I grudgingly forced myself to schedule one hour of cleaning off my desk today. As usual, it wasn't nearly as bad as I thought it would be. I didn't quite get to everything, but The Pile of Doom is gone!"

I texted Katie: "PA Report. Emptied one medium box from that pile in the spare bedroom. Mostly stuff I don't need, carefully packed away for years."

Katie: "PA Report. I cleaned out (drumroll please) the basement closet. Three large trash bags, a car stuffed with donations, a huge pile of recycling."

Me: "PA Report. I reduced my inbox by ten emails every day this week!"

God whispers, *My recovering perfectionists are Pretty Awesome.*

**Thank You, Gracious Lord, for driving out my fear. Your love is the only perfection I need.**
—Leanne Jackson

**Digging Deeper:** Isaiah 26:3; 2 Corinthians 12:9

---

# Wednesday, July 30

# SEEMINGLY INSIGNIFICANT: Loving the Way God Loves
**Do not judge, and you will not be judged.**
—Luke 6:37 (NIV)

"All your life, you've reduced people to some tiny, meaningless thing you think about them!" my daughter Lulu accused the other day. "That they use paper plates. Or eat out every meal."

Having attended high school far from home, Lulu bypassed the door-slamming and surly clairvoyance of teenagerdom. Now, almost thirty, she's catching up. And she's right. Reducing others to some absurd lowest common denominator is my worst sin.

I'm even judgmental about strangers I only read about. This morning, during my daily Bible-reading podcast, it was Rahab, the woman Joshua's spies stayed with before the Israelites entered the Promised Land. She was, in the podcast's dainty translation, "a harlot." A prostitute. Someone I had no use for. *Why were they even staying with her?* I fumed automatically as I listened. I had no use for any of them.

A friend of mine perpetually says of fellow believers whom she for any reason condemns, "How can they even call themselves Christians?"

"Isn't it actually wonderful," I respond, "that we can call ourselves Christian, even when we're not the perfect people God created us to be?"

Rahab makes an astonishing profession of faith to the men she hides: "The Lord your God is God in heaven above and on the earth below" (Joshua 2:11, NIV). She's a prostitute—*and* a believer. Soon afterward, she's welcomed into the spies' community and eventually ends up—minus that diminishing moniker, the harlot—in the lineage of Jesus Christ.

I need to see *that* part of people, their God-given highest common denominator: that God made people in his image and loves them, whether I do or not.

**Help me love as You love, Lord!** —Patty Kirk

**Digging Deeper:** Joshua 2; Matthew 1:1–17

---

# Thursday, July 31

**The end of all things is near. Therefore be alert and of sober mind so that you may pray. —1 Peter 4:7 (NIV)**

"The elk are on the move," my husband, Kevin, said as he peered over the cliff on our property to a dry lake bed below. "Let's try to photograph them."

For the past several evenings, the herd had been spotted at a spring-fed watering hole at the edge of the lake. They drank their fill before bedding down for the night in a nearby forest. Each time we had driven up, they had scattered.

Climbing into the truck, I was thankful for the diversion. I'd been receiving text messages about a granddaughter with a fever and a grandson who needed speech therapy. How could I help from so far away?

We parked at a distance and crept closer, one cautious step at a time. About a dozen mothers and calves lingered near the water.

"The sentinel," Kevin whispered, pointing to a female with her head upright, alert to any sound or movement. She stared right at us. We froze.

A frolicking calf diverted her attention. We inched nearer.

For the next half hour, we watched as three herds converged, until more than one hundred animals surrounded the small spring. The mothers cautiously sipped water from the surface, while the youngsters jumped right in, legs splashing and heads bobbing.

Through it all, the sentinel stood guard. Focused. Vigilant. Watching her, I felt challenged to do the same in prayer for my family.

When a car came speeding down the nearby road, the alarmed sentinel gave two barks of warning. In one orchestrated movement, the elk fled—hooves pounding—with the sentinel bringing up the rear.

**When I receive concerning news, Jesus, teach me to stand watch and pray for those I love. —Lynne Hartke**

**Digging Deeper:** Romans 1:9; 1 Peter 5:8

# WITH AN EVERLASTING LOVE

1 _____

2 _____

3 _____

4 _____

5 _____

6 _____

7 _____

8 _____

9 _____

10 _____

11 _____

12 _____

13 _____

14 _____

15 _____

16 _____

17 _____

18 _____

19 _____

20 _____

21 _____

22 _____

23 _____

24 _____

25 _____

26 _____

27 _____

28 _____

29 _____

30 _____

31 _____

# August

And over all these virtues put on love, which binds them all together in perfect unity.

—Colossians 3:14 (NIV)

# Friday, August 1

**Much more is required from the person to whom much more is given. —Luke 12:48 (GNT)**

When it comes to math and money management, I am all thumbs and have been since I was just a boy. I would spend all of my allowance the same day I got it on important things like bubble gum, pretzels, and comic books.

In contrast, my older brother, Tommy, was a math genius and a bit of a Scrooge, in my judgment. If I wanted to borrow ten dollars from him, I had to put up collateral and pay interest. You think I'm joking?

Today my brother is in his eighties, and he is definitely not a Scrooge. He has been a lifelong tither, plus he supports nine different mission works. In addition, he maintains four low-rent apartments, which he makes available to the needy. He has a good heart.

I solved my spending problem by marrying a woman who is like Tommy: good with money, but also benevolent. She manages our finances and gives me an "allowance" on payday, which serves as a simplified budget for me. When I have used it up, I am broke until next payday. I'm broke a lot!

From my brother and my wife, I've learned that there is a difference between being stingy and being frugal. If I want to be a generous and godly man, then I need to manage my money very carefully.

So, I have given up bubble gum and comic books ... but not pretzels.

**Lord, thank You for blessing me, so that I can bless others who are in need.** —Daniel Schantz

**Digging Deeper:** Proverbs 19:17; 2 Corinthians 9:7

---

# Saturday, August 2

**Live generously and graciously toward others, the way God lives toward you. —Matthew 5:48 (MSG)**

We were on the last leg of a Minnesota road trip, driving to the Minneapolis–Saint Paul International Airport. My two younger brothers, Dennis (known by his polka-show DJ name of "Skip") and Tim (personnel officer for Wegman's Grocery), and I pulled into the Maple Grove rest stop on Interstate 94.

As I rushed off to use the facility, I spotted a credit card lying on the brushed concrete surface. *How sad,* I thought as I passed it by, recalling a French Riviera hotel bill once charged to my misplaced card.

Upon exiting, I saw the same card, still on the ground. *What can I do?* I mused, though a nudge came that maybe I could bring it to the rest stop attendant. Yet, I passed it by.

Awaiting my brothers' return, I leaned my elbows on the roof of our compact rental car, enjoying the balmy afternoon.

My brother Skip came up, talking on his cell phone. "Hey, Kenny," he commented after completing the call, "I spotted this credit card on the pavement, called the 1-800 number to cancel, and found out nearly $5,000 was available. Sure hope whoever lost it rests easy, knowing transactions are stopped."

*Ah*... I thought (though not without a tinge of guilt), *how proud our mom would be, knowing of the big-hearted kindness of one of her sons.* And, as I told my brothers how I, too, had seen the same card and passed it by, I resolved to be more attentive to following through on the divine nudges that come my way.

**Living God, enable us to act on the gentle prods of Your Spirit in our lives today. Amen.** —Ken Sampson

**Digging Deeper:** Luke 10:25–37; 2 Corinthians 6:13; Philippians 2:3–4

---

# Sunday, August 3

**Those who are wise will shine like the brightness of the heavens, and those who lead many to righteousness, like the stars for ever and ever. —Daniel 12:3 (NIV)**

This year, my in-laws treated our family to a week on a sailboat. As I packed, the kids asked each other what they were looking forward to. "Seeing fish!" "Being with the uncles and Auntie Maddie!" "Playing in the water!"

Fun and dreamy ideas were tossed around until they thought to ask me, the one who had been before. "The sky," I said. "You'll understand what I mean when we get there."

I've written before about how I've intentionally trained my kids to look for beautiful sunsets, "cotton candy skies," we call them. Now they call out to me when they see the purples and blues start to swirl with the pinks over our backyard fence. So it didn't surprise me when the first night on the boat, one of them yelled, "MOM!! THE SUNSET!"

"Just wait!" I yelled back. "It gets better." We watched together from the top of the boat as the sky melted from brilliant blue to cotton candy pink to pitch black, then even longer as the sky flooded with more stars than they'd ever seen.

Psalm 147 says He counts and names each star; Genesis describes Abraham as having as many descendants as the stars in the sky. Suddenly those verses meant way, way more.

I gathered them close and reminded them that if God cared so much about the stars that He knew each one, He cared even more about them, His children.

**Lord, help me remember that even on my most troubled day, Your love for me is infinite and exhaustive.** —Ashley Kappel

**Digging Deeper:** Psalms 8:3, 147:4–5

# Monday, August 4

## LIFE LESSONS FROM THE BEACH:
## A Strong Anchor

**This certain hope of being saved is a strong and trustworthy anchor for our souls, connecting us with God himself behind the sacred curtains of heaven, where Christ has gone ahead to plead for us. —Hebrews 6:19–20 (TLB)**

Cannon Beach features one of Oregon's most recognizable landmarks, Haystack Rock. The arrowhead-shaped rock rises 235 feet above the ocean floor and provides a resting place for a multitude of sea creatures and birds.

While similar sea stacks litter the Oregon coastline as a result of ancient lava flows, Haystack Rock possesses a distinct quality—you can walk right up to it at low tide.

On a recent visit, my family and I explored the rock as the tide receded. Puffins and cormorants perched on the upper sides and protected their nests built in burrows and on narrow ledges. An abundance of starfish, crabs, and sea anemones clung to the rock's base. As the tide advanced and waves splashed against the stack, the starfish retreated to deeper crevices for better protection.

I followed their example and herded my gang back to the shoreline for safety. The next day we visited a sea aquarium and learned the starfish survival secret: their underside contains rows of suction-cup-like feet capable of clinging to just about anything. As we watched a starfish move across the giant wall of glass, I admired how God gifted all living creatures with unique abilities, especially for seeking shelter. He provided rocks to anchor starfish and gave His Son to anchor us.

**God, nothing is safer or stronger than You. Thank You for being our hope and anchor on sunny days and through stormy weather.** —Jenny Lynn Keller

**Digging Deeper:** Deuteronomy 32:3–4; 2 Samuel 22:1–7; Matthew 7:24–27; 1 Corinthians 10:3–4

---

## Tuesday, August 5

**And over all these virtues put on love, which binds them all together in perfect unity.**
**—Colossians 3:14 (NIV)**

Don't laugh at me, but some mornings I wake up, look at the difficult day ahead, and wish I were on Gilligan's Island with the motley, shipwrecked passengers and crew of the SS *Minnow*.

I was never a fan. I was too young. But the other day when I was putting off something or other, I got sucked into a rerun on cable. The plot was inane. The characters caricatures. The jokes painful. Yet I kept watching. There was something comforting in the silliness.

Maybe it was the utter lack of contemporary themes. Or any connection to reality whatsoever. The hapless Gilligan, the crusty Skipper, the girl-next-door Mary Ann, the glam Ginger, the pedantic Professor, and the one-percenters Thurston and Lovey Howell were like one big, happy, dysfunctional family. Why in my escapist fantasy did I want to fit in with them rather than face a hard day? The premise of the show was that they would never be rescued. They were fated to be in each other's company forever.

I pondered what my persona would be. The writer who figured out how to fashion a typewriter from bamboo? Who told stories around the fire? Maybe positive, hopeful stories that rescue was imminent? In every episode they are nearly saved except for some absurd twist of fickle fate. For them, life is just one big cosmic pratfall.

But not for us in the real world. We are saved every day, rescued from worry and fear and whatever personal shipwrecks that may befall us, by our faith. We are never so lost that we cannot be found by a God who draws us closest when our days are the hardest.

**As I face the challenges of the day, let me face them with You, Lord, rescued by Your love.** —Edward Grinnan

**Digging Deeper:** John 13:34–35; 1 Corinthians 13:13

---

# Wednesday, August 6

**May your unfailing love be my comfort, according to your promise to your servant. —Psalm 119:76 (NIV)**

Our beloved Labrador, Rugby, became ill suddenly. Dear Rugby, who spent his life in our homeschool classroom. Rugby, who carried a blanket. Rugby, who gave hugs and cared for all who entered our home. His illness was as aggressive as he was gentle. One sad Friday, our veterinarian gave Rugby three days to live.

That weekend, friends and family came to bid farewell to this caring gentleman. All the while, Rugby looked at us with brown eyes that exuded love. He wished that he could stay. We still had boys to raise and release.

On Monday morning, Rugby rested near our fireplace, wrapped in a blanket from my bed. I lay beside him. I rose to get him water and when I returned, Rugby had moved. He could barely walk, yet I found him by the back door.

And when I saw him, the years washed away.

Before me was a healthy, bright-eyed Rugby, standing sturdy and strong. Robust. Vibrant. Our eyes met, and his tail wagged like wild. "I'm glad to see you," his presence spoke. "Where have you been?" When I reached the door, I saw Rugby as sick again. Weak and frail.

Within hours, he was gone.

Although it's been months, I'm still unsure of what happened that day. But I know I experienced something extraordinary. Maybe the Lord meant to tell me that I'd see Rugby again. Or maybe He gave me a memory to treasure—one of life rather than death.

I don't know. But either way, He comforted me with His love.

**Lord, Your love falls to unexpected places, comforting me as I grieve. Amen.** —Shawnelle Eliasen

**Digging Deeper:** Job 5:11; Psalms 27:13–14, 34:18, 147:3

---

# Thursday, August 7

**How countless are your works, Lord! In wisdom you have made them all. —Psalm 104:24 (CSB)**

The first droplets from the watering can had just splashed onto the leaves of my hot, thirsty flowerbox flowers when something alive leapt up and out. I stepped back, startled. At my feet was a big brown toad. Scooping it up, I carried it back to my garden. "It'll be nicer for you here," I said, as I placed it in the shade.

By the very next afternoon, the toad was back! Which earned it a second trip back to the garden. I hoped this time it'd stay. But it didn't. When I found myself toe to toe with our flowerbox toad for the third day in a row, I really began to wonder. What was going on?

A piece of advice from a marriage counselor came to mind. "Has it ever occurred to you," he'd asked my husband and me, "that you might both be right about this?"

It was wisdom I'd thought back on again and again, because the complexity of God's creation rarely seems to miss an opportunity to remind me there are often multiple valid ways of thinking about things, in addition to just my own.

I looked again at the flowerbox. It wasn't where I'd want to be, if I were a toad. But it wasn't my journey to walk, was it? This time, when I scooped the toad up, I placed it carefully back into the place it'd chosen for itself. It, and God, knew the reason why. And that was enough.

**Thank You, God, for the complex beauty of Your creation, and for the reminder that we're all different creatures, knitted together by You, with our own unique perspectives and paths set before us.** —Erin Janoso

**Digging Deeper:** Psalm 139:14; Romans 12:6

---

# Friday, August 8

**You are a hiding place for me.**
**—Psalm 32:7 (NRSVUE)**

Several years ago now, a tropical storm ripped through southern Vermont, including the town of Woodstock, where we lived. It happened on a Sunday.

Heavy rain for twelve hours had us worried. A rivulet formed in our cellar. An hour after that, when the river across the street flooded its banks, we had only five minutes to get out.

My wife, Michal, grabbed the baby (it was her three-month birthday). I grabbed our sixty-pound dog, Max. We watched our neighbors get in their cars and flee. One of our cars was left behind in the driveway, already filled with water.

Water covered the roads, and the historic wooden-covered bridges in our neighborhood were destroyed when a storage of propane tanks shot downriver, hitting the sides of the bridges like bombs. We got out of Woodstock, to stay with friends, just before the last bridge was gone.

What would be left, whenever we could return home? We worried. I won't lie and say that we didn't. The following day, we discovered that the basement had filled completely with water, all the way up to the first-floor floorboards, and then the water flowed back out. Not much was lost. Most importantly, we knew that everything we really needed was right in front of us all the time.

**Holy One, cover me in Your wings when I am afraid.** —Jon M. Sweeney

**Digging Deeper:** 2 Samuel 22:3–4; Nahum 1:7

---

# Saturday, August 9

**Call on me in the day of trouble; I will deliver you, and you will honor me. —Psalm 50:15 (NIV)**

It was my birthday and I had just enjoyed a New Orleans-style brunch of bananas Foster French toast with a good friend. I hugged her goodbye and jumped into my car, contemplating whether I'd get my nails done then go shopping or vice versa. A kind motorist motioned for me to enter traffic in front of her. I waved gratefully and commenced to drive out of the parking space, not realizing I was in reverse gear. To my shock, I bumped the car parked behind me.

Shaking my head, I turned off the ignition and jumped out to inspect the damage to the late-model Mercedes I'd hit. I looked up and down the street, trying to spot the owner. Not seeing anyone, I debated my options. I could wait until the owner returned. I could leave a note. Or I could drive off and pretend nothing happened.

I felt a nudge in my spirit, so I slipped my name and number under their windshield wiper. Within the hour the owner called, mentioned there wasn't much damage, and thanked me for being kind enough to leave a note. A month later, when I'd almost forgotten the incident, the owner called again. I inhaled, exhaled, and prepared for the price tag of the body work I'd need to reimburse her for. In a sweet voice, she said the auto shop had buffed and touched up the paint free of charge. She thanked me for my honesty and said she was grateful for good people in the world.

I was relieved and truly thankful.

**Lord, thank You for allowing us to be vessels of Your goodness.** —Carla Hendricks

**Digging Deeper:** Psalm 55:22; Proverbs 3:5–6; Philippians 4:6–7

# Sunday, August 10

**Keep straight the path of your feet, and all your ways will be sure. —Proverbs 4:26 (NRSVUE)**

What is it about socks that make them disappear in the hollows of the washer or dryer? Never a matching pair. No, just one of them. You only realize it when you're folding the clothes and you notice that the gray sock doesn't have its mate ... or the blue sock ... or that white athletic sock. A lot of good it will do on its own.

Perhaps it's not such a quandary if you have a washer and dryer in your house. You can search in their depths and find the stubborn wanderer. Alas, we live in an apartment and do the wash in a laundry room. I used to tell myself that it was like living in an ancient village where you cleaned your clothes at the riverside, catching up with your neighbors.

When I go back in search of a missing sock, I'm hardly in the mood for chitchat, scowling all the while. But this one time ("Where's that sock?") I managed to see a neighbor I hadn't seen in a while, the two of us getting caught up. And lo and behold, I found not just the missing mate but a whole other pair. Three socks, clean and dry.

"Did you find the sock?" Carol asked upon my return.

"Yes," I replied. "And another pair." Not to mention that friend I was so glad to see. Isn't it often true that the journey you don't want to make, the thing you don't want to do, can offer unexpected benefits? Something you found before you even knew it was gone. Like another pair of socks.

**Lord, let me see You in the little mishaps of life. You are there.** —Rick Hamlin

**Digging Deeper:** Psalm 119:105; Isaiah 52:7; John 13:14

---

## Monday, August 11

## LIFE LESSONS FROM THE BEACH: Treasure

**For God's secret plan, now at last made known, is Christ himself. In him lie hidden all the mighty, untapped treasures of wisdom and knowledge. —Colossians 2:2–3 (TLB)**

In 1622, Spanish galleons *Atocha* and *Santa Margarita* battled a hurricane and lost the fight while sailing near the Florida Keys. Their heavy cargo of silver, gold, and jewels sank to the ocean bottom. Weeks later, another hurricane scattered the multimillion-dollar treasure across the ocean floor. While in the years that followed beachcombers occasionally discovered ancient coins washed ashore, three-hundred-and-sixty-plus years passed before anyone found remains of the sunken ships.

After two additional decades of following their underwater debris trails, a family of salvage divers discovered a significant portion of the ships' treasure hidden under many feet of water and sand.

On a recent visit to Key West, I toured the museum documenting the lengthy salvage operations and displaying some of the restored treasures. Although fascinated by the jewels and impressed with the divers' perseverance, neither compared to the beauty of the nearby historic church. Sunlight shining through its stained-glass windows illuminated scenes of God giving His Son to the world. Their silent but powerful message magnified the contrast between earthly and heavenly treasures, reminding me the gift from God is free, abundant, and eternal.

We don't have to be satisfied with bits and pieces found along the shoreline or spend years searching the ocean floor. The most precious treasure of all times is ever present and always within reach.

**Lord, You see our hearts and know our thoughts. Help us to seek what You value and store those treasures with You. Thank You for Your Son, the most precious gift of all.**
—Jenny Lynn Keller

**Digging Deeper:** Proverbs 2:1–8; Matthew 6:19–21; Acts 17:24–27; Romans 5:17; Colossians 3:1–2

---

# Tuesday, August 12

**Fear not, for I am with you; be not dismayed, for I am your God; I will strengthen you, I will help you, I will uphold you with my righteous right hand. —Isaiah 41:10 (ESV)**

"Rockin-Rollercoaster? What's that?" I ask my older sister, Mara, as we stare at the taunting guitar-shaped, red-and-black sign.

"No clue, but we've gotta do it. We may never have another chance!" Mara answers, speed-walking toward the line. "Let's go!"

We had known what to expect from the other rollercoasters, but this one's new, and all indoors, so we can't see what we're up against. Not a good combo, but we'll be fine, we're together.

Still hesitant, we get in line with Dad. He's fearless, more focused on taking pictures than the too-terrible-to-let-outside rollercoaster. It's our turn. Dad gets on first, sitting with a stranger so Mara and I can sit together. Instead of getting on, though, we examine the other vacationers in line.

One of them is just a kid, maybe nine years old. Mara and I make eye contact, clearly thinking the same thing: *If he can do this, a teenager and twenty-two-year-old can too!* Then he starts crying. Instantly employees appear and escort him and his family through previously invisible doors. We're pushed forward.

I'm in front, so I slide onto the rigid-but-soft plastic seats first. Looking over, I see Mara eyeing the exit. *She's gonna leave me!* I can't leave, though, that'd be too embarrassing, but I'm too scared to ride alone. Should I cry?

Before I can decide, Mara sits beside me and we're locked in. I'm not alone. My eyes are closed for most of the ride, but I'm OK. Someone I trust is with me.

**Lord, thank You for staying with me so I never face life alone.** —Rachel Thompson

**Digging Deeper:** Psalm 139:7–16;
Zephaniah 3:17

---

# Wednesday, August 13

**My spirit remains among you; do not fear!
—Haggai 2:5 (NKJV)**

Daily I pray for a neighbor teen who looks to me for stability. Last week, a doctor said she has to have her tonsils removed. Her response? An overwhelming fear. "No way! I won't!"

I'd just been reading *The Little Prince,* by Antoine de Saint-Exupéry. It's a quirky children's classic about a "little fellow" who visits Earth and befriends a Frenchman stranded in the Sahara. Though I didn't begin to understand the weird storyline, the book fascinated me, especially the first pages. The otherworldly prince makes one request of the narrator. "Draw me a sheep." (It soon becomes clear that on some other planet, not Earth, the sheep will come to life and be useful, but not here, not now.) The prince rejects multiple sketches—a sheep too sick, too old, etc.—until finally the impatient narrator draws a brick-like box. "This is just the crate," he says. "The sheep . . . is inside."

The gratified prince peers through an air hole and reports, "Look! He's gone to sleep." After I read this scene to my frightened friend, I tentatively suggested: "Imagine that your fear is like that invisible sheep. We put it safely into a box. Now let's put the box way off to the side. You know it's there, sleeping, but it's not distracting you."

Her spirit calmed. "Fear not," she whispered, repeating a phrase she'd heard in Bible stories I'd read to her. Our conversation about tonsils was tabled for another day.

**Lord, thank You that I was able to help my neighbor set aside her fear. Help me to follow my own advice—and Yours—when I am overwhelmed and afraid.** —Evelyn Bence

**Digging Deeper:** Isaiah 41:10–14

---

# Thursday, August 14

**All my springs are in thee. —Psalm 87:7 (KJV)**

Every August, I spend a fortnight nestled in the Maine woods at our one-room family cabin. It is a place of solitude, surrounded by towering pines and birches overlooking a pond. By day, dragonflies flit between lily pads and at night, loons cry eerily beneath the Milky Way.

I have been visiting this postcard scene for some fifty years now, since childhood. Back then the only on-site building was the wooden housing for a newly dug well, with its red pump head producing delightfully cold water. This pump still exists alongside the family cabin today, promising fresh spring water to anyone willing to put forth some muscle.

And, oh, how worth it! The sparkling clear, cold water flows unmatched by any kitchen faucet or bottle labeled "spring water." I pump this refreshing flow daily to stay hydrated and clean.

Like working a pump, receiving living water from the Lord requires some effort. A daily visit to Scripture and time spent in prayer can relieve spiritual dryness and bring cleansing. When I lay aside my tyrannical to-do list and drink from spiritual springs, refreshment fills my poor soul. I have become a "pour soul" who daily draws from the bounty that pours forth from the spirit of God, thus refreshing my entire being.

**How revitalizing is Your Word, oh Lord. Keep us daily drinking from Your spring.** —Lisa Livezey

**Digging Deeper:** Psalms 36:8, 46:4; Isaiah 12:3; John 4:14

---

# Friday, August 15

**. . . incline thine ear unto wisdom, and apply thine heart to understanding.** —Proverbs 2:2 (KJV)

Wilma's life was different than mine. Poverty made high school impossible, so she worked for wealthy families as a nanny, a maid, a cook. She was poorly paid, and without Social Security or a pension. I knew privilege. Yet, friendship narrowed that gap as, together, we cared for a dying friend.

Wilma was growing older, with no benefits, and on the verge of homelessness. My husband, David, called on our church to help. Church members purchased a bedraggled house and renovated it. When a church member provided back payments to secure her place on the Social Security rolls, her employers joined in to pay her fairly. On the back porch of her new home, Wilma belted out a song to heaven. There were no dry eyes among those gathered 'round.

Later, Wilma calls me, loudly praising God. Her first Social Security check has arrived. Over coffee, she shares a story from her past:

"Look at my late mother's beautiful hats," a clueless employer had said. "Choose what you want." Uncomfortably obligated, Wilma took a few hats. At the end of the day, the woman docked her pay for each hat.

I had come to understand the difficulties of day workers. Lost wages are devastating. But Wilma chuckles as she recounts this story. I understand that even in those dark, unsure days, this was a woman of innate dignity.

"Driving down the freeway, heading home . . . guess what I did . . . I sailed those hats out the window . . . one by one." We laugh, then, at the mental image of her throwing away those hats, and I saw a freedom that would never die dancing in Wilma's eyes.

Father, my heart understands the gifts Your daughter Wilma showed in such abundance. Grace, dignity, the joy of freedom. Thank You.

—Pam Kidd

**Digging Deeper:** Proverbs 1:5, 4:13; Joel 1:3

---

# Saturday, August 16

**Because He is at my right hand I shall not be moved. —Psalm 16:8 (NKJV)**

Of all my tech gadgets, none has brought me more pleasure than the little record player that sits at the righthand side of my desk. In recent years, record players have come back with a roar. I bought mine many years ago at a rummage sale, for twenty dollars, and I get records for fifty cents apiece at a thrift shop.

I love the simplicity of my player. It has just one knob, which is "on-off" and "volume." The slowly spinning vinyl is tranquilizing, and the subtle scratchy sound of the old platters makes Sinatra sound like he is singing in the rain.

I love mellow songs that calm me and do not interfere with my desk work. "When I Fall in Love," by Nat King Cole. Sinatra's lullabies, such as "In the Wee Small Hours of the Morning," plus lots of orchestrated hymns and spirituals, including "Be Still My Soul."

In a time when change seems to be the only constant, it's comforting to find pleasure from something that was invented 145 years ago.

My record player reminds me of my Bible, which has been around forever but seems as fresh as the day it was penned. Even though its values have been mocked, spurned, and twisted, those values live on in my heart. As the old spiritual says, "Like a tree that's planted by the waters, I shall not be moved."

**I thank You, Father, for the simplicity of Your Word, which gives me peace in a turbulent world.**
—Daniel Schantz

**Digging Deeper:** Matthew 5:18; Hebrews 6:19

---

# Sunday, August 17

**So pray to the Lord who is in charge of the harvest; ask him to send more workers into his fields. —Matthew 9:38 (NLT)**

While living in Indonesia, we attended an interdenominational Christian church near the factory where I worked. Since we had no pastor, several lay members took turns leading the Sunday worship service.

It was my time to lead the service and it was also communion Sunday. After the service, a woman asked if I was a pastor. When I told her I was a lay person, she scolded me and said, "Only ordained ministers can do communion." I explained that we had no pastor and were doing what we could as laity. She walked away, saying, "I will never be back here!" Although I thought she was a bit harsh,

I was troubled that I had offended and ostracized a newcomer from returning to our church. I hoped Jesus understood I knew not what I had done.

We were the only English-speaking church in town and only about 10 percent of the population was Christian. Where would we find an English-speaking minister to do the communion services? I prayed for God's help.

A couple of weeks later, I received a call from Mike, a soon-to-be coworker coming to our plant. He asked about living there, about houses and schools. He told me about his family. He asked about churches. I told him about our little church. And he said his wife was a Presbyterian minister! Mike, Lyn, and their children soon arrived. Lyn handled the special services, including Christmas, Easter, and *all* the communion services.

**Dear Lord, thank You for providing ways through situations seemingly impossible for us.** —John Dilworth

**Digging Deeper:** Jeremiah 3:15; Mark 11:24; Acts 20:28

---

# Monday, August 18

## LIFE LESSONS FROM THE BEACH:
### Discernment
**This is my prayer for you . . . that you will see the difference between good and bad and will choose the good. —Philippians 1:9–10 (NCV)**

A hot summer sun, a wide beach, and gentle ocean waves invited us to take a swim. My family hopped into the water, bodysurfed the incoming tide, and watched pelicans dive for fish farther offshore—until my seven-year-old nephew screamed.

All heads turned his way, the surrounding adults swam toward him, and his mother reached him first. Shark attack, barracuda bite, or did he step on something sharp?

Thankfully, none of the above, but the culprit inflicted a double sting. Once, when the jellyfish floated up his swimsuit leg, and a second time when he threw it as far away as he could.

Vinegar and baking soda applied to his skin reduced the pain but didn't erase the bad memory. My nephew refused to get back in the ocean. To help him understand not every water creature wanted to harm him, my husband found a website describing the jellyfish in our area.

Equipped with the knowledge most local ones were harmless, the young fella gradually returned to the water and enjoyed the ocean. As he and his brother grew into adults and made major life decisions, I prayed they applied the same principles of acquiring knowledge, discerning between good and bad, and choosing the good.

I'm blessed to say God answered my prayers. Like earthly parents, our Heavenly Father always wants the best for His children.

Lord, thank You for providing us wisdom to distinguish between right and wrong. Give us a discerning heart and a willingness to choose Your way. —Jenny Lynn Keller

**Digging Deeper:** 1 Kings 3:5–14; Proverbs 3:21–24, 16:21, 18:15; Romans 12:2

---

# Tuesday, August 19

## JOURNEYING WITH JESUS: The Bible

Then Jesus said to him, "Go away, Satan! For it is written: 'You shall worship the Lord your God, and serve Him only.'" —Matthew 4:10 (NASB)

Satan—the enemy of Christ—was out to destroy Jesus's life's work before it had begun. The young Son of God was already on the path to bringing light into the world. But first, this supernatural being—whom Jesus calls the "father of lies" (John 8:44, NASB) and a "thief" who wants only to "steal and kill and destroy" (John 10:10, NASB)—must be commanded to "Go!"

Jesus was in a weakened state. He'd been forty days in the wilderness without food. God was honing Jesus's purpose of offering His life for the forgiveness of sins. Along came the tempter. The devil coveted preeminence in the human heart. He might achieve it if Jesus broke trust with God. Jesus fought him with Scripture. Three times He responds, "It is written" (Matthew 4, NASB).

Knowing my Bible—carrying memorized passages in my mind at all times—is how I fight attacks from my spiritual enemy. I can speak God's Word, as Jesus did, and send him away.

Jesus's encounter came to mind recently when my heart arrhythmia—atrial fibrillation—was pausing long enough in converting to normal sinus rhythm there was a possibility my heart could just stop. I needed a pacemaker to help control my heartbeat—an implanted electronic device with tiny screws anchoring wires in the heart. I could feel the Adversary closing in, stealing faith, casting paralyzing fear. I spoke the Word of God, boldly joining with Jesus in saying, "Go!"

I entered my pacemaker procedure resting in the confidence of my Peacemaker—my heart in steady rhythm with His.

**God, Your Word holds power over all things. Help me learn to speak it!** —Carol Knapp

**Digging Deeper:** Matthew 4:1–11, 16:21–23; Luke 10:17–18; 1 Peter 5:6–11

---

# Wednesday, August 20

**He will wipe away every tear from their eyes, and death shall be no more, neither shall there be mourning, nor crying, nor pain anymore, for the former things have passed away.**
**—Revelation 21:4 (ESV)**

As I packed up the groceries into the shopping bags, I let out a big, long sigh. Work had been stressful, and I had a ton more to do at home—make dinner, walk the dog, do the dishes, and then jump back into work to meet a deadline.

"I hear you!" the cashier said. I read her name off her badge: Lou.

"I get off in ten minutes," Lou said. "I can't be late. I worry. When I'm late, my cat sits in the window and waits for me."

I kept bagging my groceries as she spoke. "My landlord's strict about no pets. When Mom died, everybody said, 'Bring her to the shelter,' but I couldn't do that. Mom loved her so. It's the least I could do. I'm just worried, you know. I hate to be dishonest."

"Maybe if you explained," I said.

"She's so sweet. Best cat. Misses my mother. I can tell. We both do. It's nice to have someone to grieve with and nice to have her waiting for me when I come home. Really, she's my mom's last gift to me. I hope she's not in the window right now. I'm looking for a new place. Maybe this is what I need to look for something better. What are you gonna do? Right? I really should get something better."

"Right," I said.

We parted ways, and on the drive home, my work stress and worries over meeting a deadline disappeared as my thoughts and prayers stayed fixed on her.

330

Lord, send Your love and light to help all those in grief. Comfort them and help them see Your plan. Guide them to a better place. —Sabra Ciancanelli

**Digging Deeper:** Matthew 5:4; John 14:27

---

## Thursday, August 21

**But we trusted that it had been he [Jesus] which should have redeemed Israel: and beside all this, to day is the third day since these things [the Crucifixion] were done. —Luke 24:21 (KJV)**

Recently, during rush hour, I traveled I-95 through a sizable city in Florida far from home. Confused by the GPS as to which exit was best, I decided to consult the Lord and was certain I had received an answer, only to run into an impenetrable jam of vehicles sure to make me late for a commitment.

My faith flagged. Had God really spoken, or had I listened to my own voice?

The dejected men on the Emmaus Road must have reasoned similarly. To say the least, they had been energized by Jesus's ministry, but when he was killed and they could no longer see Him, their faith was muddled. Had they been mistaken as to His lordship? Just as I initially exclaimed on I-95, "Well, Lord, I must not have heard you right," according to *The Message* Bible, the men "just stood there, long-faced, like they had lost their best friend" (Luke 24:17–18).

As He was with the Emmaus-bound men who at first were unable to recognize Him, Jesus was always with me in the hazardous traffic. Though I will never be able to see the accident He might have prevented, or the care He might have been taking to sharpen my reflexes in an unfamiliar city, as I look back on it, the time I spent in spiritual reflection while forced to wait attests to the fact that His presence with me that evening was as steadfast as the daily sunrise. Praise You, Jesus.

**Help me, Lord, to remember that You are always present, always faithful, never mistaken.**
—Jacqueline F. Wheelock

**Digging Deeper:** Psalm 23:4; Matthew 28:20

---

# Friday, August 22

**There is no fear in love. But perfect love drives out fear . . .** —1 John 4:18 (NIV)

Working as a hospital chaplain, I sometimes visit patients who challenge me on many levels. One day, a man who I'll call John asked for a chaplain visit.

The conversation began strangely. "The end of the world is coming soon, Chaplain. I can help you if you want," John declared.

I was puzzled by his words. He laughed. "Chaplain, come closer. I can help you." I declined his invitation. "You are making me angry," he snarled. His angry comment felt menacing. I wasn't sure what the cause of his anger was, but I knew I would have to be careful with him. He continued in this disturbing manner for a bit. "You glanced at the door. If you try to leave, I can reach the door before you can," he threatened.

A range of emotions pulsed through me at his words: fear, anger, resentment. I realized that I was angry with him for "exposing" my fear of him. He now had power over me. He smiled. "I know you're afraid of me," John pronounced.

Upon hearing the word *afraid*, a quote from Scripture flashed across my mind. "Perfect love casts out fear." I didn't realize I had said this out loud. "What?" John asked in confusion.

From a deep place that I still can't fathom, a sudden flood of love and compassion surged within me for this man. I could see him as a baby coming into this world fully loved by God. My fear left.

Unexpectedly, John's threatening manner dissipated. "I'm tired," he said. "I want to sleep." He turned away from me. I quietly said a blessing for him, and then thanked God for His divine intervention, and left.

**Your Words are life, O Lord. Amen.** —Adam Ruiz

**Digging Deeper:** Psalm 6:4; Romans 5:5; 1 Corinthians 13:1–3

## Saturday, August 23

**We are confident that God is able to orchestrate everything to work toward something good and beautiful when we love Him and accept His invitation to live according to His plan. —Romans 8:28 (VOICE)**

I wasn't trying to be dishonest. But I guess it was a little sneaky. I simply wanted my grandsons to try something I knew they'd like—but also knew they wouldn't try if they were aware of what it really was. So, after Xander and Oliver added the oats, raisins, brown sugar, and blend of spices to our "breakfast cookie" dough, I brought out a secret ingredient: sea sprinkles.

OK, so I took a little creative license in "rebranding" what's better known as grated zucchini. Six-year-old Xander, a bit savvier than his three-year-old brother, looked at the cup of green shavings with suspicion. Shunning most vegetables in any form other than a smoothie, Xander asked if the sprinkles were really cucumbers. Thankfully, I could truthfully answer, "No."

When the cookies came out of the oven, they were a big hit with my grandsons, sea sprinkles and all. By helping my grandsons view a dreaded vegetable in a new light, they saw it as something positive, instead of negative. Healthy became the new yummy.

I think God does the same kind of "rebranding" in my own life. Through prayer, He helps me more clearly see what's good and beautiful in what I consider negative circumstances. Often, my situation doesn't change—just like zucchini is still zucchini, even if I call it sea sprinkles—but my perspective does. That's when my heart, and my attitude, can follow suit.

Lord, give me hope and strength by helping me see life more clearly through Your eyes. —Vicki Kuyper

**Digging Deeper:** Genesis 50:20; Jeremiah 29:11; Ephesians 5:1; 1 Thessalonians 5:16–18; 1 Timothy 4:4

---

## Sunday, August 24

# WHEN DOUBT BECAME FAITH:
## The Devout Doubter

**And straightway the father of the child cried out, and said with tears, Lord, I believe; help thou mine unbelief. —Mark 9:24 (KJV)**

With my open Bible on my lap, I sat in my favorite wing chair, staring into the crackling fire. It was the place I always came for answers, but this time I couldn't summon the comforting spirit-warmth of faith.

Four years before, God had healed my body from horrendous tumor pain and prescription opioid addiction. After a lifetime of suffering, I celebrated that gift every moment. Trying to be my healthiest possible, I'd pulled a muscle while exercising. A simple over-the-counter pain medication landed me in kidney failure. I was swollen, short of breath, and so weak I could barely stand. My blood pressure spiked. Nausea and vomiting messed with my electrolyte balance; dehydration led to joint pain.

*Where was God in all of this?* I couldn't see Him, hear Him, feel Him like when I was joyously healed. *Why would He let this happen after giving me everything?* I was sixty-eight years old, a retired nurse who'd seen it all. How would this story end?

I tried to remember the times God had proven Himself faithful. With all my trials and uncertainty, He was the surest thing I'd ever known. An Unseen Hand I'd learned to trust—to count on—when life didn't go as planned. Now, the darkness of doubt consumed me. The only prayer I could conjure was a desperate plea from the deepest part of me:

**Lord, I believe; help thou mine unbelief.**
—Roberta Messner

**Digging Deeper:** Matthew 14:31, 21:21; James 1:6

---

# Monday, August 25

# WHEN DOUBT BECAME FAITH: When Time Stood Still
**My times are in your hands. —Psalm 31:15 (NIV)**

The squares on my purse calendar mocked what little faith I could muster. Everywhere I looked, my bold felt pen had blacked-out appointments I couldn't keep, deadlines I'd failed to meet, dreams that would never be.

Weeks before, those squares brimmed with possibility. Life waiting to happen. The lost years of tumor pain and opioid addiction that God had redeemed. The most I could hope for now was doing time in doctors' waiting rooms.

While most caregivers couched my predicament in gentle words, I was still a has-been, my future blacked out like the disappointments on my calendar. One day a provider I'd never met sauntered into the exam room: "All you've been through and sixty-eight years old?" he quipped. "Didn't anyone ever tell you? Your shelf life's expired." Struggling to make it to my car, my mind replayed those words, the tattered remnant of faith snuffed by doubt. It left me reeling for weeks.

How could my time be up when I'd barely gotten started? I had things to do, people to see, places to go. I hadn't counted on kidney failure. *You gave me a new life, Lord, and now* this? *Where are You anyway?*

A Voice that could be no other's whispered an answer I couldn't ignore. *You've lived those sixty-eight years, Roberta, because I had plans for you. I still have plans. Trust Me. You'll see.*

**Teach me to place my times in Your hands, Lord. To trust Your divine timing. —Roberta Messner**

**Digging Deeper:** Proverbs 16:9; Ecclesiastes 3:1, 11; Jeremiah 29:11

---

## Tuesday, August 26

# WHEN DOUBT BECAME FAITH: Doubting but Not Alone
**Turn to me and be gracious to me, for I am lonely and afflicted. —Psalm 25:16 (NIV)**

I've always tended to isolate when problems come my way. After my miraculous healing, I'd told my story everywhere. I couldn't admit I was in the pits again. *Keep your doubting to yourself, Roberta. Can't be bringing others down. That's some bad PR for God.* Prayer eluded me, except for the groanings of my spirit.

*Be gracious to me, O God.*

One evening, the guy at the diner down the road texted. "Hey, Roberta, you been sick or something? I MISS you!" Josh and I are separated by two generations. But our curiosity—our wonderings about anything and everything—unites us. That and the coffee he had waiting for me.

I set out in the pouring rain. When I pulled up at the drive-thru, Josh stretched his entire upper body out the window to pass me the gold-and-brown to-go cup. His long, dark curls were fast getting soaked. The chocolate eyes that matched the company T-shirt were already damp. "How *are* you?" he asked.

"Well, maybe a *little* better," I managed.

"*A little*?" he squealed. "That's fantastic. Visualization leads to actualization!"

I promised to stop every evening for his special brew. Next time I'd venture inside, where the two of us would ponder questions with no ready answers. God had chased me down, sicced one of his choice kids on me. The face of the Divine framed in long, damp curls, my groanings finding words:

**I've been lonely—and, yes—afflicted, Lord. But You've never, ever left me.** —Roberta Messner

---

## Wednesday, August 27

# WHEN DOUBT BECAME FAITH:
## A Calendar Called Care

**Casting all your care upon him; for he careth for you. —1 Peter 5:7 (KJV)**

In the Urgent Care waiting room, a colleague from my hospital days tottered over on her walker. "I get better, then something worse happens," she said. "Ever wonder where God is in all of this?"

It wouldn't have been so bad if I weren't asking the same question. It was there on the calendar squares in my purse, doubt detailed in black-and-white. Back at home, I learned a dear friend, Tillie, had died. She'd been a scholar and a mentor to me. When she downsized her library, she gave me first dibs. I thumbed through one of her old C. S. Lewis tomes in search of serenity and strength.

This time it wasn't Lewis who had what I needed. A yellowed page from an old calendar fell out. Printed inside each square were encouraging words from Scripture with a name of someone Tillie treasured. In her tiny script I read: *Casting all your care upon Him; for He careth for You. Call Roberta.*

I remembered that call. I'd told Tillie how I couldn't stop asking questions about the life I'd been dealt. "When I spoke at that conference, they introduced me as a researcher who leaves no stone unturned," I said. "I guess scrutiny's served me well in clinical trials. But all the research in this world can't fix the fix I'm in."

It was a long moment before the learned one spoke. "Questions . . . I've asked them too, Roberta. Sometimes we learn best by just leaning."

**In this moment, Lord, I seek only to lean on You.** —Roberta Messner

**Digging Deeper:** Psalms 37:3, 145:18; Proverbs 3:5–6

---

## Thursday, August 28

# WHEN DOUBT BECAME FAITH:
## The Things We Cannot See
**Now faith is the substance of things hoped for, the evidence of things not seen.
—Hebrews 11:1 (KJV)**

I was in the throes of kidney failure when I was asked to say a few words at my friend Tillie's memorial service. From my chair I shared stories of her quiet certainty, marveling that the hallmarks of her walk through this world were intangibles. "I know of no one who lived faith, hope, and love the way she did," I said. "Yet these are all things we can't see."

Afterward, a lady who'd taught me back in Sunday school tapped me on the shoulder. "Roberta!" she said. "I can't believe what I just heard you say." Her face twinkled with amused amazement. "You couldn't have been more than five when I tried to explain faith to you. 'It's like that chair you're sitting in, Roberta,'" I told you. "'You don't see it, but you trust it to hold you up.'"

I'd scrunched my face into a question mark and shook my pigtailed head no. "How? When? Why?" I demanded. I didn't understand why I should trust the chair to hold me up. I needed to see the proof for myself.

She recalled how the other kids went off to the cookies and punch table. When I thought the adults were out of sight, I'd jiggled the slats across its straight back, turned the little chair over, searching for clues it wasn't true. Then tried to break it.

My doubting chair.

My questioning mind soaked in the eternal truth. I had made it these sixty-eight years because of the things I could not see. God had proven Himself, not in perfect circumstances, but in every season. A hymn from that sweet used-to-be child swelled in my spirit:

**Jesus, Jesus, how I trust You**
**How I've proved You o'er and o'er**
**Jesus, Jesus, precious Jesus**
**Oh, for grace to trust You more.**
—Roberta Messner

**Digging Deeper:** John 20:25, 20:29; 2 Corinthians 5:7

# Friday, August 29

## WHEN DOUBT BECAME FAITH:
### My Faith Chair

**These have come so that the proven genuineness of your faith—of greater worth than gold, which perishes even though refined by fire—may result in praise, glory and honor when Jesus Christ is revealed. —1 Peter 1:7 (NIV)**

After several months of illness, my lab results normalized with no evidence of chronic kidney disease. My nurse-friend Gigi invited me out to celebrate. She knew about my lifelong doubting nature, of my Sunday school teacher at Tillie's funeral telling how I'd turned over the little chair for proof that faith couldn't be true. "I'll never forget when the doctor told you your cancer was gone," Gigi said with a warm smile. "How many times did you turn *that* chair over, looking for clues that they'd made a mistake?"

Through the back window of Gigi's SUV, I caught sight of a huge bow made of pink curly ribbon. When the door slid open, I couldn't breathe. It was just like the little chair from my Sunday school days. She'd unearthed it at an estate sale.

On the drive home, I kept watch on it on the floor of my passenger seat. My eyes took in my purse calendar, open to a brand-new page. I thanked God for His many provisions throughout my life, the people who'd showed up unbidden with exactly what I needed. Though I couldn't always see, hear, or feel God, He was ever working behind the scenes for my best good. I was living on *God's* calendar. Divine time.

I ran my hand over the chair's oak wood, smoothed to perfection with the passage of years. I would never turn it over again. Didn't need to. My history with God had solved the mystery. My faith had been tested and found to be true. No doubt about it.

**Faith that survives doubt, Lord, is the strongest of all.** —Roberta Messner

**Digging Deeper:** 2 Corinthians 4:7–9; James 1:2–4; 1 Peter 5:10

---

# Saturday, August 30

**[God] who alone is immortal and who lives in unapproachable light, whom no one has seen or can see. To him be honor and might forever. Amen. —1 Timothy 6:16 (NIV)**

I am not a numbers person. Mathematics confounds me and statistics almost caused me to flunk out of college. Yet, I am fascinated by scientific exploration and discovery. Recently, I read an article about our universe and discovered that the closest star to Earth—our sun—emits light that travels at 186,000 miles per second. And it takes the sun's light only eight minutes and twenty seconds to traverse the ninety-three million miles between the sun and Earth. I simply cannot fathom this magnitude of distance and time.

What totally amazed me was when I read that the Triangulum Galaxy (M33) is approximately three million light years away from Earth and is the most distant object visible to the naked eye. Consider that all of our universe is not visible to the naked eye. Current scientific theory states, "There is no reason to believe that there is anything outside of the expanding universe into which the universe expands." I must admit that my little brain just shut down as I closed my book. I was brought to my knees in the presence of sacred mystery.

Part of experiencing holiness is to be surrounded by the ultimate mystery of God. God is as intimate and knowable to us as a baby is when in symbiotic unity with her mother in her womb. Yet God is also holy because God is beyond our ability to comprehend. This is the greatest paradox of truth.

**Dear God, help me to seek to understand as much as I can. But also help me to know that the greatest truths of God are always shrouded in holy mystery. Amen.** —Scott Walker

**Digging Deeper:** Psalm 8:1–9; 1 Corinthians 13:2

---

# Sunday, August 31

. . . you know that your labor in the Lord is not in vain. —1 Corinthians 15:58 (NIV)

Susan, a woman I know from church, had been in a serious accident caused by a sudden seizure. Her small SUV had rolled and flipped before coming to rest atop a parked car. Scans at the hospital showed broken bones but also invasive cancer in the brain and throughout her body. Susan had no family except her adorable puppy, who also had survived the crash.

After surgery, followed by rehab, Susan was transferred to a residential care facility for further recuperation and radiation treatments. Our faith community rallied to help by caring for her puppy, collecting funds, and calling her on the phone. Health restrictions prohibited in-person visits, so instead we dropped off gifts for Susan at the facility's entranceway.

After hearing Susan comment negatively about the institutional food, I dropped off a Fuji apple salad—a known favorite of hers. Later that day came the text: "Please bring more salads. The food here is inedible! But no ham—you know how I like things organic and pure!"

Frustration welled up within me. Surely Susan felt alone and helpless, yet couldn't she have managed a simple word of thanks?

I offered up my response to God and recalled the words of Mother Teresa: "Do small things with great love." Then, remembering to be grateful for my own health, I prayed for generosity of spirit and an extra measure of kindness as I continued to care for Susan from afar.

**Lord, we know that You see everything. Help us to show great love in the smallest of actions, even when feeling unappreciated.** —Lisa Livezey

**Digging Deeper:** Luke 10:34; 2 Corinthians 7:1; Galatians 6:9; Philippians 1:9

## WITH AN EVERLASTING LOVE

1 _____

2 _____

3 _____

4 _____

5 _____

6 _____

7 _____

8 _____

9 _____

10 _____

11 _____

12 _____

13 _____

14 _____

15 _____

16 _____

17 _____

18 _____

19 _____

20 _____

21 _____

22 _____

23 _____

24 _____

25 _____

26 _____

27 _____

28 _____

29 _____

30 _____

31 _____

# September

Cause me to hear Your
lovingkindness in the morning,
for in You do I trust.

—Psalm 143:8 (NKJV)

# Labor Day, Monday, September 1

**Everyone's work will be put through the fire so that all can see whether or not it keeps its value, and what was really accomplished.**
**—1 Corinthians 3:13 (TLB)**

Back in the nineties, after writing more than 40,000 radio commercials (which was about 39,000 too many for one lifetime) for five different radio stations, I quit my job to stay home and write what I wanted to write.

I wrote about my life as a married mother of four and then as a single parent going through a divorce, then as a mother taking her nine-year-old son through the death of his father. I wrote about running a crash pad for airline pilots, leaving Wisconsin and moving to Florida in my fifties, remarriage in my sixties, the death of that spouse, and finally being a single grandmother who loves to travel.

I've never made as much money selling articles to magazines and newspapers as I did writing radio ads, but I love my freelance job at home infinitely more. I learned that doing what I love is more important than making more money. Instead of a job, I had a career. My at-home work also gave me much more time with my children, friends, and neighbors. Plus, every little adventure became a possible story to write.

**On this Labor Day, Lord, help me appreciate those who may not love their jobs or careers as much as**

I do, but do them anyway with devotion knowing that work itself, no matter how tedious, is what gives us our dignity. —Patricia Lorenz

**Digging Deeper:** Proverbs 12:14; 1 Corinthians 3:9

---

# Tuesday, September 2

**And whatever you do, in word or deed, do everything in the name of the Lord Jesus, giving thanks to God the Father through him. —Colossians 3:17 (ESV)**

I looked down at my notes as I ran through my argument again. I knew it by heart, but I wanted my delivery to be perfect. In a few hours, I would be standing before a judge.

Although I had been practicing law for several years, I'd not yet argued in a courtroom. The coronavirus pandemic hit shortly after I entered private practice. And, while the pandemic had since subsided, many courts now held hearings by video or phone. Remote hearings were certainly efficient. But I valued formality. In fact, I even carried my great-grandfather's pocket watch with me today.

My computer chirped, notifying me of a new email. As I read it, my spirit sank. This afternoon's hearing would be held by video. My anticipation evaporated. In a matter of seconds, everything had changed. The monumental had become mundane.

Absentmindedly, I reached into my suit pocket. My fingers touched the cold surface of my great-grandfather's watch. I retrieved it. The second hand ticked steadily—as it had for generations.

The watch's even cadence reminded me that, regardless of the hearing's change in venue, my obligations remained consistent. As a lawyer, I was obligated to represent my client to the best of my abilities. As a Christian, I was called to do all things for and through Christ. Although a videoconference was less formal than an in-person hearing, it was no less important.

So, as the watch ticked on, I began to practice my argument once again.

**Jesus, help me to do all things in Your name and for Your glory, regardless of the circumstances.**
—Logan Eliasen

**Digging Deeper:** Philippians 4:13; Hebrews 13:8

---

# Wednesday, September 3

**Then Samuel took a stone and set it up between Mizpah and Shen, and called its name Ebenezer, saying, "Thus far the LORD has helped us."**
—1 Samuel 7:12 (NKJV)

I'm in a daydreaming kind of mood. The kind that got me in trouble in grade school. Instead of focusing on what I'm supposed to be doing, I'm looking out the window. Actually, I'm looking at the windowsill in my office. A variety of objects are sitting there. A couple of stained-glass angels that catch the sun. A bundle of sage from a hike with dear friends through Sonoma Botanical Garden in California. Two jars of marbles from my youth. My great-uncle Johnny's compass. Guatemalan prayer people (made of paper). A tiny Bible with a mustard seed attached. Some healing dirt from El Santuario de Chimayó in New Mexico. And so much more.

As my eyes fall on these pieces, I remember where I've been to acquire them, the people I've been with, and even holy encounters. Each of these pieces represents significant experiences that have shaped me into the man I am today. Indeed, my office shelves, in addition to books, are filled with such items. With each gaze, each touch, something deep sinks into my soul.

Perhaps I should daydream more often and look at my computer screen less. Maybe I should loosen the grip on focus and allow the grace all around me to become present. It might just be time to not do something and just sit there. And allow the Spirit of God to seep into my soul through all I see and say:

"Thus far the Lord has helped me."

**Lord, Your people are altar builders, marking their pilgrimage to Your loving presence. Remind me to build my own altars and to use them to proclaim Your everlasting love. Amen.** —J. Brent Bill

**Digging Deeper:** Genesis 12:1–8

# Thursday, September 4

**Praise the LORD, my soul, and forget not all his benefits. —Psalm 103:2 (NIV)**

My friend Kelly and I have a tradition of celebrating our birthdays together by treating each other with manicures and pedicures at a spa. We both look forward to two hours of pampering twice a year—me paying when it's her birthday and her paying on mine.

For my birthday last September, the nail technicians we normally used were off that day, so we had two different employees. Kelly ordered the usual for us, but it was a very different experience. Instead of lots of massaging and TLC, the duo rushed us through, skipped steps, and finished our mani/pedi in half the time it usually took. Kelly paid, and we left the salon.

I could sense we both felt a little cheated, but Kelly spoke up first. I agreed that the service was subpar. The two of us complained so much that I realized when I got in my car that I'd totally forgotten to thank her. I was mortified! *I'd spent time with my best friend. I had cute pink toenails and fingernails. It was my birthday gift.* I dialed Kelly's number.

"I forgot to thank you, my friend!" That's when it hit me—all my complaining had overshadowed my feelings of gratitude.

Expressing my gratitude reminded me how blessed I really was. Not only did I receive a mani/pedi for my birthday and spend time with a beloved friend, but I also had the gift of knowing gratitude couldn't exist when I complained.

**Dear God, help me to be grateful and see the good in every situation regardless of the circumstances. Amen.** —Stephanie Thompson

**Digging Deeper:** Philippians 2:14; Colossians 3:13; 1 Thessalonians 5:18

---

# Friday, September 5

**The second is this: "You shall love your neighbor as yourself."** —Mark 12:31 (ESV)

I've lived in my twelve-story building in the Chelsea section of Manhattan for thirty-three years. Of all the neighbors I've met and loved, two- and four-legged alike, Ari next door is the finest. His high laugh penetrates our shared wall and has single-handedly banished more than one dark mood. When his partner, Miles, was dying of AIDS, my wife, Julee, and I sat with them. As the end neared, Miles asked Julee to sing his favorite song of hers, "Mysteries of Love."

Years later, when Julee passed while we were up in the Berkshires, Ari was the first to call after he saw the obit in the *Times*. I'm not sure I could have talked to anyone else. And when his older brother died, I was surprised to learn from Ari that his brother had been one of the Americans held for 444 days by Iranian hostage takers back in 1979.

These days, Ari's knees are shot—he started out as a Broadway dancer—but he is still a master chef, his second profession. There is always a warm baked good or hot dish waiting when I return to my apartment, which he watches while I'm away. I bring him an apple cake from one of the Berkshire farm stands, and I always arrange a playdate for Gracie with Ari. He keeps a slipper for her to run around his apartment with and a jar of special treats.

Good neighbors can be like family without the baggage. They start out as strangers brought into our life by chance, or so it might seem. But remember what Jesus said. He used that word *neighbor* for a reason.

**Lord, thank You for the Golden Rule and the dividends it pays in love. Good neighbors reflect Your grace.** —Edward Grinnan

**Digging Deeper:** Romans 13:10; James 2:8

# Saturday, September 6

**So neither the one who plants nor the one who waters is anything, but only God, who makes things grow. —1 Corinthians 3:7 (NIV)**

"If you name your plants and speak kindly to them, they'll grow better," advised my younger daughter, whose thumb had proven to be somehow much greener than my own.

The idea seemed a bit silly to me, but I was willing to try. I'd foolishly picked out a maidenhair fern at the nursery some weeks ago, and when the cashier told me I'd be back soon for a heartier plant after I'd inevitably killed this delicate one, well...the gauntlet had been thrown down. Now I had something to prove!

The maidenhair was already looking pretty rough by the time my daughter offered the advice, so what did I have to lose?

I tried to think of an appropriate name for this poor plant that hung on despite my unwitting attempts to kill it. Into my head popped "Miriam," the name of a friend of mine. Miriam, like my poor plant, was delicate in her way—a kindhearted soul with all the charms of a proper Southern belle—but she'd withstood trials that would surely have done in a person of lesser faith. Miriam was a survivor, which I hoped my little plant would be.

Each day, I complimented my fern-Miriam's beauty. I offered plenty of sunlight and an occasional steam bath.

Soon, fern-Miriam became strong, green, and gorgeous. Like my friend, this Miriam was resilient too.

It all made me think...if calling them by name and speaking kindly to plants help them grow, what must it do for humans?

**Lord, help me to be an encourager.** —Ginger Rue

**Digging Deeper:** Romans 15:2; Hebrews 10:24–25

**Likewise, the tongue is a small part of the body, but it makes great boasts. Consider what a great forest is set on fire by a small spark.** —James 3:5 (NIV)

Recycling bins.

As I return from a weekend away, they're in their green plastic glory. Smack in front of our home. I'd spoken two sentences as I'd left days before. "I love you all. Please grab the bins."

I pull into the drive, storm up the sidewalk, and open the front door. I'm on a mission. I feel let down. Frustrated. This one request, unattended, hurts my heart. I walk through the living room and pound down the stairs to the family room, where I find sixteen-year-old Gabriel doing homework.

"Gabe, you forgot the bins!" I shout. My words feel red and hot as they leave my mouth. Gabriel looks up. Now heat colors his face. "Mom," he says. "We cleaned the whole house. The bathrooms too."

I stand for a moment and then retrace my steps. Up vacuumed stairs to the living room, where wood floors shine. The tables are clutter- and dust-free, and my signature details are replicated. Scented candles burn spicy-sweet. Low lights make the room cozy. Piano music plays from the stereo.

And I'd missed this offering.

Suddenly the comfort of this place rejects me. I've been harsh. Angry. Unkind. I think of a recent night at Bible study—we'd read from James. A forest can flame from a flicker, and my words had burned through a blessing.

I hear footfalls behind me. "I'll grab the bins," Gabriel says. And as he heads for the door, I remember another truth from James—the Lord is full of compassion and mercy.

I'll receive both tonight. Then I'll apologize to my son.

**Lord, help me to use words with carefulness and caution. Amen.** —Shawnelle Eliasen

**Digging Deeper:** Proverbs 15:1–4, 21:23; James 1:26

---

# Monday, September 8

### Jesus said to them, "How many loaves do you have?" —Matthew 15:34 (NKJV)

On a dreary weekday, I pushed back my office chair. Everywhere I clicked, the news displayed a broken world. *Lord, I want to help, but the needs are so great and I feel so small. What can I—one person—do?*

The next morning, while snuggled in my prayer chair with a cup of coffee, I read the story of Jesus feeding the multitudes. Only this time something jumped out at me. Jesus asked them what they had. That's where the solution was to their problem. *Lord, is there something that I have that You can multiply in order to make a difference?* The next couple of days I came up with a unique list: a seed catalog, a tractor, and some acreage I wasn't using.

Through spring the feeling of being helpless dissipated as I pored over seed catalogs and placed orders, then fenced off and planted three new garden plots. I'd purposed to grow the best produce in order to give it away. By summer, the world looked brighter as plants and vines burst forth. But by fall, I still hadn't a clue where it was to go—until the day before harvest, when I learned of a family who helped homeless teens. The dad had been experiencing health challenges and couldn't work as much. They needed food. With the help of friends, I harvested between 600 and 650 pounds of produce, which we boxed up and sent. God knew what they would need beforehand and led me to help.

**Lord, thank You for teaching me to not be overwhelmed with the world, but to focus on what I personally can do to contribute. Amen.**
—Rebecca Ondov

**Digging Deeper:** Mark 8:1–9; Acts 20:35

---

# Tuesday, September 9

**And your ears shall hear a word behind you, saying, "This is the way, walk in it," when you turn to the right or when you turn to the left.**
**—Isaiah 30:21 (ESV)**

Several years ago, I invested in a robotic vacuum cleaner. I love the machine because it can vacuum every day when I don't have time. And our golden retriever, Dolly, keeps "Robbie" the robot vac busy sweeping up dog hair.

Sometimes Robbie needs help knowing where to go, so I nudge him with my foot to show him the right direction, such as under a couch. Or I block him from going where I don't want him to go, like under the Christmas tree. Occasionally, he goes in circles when he bumps into things and seems confused about which way to go. When that happens, he stops trying and cries out for help (well, he beeps) to let me know he needs me. And sometimes he just gets tired and quits until I take him to the recharger. My husband finds this humorous, but I know Robbie needs guidance.

I see similarities in myself and Robbie. God has given me a purpose and a plan and the freedom to achieve them. However, I need Him to point me in the right direction or I get lost trying to find the way on my own. I'm thankful He often blocks the wrong path, even if I don't understand why at the time. Like Robbie, sometimes I get frustrated and want to quit, crying out to God for help. And often I need recharging—motivation and encouragement—to try again.

Unlike Robbie, I have the advantage of prayer and the Bible to help guide me. Thankfully, God steps in to show me the way.

**Lord, thank You for Your guidance along life's path.** —Marilyn Turk

**Digging Deeper:** Psalm 32:8; Proverbs 16:9

**Through him all things were made; without him nothing was made that has been made.**
—John 1:3 (NIV)

"Lean *into* that chord!" the Community Band's conductor said loudly to the flute section as he signaled the rest of us to pause. "It's *supposed* to be crunchy!"

We were sight-reading through a new piece of music, and this chord had caught us all off guard. It felt abrasive and out of place. Could a sound that felt so . . . off . . . be *right*?

The thought reminded me of a conversation I'd had recently with a friend. We'd been in a meeting where there'd been a lot of respectful yet contentious debate. Not everyone's points of view agreed, and the tension had been uncomfortable. I'd voiced my concern to her after we left.

"Comfortable is not often a great goal," she'd said in reply. "It wasn't that long ago this discussion never would have happened. Its answer would've been considered already decided.

"That paradigm was tidier for some, I guess," she'd continued. "If you fit a certain mold. But it harmed *so* many others, because 'tidiness' like that's only possible when God-given voices are kept from the table.

"Which is why," she'd said then, brightening, "I'll take messy conversations like that one any day! It means more of the voices God meant to be included—are!"

I was still smiling at this memory when the conductor cued the rest of the band to join back in. This time, we *all* leaned into the chords in question. They *were* crunchy. But they were also interesting. Complex. And beautiful, just as their composer had meant for them to be.

**You are the ultimate Composer, God, and I am Your instrument. Thank You for the opportunity to participate within the beautiful complexity of Your creation.** —Erin Janoso

**Digging Deeper:** Acts 9:15–16; Galatians 3:28

---

# Thursday, September 11

**In this world you will have trouble. But take heart! I have overcome the world.** —**John 16:33 (NIV)**

A week and a day before 9/11, I was at the World Trade Center. A visiting friend wanted to see the view from the towers, but the observation deck was closed.

"We'll go up to Windows on the World," I'd said. "It's a restaurant on the 107th floor, and they have massive windows."

We got in the elevator in Tower One and felt our ears popping as we zoomed up higher and higher. The maître d' let us through, and my friend gasped at the amazing view.

Nearby, a family tried to show their visiting relative the view as well. She stayed far from the windows.

"No," she laughed nervously, "I can't!"

"Come on," I chimed in playfully. "Nothing is going to happen!"

I leaned into the window and repeated to myself, "Nothing is going to happen."

Eight days later and just eight floors below, terrorists flew an airplane into that very building.

I often think about the woman who couldn't bring herself to go near the windows, knowing people had no choice but to jump from them just days later.

I'd naively diminished her fear and the reality of life itself. God does not promise a life exempt from pain. Anything can happen at any time—blessings and tragedies alike. But God promises to walk with us each day and give us peace. So, today and all days, we must rest in those promises and the precious gift of life we're given each and every day.

> **Dear Lord, help me to rest on Your promises, when the evil in this world is too much to bear.** —Karen Valentin

> **Digging Deeper:** Psalm 23:4; John 14:27

---

# Friday, September 12

**Children's children are a crown to the aged, and parents are the pride of their children. —Proverbs 17:6 (NIV)**

The news had brought our family joy: my niece Kira was expecting her first child and my sister's first grandchild. My family had experienced years of loss as my aunts and uncles were aging, suffering from serious illnesses, and passing away. The announcement of this sweet baby on the way was welcome news.

There was a downside, however. Well into my middle-age season, I, too, was aging, and the title "great-aunt" sounded ancient to me. My sister had been trying out several titles in lieu of "grandmother"—cute names like Mimi, Gigi, and Nana. She had settled on "Ma-Ma" right before her grandbaby's birth, and we celebrated when we discovered my niece was carrying a little girl.

When news came that my great-niece had made her entrance into the world, I immediately made plans to travel to Maryland to meet her. Finally meeting precious Akari face-to-face and holding the sweet seven-pound bundle in my arms, my eyes filled with tears. I had my niece snap a slew of pictures of me holding her, then bragged to the world via my social media accounts. She was a beautiful addition to our family and lit up every space she entered.

I had long forgotten my issues of feeling old as a great-aunt, and yet I still needed a more fitting title. I eventually landed on the title "G-auntie," and Akari is my "G-niecy." I couldn't be more joyful over this precious new baby in the family, my new role, and even my new title, her G-auntie.

**Lord, thank You for new life and for the healing and joy children bring their families.** —Carla Hendricks

---

# Saturday, September 13

**Therefore encourage one another and build up each other, as indeed you are doing.
—1 Thessalonians 5:11 (NRSVUE)**

Jorge has been a dear friend ever since we were in fifth grade. He was born in Ecuador and immigrated to Southern California, where his father, Jaime Jarrin, worked for the Dodgers as the Spanish-language broadcaster on radio and TV (a job he would hold for sixty-four years).

Sure, Jorge was different from me, coming from a family that mostly spoke Spanish. He was more athletic, too, confident on the ball fields, not like me. But we were drawn to each other with a shared gift of gab. After school, we'd sit under the old oak tree, and he held me spellbound with tale after tale. I tried to keep up, recounting my own favorite movies and TV shows, occasionally breaking out in song.

Indeed, in high school we sang together in musicals and acted on stage. Even regaled the graduating seniors with a host of skits about school. And though we attended colleges on different coasts, and I settled a couple thousand miles away, we kept in touch. I even got to sing a solo at his wedding.

Not long ago, he and his wife, Maggie—and his dad, Jaime—joined us on the Guideposts-sponsored trip to the Oberammergau Passion Play. Maybe we've gotten a little grayer since then, but sitting on the back of the bus, it was like we were in fifth grade again. Too many stories to share.

A friend is a wondrous treasure, a God-given gift. That someone who helps you become who you are and who you are meant to be. Let me introduce you to Jorge.

**May I be a good friend—like the precious good friends You have sent me.** —Rick Hamlin

**Digging Deeper:** Job 6:14; Proverbs 27:9; 1 Peter 4:8–10

---

# Sunday, September 14

**For he will command his angels concerning you to guard you in all your ways. —Psalm 91:11 (NIV)**

Listening to "Angels Among Us,"* by Alabama, I was drawn into the chorus:

*Oh, I believe that there are angels among us . . .*
*They come to you and me in our darkest hours*
*To show us how to live, to teach us how to give*
*to guide with the light of love*

Memories of people who had come alongside me during my times of need poured into my mind.

---

*"Angels Among Us," written by Goodman, Don and Hobbs, Becky, sung by Alabama, RCA Records, 1993.

A few folks came only for a moment, many for a season, and others for years.

During my first trip to New York City after 9/11, I asked a woman on the subway which stop was closest to Ground Zero. She said, "I will get off with you and take you there." What unusual grace and kindness she gave to me, a stranger! Another time, just before leaving home to have surgery, I received an email from close friends saying they had come the night before to pray outside our home for my surgery. Touched by their special expression of love and wrapped in their prayers and those of others, I went to the hospital in peace!

I listened to "Angels Among Us" again. Thoughts surfaced of more people throughout my life who I believe God sent to guide, help, or encourage me. It was quite a spirit-building, faith-affirming experience. Who are those special ones in your life?

**Dear Lord, allow Your grace to extend through me to others, as others have allowed You to do for me—even when doing so is an inconvenience.**
—John Dilworth

**Digging Deeper:** Genesis 19:15; Luke 4:9–12; Hebrews 1:13–14

---

# Monday, September 15

## JOURNEYING WITH JESUS: Compass
**Because of this answer, go; the demon has gone out of your daughter. —Mark 7:29 (NASB)**

Jesus had quietly entered a house in Tyre—a city in present-day Lebanon. He was such a celebrity He "could not escape notice" (Mark 7:24). A determined woman with an ill young daughter came and "fell at His feet" (7:25).

Like any mother, she wanted her little girl healed. She was a Greek of Syrophoenician descent. Jesus tested her by saying He was sent to the nation of Israel. The unnamed persistent woman boldly replied, "Yes, Lord, but even the dogs under the table feed on the children's crumbs" (7:28).

She hungered for anything He could give. Jesus bestowed a rare compliment, saying her faith was great and to go home, where her daughter was now well. Her compass was set. She had zeroed in on Jesus.

In my public-library reading group, we discussed a historical book that presented a twisted truth of Jesus. I felt a nudge to pass my turn—something I never do. At the close of the conversation, someone noted I hadn't yet spoken.

I focused on Jesus—the words were there—saying I believe everything the Bible says about Him, and I have staked my life in His—my future, my eternity. I told how He said to love God with all the heart, mind, strength, and soul—and to love our neighbor as ourselves. "The people in this book did not do this," I ended.

My sincere belief resounded around the table. One searching woman stayed after to hear more. She, too, wanted to set her compass.

Father—by the invitation of Jesus—there are no "under the table crumbs." I have a place at Your table. —Carol Knapp

**Digging Deeper:** Matthew 15:21–28; Mark 7:24–30; John 1:9–13; Romans 8:14–17

---

# Tuesday, September 16

**I have set my rainbow in the clouds, and it will be the sign of the covenant between me and the earth. —Genesis 9:13 (NIV)**

I was directly in the hurricane's path, and though I had been brought up on the Mississippi Gulf Coast, never had I felt so threatened.

Pushing to get to my destination, I finally saw my exit from the rain-shrouded interstate. After I made my way through the wind and rain onto the street, I stopped at a red light, affording me the opportunity to pay attention to the heavens. And there it was—among the clouds and mist—a glorious double rainbow.

Too often in the past, I had found myself quietly questioning God's signs and wonders as I traveled the road of His kingdom, questions such as, "Are these rainbows just a normal scientific part of this weather pattern?" Or "Was it really God who cleared the left lane so that I could avoid a catastrophic collision?" Or "Was it just the course of nature that reverted my blood pressure readings to normal without any lifestyle changes?"

"Believe the rainbows," I said to myself as, later, the television maps in the motel showed the storm moving steadily toward us. With no clear choice as to the best plan of action, I felt an unbelievable peace. I waited during the next twenty-four hours knowing, no matter the outcome, I would choose to believe that the rainbows I had witnessed spoke to God's protection over me, and that was all that truly mattered.

After enduring the sound of high winds through the night, I woke up to calm. No bending palm trees. No power outage. No damage. With spectacular rainbows overarching my thoughts, I praised my God.

**Lord, help me to become more sensitive to the wonders You daily perform.**
—Jacqueline F. Wheelock

**Digging Deeper:** Matthew 19:26; Mark 11:24

---

# Wednesday, September 17

**My lips will shout for joy when I sing praise to you—I whom you have delivered.**
**—Psalm 71:23 (NIV)**

"I'm going to make a recorder case for everyone in my class," my daughter Olivia, nine, announced. She had come home that week with her first instrument and decided to make colorful cases to replace the burlap ones they'd received.

I was skeptical. I do not sew. But she was determined. Olivia took orders, FaceTimed her grandmother, and got going. She followed the pattern, cut the fabric, and ran the machine—the only thing I could do to help was to pin the edges to make the project go faster.

The first one took forty-five minutes. By the second day, she was making six an hour. Each night she'd fill her little tote bag with freshly made cases to hand out the next day. She didn't ask for money. She didn't leave anyone out. And I got to watch her bloom with confidence as she produced something with her own hard work.

As I tucked her in one night, I said, "Olivia, I am so proud of you. You set a goal for yourself and just made it happen. That was a lot of hard work!"

She smiled. "It is hard work, Mom, but it makes everyone so happy to get one, and now our music room is full of bright colors."

I have no doubt that God put Olivia on this earth to spread joy. I just didn't realize that she would learn to shine so quickly within the concrete walls of a fourth-grade music room.

**Lord, help me look for everyday ways to bring Your light and joy to those around me and to make the basic things in my life more beautiful.**
—Ashley Kappel

**Digging Deeper:** Psalm 4:7; Galatians 5:22

# Thursday, September 18

**Whosoever therefore shall humble himself as this little child, the same is the greatest in the kingdom of heaven.** —Matthew 18:4 (ASV)

I went through the McDonald's drive-thru to grab food on the way to my autistic son's counseling session. As I drove, my son ate happily in the back seat.

Just then, I heard his little voice ask me to open his barbecue sauce. We had been working with his teachers on my son requesting help when something is too difficult for him, so this was really great progress. Yet, thinking mostly of the inconvenience, and not wanting to have to stretch back to grab it and to return it, I asked him to please try on his own.

He responded with an amazingly articulate and sincere plea, "I don't want to destroy the thing I love, Mom. I don't want the sauce to spill or nuggets to fall."

I was so proud of him for applying the communication skills he had been developing. And my son's words moved me to see the situation through his eyes: He knew that he could not take the chance to spill or drop the sauce. This situation required help from someone he trusted.

What a beautiful spiritual lesson for me. My son was wise enough to know that asking for help was imperative in that moment, and he was unashamed to do so. So often, I think to ask the Lord for help last, after the mess I have already made.

Lord, thank You for using my beautiful son's way of thinking to gently remind me of Your help and love. Thank You that You are always willing to hear my plea for Your help, and I can do so anytime, unashamed. —Nicole Garcia

**Digging Deeper:** Jeremiah 29:13; Matthew 7:7, 21:16

---

# Friday, September 19

**And if I go and prepare a place for you, I will come back and take you to be with me that you also may be where I am.** —John 14:3 (NIV)

For the last twelve years, I have been a senior lecturer at my alma mater, Mercer University, in Macon, Georgia. I recently retired at age seventy but return to campus almost every day to drink coffee at Jittery Joe's coffee shop. I love to talk with students and catch up on my reading. I do not want to be separated from friendship and camaraderie.

Yesterday, as I watched new freshmen enter the coffee shop, I thought about my own freshman year in 1969, an unfathomable fifty-four years ago! I began to jot down the names of college classmates that soon became dear friends. I remembered my roommates, my soccer teammates, old girlfriends, favorite professors, coaches, advisors—the list went on. Then I wrote by each name where they currently live and what their professions are. I was suddenly amazed at how many of these dear friends have "disappeared" from my awareness over these last fifty-four years. I remember them clearly and fondly. But I don't know where they are, or if they are still living, or how to contact them. This was an astonishing and sad realization.

Perhaps the greatest longing within the human heart is found in the word *reunion*. We want to be reunited with all of the people that we consider dear through these many years of life. And we hold in our hearts the innate hope and faith that both life and death are leading to reunion with all whom we have loved in another dimension that we cannot now perceive. This longing is cross-cultural and universal. This longing is the heartbeat of our soul.

**Dear God, may I trust that all of life is leading to reunification. Amen.** —Scott Walker

**Digging Deeper:** 1 Corinthians 2:9;
1 Peter 1:13

---

# Saturday, September 20

**Therefore, whatever you want others to do for you, do also the same for them—this is the Law and the Prophets.** —Matthew 7:12 (HCSB)

I've hit a wall, literally. A giant wall stands in front of me, stopping me from continuing my run. I look around for options, hoping to figure out how to get over it on my own.

"Need a hand?" someone shouts, the front half of their muddy body hanging over the top. Someone else cups their hands together at the base of the wall to help give me a boost. With their help, I'm able to get to the top of the wall, where I turn around and help the next person up. Even though we're racing each other, a community is formed to help those who can't complete the obstacles on their own.

"Are you racing alone?" a woman asks on the other side, looking surprised when I nod. "Not anymore!" she declares. "You can join our group!" I stay for a moment but soon realize that their group is racing for completion, not time. I run ahead, feeling bad for leaving them but knowing they'll understand.

I complete, or at least attempt, each obstacle on the four-plus-mile course. Many times I have to stop and wait for someone to help me, though, then I try to help the person behind me. It takes more time, but that's OK.

I finish the race covered in mud, sweat, and joy. I could've finished faster if I hadn't stopped to help every now and then, but I wouldn't have finished most of the obstacles without the help of others.

**Lord, thank You for the kindness and helpfulness of others when I needed it.** —Rachel Thompson

**Digging Deeper:** Acts 20:35; Galatians 6:2

# Sunday, September 21

**Surely I have calmed and quieted my soul;
like a weaned child [resting] with his mother.
—Psalm 131:2 (AMP)**

I begin each day with an early-morning quiet time.
I usually read a devotional, pray, read and study
the Bible, and perhaps a Christian book. This time
has long been a daily highlight for me. Yet, recently,
I felt something was missing. So I asked God, "Is
there something you would like me to do in this
time that I'm not doing?" Within seconds, one
word came strongly to my mind: *listen.*

As I thought more about this answer, God added
scriptures to my reflection. "Be still and know that
I am God" (Psalm 46:10, NIV). "In quietness and
trust is your strength" (Isaiah 30:15, NIV).

This was *quiet* time with God. I had thought of
that as meaning free from distraction and noise.
Being up early, before anyone else, allowed me
to concentrate on prayer and devotions. Now I
realized that *I* had not been truly quiet. My mind
was continually talking—in prayer and reading.
I was not giving any focused time to quieting my
mind and soul and just listening to God.

So now, I have added mental quietness to my
quiet time. For no less than ten minutes each
morning I try to clear my mind, sit, and be still with
God. I begin by saying to Him, "I'm listening, Lord."
And then I wait.

God is giving me new insights, and when I become truly quiet, I no longer feel something is missing.

**Lord, thank You for telling me that our quiet time means more than no noise. May I always remember to listen to You not just then but throughout each day.** —Kim Taylor Henry

**Digging Deeper:** Deuteronomy 30:19–20; 1 Samuel 3:9; John 10:27

---

# Monday, September 22

**But ask the animals, and they will teach you, or the birds in the sky, and they will tell you. —Job 12:7 (NIV)**

My alarm didn't go off. I woke up late, and so the rest of the house woke up late too. My son Henry rushed to eat his breakfast and got dressed while I scrambled to throw together his lunch. Thankfully, he made it out the front door and caught the bus with just seconds to spare.

All was well, but that anxious, hurried feeling stayed with me, ruining the comfort of my routine and leaving me with the restless sense that something was amiss. I put on my coat and shoes and found the leash to walk my dog, Soda, and hopefully find some peace.

The sun rose over the mountains, filling the sky with gentle hues of pink and purple. Over our neighbor's field, a wedge of geese flew over the tree line. Their honks of encouragement punctuated the sky as they glided gloriously like in a scene from a movie.

*How do they manage to all get together on time?* I thought. *Is there a lead mother goose that orchestrates their travels and rallies the flock from place to place?*

I was on to another thought when a smaller flock of five geese loudly honked, flying in an unorganized jumble trying to catch up. I laughed and shook my head.

"Guess your alarm clock didn't go off either," I said to the sky—and just like that, my anxiety disappeared, and everything was right again.

**Lord, Creator of the Universe and everything good—help me to remember to trust Your perfect timing, even on days when I oversleep.**
—Sabra Ciancanelli

**Digging Deeper:** Ecclesiastes 3:11; Galatians 6:9

---

# Tuesday, September 23

**Stretch out your hand to heal ...** —Acts 4:30 (NIV)

I noticed the University of Pittsburgh student in front of the elevator. "It's out of service," I said. "You'll have to use the stairs."

That's when I saw her thigh-high brace. "I can't—" she began, but I cut her off. "I know another way," I said. I took her through back hallways and obscure passages to her classroom. "Thanks," she said, "but how did you know how to get here?"

"Oh, you know," I shrugged. I *didn't* tell her I made similar journeys nearly fifty years ago. My sister Cindy was quadriplegic but made her way around Pitt's complex campus. "ADA access" wasn't a thing back then; we had to forge our own way and find all the hidden hallways. My family took turns taking notes for her, so my exposure to college began when I was fourteen. I learned about modern art and ancient Greece, but mostly I learned how Cindy navigated the world. A wheelchair isn't defined by its wheels but by its *difference*. Cindy couldn't escape the sense of feeling different, of being judged by factors outside of her control.

I won't pretend to know what my sister felt, nor to suggest that I received some insight into the issues facing marginalized groups . . . but I learned what it's like to feel excluded, to feel different, to stand apart.

And I learned something else from Cindy: how to forge one's own way, and how to help others—those who may feel left out and excluded—to find their path too.

**Lord, our infirmities are sometimes obvious, sometimes not; allow us to see Your face in every face around us.** —Mark Collins

**Digging Deeper:** Luke 9:11; Colossians 1:28–29

# Wednesday, September 24

**He is before all things, and in him all things hold together. —Colossians 1:17 (RSV)**

We watched the weather. Hurricane Ian strengthened as it pushed through the Caribbean, growl becoming roar as it blasted the Gulf of Mexico. Right on track for the Airbnb we'd reserved on Florida's Fort Myers Beach. I was monitoring closely in case plans changed.

Boy, did plans change.

We watched the news in amazement and dismay as wind and water rose. Then video of the aftermath. What had been a beautiful community (and at least one nice-looking Airbnb) had been reduced to sand-swept rubble in a matter of hours.

The power of nature. We are helpless before it. Then I think of my God. And the fact that Ian, as brutal as it was, was a minuscule puff of breeze on a sand speck floating in an out-of-the-way galaxy in the reality of our Almighty.

We are nothing in the scope of things. Yet to God, we are everything. This is an aspect of my Savior I struggle to understand. He guides stars across the universe, He imagines galaxies and they *become*, He stirs the wind with a finger and the oceans roar . . . and He helps me find a parking place. Somehow He is concerned about my looming taxes and lost car keys.

I love Him, but more importantly, He loves me.

I can't explain hurricanes or why they happen. But I can trust God when He says He holds all things in His hands. And I can rest in the harbor of His care no matter what the weather report says.

**Lord, You are so much greater than my mind can comprehend. Guide me through the storms of life.**
—Buck Storm

**Digging Deeper:** Isaiah 4:6; Nahum 1:7; Matthew 8:26

---

# Thursday, September 25

**Everyone was amazed and gave praise to God. They were filled with awe and said, "We have seen remarkable things today." —Luke 5:26 (NIV)**

I only had a few minutes before heading off to work. Since I was housesitting for my sister, I took one last glance around, to make certain her home was in order. My eyes couldn't help but pause on the view through the massive picture window that looked out over Bear Creek Park and the entire city of Colorado Springs. Compared to my compact little condo on the other side of town, Cindy's home felt like a palatial slice of paradise, perched on the slopes of Pikes Peak.

A sudden movement just beyond the backyard fence caught my eye. It was the biggest housecat I'd ever seen! I looked again. It was no housecat.

It was a bobcat, with a tiny bobkitten in tow. In a matter of seconds, they both disappeared from my sight but not from my mind. Our chance encounter changed the tone of my entire day. I headed to work grinning from ear to ear. I couldn't stop thanking God for the gift I'd received by glancing out the window at just the right time. How many other miraculous little wonders surrounded me each day—ones I missed by leaving a minute too late, by being distracted by details, or by simply looking the other way?

That brief moment of awe became a touchstone, a reminder to keep my eyes and heart open. You never know when God's gift of the extraordinary will cross paths with what you thought was just an "ordinary" day.

**Father, thank You for every little gift of wonder You bring my way.** —Vicki Kuyper

**Digging Deeper:** Psalms 71:15–18, 104:24; Luke 5:1–26

---

## Friday, September 26

**Doesn't he leave the ninety-nine in the open country and go after the lost sheep until he finds it? —Luke 15:4 (NIV)**

Sitting at the kitchen counter, I kept trying to coax my stack of three rings off my finger on my right hand. Silly that removing these rings was one of the hardest things I faced as I prepared for surgery the next morning. With a final tug, I got them off and all three sailed across the floor.

No worries. I quickly found the first two, both gifts from my husband. But I could not find the third very special one that my mother had worn most of her adult life. Later that day, three grand-girls came to visit, and I challenged them to find it, offering a reward if found. They crawled around on the floor and covered the entire area, but no luck.

"We'll find it," I said, surprising myself with my confidence, which came from the memories of God's goodness in finding a few things that seemed gone for good.

Three months later I was pulling on a pair of knee-high leather boots and kept feeling something that stopped my progress. I reached into the boot and pulled out my mother's ring! I sat there in stunned silence. I didn't want to try to figure out how it got there. I just wanted to thank God.

**Lord, I know You care about lost things, and when I lose something, I learn to hold on to hope.**
—Carol Kuykendall

**Digging Deeper:** Luke 15:3–6, 8–10

---

# Saturday, September 27

**Be strong and courageous, fearless and enthusiastic! —1 Chronicles 22:13 (TLB)**

A few weeks before my son Andrew started chemo, he and I attended the Orlando Air and Space Show featuring the U.S. Air Force Thunderbirds. We brought lawn chairs and a giant beach umbrella, and on a beautiful Florida September day, we forgot about cancer and watched incredible performances in the sky for more than four hours.

We saw a World War II P-51 Mustang, an F-22 Raptor, stunt pilots do unfathomable maneuvers in the sky, a very loud F-18 Super Hornet demo, the Navy Legacy Flight, and thirty minutes of the Thunderbirds blasting through the clouds and reaming out the cobwebs in my heart and head.

Knowing Andrew was fearful of the cancer inside him, I was overjoyed to see him enjoying the airshow so much. He'd always wanted to be a pilot, but poor health had kept him from reaching that career goal. So that year for Christmas, I stepped way out of my gift-giving budget and bought a one-hour flight instruction and fourteen weeks of ground school for both him and his seventeen-year-old son, Ethan, who hopes to fly for the Air Force someday.

Their inaugural flight instruction was breathtaking, and it gave Andrew a sense of purpose and determination to fight the cancer so he could continue with flying lessons.

**Lord, help me to reach for the sky when problems arise, and help others reach for their dreams no matter how impossible they seem.** —Patricia Lorenz

## Sunday, September 28

**Turn back to Me—says the Lord of Hosts—and I will turn back to you. —Zechariah 1:3 (JPS)**

During the Days of Awe (the ten days from the beginning of Rosh Hashanah to the end of Yom Kippur), my husband, Keith, and I were driving across town when suddenly a car shot out of a side street and crashed into a street lamp, knocking down the pole, which barely missed us. Like everyone else on the main road, Keith hit the brakes as the young man who had been driving the now-crumpled car leaped out of it and slammed his fist down on the car roof. It was clear he was unhurt.

"He was going too fast to make the turn," Keith said. "I hope he has insurance."

Later, at Yom Kippur services, the rabbi was describing the sins we were there to repent as "missing the mark." It made me think about the car that missed the turn. Just as that driver had been going too fast, I realized much of what I wanted to ask God to forgive was the result of my not slowing down enough to make better choices. I was moving too fast to think about the consequences of my actions or words, and I had crashed just as surely as that angry young man.

I also recognized that God provided my insurance coverage by giving me the opportunity every year to get my dents pounded out. Then I started laughing. Next year, I promised myself, I would try to miss all the street lamps by slowing down to make the turns.

**You seem to have a sense of humor when it comes to teaching a lesson, Lord of Laughter, and I want You to know I appreciate that a whole lot.** —Rhoda Blecker

**Digging Deeper:** Jeremiah 26:3, 13

---

# Monday, September 29

## SEEMINGLY INSIGNIFICANT: God's Time-Spanning Love
**From one ancestor he made all peoples to inhabit the whole earth... —Acts 17:26 (NRSVUE)**

After his mom's funeral, a friend made tea for my husband and me, and read us an essay about his family written by his late father. The account went back hundreds of years, before his ancestors' emigration from Holland to Michigan, and was surprisingly detailed.

Our friend's reverence for this story evidenced his love for family members he never knew, who otherwise surely would have been forgotten. But it also—in the time-crimping way of genealogies—showed their love for as-yet-unborn him.

My friend's reading conjured the admittedly boring but occasionally equally intimate genealogies of God's children I'd been encountering in a daily Bible-reading podcast. Family professions are noted: potters, warriors, musicians, writers. Occasionally, a name blazes into realness. Mephibosheth: son of Jonathan, grandson of Saul, father of Micah, disabled in both feet from his nurse dropping him while fleeing the war in which his grandpa and dad just died. Jarha: Egyptian slave married to the sonless master's daughter to produce a grandchild.

My mother-in-law similarly chronicled my husband, daughters, and me in her wobbly cursive in two different Bibles, one of which she regularly read before her Alzheimer's and the other a fragile tome passed down by her ancestors. Someday, I hope I'll record my grandchildren's names there too, proof they've been loved since creation.

**Father, thank You for Your Word, even the boring genealogies, which evidence Your love.**
—Patty Kirk

**Digging Deeper:** 1 Chronicles 1–7; Acts 17:24–31

---

# Tuesday, September 30

**And let us run with perseverance the race marked out for us, fixing our eyes on Jesus, the pioneer and perfecter of faith. —Hebrews 12:1–2 (NIV)**

My thirteen-year-old daughter had been given a lead with a theater company thirty miles away. For months, I drove her to daily practices, and because of the distance, I stayed and wrote in a little office near the rehearsal room. During tech week and production weeks, I was on hand to help her with costume changes, makeup, and hair. There were dozens of children, and several adults, but I was the only mom in the green room, which surprised me.

I worried about what the other adults were thinking of me. Did they see me as an overprotective helicopter mom, someone who circles their child and doesn't let them out of their sight? As soon as I arrived in the building, one woman watched me the closest. It bothered me, so I asked my daughter if she wanted me to drop her off and try to kill time somewhere else, but she wanted me to stay. She had a big role and needed my help.

During performance week, when the woman finally approached me, I braced myself for what she might say. Imagine my surprise when she said, with tears in her eyes, "I wish I had been blessed with a mom like you."

That day, I realized I should not let the fear of other people's opinions dictate my actions. I do not answer to the judgment of others but to the purpose that God has given me.

**Lord, help me to not worry about what others think of me, but help me to run the race You have set before me.** —Gabrielle Meyer

**Digging Deeper:** Proverbs 12:25; Isaiah 41:10; Colossians 3:23

# WITH AN EVERLASTING LOVE

1 _____

2 _____

3 _____

4 _____

5 _____

6 _____

7 _____

8 _____

9 _____

10 _____

11 _____

12 _____

13 _____

14 _____

15 _____

16 _____

17 _____

18 _____

19 _____

20 _____

21 _____

22 _____

23 _____

24 _____

25 _____

26 _____

27 _____

28 _____

29 _____

30 _____

# October

Above all, keep loving one another earnestly, since love covers a multitude of sins.

—1 Peter 4:8 (ESV)

# Wednesday, October 1

**Remember not the former things, nor consider the things of old. Behold, I am doing a new thing; now it springs forth, do you not perceive it? —Isaiah 43:18–19 (ESV)**

"Do you still run regularly?" my friend Matt asked.

"Not these days," I said.

A year ago, I had been following a strict regimen. Every evening after work, I had run six miles. But, over time, my schedule became busier. Exercise became infrequent—then nonexistent. Now, it had been several months since I had gone for a run.

"Do you want to start again?" Matt asked. "We could be accountability buddies."

I hesitated. I wanted to start running again, but I dreaded that first run. I knew a timer would show me I was slower and a side-stitch would tell me I was weaker—quantitative and qualitative evidence of my abandoned habit.

"I don't know," I said. "I'm not even sure how far I can run now."

"Let's start with a mile each day," Matt said. "We can increase distance after a week."

Hearing the word *mile* (singular) discouraged me.

"I guess I'm back to beginner status," I said.

"Don't think about it like that," Matt said. "Focus on where you are heading, not where you've been."

Matt was right. Focusing on my past self would only prevent me from improving. I couldn't move forward if I continued to look back. I needed to change my perspective.

"When would we start?" I asked.

"Tomorrow," Matt said.

"All right. I'm in," I said—resolute that, tomorrow, I would run one mile more than today.

**Lord, help me to focus on where You are taking me and not where I have been.** —Logan Eliasen

**Digging Deeper:** Exodus 14:10–15; Philippians 3:13–14

---

# Thursday, October 2

**For the Spirit God gave us does not make us timid, but gives us power, love and self-discipline.** —2 Timothy 1:7 (NIV)

"Mom, I'm too scared to try basketball," my son Beau, five, told me. Beau had been waiting for his turn all year. He was done watching siblings; he wanted to play! Now his first game was upon us, and he was balking. "What if I can't reach the goal?" he asked.

He and I snuggled on the couch while I reminded him that everyone on his team was playing for the first time and that they lower the goal for the younger teams. In fact, it would be lower than the one in our backyard, the one he'd already made a few buckets on!

Beau mulled this over, then said, "Mom, I have one more question. Do you think I'll be able to dunk?"

Oh, how wildly we can swing! From being fearful that he wouldn't reach the goal to wondering how many dunks he would make, Beau reminded me how we can vacillate so quickly between fear and confidence. I can't help but think that God must chuckle to himself at how quickly our feelings and fears toggle back and forth.

That night, I thanked God for Beau's confidence and his willingness to trust me to guide him in the big and small things. I hope I can always encourage him to believe in himself, trust his hard work, and reach for the stars, or, in this case, an eight-foot-high orange hoop.

**Lord, help me always believe in myself and to show my children that they should have faith in themselves too, because You are always there to help us along the way if only we will follow You.**
—Ashley Kappel

**Digging Deeper:** Psalm 34:4; 1 John 4:18

---

# Friday, October 3

**For physical training is of some value, but godliness has value for all things, holding promise for both the present life and the life to come. —1 Timothy 4:8 (NIV)**

Seventeen-year-old Gabriel, a captain of his high-school team, swam his last meet recently. The season ended, and he'll graduate soon. Watching him dive from the block, streamlined and strong, I remembered his very first dive, when he was five. He sprang from the block at the whistle-sound, legs and arms flailing like a baby frog. His belly smacked the water, but Gabe, my fierce competitor, poked his head around to see where the other swimmers were. Then, even though he didn't really know how, he swam like mad.

Over the years, I've spoken a phrase to him before each meet. It's borrowed from one of his favorite movies. "Be fast and accurate," I say. "Like the patriot."

Gabriel is. His stroke is practiced. His turns are honed. He's worked on endurance and strength.

In 1 Timothy, God's Word speaks of the value of physical training, which is important but temporal, in comparison to godliness, which stretches forward from this lifetime to the next. Well-toned spiritual muscle and godly life practices benefit the believer as we work out our faith. Sanctification is a spiritual transformation. It's a renewing of the mind as we understand the Word. It's allowing that understanding to shape our living. It's a prayerful process of yielding to the Spirit to become more like the Son.

I'm thankful that Gabriel has been focused and intentional with swimming. But I'm more thankful that we can work together to grow in Christlikeness until we see our Savior face-to-face.

**Lord, thank You for drawing us to grow in godliness. Help me to live with intention and discipline. Amen.** —Shawnelle Eliasen

---

# Saturday, October 4

**So whatever you wish that others would do to you, do also to them, for this is the Law and the Prophets. —Matthew 7:12 (ESV)**

Our entire family loves to play Horseopoly—the horse version of Monopoly. But my husband and I noticed our children were very competitive, which led to hurt feelings when playing. They missed the preciousness of having fun together. We tried talking about this with them and highlighted "The Golden Rule." We noticed little change, but one Saturday something shifted with our son.

Typically, our whole family plays, but one Saturday afternoon my son, Jacques, asked to play Horseopoly just the two of us. (Of course I consented, because I can't resist buying horses!) On that particular Saturday afternoon, Jacques bought way too many horses too quickly. When he was forced to pay my "farrier" bill (the equivalent of paying a utility bill in regular Monopoly), he was a little short. I sighed and smiled at him. His sweet eyes peered at me. I said, "Jakey, you can pay me what you have and don't worry about the rest." Jacques was confused and his brow furrowed.

He said, "Mommy, why would you do that? You can win." I then told him I enjoyed spending time with him more than I liked winning. I also added, "I think you would do the same for me." Suddenly he smiled and understood why I would take less money than he owed and kindly offered to return the favor.

"The Golden Rule" lived in our Horseopoly game that day . . . and in our family Horseopoly games afterward.

**Merciful Lord, may I treat others in ways which honor You and may I be a vessel of Your grace.**
—Jolynda Strandberg

**Digging Deeper:** Genesis 21:22–23;
Luke 18:9–14; Acts 28:1–6

---

# Sunday, October 5

**I will remember the deeds of the LORD; yes,
I will remember your miracles of long ago.**
—Psalm 77:11 (NIV)

I love "old things": antique furniture, classic books, nineteenth-century houses, family heirlooms, and genealogy. My wife, Beth, must grow weary of my desire to visit every antiques store in Georgia and my penchant to look for "lost treasures" on eBay.

Yesterday, I was exploring the backyard of our home in Macon, Georgia, after an intense storm blew down an old pecan tree. Our house was built in 1854, and for many years there was an old stable and barn on the "back acre." Now it is a landscaped yard covered with grass. However, when the old pecan tree was uprooted, its deep and tangled roots ripped out of the ground, revealing old bricks of former structures, such as stables, that have been buried for years. I was fascinated.

Picking up a 150-year-old brick covered in red Georgia clay, I washed it off and held it, gleaming, in my hands. I fantasized seeing the fingerprints of laborers who manually molded the bricks. There were no fingerprints, but there were layers of profound mystery. So much is buried in the depths of time and history.

Later that night, I sat on the porch and thought how I must find ways to "tell our stories" to our children and grandchildren before they are muted in the depth of silence. Our great-grandchildren may well forget our names, but they seldom forget the treasured stories passed down through generations. Our stories are perhaps the most valuable buried treasure we can unearth and share with each other. They are the foundational bricks of every family.

**Father, may we love our family and friends by sharing our stories of deep meaning and delight. Amen.** —Scott Walker

**Digging Deeper:** Psalm 78:1–8; Matthew 13:10–13

---

# Monday, October 6

**Let no debt remain outstanding, except the continuing debt to love one another, for whoever loves others has fulfilled the law.** —Romans 13:8 (NIV)

I have a painful corn on the knuckle of the third toe of my right foot. A corn is a small, deep callus, if you haven't had the pleasure. What amazes me is the degree of discomfort one can cause, enough that it becomes debilitating if I don't treat it, which I sometimes don't until the pain gets so bad, I'm limping around the house.

The other day, waiting to see my foot doctor, I wondered what other things I don't pay attention to until the pain brings me up short. The quick answer was my conscience.

Something had been troubling me. Something I'd said to someone that I shouldn't have. I'd glossed over the remark even as I inwardly flinched. Those few ill-considered words were causing a disproportionate degree of pain. I tried to ignore it just as I often ignored my corn. The result? It only got worse.

Yet the person who I'd hurt was someone I would not likely talk to again—an anonymous insurance claims specialist on the phone. She'd probably forgotten my snarky comment, but I hadn't.

I had been unkind. No wonder it had become a throbbing regret. In the absence of being able to make a direct amends, I prayed, "Lord, forgive my words. I should always treat people as you would have me treat them, even in the heat of the moment. I was wrong."

One of my pains subsided immediately. The other would soon when the doctor called me in. I know what she would say: "You should have taken care of this earlier."

**Lord, let me guard my words. Help me restrain my anger when it flares and make amends quickly when it does.** —Edward Grinnan

**Digging Deeper:** Luke 6:35; Ephesians 4:32

---

# Tuesday, October 7

**I am purposed . . .** —Psalm 17:3 (KJV)

It was a cool fall day and we were at my seventh-grade nephew Charlie's football game. The crisp air and the cheering of parents suddenly brought me back to my early days of football, when I was around the same age as Charlie was now.

I loved the game, for many reasons: the camaraderie of the team, the encouragement of the coaches, the spirit of play. But most important, in this sport, I found my first real challenge. I was determined to never give up, and, boy, it wasn't easy to keep that inward promise.

I was tall and skinny, with a little athleticism thrown in, and I had started the sport a lot later than most of my teammates. So, I had a lot more to learn. Yet with all these very real difficulties, still my determination grew.

I rode the bench a lot at first but gradually earned my way to some playing time. I'd fall down hard, get my breath, pop up, and run back to the huddle. By the time I was a junior, I had become a real part of the team. In my senior year, I was starting in my position as an offensive guard.

In a way, it was football where I found my first success. I was knocked down more times than I can count. And I learned that when I fell down, if I just got back up, I couldn't be stopped.

I still use those lessons today in my faith, my business, and my life. Choosing God as my coach, He serves as a reminder. No matter what difficulties come, He is near. My purpose is steady. Get back up.

**Father, stay with me, keep me on Your team for life.** —Brock Kidd

**Digging Deeper:** Luke 16:4; 2 Thessalonians 2:15

---

# Wednesday, October 8

**... I am the way ...** —John 14:6 (KJV)

When I need a refresher course in the meaning of life, I go back in time to a place where a rickety bridge spans a coal-stained creek. Up ahead, an old couple, Taft and Beulah, rush to the porch, door flung wide. David and I, newly married, and with David just graduating from divinity school, had been sent here, by God's grace, to a little defunct mining community and a dying Presbyterian Church.

Seeing Taft and Beulah's house, you'd call it a shack. I see it, even now, as sacred, the doorway to a deeper life. There's a living room heated by an old woodstove. To the right is a bedroom filled to capacity by an ancient four-poster brass bed, stacked with homemade quilts. Strings hang from light bulbs, no light switches here. In the kitchen, Beulah cooks on a woodstove, where a cast-iron pan of cornbread waits for the hog out back.

Our families were shocked when we came to this forsaken Appalachian parish. We went with lofty thoughts of saving the poor. We came to learn that God sent us there so that His favored people, people like Taft and Beulah, might save us.

I lost the girl, there, whose designer bags matched her shoes, and David lost the guy who measured others by graduate degrees.

Here, God's people taught us to relish the smell of Beulah's blooming bubby bushes and the miracle of Taft's ripe tomatoes hanging on vines. They insisted that we stay for meals and teased us if we didn't, "I recon' you just came to borr-ie' fire," they'd laugh.

And so we were saved. Because once you *see* God's love so obvious in His people, there's only one way forward.

**God, Your beautiful people showed us Your Way. We thank You.** —Pam Kidd

**Digging Deeper:** Psalm 85:10; Proverbs 3:3

---

# Thursday, October 9

### The LORD thy God is a consuming fire . . . —Deuteronomy 4:24 (KJV)

The moment I crested the hill, I knew something was wrong. Though the sky overhead was a crisp azure blue, the base of Pikes Peak was cloaked in a gray haze. Smoke. My heart began to race.

It had been more than a decade since Colorado Springs had battled the Waldo Canyon fire, which burned 346 homes. It was the most destructive fire in Colorado's history, until one broke out less than a year later in nearby Black Forest, consuming 486 homes. In California, where I'd grown up, fires had devastated my hometown of Santa Rosa several years in a row. Friends had lost houses. People had lost their lives. It's no wonder the sight of smoke made me skittish. I began to pray.

Deuteronomy 4:24 instantly popped into my head. God as a consuming fire was not a comforting image. It reminded me God was wild, uncontrollable, and all-powerful. Then again, this untamable God limited Himself to live in the fragile frame of a human being— for me. Jesus was a raging fire willingly transformed into a comforting hearth, inviting me to warm my heart and soul in His forgiveness and grace.

The blaze near Pikes Peak was extinguished in record time that day, but the image of God as a consuming fire remains. However, it no longer unnerves me. It's true, I can't control God. But I don't have to battle Him. Instead, I can trust Him because love is the fuel that feeds His eternal flame.

**God, You are awesome in every sense of the word. Help me relate to You, and worship You, as both almighty and all-loving.**
—Vicki Kuyper

---

# Friday, October 10

**. . . for we do not know how to pray as we ought, but that very Spirit intercedes with groanings too deep for words. —Romans 8:26 (NRSVUE)**

The picture was proof, sitting there on Mom and Dad's kitchen counter: me singing at Carnegie Hall, a duet with my friend Joanne, the two of us looking confident and polished, the orchestra in the pit providing immaculate accompaniment. A memorable moment—and a reminder that photos don't always reveal the whole truth.

We were performing selections from Gilbert and Sullivan's *Pinafore* with the Blue Hill Troupe, an amateur musical group. We would do the whole show later in the season, but this was just a concert, no costumes, just tuxes on the men and nice dresses on the women, part of the group's seventy-fifth anniversary. A celebration.

And I was scared out of my wits. Sure, I liked to sing, but here in this hallowed hall where the finest musicians in the world had trotted out their stuff? Carnegie Hall is famous for its acoustics. What I noticed is that all the sound went out to the audience, none of that singing-in-the-shower resonance. It made me feel even more alone.

And yet, I did it. I walked up to the front of the stage with Joanne, looked to the conductor in the pit for the downbeat, and the music just came out of me, not a note wrong.

When I read in Scripture how Jesus's followers found just the right words when they were testifying on His behalf, the Spirit speaking through them, I think of that moment. In fact, we get these Carnegie Hall opportunities again and again, witnessing our faith. And somehow the Spirit comes down.

**Dear Lord, when fears overwhelm me, let Your Spirit come.** —Rick Hamlin

**Digging Deeper:** Genesis 1:2; Luke 4:1; John 14:15–17

---

# Saturday, October 11

**Your hands have made and fashioned me. —Psalm 119:73 (ESV)**

"We have finally arrived at the museum," I texted my husband, Kevin, frustrated at our late start in touring the National Gallery of Art in Washington, D.C. Our daughter, Katelyn, and I planned to see all the tourist sites while Kevin attended a conference during the day.

Our first morning had not lived up to my expectations. I had risen early with a mental checklist of museums to conquer. Katelyn—a night owl—had slept in and wanted a leisurely breakfast at a popular restaurant. How was I going to vacation with someone with a completely different set of priorities?

After breezing through several sections of the museum, we stepped into a gallery of marble statues. I found myself drawn to *The Reading Girl*.

"Look at her bare foot," Katelyn said, zooming in her camera to capture the sculpture's five perfectly carved toes peeking out from under the hem of her draped nightgown. The marble girl's book was propped on the back of the chair, as she intently stared at the stone pages. According to the brass sign, *The Reading Girl* had taken five years to complete.

Five years! I noted the details in the girl's braided hair and the carved lines in her clothing. What would it be like to hold an internal vision for so long before unveiling a completed reality? Could I have the eyes of a sculptor and appreciate the unseen beauty in others?

"Mom, let's go see the Impressionist paintings," Katelyn said, leading the way.

I linked my arm in hers. "Do you want to go to a coffee shop afterward?"

**Jesus, give me sculpting eyes to see what is inside of others and call it beautiful.** —Lynne Hartke

**Digging Deeper:** Psalm 139:13–16; Ephesians 2:10

---

# Sunday, October 12

**And now, in my old age, don't set me aside. Don't forsake me now when my strength is failing.** —Psalm 71:9 (TLB)

Today, October 12, I turn eighty years old. *How on earth did that happen,* I wonder. I remember when my dad turned thirty, and I thought he was so old. Little did I know he'd live to be ninety-eight.

Of course, we're never guaranteed a long life. My nephew Jacob died in a plane crash when he was eighteen. My mother died of ALS at fifty-seven. My stepson Joseph died at age fifty-eight of a heart attack. So when you hit eighty, you know you're on the downward side of life on this planet. And even though I'd like to remain happy and healthy and hang around for another twenty-five years, it may not happen.

Like most people, the older I get, the less I'm concerned with material needs and the more I think about preparing my heart, soul, and mind for the afterlife. I'm happy to get rid of all the stuff I've collected over the years and share it with my kids, grandkids, nieces, nephews, friends, and visitors. It's fun seeing my stuff in their homes.

But how do I prepare for life after death? Quiet walks in beautiful places. Gasping at sunsets. Getting myself to church regularly, where the peace that comes from plopping myself in that pew and participating in worship and singing is extraordinarily soothing. Kindness to strangers. Sharing my bounty. Gathering friends together. All of that stuff we can do at any age, but when we've been granted the gift of old age, there's no time like the present!

Lord, I know I'm on the fast track to being with You in eternity. Help me to make these last years the best years. —Patricia Lorenz

**Digging Deeper:** Genesis 43:27–28; Psalm 102:23–29; Ephesians 4:20–24

---

# Monday, October 13

**. . . for I have learned to be content whatever the circumstances. —Philippians 4:11 (NIV)**

I opened the door to my apartment. It didn't seem like anyone was home. "Hello?" I said, just to be sure. No one answered. I smiled, opened my arms, and plopped on the couch. Seldom do I have the opportunity to truly relax without the anticipation of someone calling me or needing my help. But just as I got comfy, the door opened. "Hi, honey," my mother sighed, looking spent. My father followed behind. I groaned, but I got up to help him out of his coat. Minutes later, my kids stormed through the door. I groaned again.

As much as I love my parents, I don't always love that they live with me—my apartment is small, my father has many needs, and my mother and I can work each other's nerves. I don't always love living with my kids either—they're loud and messy, and they eat all the cookies before I even enjoy a crumb. Sometimes I wish I lived alone.

Yet, the sad part is, in a few years, that's exactly what's going to happen: my parents will be with the Lord and my kids away at college, then with families of their own. The solitude I often crave will finally be granted, but at a heavy price. It will arrive when my family is gone, accompanied with the greatest sorrow I'll ever know. So even when I groan in the chaos of it all, within the same breath, I'm grateful.

**Dear Lord, I know that everything in life has its season. Help me to truly appreciate each one, even when it's difficult to do.** —Karen Valentin

**Digging Deeper:** Psalm 73:26; Ecclesiastes 3:1

---

# Tuesday, October 14

**Blessed are those who mourn, for they shall be comforted. —Matthew 5:4 (NKJV)**

It was a sunny Tuesday morning when my sister and I arrived at the hospice facility with my mother.

One of my mom's favorite things in life was feeling the sun's warmth on her face, so I immediately noticed the beams of sunlight streaming through the windows and French doors in her room. It was a wink from God. He was prepared to welcome my mother into heaven, and he'd welcomed us—her daughters—into a place of peace.

Being with my mom during hospice was heart-wrenching, yet we were strengthened by the many prayers of others. God's lovingkindness came through in the caring staff, the joyful music, even the chirping birds outside of her window that seemed to sing God's praises.

My mom's words became few, and eventually she became silent as she walked closer to the arms of Jesus. We slept by her bedside for two days, leaving only to slip away for meals and return within a short time. On the third day, my sister and I decided to run home to shower, pack fresh clothes, and for me to see my children who I hadn't seen in a few days. In less than an hour, I received the call that would change the lives of me and my siblings forever.

Since we're both believers, I know that I will see my mother again. She raised me to be a God-fearing woman, and, like her, I will serve Him until my very last breath.

**Lord, I'm grateful to be Your child. My greatest reward will be when You welcome me into heaven. I will serve and praise You until we meet face-to-face.** —Tia McCollors

**Digging Deeper:** Psalm 29:11; Isaiah 57:1–2; Matthew 5:4; 2 Thessalonians 3:16

---

# Wednesday, October 15

**Take delight in the Lord, and he will give you the desires of your heart. —Psalm 37:4 (NIV)**

One of my greatest joys is holding babies. When our kids got too old to cuddle, my friend Mary grieved with me. She said, "I just know heaven will be full of babies to hold!"

I volunteered once a month in our church nursery and absolutely loved it.

One Sunday, I attended another church. The next day, I stopped by that church to talk with Pastor Kristi. She had brought her baby to work because he was still nursing.

We played with him as we talked, passing him back and forth between our laps. I kept thinking that he would be mobile sooner than she expected, and meetings would go better without his participation! I wanted to cuddle him some more, but I was afraid it was too early to ask.

A month later, I was scanning my to-do list when I felt a nudge to call Pastor Kristi. I dialed her church. The secretary answered and I explained my reason for calling. There was a long pause. I held my breath, imagining her considering ways to say "no" to this creepy stranger without hurting my feelings.

Instead, she said, "Your timing is incredible! Pastor Kristi just told me that she is starting a new meeting on Monday, and could I find someone to mind the baby for that hour!"

I called Mary to tell her that I get to have a touch of heaven right here on Earth.

**Dear Lord, thank You for giving us the desires of our hearts. Even the smallest ones.**
—Leanne Jackson

**Digging Deeper:** Luke 18:16; Galatians 5:22

# Thursday, October 16

**No one is good but God alone.—Luke 18:19 (NRSVUE)**

My husband and I have a friend who's been in and out of prison for as long as we've known him. Despite surviving a tortuous childhood, he struggles to find his footing in the world or make wise choices. He is often homeless. He considers Charlie and me his second parents, but we are divided on how to help him.

When he is in prison, I feel relieved. This sounds harsh, but in prison, he does everything right. Almost as soon as he is sentenced, he applies for work, though it pays pennies an hour; when he is free, he struggles to get or keep a job. In prison, he prays and reads Scripture regularly, advocates for faith services, and encourages others. He writes to friends and is a favorite among the guards. I think he is safest and his best self in prison.

Charlie believes prison cannot be the "best" place for anyone and doesn't understand my "tough love" approach. "What about compassion?" he asked recently, compelling me to ask myself the same question.

I do think of myself as compassionate. So why *am* I so stubborn about our friend? Is it because when he's in prison, I don't have to worry about him? Because I can simply write to him, put a few dollars in his account, and feel I've done my best? Or because I don't have to dread the disappointment and worry if he fails again?

And then a really frightening question came into my mind: What if God applied my brand of tough love to me?

**Compassionate God, help me to be as merciful to others as You are to me.** —Marci Alborghetti

**Digging Deeper:** Exodus 15:1–2, 11, 13, 17–18; Isaiah 30:18

---

# Friday, October 17

**Grandchildren are the crown of the aged, and the glory of children is their fathers.** —Proverbs 17:6 (ESV)

My husband, Anthony, and I could hardly contain our laughter. We were talking with our youngest daughter, Jada, about some schoolwork she needed to complete, and she had ended her story with the statement, "I figure this way, I'll be knocking a bird with two stones."

I flashed my squinted eyes toward Anthony, while he did the same toward me. We realized what Jada was attempting to communicate: she'd meant "killing two birds with one stone."

For weeks, we chuckled over Jada's innocent faux pas. I thought about the idioms and old wives' tales I randomly assert daily, especially around my home: *It's raining cats and dogs. It's just water under the bridge. Let the cat out of the bag.*

Like family heirlooms, these verbal expressions have been passed from generation to generation.

My grandmother passed them down to my mother, my mother passed them down to me, and now I am passing them down to my children. These phrases are as embedded within me as the myriad life lessons and words of wisdom my mom shared. This is one piece of my mother's legacy that will live on through my children, and, Lord willing, through my children's children as well.

Sometimes we wonder if our ancestors' legacies will be remembered by future generations, but God provides evidence that they live on in their descendants. Jada reminded us that though my parents are gone, their legacies will never die. Also, the apple doesn't fall far from the tree.

**Heavenly Father, thank You for the opportunities to share our ancestors' legacies with our children, instilling the wisdom, strength, and love that will impact generations to come.** —Carla Hendricks

**Digging Deeper:** Deuteronomy 6:1–9; Proverbs 13:22

---

# Saturday, October 18

## JOURNEYING WITH JESUS: Water Bottle

**He said to her, "Go, call your husband and come here." —John 4:16 (NASB)**

A lone woman had come to draw water at a well. A Jewish man in that day would never speak with an unknown woman, especially a despised Samaritan.

But Jesus was eager to tell her about His "living water" (John 4:10).

It sounded wonderful. She wouldn't have to draw from the well; she'd never be thirsty again. She ran into a snag, however, when Jesus told her to go and bring her husband.

She didn't lie. "I have no husband" (4:17). Jesus laid her life before her: five husbands, and a current relationship with one not her husband. When He told her He was the Christ, she believed.

Not only did she go and bring back her companion, she brought the whole town! Jesus stayed two days in the village offering His living water—the good news of God with us.

I got a call late one evening from someone I'd met only once but had stayed in touch with. She was in the hospital dying. She was desperate. There were many broken relationships in her life. She'd once said, "You wouldn't like me if you knew all the things I've done." I urged her to call to Jesus for His forgiving, sustaining living water—and she did.

My friend survived her medical crisis, still with side effects for which we are asking healing. But most satisfying, she's now got eternity in her water bottle—water only Jesus can give.

**As the song goes, "Fill my cup, Lord, I lift it up, Lord!"** —Carol Knapp

**Digging Deeper:** Jeremiah 2:13; John 4:3–42, 7:37–39

# Sunday, October 19

**God's Spirit blows wherever it wishes. You hear its sound, but you don't know where it comes from or where it is going.** —John 3:8 (CEB)

What a surprise! Last week, my friend Joseph phoned. I hadn't seen or talked to him in more than a decade. I'd say the call was "out of the blue," though he reminded me that six months ago, I'd mailed him a gently used book for his son. "So I wanted to thank you," he said. And then the conversation took off. We caught up on our personal and professional lives. We reminisced about the church community where we'd met when he was a political science student, before he moved back to his hometown in Florida.

I reminded him of one private Sunday morning conversation. We were walking to our cars after church. I vented my frustration. "That was the worst sermon I've ever heard"—one long anecdote, untethered from a scriptural mooring, about the hospitality of a church in Vidalia, Georgia, that opened its doors to hurricane evacuees.

"I don't remember this," he said last week.

So I continued my story. "I was so startled by your response to my harsh critique. You said, 'You're kidding! That sermon spoke to me. It confirmed that I have to go back home and serve my people.' And a few months later, you packed up and left us." What a testimony to the personal force of the Holy Spirit. "Who knew? You and I both sat through what I call the Vidalia sermon. I'm there thinking, no breeze today. You're being blown away."

**Spirit of God, thank You for meeting each of us according to our need. Open my spirit to hear and see Your Word to me today and this week.** —Evelyn Bence

**Digging Deeper:** Ephesians 3:7–21

---

## Monday, October 20

**"But now bring me a musician." Then it happened, when the musician played, that the hand of the LORD came upon him.** —2 Kings 3:15 (NKJV)

Downstairs, in the room beneath me, the piano tuner strikes note after note. When the man first inspected our old upright's condition, he warned me that the process would take a while, explaining that he would need to do two complete passes of tuning every key.

"I have time if you do," he said.

I nodded, but now the droning sound is nearing the three-hour mark with no end in sight.

I remind myself that the piano desperately needs it, and my oldest, studying music composition, requires the correct pitch to master ear training, a complex skill of being able to transcribe music as you listen to it.

I am about to ask the kind and exceptionally patient man how much longer it will take when I receive an urgent email. My shoulders grow tight as I try to focus on the words in front of me. I put on headphones, but the notes come through anyway.

Finally, the striking stops. Silence permeates the house. *He must be packing up his tools*, I think.

I descend the stairs as he starts to play something. I turn a corner and stand in the doorway as he performs a Mozart allegro. His fingers create a rainbow of glorious sound, and everything in the house shifts to beauty. Even the cats come to investigate.

A sense of awe washes over me. Respect, admiration, peace, and gratitude. Gratitude for everything, every sound of every key that led to this amazing magical moment.

**Lord, I feel You with me, in me, and through me.**
**Thank You for reminding me that patience is**
**often necessary to receive amazing experiences.**
—Sabra Ciancanelli

**Digging Deeper:** Psalms 49:4, 95:1;
Ephesians 5:19

---

# Tuesday, October 21

**I am content with weaknesses....**
**For when I am weak, then I am strong.**
**—2 Corinthians 12:10 (ESV)**

My best shot at greatness arrived last year when Samuel August was born to our granddaughter, Hannah, making me a great-grandfather.

When first I saw Samuel, I was struck by his helplessness. "He can't even hold his head up," I said to my wife.

She laughed. "Well, never fear, babies have a way of getting everything they need."

I soon discovered that a baby the size of a baked ham could fill a ten-room house with such an odor that Dad called the plumber, suspecting a sewer problem.

Then there are all those specialized "cries" that babies are programmed with, like the "self-pity sob," which could break even Al Capone's hard heart. And the threatening "Feed-me-NOW-or-I-will-break-your-legs" cry, and, ultimately, the "screaming marathon" that is so shrill and lasting that neighbors have been known to call 911.

Sammy's greatest strength, however, is his smile. When he gives me that cute little grin, I am ready to give him half of my kingdom.

As a male, I want to be strong and self-sufficient, but from my great-grandson I have learned that humility is the first step to greatness. My family says that I am easier to live with and a lot more loveable when I am vulnerable and willing to be helped.

**Father, help me not to be ashamed of weakness, but to recognize the opportunities it contains.**
—Daniel Schantz

**Digging Deeper:** Psalm 73:26; Hebrews 4:15

# Wednesday, October 22

**For God has not given us a spirit of fear and timidity, but of power, love, and self-discipline. —2 Timothy 1:7 (NLT)**

The verse listed above is my life verse. Every time I autograph a book, below my name, I write down the reference 2 Timothy 1:7. This is a constant reminder to me of how abundantly the Lord has blessed me. He has loved me unconditionally, granted me His power as I deal with life's painful situations, and aided me in living a life of discipline.

Interested in finding her own life verse, our daughter, Adele, went about it in a fun way. Her birthday is May 16. Asking God to guide her, she went through the entire Bible, listing each verse from chapter five, verse sixteen. After searching through every book, she felt God was telling her the verse He chose for her was Matthew 5:16 (NIV): "In the same way, let your light shine before others, that they may see your good deeds and glorify your Father in heaven."

Inspired by the idea, I decided to check out what God's Word said for my own birthday, October 22. Because my birthday is late in the year, several books in the Bible didn't reach ten chapters. It was a fun exercise, and while I already had the one verse God had given me more than thirty years before, I was inspired and uplifted by Hebrews 10:22 (NKJV): "Let us draw near with a true heart in full assurance of faith, having our hearts sprinkled from an evil conscience and our bodies washed with pure water."

**Father God, you chose the date of my birth and have established my steps. Thank You for guiding me to that special verse that has become the benchmark of my life.** —Debbie Macomber

**Digging Deeper:** 1 Timothy 6:18; Hebrews 10:24

---

# Thursday, October 23

**Nevertheless, in the Lord woman is not independent of man, nor is man independent of woman.** —1 Corinthians 11:11 (NIV)

Randy struck up a conversation with the elderly couple seated across from us in the waiting room. I love that my husband is friendly and open.

The more we talked, the more I was struck by the similarities between us. Our men want to be early to every appointment, while we ladies want to be precisely on time. Our politics were aligned. We all had agricultural backgrounds. While I'd never met them before, there was a powerful sense of familiarity. Randy and the man knew the same people and walked comfortably down memory lane. As the men carried the conversation and we ladies filled in the gaps, I had an overwhelming impression that we were seated across from "us" in twenty years.

I could see it in the couple's mannerisms. They were committed to each other—a team. After decades together, they knew each other completely and they were content with each other. This was a true partnership. Will this be us, or is it wishful thinking?

As Randy and I continue to grow our faith together, we have both felt our marriage strengthen. Worshipping together forms a different bond of unity. It's like a maturing of love into a richer fruit. The more we fix our eyes on the Lord, the smaller and less important differences between us become. Sure, there will be bumps along the way. But even more so today than when we married nine years ago, I can see us as that couple.

**Lord God, bless our marriage and partnership. Please continue to strengthen us together in our ever-growing love for You.** —Erika Bentsen

**Digging Deeper:** Genesis 2:18; Proverbs 31:10–12; Ephesians 5:25–33

---

# Friday, October 24

**My dearly loved brothers, understand this: Everyone must be quick to hear, slow to speak, and slow to anger. —James 1:19 (HCSB)**

"Katie, I have an idea!" I proclaim, rounding the brown couch my closest-in-age sister is sitting on. Mock irritation peeps from behind her glasses as she looks up from her book.

"I literally just sat down," she says before sighing, bookmarking her book, and turning her full attention to me. "What is it now?"

"OK, so..." I start, before launching into an in-depth explanation of the new idea I had for my book. Patiently she listens, waiting for me to finish blabbing so she can return to her own book. She's been working all day—leaving at 6:30 a.m. and returning at 5:30 p.m.—so I know she's just wanting to relax for a bit, but I'm too excited and selfish, and she's too kind.

I love talking to Katie. I know she'll always listen, and she won't get mad when I interrupt her. Even though my constant pestering must annoy her, she never gets angry. Every time I come to her, she puts down her book, phone, or headphones, and listens.

While I talk, she asks questions, or reminds me of other ideas I had that would contradict this new one. Every now and then she stops me and gives a suggestion or tells me something is cliché. Once I finish, she gives more feedback, mixing constructive criticism with encouragement.

Finally I leave, letting her return to her book for a few minutes before I think of a new idea and she hears me rounding the corner with another "Kaaaaaatieeeeeee."

**Lord, thank You for Katie's listening and patient nature.** —Rachel Thompson

**Digging Deeper:** Philippians 2:4; 1 Peter 4:8

# Saturday, October 25

**Be completely humble and gentle; be patient, bearing with one another in love. —Ephesians 4:2 (NIV)**

Excitement mounted as we ran through the dress/tech rehearsal for our church musical revue. Opening night tomorrow! We had already sold out, and no wonder. We had talent to spare: trained voices, guitarists, pianists, comedians. Even the choir director donned top hat and tails to tap "Puttin' On the Ritz."

I had been recruited to write patter that connected and introduced the acts, however loosely. The task had seemed simple enough until our lead bass singer, grumpy at the best of times, criticized his intro-duction. "You left out the video!" he thundered. "Give me the video first!" I knew he liked to be perfect, but did he have to be so hard on me? I tried to appease him and quickly wrote stage instructions. Then he fussed about something else.

I hissed to the choir director, "What does he *want*?"

Very quietly he responded, "Just to be loved. What we all want."

The revue generated applause and a tidy profit for outreach. As for the singer, he disappeared from choir when his health took a turn. Perhaps he had been fearful of his prognosis when he lashed out.

This happened years ago, and I confess, I've forgotten his name, but I have not forgotten my choir director's gentle reprimand. We all want love, especially when we don't know how to ask for it.

**Merciful God, forgive me when I put my own feelings before those of another. Tune me in to unvoiced pain.** —Gail Thorell Schilling

**Digging Deeper:** 1 Corinthians 13:4; Galatians 5:22–23; Colossians 3:12

---

# Sunday, October 26

**A good name is better than fragrant oil.**
**—Ecclesiastes 7:1 (JPS)**

I was never happy with the Hebrew name, Rivka, that my parents had given me at birth, but I didn't think there was much I could do about it. Then my friend Barbara told me that she was going to change her given name. "I am not Barbara," she said. "That was my older sister, who died before I was born. I just inherited it." I decided that made sense.

The next week, on Shabbat, I spoke to the rabbi, who said it would be fine to pick a new Hebrew name. "What name would you like?" he asked me. All I could say was, "I'll get back to you on that."

I looked up Hebrew names starting with "R," because I thought there was some kind of tradition that Hebrew and "regular" names should begin with the same letter. There were a lot of them. When we had picked my husband Keith's Hebrew name, he had very few to choose from, and that made his choice much easier. The problem was that none of the "R" names seemed to fit me.

Then another friend pointed out that I was holding tightly to a tradition that didn't make sense any longer. "You can pick what says 'you' to you," she said. The choice of Hebrew names opened much wider for me, and I tried on a lot of them before one fit perfectly. My Hebrew name is now "Batya," which means "daughter of God." And it does make me happy.

**I hope You don't think I'm disrespecting my parents, God. It's just that they didn't know who I was going to become, and You did.** —Rhoda Blecker

**Digging Deeper:** Exodus 3:15; Isaiah 43:1

---

# Monday, October 27

**Be strong and of good courage; do not be afraid, nor be dismayed, for the LORD your God is with you wherever you go. —Joshua 1:9 (NKJV)**

My friend Susan was elated, having purchased a new car for the first time in her life. She was forty-five years old, and had always bought inexpensive junkers, mostly because she doesn't like borrowing money. But this time, Susan wanted a new car. She had a new job and wanted a car that would withstand a longer daily commute. She bought it and she loved it.

Then it snowed. Susan was new to living with snow, and she didn't know how to drive in it. I asked her what went wrong that day. "The car started to slide on the snow and ice. I slammed on the brakes."

"Oh no!" I replied. I've been on snow for as long as I've been driving and know that slamming on the brakes is probably the worst thing one can do. "Yes," she said. "The car spun around completely and then slammed into a wall."

But then Susan said something I've always remembered: "When I was scared, I forgot about God. I always say that I turn to Him for help, but in that moment, I didn't. Slamming on the brakes was like forgetting who I am."

What a wonderful way that was to say something so simple about the Christian life. Remember who you are—a child of God—even when you're frightened.

**When I am afraid, Lord, remind me to listen for Your voice and look for Your hand.** —Jon M. Sweeney

**Digging Deeper:** 2 Timothy 1:6–7

---

# Tuesday, October 28

## SEEMINGLY INSIGNIFICANT:
### Learning as Jesus Learned
**Let the wise, too, hear and gain in learning and the discerning acquire skill. —Proverbs 1:5 (NRSVUE)**

Whenever I explain something in class, I ask questions to ensure everyone gets it, typically ignoring the immediate hand in the air from someone keen to be the one with the answer. Every class has this student, always desperate to be called on.

If all students were like that hand-raiser, if my classrooms pulsed with straining arms punching right answers into the empty air above intent faces, I might like it. Indeed, when I eventually let the hand-wavers speak, their responses sometimes dazzle me. Still, as a teacher, I'm more thrilled by those other students' struggling answers, which demonstrate that real learning—that is, undergoing a change in thinking—is actually happening. Every semester, I struggle spiritually and pedagogically to love the class's inevitable know-it-all, who never seems as motivated to learn or think as to be publicly right.

I wonder if the temple teachers struggled to love twelve-year-old Jesus that time his parents accidentally left town without him and returned to find him "sitting among" them. Luke says, "Everyone was amazed at his understanding and his answers," but that doesn't necessarily mean they actually liked this smarty-pants in their midst. As an adult, Jesus amazed—and outraged and enraged— many other teachers with his understanding and wise answers to their questions, so much so they sought to kill him.

Luke helpfully addresses my question by revealing that Jesus wasn't magically all-knowing from babyhood, but deeply engaged in learning. His parents find him that day not only wowing his teachers with smart answers, but "listening to them and asking them questions." As a result, Luke concludes, he "increased in wisdom."

**I want to teach and learn as You did, Jesus. Help me!** —Patty Kirk

**Digging Deeper:** Proverbs 1; Luke 2:41–52

---

## Wednesday, October 29

**The heavens declare the glory of God, and the sky above proclaims his handiwork. —Psalm 19:1 (ESV)**

"Ready to turn off our flashlights?" My husband, Kevin, asked as he settled into his camp chair at a viewing point near our cabin in northern Arizona.

"I would rather be in my warm bed, reading a book," I grumbled, "than out in this chilly night air."

Kevin just shook his head at my negative attitude. He turned his eyes toward the northern quadrant of the night sky to search for Hercules, the constellation nearest the new Tau Herculids meteor shower. If visible, astronomers predicted a spectacular light show as the Earth traveled through the debris from a disintegrating comet.

If. *If* was the cautious qualifier. Since the meteor shower was new, nobody knew the outcome. As someone who had tried to view other meteor showers in the past, only to be hindered by cloud-covered or light-polluted skies, I understood the caution. But this time, we sat miles from the nearest city on a moonless night, so we hoped for the best.

429

Kevin and I settled in to wait under the canopy of thousands of stars. Night sounds echoed around us. Croaking frogs from a nearby spring. Chirping crickets. A hooting owl.

"There!" Kevin said, pointing to a brief light trail in the night sky.

I held my breath, searching the heavens. Minutes passed. "There's another," I gasped, focusing above me. "And another!" We documented six more meteors in thirty minutes. If I had stayed home with my book, I would have missed the opportunity to witness the heavens interacting with Earth.

**Jesus—as the One who holds the heavens but knows my name—I step forward in hope in the uncertainty of this day, knowing You have plans to intersect my life in beautiful ways.** —Lynne Hartke

**Digging Deeper:** Psalms 8:1, 111:2

---

# Thursday, October 30

**...be humble and consider others more important than yourselves. —Philippians 2:3 (CEV)**

Folks pushed shopping carts past me as I put a can of Libby's brand green beans in my cart. I'd volunteered to head up the Boxes of Blessings program for church, where we would be putting together twenty-five Thanksgiving food boxes to give to folks who needed a hand up for the holidays.

Although it was only October, today was the day I'd be placing the food order with the grocery store.

I glanced at my long grocery list, then at prices on the cans and sighed. *Inflation has made this crazy expensive—we're going to have $1,500 to $1,600 in these! What about the church's budget?* I put the name brand back on the shelf and I reached for the plain label. But I thought, *I want them to feel special, not second-rate.* I stood there for several minutes wrestling about the budget versus the message. Then a still small voice whispered, "The people need to know that they are valued. Buy the name brands." *OK, God.* I whisked through the store, gathering one of each for the SKU numbers, then placed the order.

Weeks later, when I went to pay, I was shocked at the total. Turning to the manager, I mentioned to him that something was wrong. The bill was a lot less than what we had anticipated. He smiled. "Between the time you placed the order and now, the name brands went on sale." They ended up being cheaper than the plain-label cans.

**Thank You, Lord, for encouraging me to send the most important message to others, that they are valued. Amen.** —Rebecca Ondov

**Digging Deeper:** Proverbs 3:27; Hebrews 13:16

---

## Friday, October 31

**The spirit of man is the candle of the Lord.**
**—Proverbs 20:27 (KJV)**

I struck another match, attempting once again to light my daughter's jack-o'-lantern candle. Still no luck. "What's wrong with this thing, anyway?" I grumbled. A closer look revealed the problem: there was no wick.

Just then, my daughter came bursting outside, decked out in her "Batcat" costume—the very picture of little-kid excitement. But all I could think was: "She's gotten so tall!"

There'd been so much growth and change lately—for Aurora, and for our relationship. When she'd been smaller, I'd delighted in the close intimacy we'd shared. As someone who has always struggled to connect with others, I'd wished it could stay that way forever.

But lately, I could feel her wordless, bigger-kid questions. "Do my feelings make sense to you, Mama? Is there room for the different things I think and feel?"

Of course, I always *meant* for there to be. But intentions were no longer enough. I needed to figure out how to connect with this more grown-up version of who God had designed my daughter to be.

But, *what if I couldn't?* I worried. What if, like this defective candle, I just didn't have what it'd take?

A thought pinged. *I wonder, though* ... I dug my fingernail into the candle's top. And there—just below the surface—was the wick! It lit easily. As the pumpkin's friendly face blazed to life, I smiled, encouraged. The candle hadn't been missing a thing. It'd just taken a little extra work to find what'd been right there all along.

I know, God, that my daughter and I are both the work of Your hands. Please bless my relationship with her as I seek, always, to be the parent she needs me to be. —Erin Janoso

**Digging Deeper:** Psalm 139:13; Philippians 4:13

## WITH AN EVERLASTING LOVE

1 _____

2 _____

3 _____

4 _____

5 _____

6 _____

7 _____

8 _____

9 _____

10 _____

11 _____

12 _____

13 _____

14 _____

15 _____

16 _____

17 _____

18 _____

19 _____

20 _____

21 _____

22 _____

23 _____

24 _____

25 _____

26 _____

27 _____

28 _____

29 _____

30 _____

31 _____

# November

And so we know and rely on the love God has for us. God is love. Whoever lives in love lives in God, and God in them.

—1 John 4:16 (NIV)

# Saturday, November 1

**Though your sins are like scarlet, they shall be as white as snow; though they are red as crimson, they shall be like wool.** —Isaiah 1:18 (NIV)

A few months ago, I spilled a large mug of hot tea on my ivory-and-beige upstairs carpet. Unfortunately, it was a Red Zinger mix that soaked a foot-wide circle and sprayed reddish spatters much farther. I tried commercial cleaner, baking soda, even vinegar. The stain lightened but remained glaringly visible.

Covering the stain with a rug wasn't feasible. My carpet was out of stock, so I couldn't have the ruined part replaced. I was resigned to living with the ugly reminder of my carelessness. Then a friend advised me to treat the carpet every day "for as long as it takes." Progress was slow, but six weeks later every trace of the stain was gone.

The daily cleaning process gave me time to think about the stains in my life. There are sins I commit on an almost daily basis: anxiety, gossip, snap judgments. Sometimes I harbored ill will in my heart. When I accidentally came home with a greeting card I didn't pay for, I kept it because the store was fifty miles away. I wasn't always nice.

Thankfully, God doesn't make me wait for His forgiveness. When I confess, He willingly and immediately forgives both the little spatter sins and the big Red Zingers. And when I called the store about the greeting card, they forgave me too.

**Merciful Father, thank You for the grace that is greater than my sins. Help me keep a rein on my tongue and a loving attitude in my heart as I strive to walk closer to You each day.** —Penney Schwab

**Digging Deeper:** Psalm 51:3–4; Luke 18:9–14; Ephesians 4:32

---

## Sunday, November 2

**And the Scripture was fulfilled which says, "Abraham believed God, and it was accounted to him for righteousness." And he was called the friend of God.** —James 2:23 (NKJV)

We remember deceased loved ones in personal ways: a funny story, meals they loved to cook, or a special moment that we know will never be repeated. My mother-in-law, Nereida, was a praying woman. Talking to God daily was like breathing for her, or being with her best friend. In prayer, she shared her cares, joys, worries, and heart's desires. Nothing was too small or big for God.

Nereida prayed on her knees till she died at eighty-eight years old. This was her faith and personal tradition. In the latter years, she used a small, decorative pillow to kneel. She prayed before sunrise and late at night. When I remember Nereida, I think of the words used to describe Abraham in Scripture: "friend of God." Her relationship with the Divine was a love relationship—she saw God as a trusting best friend who was dependable, reliable, and caring.

The morning my wife, Elba, and I were planning to drive her to the hospital for surgery to remove a cancerous lump from her lung, she was up long before us praying. That day was the last time she prayed at home and on her knees. Although the surgery went well, a week later her heart gave out. But even in her dying bed, we prayed together. What a blessing to be remembered and called a "friend of God."

**Lord, teach us to be Your friend, keeping nothing from You and trusting everything to You.** —Pablo Diaz

**Digging Deeper:** Exodus 33:11; John 15:13–15

---

# Monday, November 3

**Live full lives, full in the fullness of God.**
**—Ephesians 3:19 (MSG)**

My final Guideposts ministry visit was to White River Junction Veterans Affairs Medical Center, in Hartford, Vermont. Upon entry to the hospital, a matter-of-fact, all-business counter agent led me to the chaplain's office. I noted a distinct softening of the agent's expression after having encountered the chaplain.

Chaplain Lorna, in the midst of an intense telephone conversation, directed me to wait in an outside foyer. After an extensive phone discussion, the chaplain invited me in.

I began with a presentation of our Guideposts booklets and magazines, only to be interrupted by facility engineers. Their picture-hanging project in the chapel was complete.

But then, with full-throttle, total attention and awareness, Chaplain Lorna shared the unique nature of her White River, Vermont, pastoral ministry and asked focused questions on the multi-faith appeal of our publications and how to order. On the spot, she went to our website and placed a significant booklet request.

Upon leaving, I asked whether I could lead her in a prayer. I bowed my head in a word of gratitude and support, and then I prepared to depart.

Before I could go, Chaplain Lorna, with locked eyes, impassioned heart, and a deliberate, intentional manner, blessed me with words that inspire me to this day: "Guide the pathways of this Your servant, O Lord. Keep him safe and secure in Your hands. Be his ever-present helper and friend."

I walked away, grateful and inspired by the privilege of having been in the sacred presence of one of God's true servants.

**God, our provider, enable us to offer Your expansive grace, sanctuary, and calm assurance to those we encounter this day. Bless especially our Veterans Affairs chaplains. Amen.** —Ken Sampson

**Digging Deeper:** Isaiah 11:9; 2 Corinthians 4:6

---

# Tuesday, November 4

**He will be the stability of your times.**
**—Isaiah 33:6 (NASB)**

I was struggling to get my young daughter down for a nap in the small hotel room. It didn't help that my son was bouncing off the walls with excitement, laughing, and chatting nonstop. Why should I expect any less? After all, we were on vacation at an amusement park, the so-called Happiest Place on Earth. I gave my husband a warm, knowing smile and sat back in an overstuffed chair, wholeheartedly content, as I surveyed the happy, chaotic scene.

I awoke with a start—alone in my own queen-sized bed. My marriage had ended more than a decade ago. My children were grown and now had children of their own. For a moment, my heart sank to find myself on the sunset side of that happy scene in my dream. But an unexpected wave of gratitude suddenly swept through my melancholy, washing it away.

My dream wasn't a snapshot of an actual moment. It was a patchwork of cherished memories, a celebration of a season of life I'd been blessed to have experienced. My brain was still enjoying the past, while incorporating that story into my present. Yes, my life looks a lot different than it did thirty years ago, but so does everyone's. Each new season is a time of saying "hello" to new people, places, and experiences, and "goodbye" to others. The one and only thing that remains the same is God. Being in His presence is the "happiest place on earth," regardless of where I am.

**Lord, happiness may ebb and flow throughout the story of my life. Thank You that Your presence is**

a constant from beginning to end—and beyond.
—Vicki Kuyper

**Digging Deeper:** Psalms 16:11, 63:6–7; Ecclesiastes 3:1–8, 7:14; James 1:17

---

# Wednesday, November 5

**Jesus Christ is the same yesterday and today and forever. —Hebrews 13:8 (ESV)**

Not long ago, I underwent tests and brain studies for a book I was writing about my family's possible susceptibility to a heritable form of dementia, my mother's journey with the disease, and my own uncertain future.

Not everyone wants to know the future. If there is a ticking bomb concealed in my brain matter, do I want to know? Science now understands that the underlying pathologies of Alzheimer's are present decades before the disease manifests clinically.

Knowing is one thing. *Wanting* to know is quite another. Wanting to know is what makes us human, I think. Wanting to know the future, wanting to know love, wanting to know ourselves, wanting to know God. If I am to follow my mother and all her sisters into that miasma of Alzheimer's, do I want to know it?

The jury is still out on the fate of my brain, though there have been some troubling signs. I struggle from time to time with my memory and cognition, and though that could be the normal vagaries of aging, my neurologist notes in his last report that the diagnosis of Alzheimer's cannot yet be ruled out.

The other day I found myself staring at a bottle of cilantro that I intended to return to the spice cabinet but, instead, I had opened the dishwasher. What made me do such a thing? Was this the future?

*No,* I thought. Of what use would faith be if we knew our futures? Isn't trust in God how we accept the unknown? And the unknowable? The only certainty we are given is that God awaits us. That is all I need to know.

**Lord, help me to face the unknown with that knowledge that You are with me now and tomorrow and always.** —Edward Grinnan

**Digging Deeper:** Psalm 121:3–8; Philippians 4:6–7

# Thursday, November 6

**You light a lamp for me. The LORD, my God, lights up my darkness. —Psalm 18:28 (NLT)**

If you've ever seen a dog chasing its tail, you've probably wondered who (or what) could be in the dog's "mind." But sometimes the darkness of this world can so disorient us that we question whether we aren't moving in fruitless circles.

The miraculous certainty about walking with Christ is that even if sometimes we can't figuratively see him, causing progress to seemingly elude us, we know that we are ever moving forward because we know who's out front. Though darkness may appear to rule at times, one has only to recall whom they follow—whose voice whispers comfort in their ear—to know that a clear, straight path will emerge in time if they stay close behind the Savior. Paraphrasing my pastor's words, the default state of an area is always darkness, until light shows up.

Sadly, there will always be those who will choose to run around in the dark circles of this world, chasing their own belongings and refusing to pursue the Light. But as believers, no matter the circumstances, we delight in the fact that the Light with its inherent direction is eternally right in front of us.

In a world where one could be persuaded that darkness is winning, sending us into a downward spiral of despair, it is comforting to know that we are connected to Jesus even when He seems hidden and our vision becomes dimmed. What a promise that we all have access to a perfectly self-directed Savior! And like the sun, when He rises in us, darkness has no choice but to flee.

**Heavenly Father, when the world seems ensconced in darkness, help me remember that You have already sent the Light.** —Jacqueline F. Wheelock

**Digging Deeper:** John 1:3–4; Hebrews 12:13

# Friday, November 7

**O Lord, thou hast searched me, and known me.**
**—Psalm 139:1 (KJV)**

As a young teacher, I became friends with Susan, the art teacher across the hall. Susan was a tiny woman with a giant faith. She often shared with me her prayers for her three children.

Because my girls were still little then, I couldn't imagine my own daughters as teens and young adults, as Susan's children were.

By the time my girls grew up, Susan was gone. She died of cancer several years ago.

How often now have I thought back to the things Susan taught me about parenting! I'm grateful for the stories she shared about how she trusted the Lord with her young adults and how she prayed that she'd buried His Word deep inside their bones.

Recently, I looked up Susan's daughter, Rebekah, on social media and told her how fervently her mother had prayed for her and her brothers. I saw on Rebekah's page that another friend of Susan's had shared how, on her birthday each year, she read Psalm 139 because Susan had modeled that for her. Rebekah was old enough now to understand her mother's impact on those around her, and she thanked me for reaching out.

Today, as I pray for my now-grown children, I'm also praying for Susan's three, because that's what Susan would be doing if she were here. And I'm thanking the Lord for blessing me with Susan long before I knew how blessed I truly was.

Father, thank You for Susan, who modeled godly parenting for me before I knew how much I needed her wisdom. Please bless my own children and hers as well. —Ginger Rue

**Digging Deeper:** Psalm 119:9; Proverbs 1:5

---

# Saturday, November 8

... one's nationality or race or education or social position is unimportant; such things mean nothing. Whether a person has Christ is what matters, and he is equally available to all. —Colossians 3:11 (TLB)

"Where were you, Dad?" my son asked.

"I was in high school."

"No, Dad. Where were you on the issue?"

We were driving to visit my mom in Alabama. Johnny was asking me about growing up there during the time of racial desegregation.

I told him that as a young boy, I noticed there were separate water fountains and restrooms. Even as a child that seemed wrong to me. I asked my mom about it and she said that all people are God's children—equal in His sight and equal in His love.

I explained to Johnny that I was in high school when desegregation came. Everyone's emotions were running high. It was change, and the change brought resistance. I also shared that after our school was integrated and we got to know each other, emotions melted into friendships for many.

I also said that, after years of living and working in foreign countries, my life has been so enriched and my world enlarged through encounters and friendships with people from many nationalities, races, backgrounds, experiences, and perspectives different from my own.

That conversation with my son caused me to realize that many people in my life who I treasure are there because we both looked past our differences to embrace the best that we have in each other.

**Dear God, help each of us take the necessary steps to rise above any barriers that separate us from the love and grace You shower upon us through a kaleidoscope of people!** —John Dilworth

**Digging Deeper:** Matthew 22:37–40; Romans 8:39; 1 Corinthians 12:12

---

# Sunday, November 9

**And they, continuing daily with one accord in the temple, and breaking bread from house to house, did eat their meat with gladness and singleness of heart. —Acts 2:46 (KJV)**

I've just seen a survey that says I live in the county that ranks number two nationwide for "where Americans are happiest." Scoring considers personal finances and the vaguely defined qualities of "well-being and quality of life." Do I qualify? I live on a modest budget, drive an old sedan, stay pretty close to home, and count up a host of nothing-much-special days. Happy? I'm not sure, but last week I told someone that I felt more contentment than ever before.

This might be why: Every Sunday, our church service ends with a line from *The Book of Common Prayer* that asks God to "grant us strength and courage to love and serve" Him "with *gladness and singleness of heart*." In the past year, I've claimed this request for *gladness*, a King James noun that doesn't even get its own dictionary definition. To me it bespeaks a deeper, richer emotion than happiness.

In Acts 2:46, "gladness and singleness of heart" refers to believers tending their daily routines, even eating home-cooked meals. My trusty prayer book drops it into the "sending forth" prayer that challenges us to go "into the world in peace," until we gather again to ask the Lord's blessing. *Gladness and singleness of heart.* It undergirds the contentment I recently identified as it helps me stay focused on the ordinary tasks at hand.

**Lord, I thank You for the lines of Scripture that inspire my prayers and, in turn, direct and define my days.** —Evelyn Bence

**Digging Deeper:** Psalms 100, 119:105, 169–176

---

# Monday, November 10

**And the light shineth in the darkness . . .**
**—John 1:5 (KJV)**

It sounds like a Bible story, except that it happened near an isolated Montana cabin. Women friends gather there for a retreat. Night falls as an unrelenting rain beats down.

Then, a catastrophe. One of the women suffers a diabetic crisis. An ambulance is called.

But wait, the cabin is on a narrow unlit road, beyond an unmarked bridge.

So, my friend Marie Ann reacts in a way that to her is natural. She lights a lantern and steps into the darkness. Through the rain, she makes her way to the bridge. She holds the lantern high to direct the ambulance. A crisis is averted.

I write to Marie Ann, a *Walking in Grace* reader, and ask if I can share her story. She emphasizes that she is the "least medical person she knows," so, to her way of thinking, it was obvious that she should hold the lantern.

You might think I'm fixated on this story because the Bible often refers to a lamp as God's Word. But, no, like Marie Ann, I just want to be the one who holds the lantern.

All in all, I'm a pretty average person, with no shining skills, and so I guess I'm a likely choice to be a lantern holder.

I imagine the lantern tucked away, maybe in our messy garage. I pull it out and trim the wick. I make sure matches are nearby. It's a metaphor, I know. But in my mind, I want to be ready for the time when God calls me out into the storm to help another.

**Father, let me be Your lantern when
Your time is right.** —Pam Kidd

**Digging Deeper:** John 8:12; Ephesians 5:8

---

# Veterans Day, Tuesday, November 11

**...God is making new life, not a day goes by without
his unfolding grace.** —2 Corinthians 4:16 (MSG)

This past October, I met U.S. Army veteran and friend
Perry Baltimore III on the Appalachian Trail in the
nearby Hudson Highlands.

I've known Perry since our first Army duty
station. He served as a field artillery officer for
twenty-seven years and recently retired after
twenty-five years as founding CEO and president
of the Marshall Legacy Institute, furnishing mine-
clearing dogs to war-ravaged nations around the
globe. In celebration of his retirement, Perry was
walking the Trail from his home state of West
Virginia to Maine.

After hiking an invigorating four miles on the
brisk afternoon, we linked up at the Appalachian
Market with Perry's United States Military
Academy class of 1970 classmate Dave Herring.
Veteran Dave had just driven ten hours from
Michigan to pay tribute to Perry's faithful, God-
guided decades of service.

A wet snow was falling as we convoyed up to
Fahnestock State Park Campground. After Perry and
Dave set up their micro-weight tents, we hovered

around the campsite table and shared a soggy Meal Ready to Eat (MRE) of beef jerky, hot cocoa, and chicken and noodles.

Then Dave asked me to take a photo. In recognition of Perry's being voted by class of 1970 members as the esteemed graduate for the year 2022, he presented Perry with an inscribed coin of excellence.

Never mind the snow falling and no fanfare or applause of crowds. I was eyewitness to a power-packed moment, rich in significance. And I was grateful to applaud, by my presence and attention, the God-honoring calling of my dear friend.

**Eternal God, give us sensitivity to celebrate the grace of Your presence in Your children. Bless all our Armed Forces veterans this day. Amen.** —Ken Sampson

**Digging Deeper:** Psalm 46; Romans 2:10; 1 Thessalonians 5:12–13

---

# Wednesday, November 12

**Have I not commanded you? Be strong and courageous. Do not be afraid; do not be discouraged, for the Lord your God will be with you wherever you go. —Joshua 1:9 (NIV)**

While I work with a lot of loving and caring folks, I'm not always sure what their faith practices are, and as a result, I am often shy about sharing my beliefs about the Lord.

One day, a colleague, Symara, shared with a small team of colleagues that she had received some unforeseen medical news that obviously distressed her. Many people in our group messaged her that they "wished" her the best or offered her "good thoughts."

Without knowing whether my colleague was a believer, I told Symara that I would pray for her and would ask my church's prayer group to add her to our list of folks in need of prayer. I alerted her that they would only have her first name and wouldn't need to know any of the circumstances. They would only know that she was in need of prayer.

Symara immediately sent me a note of thanks and told me how touched she was that I would pray and ask others to do the same on her behalf.

Some days later, in a larger meeting, Symara quietly told the group that she was grateful for what I had done for her. Following the meeting, when another person asked me for the back story on her gratitude, I told them that I offered to pray for her and added her to my church's prayer list. The person, who didn't know I was a believer, seemed surprised. And just like that, without making a big pronouncement, I shared my belief.

**Lord, I am thrilled to give all the glory to You for Your provision and for my courage.**
**—Gayle T. Williams**

**Digging Deeper:** Matthew 14:27;
1 Corinthians 16:13

# Thursday, November 13

**Come to me, all you who are weary and burdened, and I will give you rest. —Matthew 11:28 (NIV)**

I had pushed myself to the limit. I had written seven books in twelve months, and I had just released the fourth book that year—with my dream publisher. I should have been ecstatic. But I was feeling overwhelmed and exhausted. And then, I had a panic attack.

Ten years ago, I had dealt with panic attacks and overcome them. Or so I thought.

As one panic attack turned into numerous over the course of a few days, I was devastated. The thing I had conquered suddenly felt like it was conquering me. Depression, hopelessness, and fear were constant companions. I had worked so hard to be at the top of the mountain, but I suddenly found myself in the valley once again.

The most debilitating thing about panic attacks is the belief that they are harmful and destructive—and the fear that they will happen again. So, I started to change my perspective. I started to see them as helpful warning signals, telling me that I had pushed myself too far.

As soon as I saw the negative emotions as helpful and not harmful, I was able to move beyond the fear and take a good look at what I needed to change. I had been pouring myself out for months without taking time to refill. So, I decided to start doing the things I loved again. I journaled, read my favorite books, and watched old movies. As I did, God helped me to find the peace and joy I had lost.

**Lord, remind me to see negative emotions as warning signals and direct me back to the peace and joy that only You provide.** —Gabrielle Meyer

**Digging Deeper:** Psalms 61:1–2, 139; Isaiah 40:31; 2 Timothy 1:7

---

## Friday, November 14

**The Lord kills, the Lord gives life. Some he causes to be poor and others to be rich. He cuts one down and lifts another up. —1 Samuel 2:6–7 (TLB)**

In one four-day period, my youngest son, Andrew, started six months of chemotherapy, my friend Barbara died, I attended my stepson Joseph's funeral, and I flew to New York to visit my dear friend Brenda, who was suffering with cancer and exhaustion from chemo.

Life was heavy that week. But in my desperate attempt to be more positive, I listed things coming up. I would be visiting Andrew and my daughter Jeanne and their families for the Christmas holidays, Andrew's birthday in late December, New Year's Day, and an additional week in January. Then I was leaving with my brother and sister-in-law on a trip to Australia and New Zealand.

As I prepared for the coming weeks, I started thinking about Jesus's short thirty-three-year life.

I wondered if he had ups and downs. I'm sure he looked forward to meeting people and performing miracles. But I bet he dreaded the long, sandy, thirsty walks in between all the towns in the Holy Land. I'm sure he was looking forward to the Last Supper, but dreading the Crucifixion. Good times and bad times all seem to have a place in our lives.

Now when I have a sad week, I tell myself to plan an event with friends or family: dinner out, a card game, a movie, or a tour of an interesting attraction like the Beatles museum, the glass-blowing place, Gatorland, or the murals in St. Pete. I learned that planning and doing cure discouragement and whining.

**Father, push me toward the light of hope, where joy lives.** —Patricia Lorenz

**Digging Deeper:** Genesis 40:6–15; 1 Samuel 1:18; Ecclesiastes 3:1–8

# Saturday, November 15

**Therefore do not worry about tomorrow, for tomorrow will worry about itself. Each day has enough trouble of its own.** —Matthew 6:34 (NIV)

I grabbed another handful of photographs and flipped through the series of disjointed images. Graduation party. Christmas morning. Family reunion.

I looked at my watch—it was later than I had thought. My mom and I had been sorting family photos all afternoon. But I still had to grocery shop and do laundry for the upcoming week. While I had enjoyed this rare time alone with my mom, I felt distracted by those undone chores.

I resumed sorting photos by date until I reached a landscape shot—a picture of a lake.

"When was this taken?" I asked. I'd been estimating photo dates by looking at hairstyles, heights, and clothing trends. But this photo had no human subjects.

"No idea," my mom said. "You can toss it." She gestured to a pile of photos—pictures of landscapes and wildlife. None contained people.

"I feel bad throwing these away," I said. "Somebody must have taken them for a reason."

"I'm sure they did," she said. "But, over time, it becomes clear what's really important."

I watched her sort photos of family and friends. Curating memories of people.

And, suddenly, I understood the flaw in my perspective. All day I had been distracted by my undone chores—things I wouldn't remember even a week from now. Instead, I should have been focusing on my time with my mom.

So I laid the landscape photo with the others that no longer mattered. And I resolved to focus on what was truly important.

**Spirit, help me to distinguish between what matters and what does not. —Logan Eliasen**

**Digging Deeper:** Philippians 4:8; Colossians 3:2

# Sunday, November 16

**Why, you do not even know what will happen tomorrow. What is your life? You are a mist that appears for a little while and then vanishes.**
**—James 4:14 (NIV)**

My husband, Brian, and I had been planning this night literally for years. Finally, we were getting ready to go see the Broadway show *Hamilton*. Every show was sold out when I realized I had made a gross miscalculation.

"We don't get to go?" the kids asked. They knew every word on the soundtrack, but I hadn't counted on them wanting to see the actual musical! The tickets were already purchased. So we kissed them goodnight and headed to the evening show.

As I watched, I couldn't help but think, *James would love this,* or *Olivia would flip!* Only Beau, five, seemed to understand that three hours in silence might be a tall order.

I prayed, "Dear Lord, help me remember next time not to let a chance pass." The next morning, I checked the ticket website. That's when I saw it: three second-row tickets for the show that afternoon. "Don't miss it," I heard a Voice inside my head whisper.

So, I did it. For three hours, my eldest two kids and I sat mesmerized as the tale of our founding fathers unfurled in front of them.

That day, I felt the moment of peace when you know you've made the right decision. It's not often I get that, but that day I was glad I listened to the

Voice, even if it did mean my house was filled with duels for weeks after.

**God, thank You for second chances to experience the beauty of Your world. Help me to listen to the nudges You send.** —Ashley Kappel

**Digging Deeper:** Lamentations 3:21–23; Colossians 3:17

---

# Monday, November 17

**And the Word was made flesh, and dwelt among us.** —John 1:14 (KJV)

The last silent movie from Hollywood came out in 1935, thankfully, but you would never know that if you watch YouTube. I find a lot of helpful car repair videos online, but there is one type that infuriates me: the silent YouTube, created by the amateur mechanic.

As I watch one of these muted videos, I am instantly lost. "What is he spraying on that brake bolt? Is that cleaner, or oil, or sealer? The wrong liquid could be fatal. How tight is he torquing that bolt? If it comes loose, it could cause a wreck."

I can hear the mechanic breathing as he films his work, so why doesn't he just explain these things? I'll bet he doesn't watch the Super Bowl with the sound turned off.

These wordless videos have helped me to appreciate the effort God made to communicate with us humans using both images and words. He

457

sent His Son to Earth so that we could see Him, but He also gave us a Book that contains 783,137 words in the King James Version, explaining His will in meticulous detail.

To me, life seems less like a video and more like one long conversation, where the right word can be worth a thousand pictures.

**Lord, give me the words I need to repair the broken people around me.** —Daniel Schantz

**Digging Deeper:** Proverbs 10:20–21; John 1:15–18

---

# Tuesday, November 18

**In your unfailing love you will lead the people you have redeemed. —Exodus 15:13 (NIV)**

I once worked with at-risk youth in a middle school. Jonny was one of these kids. He was the leader of a gang, although he still attended classes occasionally.

One day, Jonny angrily stormed into my room and sat in a corner far from everyone. I walked toward him, unsure what to say. Suddenly, Jonny whispered, "I don't know how to read or write." He looked up at me with tears in his eyes. "Please don't tell anyone," he pleaded. "I won't," I said. My heart broke for Jonny. Gang life made him appear strong, but an inability to read and write had left him feeling humiliated and powerless.

We spoke after class. With his permission, I talked with his favorite teacher, Ms. Jenny, who agreed to tutor him after school. Since I was already mentoring students at the housing project where Jonny lived, I continued helping him.

Jonny made progress despite some detours and U-turns. One day, I told Jonny that admitting he couldn't read or write took more courage than all the drive-by shootings he had been involved in. Looking into his eyes, I saw that he understood. Not everyone can stand in front of another human being in total vulnerability as he had done.

A year later, Ms. Jenny told me that Jonny was in therapy and that he had transferred schools so that he could get more specialized tutoring, which, fortunately, also helped him avoid his ex-gang.

Jonny had kept his truth hidden in the dark for a long time. But once he exposed it to the light, his life turned around for the better.

**Lord Jesus, pour out Your Spirit on us. Amen.**
—Adam Ruiz

**Digging Deeper:** Deuteronomy 31:6; Matthew 14:27; 1 Corinthians 16:13

---

# Wednesday, November 19

**As we have therefore opportunity, let us do good. —Galatians 6:10 (KJV)**

Boarding the plane, I was focused on my phone, trying to fire off as many work emails as I could before being seated.

Up ahead, there was a lady on one of those scooters built for people who were unable to walk long distances. Nearing the entrance to the plane, the flight attendant took the scooter to check it. The lady was OK to walk but was limping badly. My phone buzzed and I began typing out a response to yet another business email. I felt a gentle nudge behind me as an older man politely said, "Excuse me," and began walking past me heading toward the front of the line. He got only as far as the hobbling woman. "Can I help you carry your bag or anything?" he asked.

I felt a sudden twinge of shame.

A young man in front of me turned around and looked at me with a sheepish smile. "I should have asked her that."

Before I could respond, the man in front of him said, "I was closer, I should've asked." Embarrassed, I looked at the man who offered to help after he walked past the three of us. He was smiling, obviously pleased that he was able to help another in need. My embarrassment turned to admiration for the man who acted.

Suddenly, all those messages on my phone didn't seem as important as a lost opportunity to help another. I remembered Jesus's reminder in Matthew that when we reach out a helpful hand, we are reaching out to Him.

I put my phone in my pocket. I didn't want to miss the next chance He offered me to do something good.

**Father, keep me focused on life beyond my phone.**
—Brock Kidd

**Digging Deeper:** Isaiah 58:10; Matthew 25:40

---

# Thursday, November 20

**Encourage each other. —2 Corinthians 13:11 (NLT)**

I clicked Enter. The advertisement for the Boxes of Blessings posted to Facebook. *Lord, please have the people who You've chosen sign up.* It was a week before Thanksgiving and I was heading up our church's food box giveaway.

My church had gathered together to create an experience of sharing God's love to our community. Aside from a turkey feast in each box, there would be a Bible, handwritten notes of encouragement with scriptures, and a community resource sheet. On pickup day, there would be a prayer box where they could drop prayer requests, and folks from the congregation would be there to pray for them if they wanted. The youth group kids would even carry the boxes out to their cars. *Lord, send those whom You want us to reach.*

Each call touched my heart. I received one from a grown daughter calling for her mom, who lived in a low-income apartment. The apartment would be having a potluck in their community room for Thanksgiving. Her mom didn't have anything to bring, but now she did. When I hung up, I wept. A woman who had nothing was going to share it all.

And I wasn't prepared for the text I received after the giveaway: "I just wanted to thank you all for the handwritten letters you put in your Thanksgiving Box. You all had me in tears. I didn't realize how much I needed to hear those things."

**Lord, it amazes me how when we prayerfully reach out with Your love that Your love comes back to encourage us. Thank You. Amen.** —Rebecca Ondov

**Digging Deeper:** Romans 1:12; Colossians 2:1–3

---

# Friday, November 21

**Behold, how good and how pleasant it is for brethren to dwell together in unity! —Psalm 133:1 (NKJV)**

We drove up to the enormous house on the edge of a lake for our annual artists' retreat with Creator's Haven, a nonprofit that gives women artists the space and encouragement to create.

I left my bags in the car and ran inside to find the other women for a collision of hugs and a collective scream.

"This place is amazing!" I shouted.

I bounced around the house with childlike excitement, inspecting the various areas. I gasped at the spacious kitchen, where pairs of us would alternate cooking; the living room with comfy couches, where we'd share our works in progress; and the pool and river deck, where I'd spotted the perfect place to write and paint.

That evening, after a spectacular homemade meal, we sat together in the living room, spontaneously singing and howling with laughter. We hadn't even had a full day with each other and I already felt inspired and renewed.

"To think, I'd almost missed out on all of this," I said to our newest member, sharing how I'd declined my first invitation due to financial difficulties at the time. "If not for the scholarship offered through donations to the organization, I would have never known how much I needed this in my life."

"God knew what you needed," she said, "and He made a way."

**I praise You, Lord, because You know me more than I know myself!** —Karen Valentin

**Digging Deeper:** Matthew 6:8; Ephesians 2:10

## Saturday, November 22

**You, Lord, give true peace to those who depend on you, because they trust you. So, trust the Lord always, because he is our Rock forever. —Isaiah 26:34 (NCV)**

I get a kick out of recalling the hilarious moments in my children's lives.

One that I remind them about often happened at a popular fast-food restaurant. Like most mothers, I taught my children about stranger danger. I wouldn't say they were fearful, but they were definitely cautious. One afternoon, I packed up my three little ones for a lunch outing. After ordering, I settled my then seven- and five-year-olds at a table and hurried away to change the baby's diaper. My heart dropped when I returned and didn't see my children. Until I spotted them crouched under the table. One of the workers approached me, apologetic yet amused. When she'd come to the table to deliver our food, my children screamed and ducked under the table.

Simply put, my children didn't trust people they didn't know.

Now that they're teenagers, I've used the laughable moment several times to remind them about their relationship with God when they are questioning circumstances in their lives. They know Him. He's not a stranger. His intentions for them are good and pure, and He will never lead them into danger. His Word says that God is our friend, protector, and shelter. He—above anyone and everyone else—can be trusted.

**God, I want to know You more every day. You're no stranger to my desires. You know me so deeply that You've numbered the hairs on my head. I trust that You know what's best and that Your plans are to prosper me and give me a future.** —Tia McCollors

**Digging Deeper:** Joshua 1:9; Psalms 20:7, 118:8; Romans 15:13; Hebrews 13:5

**The way of the righteous is like the first gleam of dawn, which shines ever brighter until the full light of day. —Proverbs 4:18 (NLT)**

"How long have you lived here?" I asked Mary, a white-haired woman, who sat huddled in a corner at an event where I was speaking in southern Arizona.

"My husband and I moved here in 1983." She stared over my shoulder to a past I could not see. "I never wanted to leave the Midwest, but he was determined to come."

"I'm from the Midwest too. We came over thirty years ago, but I still miss all the vibrant green."

"I am still waiting to find beauty in the desert," she replied, gloom and doom dripping from her words.

"It took me awhile to see past all the brown too," I said, adopting my best Arizona tourism voice. "The saguaros blooming in the spring. The baby quail." I ticked off a few of my favorites. "And how about the incredible desert sunsets?"

I was determined to reach this hunched-over woman. She admitted her husband had died twelve years ago. "Why didn't you leave?" I asked, as I dropped the hype and spoke with simple kindness.

"I couldn't leave my church. And my friends are here."

"So, you found beauty in the desert after all."

Light as bright as any desert sun dawned in her eyes, as Mary let me take her arm and lead her to a table where her beautiful friends were waiting.

**When I become stuck, dear Jesus, rehearsing the sad lines of the past, help me see how You are leading me into a light-filled future.** —Lynne Hartke

**Digging Deeper:** Psalms 37:18, 97:11

---

## Monday, November 24

## SEEMINGLY INSIGNIFICANT:
### Thirst-Sating Faith
**The woman said to Him, "Sir, give me this water, that I may not thirst, nor come here to draw." —John 4:15 (NKJV)**

Every morning, I scrutinize photographs accompanying *New York Times* stories, hoping to understand the people they're about. I open each in a new tab and enlarge it further to examine tiniest details.

Today, I've homed in on a large, ancient-looking clay jug among the plastic clutter on somebody's roof in Jordan. *What's this?* I text, with a pic, to a friend who oversees a Jordanian archeological dig. *Water jug*, he responds. *Just like the Byzantine ones we dig up.* Water's scarce there, and such jugs, with a cup on a string, are set out for thirsty passersby everywhere. They haven't changed in millennia.

That heavy clay jug, then, is what the Samaritan woman has at Jacob's Well—just thirteen miles from my friend's dig—during her midday conversation with Jesus. From my first days as a believer, her story in John 4 has drawn me. Alone in a remote-seeming place, with a stranger whose culture she disapproves of, she sounds so feisty. When he offers living water, she sasses, "You have nothing to draw with, and the well is deep" (John 4:11, NKJV). That jug, she thinks, is her power. Moments later, though—in her excitement to tell others about this man who intuited her own thirst and sated it—she leaves it behind.

That's the thirst-sating faith I want. So powerful that I leave behind all the power I think I have to tell others about it. So powerful that people run after me to drink it for themselves.

**Grow my faith, Jesus!** —Patty Kirk

**Digging Deeper:** John 4

---

# Tuesday, November 25

**Give thanks in all circumstances, for this is the will of God in Christ Jesus for you.**
**—1 Thessalonians 5:18 (NRSVUE)**

Two days before Thanksgiving, I was chewing an oatmeal cookie and pondering all the good things I'd be eating very soon—pumpkin pie, stuffing, cranberries—when I felt something hard in my mouth. I twirled my tongue around and then spit it out. Part of a tooth, a back molar, and the chipped ancient crown.

*How will my dentist be able to see me at such short notice?* I thought. I called his office. Told my sad story to his assistant. "Can you come in at eight o'clock tomorrow morning?" she asked.

"No problem."

I figured I'd be out of commission all week, my cheek numb, possibly an emergency trip for a tooth extraction or root canal.

The atmosphere in the office was calm, the staff warm as ever. After a shot of Novocaine and some probing, my dentist announced, "You'll need a new crown." He put in a temporary, and we scheduled an appointment for the following week, as I hummed the old hymn, "Crown Him with Many Crowns."

Thanksgiving wouldn't be ruined after all. I could feast to my heart's delight, chewing a bit more on one side than the other. And I was only too glad to tell the other guests what I was thankful for this year. "I chipped a tooth and I've got a temporary crown." My listeners didn't think that sounded so good. "No, no," I insisted. "It's great. The crown chose just the right moment to break. Think of how bad it would have been if it had happened today."

Paul was right: there's always cause to give thanks.

**I will never tire from giving thanks to You, Lord.**
—Rick Hamlin

**Digging Deeper:** Psalm 107:1;
Colossians 3:15

**Forgetting the past and looking forward to what lies ahead, I press on to reach the end of the race and receive the heavenly prize for which God, through Christ Jesus, is calling us.**
**—Philippians 3:13–14 (NLT)**

My phone buzzes. I don't want to look. I know who it will be—my son, asking me if I'm ready to work out.

"Ugh," I say.

My wife laughs. "Just go."

I call him. "We doing it?"

Same reply as always. "Every day."

I meet him in our garage gym. The evening ritual. He pushes me and, as usual, somewhere in the suffering I actually start to enjoy it. I especially enjoy spending time with my grown and married son. And I love the fact he still wants to hang out with me.

They say life is a marathon. There are highs and lows. There are storms and sunny days. But the road stretches out before us, never wavering. Sometimes our legs get tired—at least mine do.

A particularly steep hill looms and I look over at my lifelong Running Companion. "Are we doing this?"

He says the same thing he always does. "Every day."

And, so, we do. And somewhere along the way I begin to enjoy it. Not the climb, maybe, but the company is perfect.

Well, my phone just buzzed, guess I gotta go. After all, it's abs day. I sure don't want to miss that one . . . Ugh.

**Dear God, thank You that we don't run this race alone. That You are lockstep with us every mile. And that You are the prize at the finish line. I will press on.** —Buck Storm

**Digging Deeper:** Psalm 127:3–5; 1 Timothy 4:8

---

# Thanksgiving, Thursday, November 27

**Enter his gates with thanksgiving and his courts with praise; give thanks to him and praise his name. —Psalm 100:4 (NIV)**

For the last twenty years of their lives, my parents spent Thanksgiving with us. It was a special time for Mom and me. As a young adult, we didn't always have the strongest of relationships. That changed over the years as we worked together preparing a huge meal for Thanksgiving. Mom and Dad would arrive from the other side of the mountains early Wednesday morning and the fun would begin as we traded stories along with our traditional recipes handed down from one generation to the next.

As we worked together, we laughed and cried and formed a bond that had escaped me in my youth. Those twenty years of cooking with Mom were some of my best memories I have with my mother.

Thanksgivings didn't seem the same after Mom passed. I missed her something fierce. The hole in my heart felt huge. The Wednesday before Thanksgiving, the first year after Mom passed, I sorted through the recipes I'd compiled with little enthusiasm. The front door opened, and I heard voices in the foyer. It was my two daughters, Jody and Adele. Knowing how much I missed Mom, they came to help and said it was time I passed on the family recipes to them. As we worked together creating new memories for the first time, I felt my mother's presence more than her absence. She was right there with us. And so it continues to this day, one generation to the next, sharing recipes, making memories, building bonds of love.

**Father, my heart is full of thanksgiving for those precious years You gave me with my mother and even more so for the time I've had with my daughters.** —Debbie Macomber

**Digging Deeper:** Psalms 26:7, 42:4

---

# Friday, November 28

**Our law does not judge people without first giving them a hearing to find out what they are doing, does it? —John 7:51 (NRSVUE)**

Recently, I received this prayer request from a local church about Sarah, a teacher on mission in Africa. "Please pray for the government to pay Sarah her salary or she will have to let her household cleaning and cooking staff go." I stopped abruptly. With all the problems in this world, they want me to pray that someone won't have to clean and cook for herself?

After rolling my eyes, I resumed reading. "Sarah's household staff depends on her income to feed and house their own impoverished families."

I learned that it is possible to blush with embarrassment even when alone in the room. While I lived my comfortable life, not only did Sarah have the courage to go on mission and use her teaching skills to help disadvantaged kids, she was also employing and supporting village families. Sarah ought to be rolling her eyes at me!

I realized that my quick judgment was born of guilt. Before college, I'd wanted to join the Peace Corps, but my parents were terrified when I merely mentioned this idea. I quickly—maybe too quickly—decided it wasn't worth upsetting them. In surrendering so easily, I gave up the chance to do God's work in a vigorous, meaningful way. But now He was offering me a chance to pray for someone doing that work, to join in the work in a different way. I wouldn't give that up.

**Lord, it's hard to pray—or help—when guilt makes me cynical. Keep my eyes and heart open and fixed on You.** —Marci Alborghetti

**Digging Deeper:** Matthew 7:1–5, 7–8; Luke 22:24–27; Romans 1:8–9

**I keep my eyes always on the L**ORD**. With him at my right hand, I will not be shaken. —Psalm 16:8 (NIV)**

For almost twenty years now, on the Saturday after Thanksgiving, our local churches have their holiday sales featuring local craftspeople, hobbyists, and artisans.

My mom, sister, niece, and I go from one church sale to the next doing early Christmas shopping.

I always look forward to the work of a retired fireman who whittles old wooden thread spools into Santas. I have a growing collection of his treasures from every year he's been there.

Today, as I approached my whittling friend, I noticed that he had a new addition to his offerings, an odd-shaped, abstract cross. I picked it up.

"It's a comfort cross," he said. "Go on, grasp it."

The cross fit perfectly in my hand. I rubbed the buttery smooth wood with my thumb.

"I tried a dozen designs and altered the one I liked best. This one's wife-approved and God-approved." He smiled. "You hold it when you pray. Reminds you you're not alone."

I bought four—one to keep and three to give as gifts. Later, in the car, I noticed the man had delicately wood-burned his initials and a heart into the handle. I clasped the wooden cross in my hand, and just like he said, I felt closer to God—and all the people who make this holiday season filled with love and blessings.

Lord, as we approach the busy days ahead of holiday gatherings and shopping, slow me down and help me feel the comfort of Your love and the love of those around me. —Sabra Ciancanelli

**Digging Deeper:** Psalm 145:18–19; Romans 15:13

---

## First Sunday of Advent, Sunday, November 30

## FILLED WITH HOLY ANTICIPATION: God's Great Gift of Love
**The true light, which enlightens everyone, was coming into the world. —John 1:9 (NRSVUE)**

The little two-lane country road in front our house looks like a highway today. It's crowded with cars, SUVs, and pickup trucks heading west and then returning to the east. It's the first day that Jay's Christmas Tree Farm is open.

It's a pleasant day, and on days like this, I enjoy taking my utility cart out to the road to pick up decorative rocks from the recently harvested field next door. Today, I'll work close to the road so I can see the cars and the people in them. They are driving slow as they look for the tree farm half a mile farther west. Many of them wave. There are lots of smiling faces. They're anticipating finding that perfect tree for this perfect season. In about thirty minutes to an hour, they'll be coming back past with a freshly cut tree tied to the roof or in the bed of the truck. Most of them will still be smiling, full of hot chocolate served by David Jay and his family. And still full of anticipation too.

Seeing them warms my heart. While many of the people with their trees aren't thinking about Advent, I am. In the darkness of these days, both metaphoric and real, I need anticipation for that which is good and pure and life-giving. For Advent. For the Everlasting Love of God. For the Light that is to come into this world.

**Great Lover of our Souls, grant me a feeling of holy anticipation this Advent season. Keep my heart centered on Your great gift of love, whose coming into the world we celebrate.** —J. Brent Bill

**Digging Deeper:** Isaiah 9:6–7

### WITH AN EVERLASTING LOVE

1 _____

2 _____

3 _____

4 _____

5 _____

6 _____

7 _____

8 _____

9 _____

10 _____

11 _____

12 _____

13 _____

14 _____

15 _____

16 _____

17 _____

18 _____

19 _____

20 _____

21 _____

22 _____

23 _____

24 _____

25 _____

26 _____

27 _____

28 _____

29 _____

30 _____

# December

For great is your steadfast love toward me . . .

—Psalm 86:13 (ESV)

# Monday, December 1

**But you, Lord, are a compassionate and gracious God, slow to anger, abounding in love and faithfulness. —Psalm 86:15 (NIV)**

Despite her worsening dementia, Mom wanted to stay in her four-bedroom house. After ten years of helping her long-distance, I was tired and discouraged.

Every month I drove 508 miles from Indiana to Virginia. I found Mom's bills piled on her bed and paid them. I taught and retaught her to operate her thermostat. I shared the frozen meat she'd bought from a salesman at the door with her friends and neighbors. I arranged for Meals on Wheels. I paid a caregiver to be there evenings and weekends, then all day.

Mom used to say, "When I don't know where I am, move me near you." But whenever I brought that up, she resisted. We toured assisted living facilities near her, including one where her church friends lived, but each time she balked at making a deposit. She'd end the discussion with, "I like my house."

As I prayed about it, I felt a nudge to put myself in Mom's place. *If you couldn't recall what happened an hour ago,* God seemed to say, *how could you imagine a different home?* I toured the new assisted living facility three miles from my house. I picked out an apartment and made a refundable deposit.

Mom spent Thanksgiving with us, and the next day I showed her the apartment. I asked if she'd like to live there. She looked around and nodded. "I'll try it for the winter."

A few days later, Mom said, "I like living near you."

**Thank You, Lord, for moving me to see my loved one with Your grace and compassion.** —Leanne Jackson

**Digging Deeper:** 1 Corinthians 13:12; Ephesians 6:2

---

## Tuesday, December 2

**Honour and majesty are before him: strength and beauty are in his sanctuary. —Psalm 96:6 (KJV)**

Children from several denominations and some who don't attend anywhere come to Joy Club, our church's weekly after-school program. I teach third graders, and I've learned that Christmas traditions vary greatly. Some churches don't allow seasonal decorations, while my congregation goes all out. Green garlands and sprigs of holly decorate the kneeling rail. The Advent Wreath is splendid with its purple, pink, and white candles. Brilliant red poinsettias adorn the altar. But last year, I thought the handmade gold and white ornaments looked frayed and old—not surprising since I'd helped make them fifty years earlier. Thinking that far back made me feel frayed and old too.

During the last Joy Club session before Christmas, I took my class to the church sanctuary for prayer time. I hadn't planned to plug in the tree lights, but since the light was dim I did. The response was shocking. Talking stopped. Mouths dropped open. The kids began gently touching the ornaments—the Lamb, Rose, Latin cross, Crown of Thorns—and listening while I explained the meaning of each Christian symbol. "This is the most beautiful thing I've ever seen," one girl said, her eyes shining.

I thought the ornaments had lost their luster. But viewed through the eyes of children, they were just as magnificent as when they were new. "It *is* beautiful," I replied. And when we prayed, I thanked God for providing the much-needed touch of awe and beauty for the children and also for me.

**Thank You, Awesome God, for unexpected moments of beauty that touch our souls.**
—Penney Schwab

**Digging Deeper:** Psalm 29:1–2; Isaiah 61:2–3; John 1:14

---

# Wednesday, December 3

**Indeed, you will be judged by the very standards to which you hold other people. —Matthew 7:2 (VOICE)**

I was busy selling shoes at a pop-up sale, while my sister was busy shopping. Since I couldn't leave my Chanel, Gucci, Valentino, Manolo, and Jimmy Choos, I asked Cindy to find a new lipstick for me in the makeup section. Something not too bold, not too bright, and not too dark, with just a hint of warm, natural color. She returned with the perfect hue.

Delighted with her find, I checked the name on the tube, so I could purchase the same color in the future: Uptight. I was immediately offended. *Just because I don't want to look garish, goth, or like I'm trying to act thirty years younger than my age, doesn't mean I'm uptight! How dare this company judge me that way. They don't even know me!*

Immediately, God's Spirit shined a spotlight on the hypocrisy of my own thoughts. How many times—every day—had I mentally judged others without knowing them? I made assumptions about people according to their sex, their age, their appearance, how they spoke, and even by how much they spent on the shoes it was my job to sell them. I may have never spoken my judgments aloud, but they were there, coloring the way I viewed those around me. I was not only uptight, but judgy. Once again, God taught me that He can use anything, even lipstick, to temper my heart with much-needed grace.

**Father, help me see each person around me with eyes filtered by Your love and grace, instead of judgment and comparison.** —Vicki Kuyper

**Digging Deeper:** Isaiah 11:1–5; Luke 6:37–38; John 7:24; Romans 2:1; Galatians 6:4

---

# Thursday, December 4

God, teach me lessons for living so I can stay the course. . . . Guide me down the road . . . —Psalm 119:33–34 (MSG)

Portsmouth Naval Shipyard, on the eastern New Hampshire/Maine border, is a compact warren of four- to five-story industrial buildings, alleyways, docks, cranes, and congested, winding streets. I was thankful to navigate to building H-23, the shipyard's Helmsman Inn, while on a final Guideposts military liaison trip.

"Any recommendations for a good restaurant?" I asked the inn's counter officer, Jeanne, after I received my room key. "Robert's Maine Grill, on Route 1 heading north" was the pleasant agent's reply. She then gave tricky verbal directions. Sensing my confusion, Jeanne took another approach.

"Just follow the railroad tracks to Gate 1. Then, you'll be right on Highway 1 heading north." With a map and blue felt-tip pen, Jeanne hash-marked tracks on roads leading to the gate.

With hesitation, I followed the route. The steel rails under the tires of my 2013 Chrysler 200 made for erratic steering as I navigated the misaligned pavement. I can still feel the uneven grooves.

The tracks sandwiched between the Relief Valve Recreation Center and historic Peace Treaty Room, then made a right at the credit union. Just ahead, down the quarter-mile incline, was Gate 1.

Though the road wasn't pretty, following Jeanne's railroad markings made the difference. I enjoyed my seafood dinner of clam chowder with fish and chips while overlooking the wetlands of the Kittery, Maine, coast. And, reflecting on eight-and-a-half years of exceptionally satisfying Guideposts military liaison service, I was grateful.

**Ever-faithful God, when our way seems erratic and muddled, grace us with assurance that You guide us through. Channel our actions this day, that the protection of Your goodness may guard our way. Amen.** —Ken Sampson

**Digging Deeper:** Deuteronomy 31:6; Psalm 16:11; Isaiah 49:8–12

---

# Friday, December 5

**Who teaches us more than the beasts of the earth, and makes us wiser than the birds of heaven?** —Job 35:11 (NKJV)

It pleases me no end that my dog considers me a great cook. She is interested in everything I make and always sits by my side when I eat. She has a look that says, "I bet that tastes *really* good." Then she stares, mesmerized, through my last bite. If perchance a bit of food drops from my plate, she is on it like a starved jackal.

Usually, I put a bowl on the floor by where I sit at the table and fill it with bits of chicken or string cheese so that Gracie feels as if she is sharing in my meal.

Several times a week, I boil eggs so she can have "teatime" after our daily hike. "Do you want your egg?" I'll ask. She knows that word like she knows her own name.

I also poach free-range chicken breasts in organic chicken broth, bits of which I add to her prescription dog food throughout the week. I find amazing satisfaction in watching her eat, though never for long, because the food is gone in the blink of an eye punctuated by a demure eructation.

I know what you're thinking: this man is crazy. Maybe I am. But if it wasn't for me, Gracie wouldn't eat. Being able to take care of her in that most fundamental way, to nourish her, is one of the great blessings of my life. The first thing I do every morning is take care of another living being, one I love very much. It is how God trains me to care.

**Lord, You gave us dominion over the animals. But You have also given them dominion over our hearts.** —Edward Grinnan

**Digging Deeper:** Genesis 1:21; Job 12:7–10

---

# Saturday, December 6

**As a mother comforts her child, so I will comfort you; you shall be comforted in Jerusalem.** —Isaiah 66:13 (NRSVUE)

"Don't wake the baby."

This phrase is printed on a lovely piece of music our choir is singing.

If you had just wandered into the rehearsal and looked at that xeroxed sheet you might have asked yourself, "What's this about waking a baby?" It's not like we were rehearsing next to the nursery. And there wouldn't be any kid in there at this hour. Not at 7:30 at night.

If you've ever sung in a choir, or played in a band, or took piano lessons as a kid, you became familiar with the usual directives in music, often about volume: double or triple "f's" for "fortissimo," very loud; double "p's" for "pianissimo," very soft; and then "mf" and "mp" for "mezzo-forte" and "mezzo-piano," a little louder or a little softer. Other times the terms are about tempo or expressiveness: "andante," "allegro," "adagio." But "Don't wake the baby"? I'd never seen that on a piece of music.

Except here, in this choir, with Christmas coming up, we knew what it meant. Our director has used that phrase before, not just about volume but about tone and mood. Perhaps if the word were capitalized—Baby. Yes, that Baby. The Christ Child.

Not for nothing are some of our favorite carols like lullabies. You want to lean into them and sway: "Silent Night," "Away in a Manger," "O Little Town of Bethlehem." Don't wake the baby. Good advice for life. Singing and living so that the babe in the manger can sleep undisturbed, knowing that all is well.

**I come to You, Lord, full of confidence and trust, like an innocent baby in his mother's arms.**
—Rick Hamlin

---

## Second Sunday of Advent, Sunday, December 7

## FILLED WITH HOLY ANTICIPATION: The Light of Christ

**The people who walked in darkness have seen a great light; those who dwelt in a land of deep darkness, on them has light shone. —Isaiah 9:2 (ESV)**

The Christmas tree is up. Though every year Nancy says we'll get a smaller one next year, we never do. So, another eight-and-a-half-foot tree is situated in the middle of the two-and-a-half-story picture window in the great room.

We're already talking about tomorrow, when various ladders and step stools will come out and decorating will commence. The lights will be tested and ready to wind around the tree. Popcorn and cranberries will be strung tonight. And various ornaments, all with some special history, will come out of storage.

We know it'll be a full day tomorrow. But we're looking forward to it. Most of all, we're anticipating the moment at dusk when the house lights are shut off, the tree lights are plugged in, and the darkness of the room is filled with their glow. What joy! We need joyous light.

In this same way, we anticipate the coming of the Light of Christ into the world. The tree and various lit garlands are just symbols, though very real, of that which we hope for. Great love is poised to come into this world. Yes, obviously Christ has come—centuries ago. But at this season we celebrate love born anew, fresh in the form of the babe in Bethlehem who filled the stable, and thence the world, with holy Light.

**Oh Light of our souls and this world, we need You in this darkness. Both these literally dark days and the metaphorical ones that surround us. Bless us with Your illumination—and anticipation of even more light. Amen.**
—J. Brent Bill

**Digging Deeper:** Isaiah 60

---

# Monday, December 8

**A generous person will prosper; whoever refreshes others will be refreshed. —Proverbs 11:25 (NIV)**

My friend Susann had a benign tumor on her liver. It was large and painful but operable. For weeks I had texted and called, peppering her with questions. When was the surgery scheduled? How long would recovery take? Would she travel for the robotic surgery she'd told me about?

During one of my check-in calls, she mentioned her disappointment over being sick during Christmas. She loved decorating her home during the holidays, and this year she didn't have the mental or physical energy to spread holiday cheer around her home, even with the help of her husband and young son.

Then came the moment I'd been waiting for—my opportunity to do something to help. She asked if I could help decorate her Christmas tree. Thrilled to finally have a tangible way to help, I responded with an enthusiastic "yes," and made plans to visit the following weekend.

When my husband and I arrived, Susann's home was warm, visually and physically. Her husband had lit a comfy fire in the gas fireplace and had purchased a lovely full tree that stood tall in the corner of the family room. Pushing through intermittent abdominal pain, Susann provided verbal directions, decorating her tree with the use of my hands. She shared stories behind the ornaments I placed on the tree—where she'd purchased special ornaments and which family member or friend had gifted her with others. Afterward, she was pleased with her fully decorated tree, and I was grateful to have found a way to help my friend through a challenging Christmas holiday.

**Lord, may we seek to be Your hands and feet, helping others when they are most in need.** —Carla Hendricks

**Digging Deeper:** Philippians 2:1–8; 1 Thessalonians 5:11

---

# Tuesday, December 9

**For where your treasure is, there will your heart be also.** —Luke 12:34 (KJV)

From Ebenezer Scrooge to his namesake, Scrooge McDuck, our literature is peppered with fictional misers. But misers are very real. The Bible refers to the concept as a "sore evil," and history's long list of wealth hoarders interchanges "miser" with "misery."

As a financial consultant, I've never had to deal with a true miser, for the simple reason that it would be unlikely for a miser to trust anyone with their hoarded riches.

But I have learned something important about wealth in general, and I've found the Bible to be on the money when it comes to its advice. From withholding corn (Proverbs 11:26) to ignoring the needs of others (1 John 3:17), unhappiness seems to be the bottom line.

Not unlike the Bible, one of the great advantages of the investment business is the window it offers to contentment. I see it every day in the people I serve. There are those who are desperate to hold on to all their money. No matter how much their portfolio grows, they never seem content. Then, there are those who are always ready to let go and give. These tend to be my happiest clients.

In the Charles Dickens story *A Christmas Carol,* the reader is treated to a moment of great satisfaction when old Ebenezer discovers the wild joy of giving. Or as the Bible puts it, he discovers that "It is more blessed to give than to receive" (Acts 20:35).

Today, I consider the misers with sadness. And then, I smile, remembering with a happy heart what I've learned in my business: "God loveth a cheerful giver" (2 Corinthians 9:7).

**Father, I want to be one of the givers who makes Your world a happier place.** —Brock Kidd

**Digging Deeper:** Ecclesiastes 5:13; Luke 6:38

---

# Wednesday, December 10

**Remember not the former things, nor consider the things of old. Behold, I am doing a new thing. —Isaiah 43:18–19 (ESV)**

Our farmhouse was built in 1908. Optimists would call it old-world charm. Realists would look at it and see constant repair and update.

I'm a do-it-yourselfer. When the time came to extend a gas line, I figured I was up to the task. I surveyed the job and made a list of parts I would need.

*Hardware store trip one . . .* Feeling good. I go down my list. I'm an old pro, so I pick up a few extra parts. I ditch my diet and grab a candy bar at the checkout to celebrate.

*Trip two . . .* Feeling less than good. Forgot parts. Regretting the candy bar. Thumb throbbing from smashing it with channel locks.

*Trip three . . .* Did you know that an old ½-inch gas line can be a completely different size than a new ½-inch gas line? I do now. I also know my next couple of days will be spent creating the whole gas run from scratch. I mentally add up the cost of my again-full cart and give the candy bar rack a dirty look.

They say that men plan and God laughs. I must give heaven a lot of joy. But I think God relates as He works on the old house that is my life. New parts never fit with the old. There's a whole lot of tearing out and starting from scratch. He seems to have a much better attitude about rebuilding than I do. He is infinitely patient and never smashes His thumb.

As for me, I see the back steps are peeling. You know, a candy bar sounds kind of good.

**I'm so glad You are God and I'm not. Thank You for Your patience.** —Buck Storm

**Digging Deeper:** Ephesians 2:10; Philippians 2:13

---

# Thursday, December 11

**For I, the LORD, love justice; I hate robbery and wrongdoing.** —Isaiah 61:8 (NIV)

Nancy Drew came into my life when I was eight years old, and nothing was quite the same again. My mother gave me two of the yellow-spined books for Christmas, and soon after unwrapping them, I was curled up in the corner of the sofa, with a candy cane in one hand and *The Secret of Red Gate Farm* in the other. I quickly lost myself in the adventures of the titian-haired girl detective and her two bosom chums, Bess and George.

I have loved mystery novels ever since.

A bookstore manager in my hometown once told me that along with children's books, mysteries and thrillers are the holiday season's biggest sellers. This didn't surprise me. After all, at Christmas many of us contemplate peace on earth. It makes sense that we want to read about justice-seeking sleuths relentlessly pursuing villains who shatter society's *shalom*—peace. If nothing else, well-written mystery novels reinforce our moral education. I think most of us long for truth and justice and "rightness" in our stories and in real life.

In his book *Not the Way It's Supposed to Be*, author Cornelius Plantinga writes that "at some level of our being, we know that goodness is as plausible and original as God, and that in the history of the human race, goodness is older than sin." Maybe that's why cold winter evenings still find me curled up in the corner of the sofa reading a mystery novel, hoping that the Lord's justice and goodness will prevail.

**Dear Lord, help me to strive to live up to Your standards of righteousness in all that I do.**
—Shirley Raye Redmond

**Digging Deeper:** Hosea 12:6; Amos 5:24; Micah 6:8

---

# Friday, December 12

**A new command I give you: Love one another.**
—**John 13:34** (NIV)

For many years, my sister, Lydia, and I would have regular conversations about God, Scripture, and faith. Her love for God was strong, fervent, and unwavering. She was a witness to me of a life lived with joy, gratitude, and faith.

In time, her health began to decline. Our final conversations were filled with both appreciation and sadness. "I love you, Adam," she would say to me as death approached. "I love you," I would respond. "Adam, why could we never say this before? Mother or Father never said that to me. Why was it so hard?" I would always respond the same way. "We're saying it now. It doesn't take away the pain of not hearing it as children, but we're saying it."

I wanted to affirm the pain she felt from the words not spoken to her and yet offer her hope. "You did with your children what Mother and Father couldn't do with us. And now they're expressing love to their own children. Maybe that's the lesson: we're not bound by the limitations of one generation."

The last time I spoke with Lydia, she was very weak. When her husband passed the phone to her, I simply said, "I love you" and she replied very weakly, "I love you too."

She died a few days later, surrounded by her family.

To this day, I hope that when she entered God's presence, our parents were also waiting. And as they beheld Lydia and rushed toward her, I'm sure the first words they said to her were, "Oh, Lydia. We love you so much!" And somehow, I believe all things were made well in that moment.

**O Lord, how happy we are that we can call You Abba, Father. Amen.** —Adam Ruiz

**Digging Deeper:** Exodus 15:13; Isaiah 54:10; Matthew 12:18

---

# Saturday, December 13

**So shall my word be that goeth forth out of my mouth: it shall not return unto me void . . . —Isaiah 55:11 (KJV)**

We donned bathrobes, created rope belts, and used sticks as canes. My friend and I, both second graders at the time, were presenting a play about the Wise Men for my Aunt Becky. We stood in the hall outside her open bedroom door, amateur thespians acting with all our hearts.

Aunt Becky lay there listening from her hospital bed in the spare room. Only twenty-seven years old, her brain cancer had returned, and my mother, a nurse by profession, was lovingly caring for her dying sister-in-law.

Young as I was, it didn't occur to me that Aunt Becky's advancing illness might inhibit her ability to appreciate our grand hallway productions. She was mostly quiet, yet sometimes would speak a phrase or two in her last months on earth.

Once I heard her recite the passage, "He leadeth me beside the still waters," from Psalm 23. Another time, "Blessed are the poor in spirit," from the Sermon on the Mount. Clearly, verses memorized in healthier times were surfacing despite the inroads of cancer within her brain.

Aunt Becky passed away fifty years ago, but the memory of her quoting Scripture remains printed indelibly upon my mind, challenging me to memorize the Word of God.

**Lord, help us to learn Scripture by heart consistently and faithfully. Thank You that Your words never pass away.** —Lisa Livezey

**Digging Deeper:** Joshua 1:8; Psalms 37:31, 63:6, 119:97; Luke 2:19

---

# Third Sunday of Advent, Sunday, December 14

## FILLED WITH HOLY ANTICIPATION: Divine Source of Hope

**Now faith is the assurance of things hoped for, the conviction of things not seen. —Hebrews 11:1 (ESV)**

The littles, as I call them, are here at the farm. They are enjoying the big Christmas tree and all their GiGi's (as they call my wife, Nancy) decorations. And the decorations are plentiful. Lighted garlands draping down from the loft and over windows and doors. Crèches from around the world abound.

They're busy chattering among themselves about what presents they'll get and the things they're looking forward to. What do we hope for, long for this Advent season? I wonder about that as I sit in my chair by the fire and feel the kids' anticipation and excitement. Their feelings are palpable, unlike mine, which, like the Christmas presents appearing under the tree, are wrapped tight.

Still, my faith is one of hope. And the carol in my heart is "Come, Thou Long Expected Jesus": "Come, Thou long expected Jesus / Born to set Thy people free; / From our fears and sins release us, / Let us find our rest in Thee."*

I feel that longing deep in my soul. So I join in with their youthful enthusiasm. I find myself sitting on the floor by the tree as they bring me the little Christmas rocking horses that reside there. Or point out a bird in the limbs of the tree. And I make up some fanciful thing that I want for Christmas—a purple unicorn. Kaley, who loves unicorns, laughs and calls me silly. No more silly than what I do long for: "Joy of every longing heart."

**Divine source of all our hope, remind me during this season that my faith in You is one of hope in that which is eternally true and loving. Amen.**
—J. Brent Bill

**Digging Deeper:** Psalm 25

---

*"Come, Thou Long Expected Jesus," written by Charles Wesley, composed by R. H. Prichard, and arranged by Tom Howard, 2009.

# Monday, December 15

**For where your treasure is, there your heart will be also. —Matthew 6:21 (NIV)**

"Excuse me, I think you're in my seat," a middle-aged woman said as she held out her boarding pass to the man sitting across the aisle from me. She and her husband had been assigned seats 12 B and C, but the man sitting there had also been assigned 12 C for Flight 527 from Chicago O'Hare to Newark Liberty International Airport.

A flight attendant intervened. Since the seated man was traveling alone, he was upgraded to first class for free. Those of us around him whooped. What a blessing!

He stood and started to take his carry-on from the overhead compartment. "I'm not sure if there's room up there for your bag," said the flight attendant. "You may need to leave it here."

As the man made his way up the aisle, a guy in front of me quipped: "You could decline the upgrade. If it were me, I'd want to stay with my stuff."

The flight attendant reassured the passenger. After all, the bag and the man were headed to the same destination. The man moved up to first class, but I couldn't let go of the comment. *How many blessings in life had I given up because stuff seemed more important? Would my attachment to the things of this world cause me to decline an extravagant offer?*

Once we were airborne, the flight attendant transferred the bag into first class. As I watched, I made a mental note to leave the details to God and embrace opportunities along life's journey, instead of my stuff.

**Dear Lord, help me to receive Your blessings with open arms while trusting You with anything I may need along life's way. Amen.** —Stephanie Thompson

**Digging Deeper:** Ecclesiastes 5:11; Isaiah 55:2; James 5:1–3

---

# Tuesday, December 16

**Ask and it will be given to you; seek and you will find; knock and the door will be opened to you. For everyone who asks receives; the one who seeks finds; and to the one who knocks, the door will be opened.** —Matthew 7:7–8 (NIV)

When my wife, Elba, and I lived in California, we met Pastor Ramon and his wife, Annie. We had an instant connection. They, too, shared the same Puerto Rican cultural heritage and faith experience as we did. Our families enjoyed meals, worship, and parties together. Before we returned to the East Coast, we said farewell but never imagined losing contact with them.

Several years later, I began searching for them on social media but without any success. The only thing I recalled was that they wanted to move back to Puerto Rico. I contacted a friend of mine—who is a pastor on the island—to get information about them. The effort was fruitless, yet I never gave up the hope of reconnecting with them.

While attending a Presbytery meeting in Naples, Florida, a pastor named Edwin—originally from Puerto Rico but now living in the USA—was the guest speaker. After his presentation, I shared my story. He offered to contact his colleagues. A few days later, he sent their contact information.

I called the number and left a voice message. The next day I received a call. After twenty-two years, we had finally found each other. Ramon and Annie, who now live in Florida, had also been searching for us. Our hearts were filled with exuberant joy.

It took a long time to reconnect with our friends, but it was worth the effort. Asking, seeking, and knocking on doors opened the way for God to answer our prayer.

**Lord, help us to not give up asking, seeking, and knocking even when it seems impossible.**
—Pablo Diaz

**Digging Deeper:** Deuteronomy 4:29; Luke 18:1

---

# Wednesday, December 17

**Do not let your hearts be troubled. You believe in God; believe also in me. —John 14:1 (NIV)**

The texted pictures from the hospital communicated more than the words that came with them about my dear friend Janis.

It was Christmastime, a traditionally joyous season in her extended family. Janis was known for hosting festive gatherings in the family's beautifully decorated home. But this year was different. For decades, Janis tried to chase cancer out of her body. This year she was tired, and the picture showed her family gathered around her hospital bed.

A week before Christmas, I got a picture of Janis in her hospital bed with both arms raised straight toward heaven. The simple message: "Our dear Janis passed away today." Oh, so close to Christmas. A friend who was at the hospital shared what she heard one of Janis's daughters say: "I'll never be able to celebrate Christmas the same way again." I felt sad too; Christmas seemed to be over too quickly. I decided to linger longer in the twelve days of Christmas, a time frame that marks the Magi's journey to see and celebrate Jesus's birth. It's a time Christians celebrate God's promises that Jesus came to fulfill.

I celebrated that He came to connect heaven to earth so Janis, in a holy moment, entered eternity to be with Jesus. I began seeing the timing as a gift to always remember how Jesus opened the gates of heaven where Janis's family will someday be together again.

The twelve days of Christmas always ends with a great celebration known as Epiphany on January 6. Shortly after Christmas, I got a message that Janis's service would be on January 6!

**Lord, comfort all those missing loved ones this Christmas. Thank You that Your comfort embraces both grief and joy.** —Carol Kuykendall

# Thursday, December 18

**For God gave us a spirit not of fear but of power
and love and self-control. —2 Timothy 1:7 (ESV)**

My daughter has a cat named Jimmy Hiss. My dad
(who lives next door) has a 110-pound Labradoodle
named Rufus.

To put it mildly, Rufus and Jimmy Hiss are not on
friendly terms. The scene had played out at least a
dozen times: Rufus spots Jimmy Hiss out of the corner
of his eye, Rufus darts after him, Jimmy Hiss goes up a
tree. We have found ourselves pulling out our ladder
to fetch our trembling cat time and time again.

Then one day, Jimmy Hiss didn't run. Instead, he
arched his back and clawed Rufus right in the nose
as he ran after him. The entire street could hear
Rufus's yelping as he ran back home.

Jimmy Hiss, on the other hand, followed him
down the street and found a comfortable spot right in
the middle of my dad's driveway. That is now where
Jimmy Hiss can be found resting on most days.

Don't worry—Rufus was fine. I'm sure his
Labradoodle pride was a bit injured to be beaten up
by a cat, but he had no long-term injuries.

But Jimmy Hiss? Well, he was more than fine.
Instead of turning and running when that giant
barking dog darted after him, Jimmy Hiss had

fought back. He had faced his giant. He had thrown his stones.

And you know what? That giant Labradoodle wasn't nearly as terrifying as he seemed. Sometimes those giants that seem so scary are actually just fluffy old Labradoodles, and by standing up to them, we are able to overcome our fears and move forward in strength.

**Lord, You made all of the creatures of this world and teach us such beautiful lessons through their presence in our lives. Thank You.** —Erin MacPherson

**Digging Deeper:** Psalms 55:22, 91:1–2

---

# Friday, December 19

**Then Jesus called the children over to him and said to the disciples, "Let the little children come to me! Never send them away! For the Kingdom of God belongs to men who have hearts as trusting as these little children's."** —Luke 18:16–17 (TLB)

When the teenager in our small congregation left for college, we had one baby and two attendees under thirty. We missed having kids! Without them, the church had no future, but we didn't know how to attract families with children.

Then a mother with two toddlers moved to town. Another baby was born. With prayer and guidance from a new pastor and his wife, we determined to make sure infants and children were welcome, including when they cry or misbehave. We invited people to worship. We held Sunday school each week, sometimes for one child. Children's Time became a part of every church service. A Christmas program with two participants was meaningful for all of us.

We are making progress. Last year, eight kids were in the Christmas program. A young piano student and his grandma sometimes play service preludes. Two ten-year-olds often light the altar candles, and children regularly do special worship music. We're planning to start a second Sunday school class.

We're still a congregation with mainly senior citizens. But we're also a church where children are learning to love Jesus and know they are valued members of the Body of Christ. When I see them kneel at the altar to pray or hear their voices ring out in song, I *know* their future, and ours, is safe in God's care.

**Jesus, friend of children, thank You for the privilege of helping children come to know You as Savior and Lord.** —Penney Schwab

**Digging Deeper:** Proverbs 22:6; Mark 9:36–37; Galatians 3:26

---

# Saturday, December 20

**Precious in the sight of the LORD is the death of his faithful servants. —Psalm 116:15 (NIV)**

We walked slowly in the cold December air through Arlington Cemetery. Paul, my grandfather-in-law, was being laid to rest with full military honors, which meant that we—his children, grandchildren, great-grandchildren, and friends—were called to walk behind the caisson.

The walk wasn't hard—about fifteen minutes of rolling hills through the seemingly infinite immaculate rows of headstones. But it was moving. While we had prepared for a somber stroll, we noticed that his children started to tell stories about Paul, bringing each other to tears and laughter, in turn.

Seeing them arm in arm, snuggled against the biting wind, reminded me how God calls us to bear one another's burdens. In this case, the burden we shared was the heavy goodbye to a beloved father, grandfather, and friend. But, as often happens, it turns out that as we shared the burden, it grew lighter. The laughter of memories and family lore returned. We remembered Paul as he lived—lovingly and with a steady hand.

That afternoon, as the family members took turns speaking at the memorial, it was clear that Paul's legacy as the family patriarch was being passed down to the living members, a mantle they took up with grace, if a bit tearfully.

How blessed we were, that day, to be reminded that a funeral on earth is but a homecoming to our eternal home in heaven above.

**Lord, thank You for days that remind me to lean on those I love so that I can remember to be strong for them when they need it. Bolster me,**

bolster them, and say hello to my favorite Marine when you see him. —Ashley Kappel

**Digging Deeper:** Matthew 5:4; John 11:25–26

---

# Fourth Sunday of Advent, Sunday, December 21

## FILLED WITH HOLY ANTICIPATION: Room in Our Hearts

**We know that the whole creation has been groaning as in the pains of childbirth right up to the present time. —Romans 8:22 (NIV)**

It's the calm before the storm. Literally and figuratively. As I write this, our part of Indiana is under a winter storm warning—six inches of snow, winds of forty miles per hour, and wind chill temps around minus twenty! I've been preparing. Getting the bird feeders filled. Fixing a place for the farm cats in the garage. Stocking up at the grocery.

As I do that, I wonder about the preparations that were being made in Bethlehem all those years ago. An influx of visitors was about to overwhelm the tiny town. And, as they prepared, did any one of them have any idea that something miraculous was about to happen? Oh, merchants were expecting good things, I suppose—sales of goods to the travelers. Families setting up a first-century Airbnb in hopes of extra shekels. Still, the only ones truly preparing for the miraculous were Mary and Joseph as they made the ninety-mile trek from Nazareth to Bethlehem.

As I think about that, I decide to pause and get ready. Physically, I prepare for the storm. Spiritually, I prepare for the coming of the Christ. In the same way I've stocked our kitchen pantry, I do things to feed my soul in readiness. I take time for quiet contemplation. I pick up a favorite Advent collection of readings. I put on familiar, soothing seasonal music.

I wait in silence. In warmth. And I prepare a place for the baby safe in my heart.

**God of Glory, still my soul and help me prepare room in my heart for You. Not just for Your coming into this world, but for all of my days. Amen.** —J. Brent Bill

**Digging Deeper:** Matthew 2:4–6

---

# Monday, December 22

**Rejoice with those who rejoice, weep with those who weep. —Romans 12:15 (ESV)**

On the way home from a doctor's appointment, my daughter, JoElla, surprised me by asking, "Why don't you like Christmas?" Stunned, I replied, "Who says I don't like Christmas?" She then described how I didn't seem to really enjoy the revelry of the season or get very excited.

Faced with the hard truth, my eyes welled. I explained to her that Christmas can be hard for some people who have lost loved ones. She understood I lost my daddy years before on December 22, and even after eighteen years, it still felt raw to me.

For several days after JoElla's Christmas question, I took a look back at my actions. Christmas had become associated with trauma and grief for me, and I never really noticed. Changes were in order. I started to focus on the joy of my childhood Christmases. I shared with JoElla and my son Jacques how my family would go to church on Christmas Eve and would celebrate Jesus's birthday after church. Every year, we had a pound cake topped with cream for His birthday and would make a wish for the coming year. I shared with my children how my daddy loved the music of the season. I noticed my heart shift when Jacques said, "Is that why we go to church on Christmas Eve?"

Indeed, my parents were the very reason I have Christmas traditions, a realization that brought me joy. This year, instead of focusing on loss, I delighted in rediscovered family traditions. Grief still exists in this season for me, but this Christmas, my heart held joy too.

**Father, be with me as I seek to rejoice in life with those whom I love.** —Jolynda Strandberg

**Digging Deeper:** Genesis 29:29–37; Nehemiah 1:4–11; 1 Corinthians 7:29–31

---

# Tuesday, December 23

**And she gave birth to her firstborn son and wrapped him in swaddling cloths and laid him in a manger, because there was no place for them in the inn.** —Luke 2:7 (ESV)

I hoisted my duffel bag onto the motel bed. This was not how I wanted to spend Christmas.

I had saved vacation time all year in anticipation of spending the holidays with my family. Then, days before Christmas, my dog, Sport, contracted kennel cough.

Sport was on the mend now. But the vet had warned he was still contagious, and I couldn't risk exposing my parents' new puppy. So I had booked a motel room near my parents' house. Sport and I would stay at the motel, and I would visit my family when able.

My phone rang. It was my mom.

"Did you get checked in?" she asked.

"Yes," I said. "I'm letting Sport acclimate to the room. I'll stop by in a bit."

"Is he doing OK?" she asked.

Sport wagged his tail, then gave a raspy cough.

"He's holding up," I said.

"Are you doing OK?" she asked.

I sighed. "Yes," I said. "But I wish this hadn't happened."

"It isn't an ideal Christmas," she said. "But it can still be a good one."

I thought of the first Christmas. For Mary and Joseph, it was anything but ideal. The couple was far from home. The inns were full. Surely Mary wished to lay her firstborn in a cradle rather than a feed trough. Yet infinite goodness came from that unconventional birth.

My mom was right. "If the first Christmas occurred in a barn, I suppose I can celebrate in a Super 8," I said.

**Jesus, help me to praise You in all circumstances.**
—Logan Eliasen

**Digging Deeper:** Isaiah 53:2–3; Matthew 8:20

---

# Christmas Eve, Wednesday, December 24

## FILLED WITH HOLY ANTICIPATION: Prayerful Watchfulness

**Now Joseph also went up from Galilee . . . in order to register along with Mary, who was betrothed to him, and was pregnant. —Luke 2:4–5 (NASB)**

"Christmas time is here," sing the Peanuts kids softly from our stereo. Well, it is almost. It used to be that Christmas Eve was a bustle of activity. A trip to town for the Christmas Eve service at the Quaker church. A cousin's family coming over for a big feast and merriment. But tonight, it's just my wife, Nancy, and me. This slower, quieter Christmas Eve suits us.

I do think of our grandchildren and back to past holidays with our kids, who by this time would be in a kind of frenzy about Christmas morning tomorrow. I remember my own anticipation as a youngster. What would I find under the tree? And at my grandparents' house? What special food would be prepared? I wanted to go to bed so that the next morning would arrive sooner but was too wired to sleep.

Not us, now. We're relaxed. Listening to music. We talk of Christmas Eves and Christmases past.

We look at the cards we've received and talk about the messages therein. We remember good times with the families who sent them. We recall the Bible stories of this season.

But tonight, in this prayerful watchfulness, we rest in the knowing what those two thousand years ago in Judea did not—this is the eve of the dear Savior's birth. Tomorrow, metaphorically at least, the world will be reborn. The Light and Love the world has been waiting for will arrive.

**This may not be a silent night outwardly, O Lord. But aid me in making it so in my heart. Help me to carry some stillness as I await the announcement of the Savior's birth. Amen.** —J. Brent Bill

**Digging Deeper:** 1 Samuel 3:1–10

---

# Christmas, Thursday, December 25

## FILLED WITH HOLY ANTICIPATION: Glad Tidings for All People

**But the angel said to her, "Do not be afraid, Mary; you have found favor with God. You will conceive and give birth to a son, and you are to call him Jesus." —Luke 1:30–31 (NIV)**

Christmas morning has dawned gray, cold, and with a blanket of snow covering the ground. I start the coffee and put Garrison Keillor's *Now It Is Christmas Again* CD in the player. I turn on the tree lights along with all the other garland and mantel lights as the sound of singing fills the room. "There are angels hovering round."

As I pour coffee and wait for my wife, Nancy, to wake, I feel the angels hovering. Those who have celebrated Christmas in this house for so many years. Those who have passed from this life to the life eternal, borne safely there thanks to the little baby whose birth two thousand years ago we celebrate. And perhaps the angels who proclaimed that holy birth. Perhaps, just perhaps, "still their heavenly music floats / O'er all the weary world."

I hear Nancy coming from the bedroom, and she smiles at the music and soft lighting on this gray morning. She pauses at one of her crèches. The baby is there. Come at last.

And the angels hover round. They've come, as the song says,

*To carry the tidings home,*
*To carry the tidings home,*
*To carry, carry the tidings home*

that God blesses us. Every one. Glad tiding of great joy, indeed!

May the miracle of Christ's birth bless your life with special joy this season—and always.

**While the herald angels may have departed, God, keep their message of glad tidings for all people resounding in the ears of my soul today—and always. Amen.** —J. Brent Bill

**Digging Deeper:** Luke 2:1–20

# Friday, December 26

**Bless them that curse you.** —Matthew 5:44 (KJV)

Returning from vacation, we found ourselves in a faraway airport.

My wife, Corinne, and I were exhausted, and the kids were even worse off. It was almost time to board for home when the announcement came: "Flight delayed." Then another hour, another delay.

*Frustration* was a vast understatement.

Standing in line with other exasperated people, I couldn't help but notice the rudeness of the lady at customer service. Passengers were looking for honest answers. She was brushing them away. When it was my turn, I put on my most "charming" face but the result was no better. She made me feel I was a meaningless bother.

My children, exhausted and hungry, had melted into a sort of constant whine. Corinne, usually calm, looked as though she was nearing the end of her rope. I had a sudden urge to yell . . . and then I remembered Mom's rose.

Grocery shopping, Mom had handed the clerk her check, which was somehow devoured by the moving checkout counter. The clerk then let out a long, angry string of words blaming Mom for the mishap.

Embarrassed and stunned, we were almost to the car with our groceries when my mom stopped, returned to the store, and picked a rose from the floral department. "This is for you," she said, as she paid, and handed the clerk the rose. In the car, she said, "We have no idea what that woman's suffered through." She never realized that the "Mom's Rose" story would stick with us for years.

That's why, at that very moment of frustration and impatience, I stood with my family, in front of the airport vending machine...picking out the perfect rose.

**Father, remind me to replace anger with forgiveness.** —Brock Kidd

**Digging Deeper:** Proverbs 19:11; Ephesians 4:32

---

# Saturday, December 27

**Therefore, as God's chosen people, holy and dearly loved, clothe yourselves with compassion, kindness, humility, gentleness and patience.** —Colossians 3:12 (NIV)

The goodness of the Lord can be found in the oddest places, if we just look.

When my elderly and infirm father's eyeglass frames broke, I visited a new eyeglass store to see if they might have frames to fit his lenses.

Tierre, one of the store's managers, looked at a few frames to see if they might fit. As she did, I told her that I had hoped to find something to help him resume his avid reading and puzzle-solving.

None of the first few frames fit, so I thanked her for trying and prepared to leave. Tierre then scoured each display case, seeking just the right frame. It seemed to me that this search was becoming futile, but Tierre kept looking. When she had examined every frame in the store, I again thanked her and made my way to the door.

Tierre then took the broken frame and went to her desk, using wire and tape to hold my dad's eyeglasses together. They didn't look great, but they worked! And my dad was so happy with this temporary fix until we were able to fully replace his glasses.

Later, I returned to the store with a note of thanks and a small gift for Tierre for all that she had done for a man she had never met. We exchanged phone numbers, and we now check in on each other from time to time. I am so very grateful to Tierre and her kind, God-loving heart.

**Dear Lord, I thank You for placing Your servants right in my path, helping me to clearly see Your grace and mercies every day.** —Gayle T. Williams

**Digging Deeper:** Job 10:12; 2 Corinthians 6:6

# Sunday, December 28

**I shall rejoice with all my heart when your lips speak right things. —Proverbs 23:16 (JPS)**

After my husband, Keith, died, I couldn't understand what I was still doing here. Indeed, my nun friend Mother Cat had told me that the nuns had prayed that Keith and I would die at the same time, because they could see how dependent we were on one another. *Clearly,* I thought, *that hadn't panned out.*

Of course, there were routine activities every day—feeding the animals, paying the bills, sweeping, laundry, and remembering to eat—the kind of things that felt mechanical, not meaningful. Torah study was a bright spot of meaning in the week, but it was only an hour, which left 167 hours still to live through. Sometimes I would take a moment in the morning to ask God, "Are You going to tell me today what You want me to do?"

One day, I was asked to teach some classes. Then one of the people for whom I act as spiritual director referred me to some acquaintances who were interested in spiritual direction. And fairly quickly after that, I was able to join a new networking group. When I discovered the Christians in the group wanted me to talk about Judaism, it occurred to me that I hadn't been paying attention. God had been telling me all along what I was still here for—to use my words aloud or on paper to try to make the world a better place. As Keith had often said to me, "Words are your life." I thought *he* was my life, but it turned out he was right.

**If I don't notice Your messages, please be patient with me. Oh, and God—maybe You could shake me a little harder when You see I've lost the plot.**
—Rhoda Blecker

**Digging Deeper:** Job 42:4; Isaiah 30:8

# Monday, December 29

**Have I not commanded you? Be strong and courageous. Do not be afraid; do not be discouraged, for the LORD your God will be with you wherever you go. —Joshua 1:9 (NIV)**

"Mami, you should ski this time," my son encouraged me on our trip. "I want you to have fun too!"

Long before I began taking my kids each winter, I'd already stopped skiing for years. New knee issues had overlapped old ones, so I was happy to let my kids ski with family while I sat in the lodge.

"Well," I said to my son, "my knee has felt good for a while. Maybe I'll try."

Riding the ski lift, my stomach was in knots. *What am I doing?* I thought. *I'm too old and broken for this!* My first attempt confirmed those thoughts. I was slow, scared, and worried about my knee.

"Go ahead," I'd told my boys. "Don't wait for me." They zoomed ahead as I'd done years before.

I was practically in tears as I crept down the hill. "I'll never know that feeling of flying over the snow again," I whined to myself. "That part of my life is over. I'm old and broken, just as I thought."

Since I'd already paid, I went back on the lift regardless. The second run was slow, but not as slow as the first. Again, and again, I went up the mountain, each run faster and more confident than the one before. For years I'd convinced myself of my limitations, without even trying. I was grateful I'd pushed through those thoughts, because when I did, I skied alongside my kids, racing down in complete exhilaration.

**Lord, help me to move beyond negative self-talk and discover my true potential.** —Karen Valentin

**Digging Deeper:** John 14:27; 2 Timothy 4:22

---

# Tuesday, December 30

*...he has blocked my ways with hewn stones, he has made my paths crooked.* —Lamentations 3:9 (RSV)

As I have noted in this space before, the Collins household celebrates the New Year with plumbing problems. OK, we've missed some years, but not many—somewhere between Thanksgiving and Epiphany, the water will stop flowing, the sink or tub will back up. This is followed by useless plunging, then useless chemicals, then the plumbing snake, which I have nicknamed Jake. (I'm sure Jake has a nickname for me, but let's move on.)

I have sent poor Jake on many missions; he resists mightily, refusing to bend around elbows or taking the wrong turns at every tee. After much twisting and cajoling, Jake finally finds the culprit and brings the clog to the surface for inspection.

What emerges is a disturbing mess full of things that shouldn't be there—bottle caps, plastic rings from milk jugs, paper clips. Once, I think I unearthed an old Chevy.

By coincidence, the end of the year also corresponds with my own obstructions:

relationships no longer flowing smoothly, overdue apologies blocked by pride. There is much to be cleared out—mostly my head, which is a disturbing mess full of things that shouldn't be there . . . but there's no Jake the Snake to help me. Instead, I have to rely on an ancient tee called a cross, where the most important work has already been done for me.

**Lord, let Your "judgment run down as waters, and righteousness as a mighty stream" (Amos 5:24, KJV). Help this sinful sailor to navigate the tricky currents that lay ahead in this and every year.**
—Mark Collins

**Digging Deeper:** Psalm 78:16; Micah 1:4

---

# New Year's Eve, Wednesday, December 31

**And let us run with perseverance the race marked out for us. —Hebrews 12:1 (NIV)**

A text chimed. "Wanna run three hundred miles with me next year?" my sister asked. It was almost New Year's. She was apparently in full-fledged resolution mode.

I'd loved running once, but that'd been years ago. I doubted I could run one mile anymore, let alone three hundred. "Yeah, right," I typed back. "Three hundred's *so* many!"

"Not all at once!" she replied. "We'd take all year! Just six-ish miles a week!!"

Six-ish sounded less scary, and I knew I needed to exercise more.

"OK, let's do it," I answered finally, with more confidence than I felt.

My January's total was only 25.14 miles—a daunting nothing compared to 300. But it *did* satisfy that six miles/week breakdown. Focusing on this smaller number helped keep me motivated.

As the weeks wore on, I started noticing that during my runs, with my body and the busy part of my mind distracted by exertion, the rest of my brain seemed to actually work better. Priorities felt clearer, and solutions to problems became more accessible. I also learned they provide an ideal opportunity for prayer. There's no other time that I feel more connected and able to listen for that still, small voice of God.

And then there was the lesson that small numbers, repeated over and over again, can really add up. On December 31, I finished, not my three-hundredth, but my four-hundredth mile of the year. Sometimes, it turns out, it's by focusing on the small goals that we're able to accomplish the biggest ones.

**Thank You, God, for showing me that it's often the small things in life that, taken together, become the big things.** —Erin Janoso

**Digging Deeper:** Proverbs 3:6; Matthew 25:21; Hebrews 11:6

# WITH AN EVERLASTING LOVE

1 _____

2 _____

3 _____

4 _____

5 _____

6 _____

7 _____

8 _____

9 _____

10 _____

11 _____

12 _____

13 _____

14 _____

15 _____

16 _____

17 _____

18 _____

19 _____

20 _____

21 _____

22 _____

23 _____

24 _____

25 _____

26 _____

27 _____

28 _____

29 _____

30 _____

31 _____

As with so many people in our country and around the world, this was a year of continuing recovery and renewal for **Marci Alborghetti** and her husband, Charlie Duffy. Even as they grieved for lost loved ones, including Marci's mother and a beloved former teacher, they continued to feel God's love and mercy as they prepared to move into a new apartment and welcomed a new pastor to their New London church. Marci notes, "The Lord has given us some valleys and mountaintops, and now we're hoping for some rest on His calm plains!"

**Evelyn Bence** of Arlington, Virginia, writes: "Two kinds of music brighten my days. As I pen this short bio, I tune my ear to the NPR classical station playing the last full-blast chords of 'The Organ Symphony,' by Camille Saint-Saëns. Then the sudden quiet is broken by songbirds making merry outside my screen door. I surprise myself—that a suburban girl has grown accustomed to a more urban life and its colorful characters, including children knocking at my door asking to borrow a stapler or maybe aluminum foil. I still organize a senior-lunch program at my small church—a true potluck, no alphabetical assignments. If there's no variety, we just laugh and enjoy, thankful for abundance."

God's everlasting love shines brighter than ever as **Erika Bentsen** continues her volunteer work with a rural ambulance service. "There are calls where all I'm doing is literally holding someone's hand to comfort them on a run to the hospital," she says. "Our crew has prayed for patients after particularly difficult runs." BlueDog remains her constant companion. "He gets so excited when we go out to feed or move water in the morning. As far as he's concerned, the earlier we go out the better. It's like he's fifteen going on three. I praise God for the love of dogs. Love flows both ways." She still manages to find time for illustrating. She welcomes readers to check out her latest projects at erikabentsen.com.

**J. Brent Bill** is a photographer, retreat leader, and Quaker minister. He's also the author of numerous books, including *Amity: Stories from the Heartland* and *Life Lessons from a Bad Quaker*.

Brent is a graduate of Wilmington College and the Earlham School of Religion. He is recognized as one of the most important communicators of the spirituality of the Quaker tradition today. He is a member of *Spirituality & Practice*'s "Living Spiritual Teachers Project."

He has been a local church pastor, a denominational executive, and a seminary faculty member. He lives on Ploughshares Farm, about forty acres of former Indiana farmland being converted into tallgrass prairie and native hardwood forests.

You can follow him on Facebook or through his website: brentbill.com

"So far, I've managed to avoid becoming a crazy cat lady," **Rhoda Blecker** says, "but somehow every morning is a mammal morning. The day starts with fresh water for the cat, then a visit to the backyard with the dog, during which I leave carrots for the wild bunnies. Once back inside, food and fresh water for the dog. Then out onto the deck to give the wild squirrel gang peanuts and black oil sunflower seeds, which I use to bribe them to stay away from the birdseed and suet. In so many ways, it's heartening to start the day surrounded by so much warm, furry life. I feel needed every morning, which lets me start the day in a very good mood."

**Sabra Ciancanelli** of Tivoli, New York, writes, "The very first devotion I ever wrote was about my son Solomon taking his first steps. We were in my mom's living room when the momentous event happened. Up to that point, Solomon teetered on the brink of taking his first step for weeks, edging forward, holding on to a table or couch but refusing to go beyond the point of letting go. On this day, he had taken off his shoes and held one in each hand, which must have given him the sense that he was holding on to something stable enough to hold him, and it did. Solomon walked across the room with ease. Amazingly, Solomon is on the verge of another major milestone—entering his senior year at college—just as my youngest, Henry, begins his senior year in high school, and I'm reminded of this important lesson of trust and letting go as we all embark on the next big steps of our future. Trust and letting go is an ongoing challenge for me, and yet I find myself, with the help of God, getting a little better at it, one step at a time."

"Good thing God's love is everlasting," muses **Mark Collins** of Pittsburgh, Pennsylvania, "because there are times when everything else feels about as solid as cotton candy. Last year, our household appliances went down one by one, apparently succumbing to some weird mechanical contagion...all except the decades-old clothes dryer. Despite years of neglect, it still works, still does its job, the flame still burns. There's probably a metaphor in there about paying attention to the things I rely on, but I'm too busy fixing the dishwasher." Mark shares the household appliances with his wife, Sandee, who is also still working and still patiently responding to Mark's question about where on God's green earth did he put the 10mm wrench. It was just here a minute ago...oh, right there. OK. Thanks.

"It's hard to believe this is my twentieth year as a *Walking in Grace* contributor," says **Pablo Diaz** of Naples, Florida. "I'm blessed and humbled to share with you my faith journey and life lessons over the years. Recently, one of the readers and mother of a family at our church was at worship and introduced herself to me. She was delighted to make a personal connection after so many years of reading my devotions. My heart filled with gratitude to be part of this wonderful family. Thank you all for your prayers and support. The interim ministry continues to be rewarding but soon will need to move on to another setting. My wife, Elba, is enjoying her retirement and loves volunteering at the hospital, thrifting, and Zuma. Yet the most precious family gift is the weekly talks with my elderly father—we are blessed to still have him in our lives."

"My wife, Pat, and I have been enjoying great times with family and friends," says **John Dilworth** of Massillon, Ohio. "After forty-five years, we attended a gathering in Arkansas of dear friends from the Azores—where Pat and I met, and we all worked. It is amazing how quickly, after so many years, we picked right up where we had left off. We also enjoyed reunions in Florida with each of our families. For Pat's family, it was the first time everyone was able to be together since our wedding day. We finally made it down to Washington, D.C., to see the cherry trees in bloom—something we had postponed way too long. While we were there, we enjoyed spending an afternoon at the Library of Congress. And on our way home to Ohio, we marked another item off our list by visiting the Flight 93 Memorial in Pennsylvania."

"This year, God has been teaching me about who He is," says **Logan Eliasen** of Des Moines, Iowa. "I'm learning that He is worthy of my praise regardless of my circumstances. The year has held seasons of joy, but also stretches of loss. What a blessing it is that the same God who is enthroned above walks with me even through the valleys."

"It seems that learning-curve life has been the norm for some time now," says **Shawnelle Eliasen** of LeClaire, Iowa. "I learned how to live without littles when my boys grew up. I learned how to leave a home I loved when we moved across the river. But this past year has brought the most change of all." Shawnelle's youngest son began public high school, ending Shawnelle's twenty-two-year home teaching journey. "I wanted to help people during troublesome times," she says. "So, I went to school to become a phlebotomist. It was an unlikely choice for someone who was afraid of blood, but I remembered how a calm presence benefitted my boys when they needed frequent draws because we lived in a century-old house." Shawnelle soon found that it was a tough skill set to master. "I pray over my patients, and I lean hard into the Lord for provision and courage every single day. I hope to gain confidence, but there is something so lovely about being completely dependent on God's sweet grace."

This past year has been one of great change for **Nicole Garcia** of Valrico, Florida. "Mourning has been part of my story, but so has a new dance of joy," says Nicole. "Grief has battled with my courage. I have had to let go of longtime relationships to move forward in a healthy way. Through it all, I remind myself daily that I am the daughter of a king. I honor my role as mother to my two boys, who are now thirteen and nine years old. We enjoy going to the beach, learning the piano, and making memories in the big and the small moments of each day. I am learning to let go of the pictures in my mind of what I thought I needed and letting God show me that He always meets my needs. I embrace this new year with His promise of resurrection to my broken places. My peace during turmoil is to stay ever present in His love and promises for me."

*Guideposts* Editor-in-Chief and Vice President of Strategic Content **Edward Grinnan**, of New York, New York, is currently enjoying the publication of his most recent book for Guideposts, *A Journey of Faith: A Mother's Alzheimer's, a Son's Love, and His Search for Answers.* His moving memoir explores the history of the disease in his own family, his mother's battle with dementia, and his own susceptibility to the disease and the possibility he might be experiencing early symptoms. "Millions of families are going through this battle. Alzheimer's is the number-one health fear of people over fifty, though cancer and heart disease kill more. It is the health issue of our time. Where I found inspiration and hope was in the power of faith and love to transcend even this devastating disease. Alzheimer's destroys the mind but not the soul."

He and Gracie, his golden retriever, are spending more time in the Berkshires of Western Massachusetts since the passing of his wife, Julee. "We're out on the trails every day. It's good for our souls and our bodies, though sometimes I have trouble keeping up!" Catch Edward's blogs and videos at guideposts.org and his meditative sleep stories on the Abide app.

**Rick Hamlin** and his wife, Carol, live in the same New York City apartment they bought almost forty years ago in upper Manhattan. "We might be in a busy, crowded city, but the calming presence of nature is never far away," says Rick. In the mornings, he runs in the park with its spectacular views of the Hudson River, not to mention the flowers in the heather garden. At the end of the day, he has a favorite spot to sing a prayer as he watches the sun sink behind the Palisades. He and Carol sing in their church choir, and on Saturdays he likes volunteering at the church's soup kitchen. "The guests feel like part of our worship community." Their younger son, Tim, is a newly ordained Episcopal priest, and their older son, Will, is a brainiac working for Pinterest. Husband, dad, writer, published author, but the role he's particularly proud of is grandparenting. "Just call me Gramps," he says.

 **Lynne Hartke** explores desert trails with her husband, Kevin, and rust-colored mutt, Mollie, in Chandler, Arizona, where they are on staff at a church and where Kevin is also the mayor. She anticipates additional adventures near the 100-year-old cabin they purchased in an old-growth forest in northern Arizona. A breast cancer survivor, Lynne was named a Voice of Hope with the American Cancer Society in 2018. Lynne is a speaker and author of *Under a Desert Sky: Redefining Hope, Beauty, and Faith in the Hardest Places*. The couple has four grown children and four grandchildren. Connect with her at lynnehartkeauthor.com.

"I keep expecting life to slow down," says **Carla Hendricks** of Franklin, Tennessee. "With the bookends of aging family members on one end and children that still need us on the other, life feels as busy as ever. Our adult sons continue to pursue their passions and dreams, as my husband, Anthony, and I advise and cheer them on. Our teen daughters continue to excel in high school and practice their driving skills, while I coordinate their extensive social calendars. Anthony reentered the corporate world after several years in nonprofit and church ministry. I continue to serve and advocate for foster youth through a nonprofit dedicated to family preservation. I spend downtime writing for local publications, completing a middle-grade novel I dream of publishing, and contributing to *Walking in Grace* each year. When I manage to carve out additional time, I'm reading an amazing book or watching Netflix or Disney + with the family."

"One of my blessings this past year was the publishing of my second book, *Do I Still Matter? The Secrets of Aging with Faith and Purpose.* This book is a Christian guide for living the potential of our older years. My prayer is th at it will be a reassurance for all in this stage of life."

**Kim Taylor Henry** of Elizabeth, Colorado, says. You can learn more at Kim's website, kimtaylorhenry.com, or send her an email at kim@kimtaylorhenry.com.

"With three adult children, their spouses, and now eight grandchildren, my husband and I were again incalculably gifted with nearly continuous times of family togetherness—celebrating; playing; cheering at their soccer, ice hockey, and lacrosse games and horse shows; talking; laughing; walking; hiking; family dinners; and so much more. God's everlasting love for us was abundantly demonstrated in His gift of our everlasting love for each other. For me, there is no greater joy on this earth than sharing life with my family. I am blessed indeed."

"Twenty years ago, I looked forward to the empty nest everyone talks about," says **Leanne Jackson** of Fishers, Indiana. "One daughter was in college; the other had graduated and moved away to her first job. I was also the primary caregiver for my mother and my aunt, who both had dementia and lived on opposite coasts. What empty nest? Now my aunt is in heaven and Mom lives in memory care near me. My husband, Dave, and I are grateful that his pancreatic cancer gives him calm hours or days between pain attacks. Who cares about an empty nest when our hearts are full of God's everlasting love?" Leanne invites you to visit her at leannejacksonwrites.com.

It's been a year of positive growth for **Erin Janoso**'s household. Daughter Aurora is in the fourth grade now, and continues to love school. She's excited she's finally started oboe lessons. She declared with certainty at three years old that this was the instrument she would play, and she's never wavered. Erin's husband, Jim, continues to travel to Alaska, Montana, and Antarctica for his microscopy business. Erin is also spending time on the University of Alaska Fairbanks campus this year. After a couple of decades off from college, Erin is taking some classes within UAF's Music Department. Her music theory and ear training courses are non-degree-seeking for now, but she's open to wherever that path might lead in the future. She also continues to play her trumpet and volunteer on behalf of music education in Fairbanks. She remains ever grateful for the opportunity to work hard at something that feels so personally meaningful.

 As her kids grow, **Ashley Kappel** finds the need to remind them daily that as much as she loves them (which is a lot!), God loves them even more. Ashley filled her year with parenting three (ages nine, eight, and five), volunteering with area schools, and working as a senior editorial director, as well as cheering on the kids at softball, baseball, T-ball, soccer, basketball, and whatever else they decide to try! The *Walking in Grace* theme for 2025, God's everlasting love, has been especially important to Ashley's family this year, as they lost their golden retriever mix, Colby, to cancer in October.

 **Jenny Lynn Keller** is an award-winning author who transforms her family's rowdy adventures into stories filled with hope, humor, and plenty of Southern charm. Follow their fun on her weekly blog at jennylynnkeller.com and on facebook.com/jennylynnkeller. Her beloved true animal stories appear in Callie Smith Grant's compilations *The Horse of My Dreams*, *The Dog Who Came to Christmas*, *The Cat in the Christmas Tree*, and *The Second-Chance Horses*.

"Earlier this year I asked my father, a retired minister of thirty-eight years, if he would be interested in doing a father/son Bible study," reports **Brock Kidd** from his hometown of Nashville, Tennessee. "Because of our busy schedules, we don't meet as often as we would like, but we both set timers on our phones to go off every morning at the same time. The message "Re-Center with Dad" pops up every morning at 10:30. It is a little thing, but has become a powerful reminder to give God a little more attention in my life, even in the middle of a crazy day." Brock is entering his thirtieth year in the wealth management business and loves family time with his wife, Corinne; sons, Harrison and David; and daughters, Mary Katherine and Ella Grace.

"It's always been difficult for me to get my head around the concept of grace," says **Pam Kidd** of Nashville, Tennessee. "Life doesn't usually give us things for free or shower us with things we don't deserve. But God's grace does. He gives freely. He expects nothing back. It's a truth we need to hold close. I consider my life. I did nothing to deserve my husband, David; my parents; my children. But everything I have can in some way be traced to simple grace. Sure, there's been confusion and heartbreak along the way, but when I look back, God's grace was always working, for good. I take my daily walk in the park. Everything's free here. The trees, the birdsong, the breeze. I think of my family. They are going in all different directions, making mistakes and fixing them, and they are learning along the way. I smile, knowing God's grace is always one step ahead."

After a year of agonizing indecision, **Patty Kirk** exchanged her job as an English professor for that of a staff accountant at her husband's CPA firm—way more money for just one day per week of entering information into QuickBooks—in order to spend more time on writing. She misses teaching and interacting with students but is excited about two novels and other writings she has in the works. Lulu and her longtime boyfriend, Seho, got married in a justice of the peace ceremony—which in Berkeley, California, where they live, was via Zoom. Charlotte and her husband, Reuben, bought a townhouse in Seattle. Both work remotely, but Charlotte's workplace is local, so she rides her scooter to the office for occasional meetings.

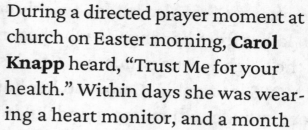

During a directed prayer moment at church on Easter morning, **Carol Knapp** heard, "Trust Me for your health." Within days she was wearing a heart monitor, and a month later had pacemaker surgery (which she calls her peacemaker)—overseen by her true Peacemaker—His faithfulness present in a miracle device. Carol and her husband, Terry, added to their twenty grands with the spring birth of their first great-grand—Ariana. They hope to meet her when family gathers in Florida for grandson Caleb's fall wedding. First, Terry's fourth spine surgery. Carol's train trip to California to visit her ninety-five-year-old Uncle Bob was a true gift. Her uncle—still playing golf—lost his sight only three months later. "His attitude remains vibrant and trusting in his Savior. He and Terry are my best models for the faithfulness of God, and faithfulness to God."

"The global pandemic is behind us, but I am still trying to climb out of some of my 'hermit hole' habits," **Carol Kuykendall** admits. "It's pretty easy to enjoy going to church in my jammies, sipping my coffee as I sit next to my husband, Lynn, at our kitchen counter with our dog at my feet. Zooming church is still tempting too often." Carol also leads a weekly small group of ten ladies from her church, who began Zooming at the height of the pandemic. Carol is still active in MOPS leadership. Carol and her husband live close enough to their ten grandchildren and their eight moms and dads, so they are making the most of their opportunities to celebrate birthdays and graduations and holidays because their numbers are dwindling. Three grandchildren are already off to college.

"You never know where a new year is going to take you," **Vicki Kuyper** writes, "and this one marked an end to watching my three granddaughters several days a week and began a season of selling shoes at a pop-up sale. You're never too old to learn something new! I still see Lula, Shea, and Taylor frequently, but now it's more for play-dates than 'babysitting,' which is a welcome change. Thankfully, this year's busy schedule still afforded me time for some wonderful adventures, including a trip to the Galapagos Islands, a photo safari in Zambia, and a couple of visits to California to spend time with my two grandsons, Xander and Oliver. As always, writing continues to fill the quiet moments of my life. As a new year begins, my mind is buzzing with curiosity over where God will lead me this year in terms of writing, travel, and spending time with those I love."

**Lisa Livezey** is a freelance writer and spiritual blogger who seeks to encourage those laboring in life's daily trenches. Her devotional writings reflect spiritual insights gathered like wildflowers along a winding path. Lisa has a degree in journalism, lives in the Philadelphia suburbs, is wife to David, a mother of five, a grandmother, a civic and church volunteer, and has served in educational capacities on local boards. She feels especially blessed to have helped her daughter raise a flock of sheep and to have cared for her parents and in-laws in their sunset years. Lisa seeks the Lord daily by attending church, praying, reading Scripture, and sitting contemplatively in beautiful chapels. She enjoys being active, especially when sailing the Chesapeake Bay, kayaking in Maine, and visiting her grandkids in Scotland. She publishes a weekly photo devotion at lisalivezey.com/olivetree and enjoys hearing from her readers.

Unlike some seniors, **Patricia Lorenz** says the older she gets, the older she *wants* to get. "This year I'm definitely hitting the geezer category, turning eighty in October. But I have my sights set on making it to at least 105." Patricia says if she's granted another twenty-five years, she hopes to continue writing, speaking, painting, working out in the pool, swimming at least two hours a day, playing cards with friends, meeting new friends, volunteering at the airport, and exploring parks, from tiny neighborhood parks to city, county, state, and national parks. But most of all, Patricia loves traveling to visit her four children and nine grands scattered all over the country. "Now that I'm single again, having outlived three husbands, I'm always on the lookout for an interesting travel companion, especially for overseas travel."

**Debbie Macomber** is a #1 *New York Times* bestselling author and one of today's most popular writers, with more than two hundred million copies of her books in print worldwide. In addition to fiction, Debbie has also published three bestselling cookbooks, an adult coloring book, numerous inspirational and nonfiction works, and two acclaimed children's books. Celebrated as "the official storyteller of Christmas," Debbie's annual Christmas books are beloved, and five have been crafted into original Hallmark Channel movies. She serves on the Guideposts National Advisory Cabinet, is a YFC National Ambassador, and is World Vision's international spokesperson for their Knit for Kids charity initiative. A devoted grandmother, Debbie and her husband, Wayne, live in Port Orchard, Washington, the town that inspired the Cedar Cove series.

**Erin MacPherson** is in the process of trading in her minivan for a still-not-very-cool sedan as she gets ready to launch her oldest son into college and her youngest into high school. She lives in Austin, Texas, where she spends her days watching soccer (both her kids' and Austin FC), reading books, and scheming ways to find the best chips and queso in Texas.

"I'm a country girl living in a city world," says **Tia McCollors** of Conyers, Georgia. "The older I get, the more I realize that I enjoy the simple things in life. I don't need the theatrics, don't consider myself a materialistic person, or have to constantly be on the go. Simple is good. My children are older now, and with that comes a certain amount of freedom. They—especially the teenagers—are wrapped up in their own worlds with their friends and extracurricular activities. They've become more self-sufficient, which has given me the time to rediscover who I am. And I'm loving every minute of it. I still sometimes shed tears when I think about my mother going home to be with the Lord. But I'm living. And living well. Thank you, Father." Tia continues to enjoy being a part of the Guideposts family and appreciates the many emails she receives from devoted readers. You can connect with Tia online at TiaMcCollors.com, through her "Fans of Tia" Facebook page, or follow her on Instagram @TMcCollors.

When **Roberta Messner** of Huntington, West Virginia, experienced a bout of doubt like no other this past year, the words of Jeremiah 31:3 became especially precious. "I wondered where God was in everything, if He'd forgotten all about me," the self-proclaimed "devout doubter" says. "I discovered He'd been working everything for my good, even when it seemed He was nowhere around. That I'd been held by that everlasting love, both God's and the love of His children, who He sent to remind me. And in the unexpected people and provisions He'd arranged just for me." Her devotional series, "When Doubt Became Faith," chronicles that journey. Roberta, who'd always been a questioner, found herself ashamed that she was doubting God. She was amazed to discover that doubt is not the opposite of faith, but rather a critical part of it. "Doubting took me deeper in my walk with God," she says. "I began to know Him in a more personal, intimate way than ever before. God proved Himself dearer in the doubting places."

**Gabrielle Meyer** grew up above a carriage house on a historic estate near the banks of the Mississippi River, fueling her passion for the past. As a teenager, she discovered her interest in genealogy and traced her ancestors back to the original settlers in Jamestown, Virginia, in 1607. As a young woman, she went on to work for the Minnesota Historical Society, where she fell in love with the rich history of her state and began writing fiction and nonfiction inspired by real people, places, and events. She currently resides in central Minnesota on the banks of the upper Mississippi River, not far from where she grew up, with her husband and four teenage children. By day, she's a busy homeschool mom and small-business owner, and by night she pens fiction and nonfiction filled with hope. Her work currently includes historical and contemporary romances, cozy mysteries, and home and family articles. You can learn more about Gabrielle and her writing by visiting gabriellemeyer.com.

"My year brimmed with gardening," says **Rebecca Ondov** of Hamilton, Montana. She created several new vegetable garden plots, picked apples from her young fruit trees, and many mornings she wandered through her bramble patches, popping fresh raspberries in her mouth for breakfast.

Landscaping around her cottage has been an ongoing dream. She says, "My favorite is to walk under the arbor leading into my yard. The climbing roses have grown so tall that they spill over the top. Halfway through I pause and inhale their rich scent. For a heavenly moment, I feel as if I'm wrapped in God's everlasting love." In her spare time, you can find her kayaking high-mountain lakes, hiking with Willow, her German shepherd, by her side, horseback riding, or pulling weeds. Rebecca delights when her readers connect with her on social media. To find out how, go to her website: RebeccaOndov.com

**Shirley Raye Redmond** has sold articles to such publications as *Focus on the Family Magazine*, *Home Life*, *The Christian Standard*, and *Chicken Soup for the Soul*. Her writing has

appeared in multiple Guideposts devotionals as well as two of Guideposts' mystery series. Her children's book *Courageous World Changers: 50 True Stories of Daring Women of God* (Harvest House) won the 2021 Christianity Today Book Award in its category. Her most recent book is *Brave Animal Stories for Kids: 50 True Tales That Celebrate God's Creation* (Harvest House). She has been married for forty-eight years to her college sweetheart, Bill. They are blessed with two children and five precious grandchildren. Shirley Raye lives in northern New Mexico, where she enjoys stuffed sopapillas with chicken and green chiles. She loves hearing from readers through her Facebook page or via her website at shirleyrayeredmond.com.

 **Ginger Rue** is working this year on trusting God more. "I'm a Type A person who wants to fix everything all the time, get things done," she explains. "But God keeps reminding me that I'm not the one in control; He is." Ginger asks *Walking in Grace* readers this year to pray for her mother, who's been dealing with health issues. "Mother is the original supermom, so please pray that she can also learn to slow down and lean on the Lord's strength."

**Dr. Adam Ruiz** is a board-certified hospital chaplain, primarily in pediatric and women's services. He has a doctoral degree in pastoral counseling from Louisville Seminary and a master's degree in pastoral ministry from the Oblate School of Theology in San Antonio, Texas. He is bilingual and bi-literate (Spanish), and is currently working on improving his French. He is married to Denise and enjoys reading, writing, traveling, and spending time with his family.

"My wife, Kate, and I remain anchored in our Cornwall Presbyterian Church and community," says retired Army chaplain **Kenneth Sampson** of Cornwall on Hudson, New York. "In June, I retired after eight-and-a-half part-time years in the Guideposts Military Liaison position. The final two ministry visits to Kentucky and the Boston area were especially dear. Steady participation in local Newburgh ministerial and Reformed Church in America fellowships, along with periodic preaching, offer opportunities to engage my ordination vows in significant and community-touching ways. At this stage in life, we especially savor the deep friendships and relationships God has drawn us to along the way. Additionally, as if living near deer is not spectacular enough, this past September we celebrated spotting a record-breaking seventeen praying mantises on shrubs in our front yard!"

**Daniel Schantz** and his wife, Sharon, of Moberly, Missouri, have enjoyed fourteen peaceful years of retirement, which they regard as the crowning expression of God's love in their lifetime. A second great-grandson was delivered to them by granddaughter Rossetti on Dan's birthday. He is a feisty little boy, with black hair and ebony eyes. This year, Sharon participated in the Missouri "Shop Hop," traveling to various fabric shops around the state to collect free patches needed to make a Missouri Quilt. All year long, Sharon creates colorful quilts, which she then donates to IDES, a relief organization. They auction off the quilts and use the profits for relief work. Dan is slowing down in his gardening and tree planting. This year, he just grew Better Boy tomatoes and set out some Arnold Promise Witch Hazel trees.

**Gail Thorell Schilling** of Concord, New Hampshire, trusts God's everlasting love to watch over her family thousands of miles away in Los Angeles, Singapore, and Turkey—

and her while she's traveling to see them all. Back at home, she's grateful for video calls that let her share in her grandchildren's activities—piano practice to new chicks to daredevil tricks. She's especially gratified that her grown children check in on each other, both for celebrations and tough times. "Raising children who love each other and who are decent citizens... what more could a mother wish?" Gail continues to work with her church hospitality team, memoir writers, and New Americans. Follow her at gailthorellschilling.com.

"The highlights of my year were the birth of Talyn Dawn, my first great-grandchild, to grandson David and his wife, Robyn, and the marriage of grandson Mark to Corrine Quick," writes **Penney Schwab** of Copeland, Kansas. "Other joys were having all my immediate family together at Thanksgiving; attending a production of *The Lion King* in Wichita; enjoying a marvelous Andrea Bocelli concert in Oklahoma City; and time spent visiting with family and friends. My major project was getting the farmstead cleaned up. My walking companion, Pepper, serenades me by barking at coyotes at least two hours each night. I'm thankful our family is mostly doing well;

for good health; and a wonderful church home. I appreciate the encouragement I receive from *Walking in Grace* readers, friends, and family. Almost daily, I'm the recipient of a kind act or cheerful word that reminds me of God's grace and everlasting love."

 **Buck Storm** didn't exactly tell the truth on the Los Angeles apartment application when he and his wife, Michelle, married in 1989. He listed his profession as "writer." He figured it wasn't much of a stretch—after all, he wrote songs, and would get to books eventually. But life often sidetracks. Those songs wound up taking him and Michelle around the globe. It took twenty-five years and a lot of miles for Buck to become a novelist but, several books in now, he finally made good on that application. Buck spends his days writing and spending time with Michelle, his grown children, and two granddaughters. His nights are often spent out playing music with popular Northwest band The Buckley Storms, a songwriting collaboration project with his son, Ransom. Buck is an award-winning literary fiction author, musician, and traveler. His books and songs have made friends around the world.

**Jolynda Strandberg** serves as a director of religious education and has spent twenty-six years as a civilian with the military. She and her family reside in Clarksville, Tennessee. This year, she and her family welcomed a cute little quarter horse into the family named Ellie, who has stolen her family's heart.

**Jon M. Sweeney** is an author who has been interviewed by NPR and the BBC, and on television on *CBS Saturday Morning*. His book *The Pope Who Quit* was optioned by HBO. He also edits other people's books, as well as a magazine published bimonthly called *Living City*. In the last year, he's watched his youngest child turn twelve, his Milwaukee city sunflowers grow to more than seven feet in height, and his dog, Juno, learn to almost dribble a basketball (seriously).

**Rachel Thompson** is a senior at John Brown University, majoring in English with an emphasis in creative writing and a minor in computer science. Rachel says,

"At JBU, I'm on the cross-country and track and field teams, and I was just hired this past summer as a client support specialist, so after I graduate in May, I'll move into this position full-time. I'm the youngest of eight, and my mom homeschooled all of us all the way through high school, so my siblings and I are really close. When I have spare time, some of my favorite things to do are reading, writing, baking, playing games, and spending time with my family."

 After their daughter left for college, **Stephanie Thompson** and husband, Michael, were empty nesters for about six months before Michael's grandmother moved in. "We both love her dearly and begged her to come live with us after the death of her son," explains Stephanie. "Mam Ma is congenial and we've always gotten along well, so I had few concerns about personality clashes. But I was worried that she would be disappointed in or judge my lax domestic routine." When Stephanie confided her cleaning challenge, Mam Ma had a wonderful suggestion: "Why don't I hire us a housekeeper to come twice a month?" "It was a win-win for us both!" says Stephanie. It's been a year now, and the three of them live happily

in a clean house in an Oklahoma City suburb with a schweenie (shih tzu/dachshund mix) named Missy and two fine felines—Mr. Whiskers, a long-haired tuxedo stray that has stayed for the past decade, and Ron, a playful orange tabby they adopted in 2020.

"How amazing that my husband, Chuck, and I will celebrate our seventeenth anniversary this year!" writes **Marilyn Turk**. "Meeting when we were middle-aged empty nesters, I found out what love truly was and knew that God had put us together. Not only has our love grown, but we have been blessed to have a loving family that has grown too, adding daughters-in-law and grandchildren." Marilyn and Chuck's golden retriever, Dolly, has added to the love in their lives.

Marilyn continues to write Christian historical fiction novels showing how faith works in the lives of her characters. In addition, she continues to direct the Blue Lake Christian Writers Conference. "God continues to bless our 'little conference in the woods' with His presence, giving us mutual love and support for each other and creating a family atmosphere. Seeing others receive blessings by attending the conference has also been a blessing, a reward, and encouragement for me."

 "When I saw my oldest sister on the hospital bed, I wanted to hold her tight. But her body was filled with too much pain for the hugs we were accustomed to," says **Karen Valentin** of New York, New York. "She was toward the end of her battle with ovarian cancer, and with it, near the end of her life. I dreaded this visit. Cancer is easier to deal with miles away. But it was time to face my beautiful sister, and this awful disease. That week, with my family and sister, I sobbed and laughed harder than I had in years. I cringed watching her struggle with pain, then filled with pride at her strength as she danced in her hospital gown. I heard her desperate wish to live, while also voicing her peace with death—whatever God willed. Tears, laughter, pain, joy, struggle, and surrender are all-encompassing in our human experience. More than anything, that's what I learned as I visited my sister in her last days. It was dreadfully heartbreaking, but it was indescribably beautiful too. This is the gift of life—the highs, the lows, and everything in between—and I'm thankful for it all."

"This has been a good year for my wife, Beth, and me," says **Scott Walker** of Macon, Georgia. "I retired from Mercer University two years ago and have adjusted well to this new chapter of life. We live close to the Mercer campus, so I still go to the university coffee shop almost every day to talk with students and read or write. Beth and I try to visit with our three adult children and four grandchildren as much as possible. The joy of family never ceases, and the importance of friends and relatives becomes more important as we enter our seventh decade of life. Relationships are the heart of human happiness. I am also grateful for the silent conversations that I have with *Walking in Grace* readers and writers. You bring much joy to my life, and I often pray for my Guideposts family. May God be in the midst of all of us."

**Jacqueline Freeman Wheelock** is the youngest of six girls (three of whom she does not remember without their spouses), and though she is a senior now, Jacqueline's older sisters, were they not deceased, would probably still be describing her as having "baby-of-the-family" syndrome—demonstrated in such occurrences as claiming that final coveted cookie, always being the last to admit it was her turn to wash the dishes, and so on. Though she has always been one for good humor and loves to make people laugh, she esteems nothing else in her life more than her walk with God, always seeking His wisdom and always looking for better ways to grow in Him. Having met at Southern University in Baton Rouge, Louisiana, and married in 1969, she and her husband, Donald, make their home in central Mississippi. They are the parents of a son and a daughter, as well as the doting grandparents of two granddaughters.

 **Gayle T. Williams** is a native New Yorker who grew up as a member of Harlem's historic Abyssinian Baptist Church, where her family worshipped. These days, she is a member of New York Covenant Church of New Rochelle, New York, where she has truly been led to her own personal relationship with Christ. While she has covered a variety of exciting and interesting news topics as a reporter, writer, and editor for magazines and newspapers for the past thirty years, it is her work for Guideposts that truly feeds her soul. Still a news junkie, she enjoys spending time with her husband, two adult sons, sisters- and

brothers-in-law, nephews and cousins, and her "framily"—friends who have become family. Music is a backdrop to most of her life, and continues to be a primary connector between Gayle and Terry, her husband of thirty-six years.

# SCRIPTURE REFERENCE INDEX

**ACTS**
2:46, 446–447
4:30, 378
16:14, 69
17:26, 386
20:35, 489

**AMOS**
5:8, 268
5:24, 518

**CHRONICLES 1**
22:13, 383

**CHRONICLES 2**
16:9, 130

**COLOSSIANS**
1:17, 380
2:2–3, 317
3:11, 445
3:12, 513
3:14, 303, 309
3:17, 350

**CORINTHIANS 1**
3:7, 355
3:13, 349
11:11, 421
13:4, 95
13:12, 162
15:58, 139, 344
16:14, 84

**CORINTHIANS 2**
3:13–15, 192
3:18, 4
4:16, 449
6:2, 240–241
6:18, 125
9:7, 490
12:10, 51, 418
13:11, 461

**DANIEL**
12:3, 306

**DEUTERONOMY**
4:24, 402
6:5–7, 230
31:6, 183
31:8, 259

**ECCLESIASTES**
3:1, 7
3:11, 14
4:9, 62, 173
7:1, 425

**EPHESIANS**
3:19, 438
4:2, 123, 424
5:2, 27, 45
6:10, 175
6:13, 146

**EXODUS**
3:4, 291
15:13, 458
20:15–16, 278

**GALATIANS**
1:6–7, 100
5:22–25, 61–62
5:25, 53
6:9, 157
6:10, 167, 459

**GENESIS**
2:2–3, 217
2:3, 47
2:7, 90
3:9, 92
8:6–7, 87
9:13, 369
16:13, 78
21:19, 11

**HAGGAI**
2:5, 320

**HEBREWS**
3:4, 133
6:19, 210
6:19–20, 308
10:22, 420
10:24–25, 272
11:1, 116, 340, 495
11:6, 26
12:1, 518
12:1–2, 387
13:2, 229
13:8, 441
13:20–21, 103

**ISAIAH**
1:18, 106, 225, 436
6:8, 75
7:11, 110
9:2, 153, 486
11:6, 246
26:3, 210
26:34, 463
30:15, 376
30:21, 359
33:6, 439
41:10, 267, 318
42:9, 194
43:1, 178
43:7, 295
43:18–19, 392, 490
46:4, 107
55:11, 494
55:12, 232
58:10, 94
61:8, 491
65:24, 19
66:13, 484

**JAMES**
1:5, 191, 235
1:19, 172, 422
1:25, 221
1:27, 208
2:23, 437
3:5, 357
4:14, 456
5:13, 226

**JEREMIAH**
1:5, 234
29:11, 115
31:3, 111
31:13, 174

**JOB**
5:18, 165
12:7, 377
35:11, 483
38:22, 40
42:2, 64

**JOEL**
2:24, 200
**JOHN**
1:3, 361
1:5, 36, 447
1:9, 474
1:14, 457
1:46, 16
3:8, 416
3:16, 258
4:10, 415
4:11, 467
4:15, 466
4:16, 414
4:17, 415
4:32, 119
6:35, 55
6:67, 99
7:24, 22
7:51, 471
8:1–11, 192
8:32, 50
8:44, 328
10:10, 328
13:34, 492
14:1, 499
14:3, 373
14:6, 401
15:12, 150
15:13, 207
15:15, 166
16:32, 152
16:33, 261, 362
17:3–4, 280
19:11, 147
**JOHN 1**
3:1, 31
3:17, 112, 489
4:7, 1
4:18, 296, 332
4:19, 171, 185
5:11, 67
**JOSHUA**
1:6, 263
1:9, 426, 450, 516
2:11, 298
**JUDGES**
5:31, 56

**KINGS 2**
3:11, 80
3:15, 417
6:22, 227

**LAMENTATIONS**
3:9, 517
**LEVITICUS**
27:30, 275
**LUKE**
1:30–31, 510
1:37, 129
2:4–5, 509
2:7, 507
5:26, 381
6:37, 297
10:37, 239
11:34, 164
12:34, 488
12:48, 304
15:4, 382
18:13, 74, 271
18:16–17, 502
18:19, 412
24:6, 154
24:15, 252
24:17–18, 331
24:21, 331

**MARK**
6:38, 283
7:24–25, 368
7:28, 368
7:29, 367
9:24, 335
10:15, 184
10:20, 113
11:17, 196
12:31, 354
14:8, 23
**MATTHEW**
1:2, 18
4:10, 328
5:3–12, 62
5:4, 409
5:16, 420
5:44, 512
5:45, 143
5:48, 305

6:21, 497
6:26, 131, 180
6:27, 199
6:34, 454
7:2, 480
7:7–8, 498
7:11, 111
7:12, 374, 396
8:2, 212
9:38, 325
11:28, 452
12:36–37, 292–293
13:16, 85
14:16, 42
15:34, 358
17:20–21, 236
18:3, 52
18:4, 372
18:20, 244
25:35, 102
25:40, 265
25:45, 289
28:19–20, 149
**MICAH**
6:8, 203–204

**NEHEMIAH**
9:20, 181

**PETER 1**
1:7, 260, 342
4:7, 299
4:8, 391
5:5, 248
5:7, 339
**PETER 2**
1:5–7, 62
**PHILIPPIANS**
1:6, 264
1:9–10, 326
2:3, 430
2:4, 96
3:13, 6
3:13–14, 122, 469
4:6, 15, 160, 218
4:7, 210
4:8, 195
4:10, 73
4:11, 24, 408
4:13, 262

560

**PROVERBS**
1:5, 427
1:7, 118
2:2, 322
3:3, 128
3:5, 279
3:27, 12, 58
4:18, 465
4:23, 48
4:26, 316
8:35, 188
11:25, 487
11:26, 489
13:17, 34
16:3, 205
16:23, 187
17:6, 363, 413
18:13, 172
18:24, 46
19:21, 282
20:27, 431
23:16, 514
28:20, 242

**PSALMS**
1:3, 39–40
13:5, 253
16:8, 324, 473
17:3, 400
18:2, 219
18:28, 442
18:35, 20
18:36, 150
19:1, 429
19:2, 86
20:2, 204
25:16, 337
28:7, 222
30:5, 211
30:12, 104
31:15, 336
32:7, 158, 313
33:13, 70
34:18, 78
35:9, 28
37:4, 410
39:2, 109
40:3, 38
46:1, 288

46:10, 2, 376
47:1, 9
50:15, 314
51:10, 70
52:8, 250
55:2, 287
66:20, 65
71:9, 406
71:23, 370
77:11, 397
86:13, 477
86:15, 216, 478
87:7, 321
90:17, 177
91:2–3, 284
91:11, 366
94:8–9, 57
96:6, 479
100:4, 470
100:5, 285
102:7, 144
103:2, 353
103:20, 141
104:24, 312
107:43, 10
116:15, 503
118:24, 251, 269
119:1, 243
119:10, 189
119:33–34, 481
119:73, 405
119:76, 310
121:1, 79
121:1–2, 89
121:5, 35
126:2, 273
126:6, 293
131:2, 376
133:1, 462
139:1, 444
139:7–8, 81
143:8, 348
147:3, 91, 142, 161

**REVELATION**
21:4, 329
21:22, 135

**ROMANS**
5:4, 231
6:5, 156
8:18, 223
8:22, 505
8:26, 404
8:28, 333
8:31, 247
12:2, 30, 60
12:12, 120
12:15, 506
13:1, 66
13:8, 398

**SAMUEL 1**
2:6–7, 453
7:12, 351
23:28, 36
**SAMUEL 2**
22:31, 255
**SONG OF SOLOMON**
4:7, 71

**THESSALONIANS 1**
4:13, 134, 160
4:16, 160
4:17, 161
5:11, 365
5:18, 467
**THESSALONIANS 2**
2:16–17, 276
3:16, 98
**TIMOTHY 1**
1:5, 202
4:8, 394
6:16, 343
**TIMOTHY 2**
1:5, 238
1:7, 32, 137, 393,
   420, 501
2:19, 198
4:7, 3
**TITUS**
3:5, 138

**ZECHARIAH**
1:3, 385

# AUTHORS, TITLES, AND SUBJECTS INDEX

9/11 (September 11 attacks), 362, 367

Acceptance, 139

ADA (Americans with Disabilities Act), 379

Addiction. *See* Illness

ADHD (attention deficit hyperactivity disorder), 129

Advent, 209, 474–475, 479, 486, 495–496, 505–506

African American history, 241

Alborghetti, Marci, 11–12, 74–75, 147–149, 196–197, 278–279, 412–413, 471–472, 523

American Red Cross, 76

Amish community, 179

Angels, 141–142, 366–367, 510–511

Anger, 75, 124, 148, 261, 332–333

Anxiety, 235, 378, 436. *See also* Stress

Ash Wednesday, 90–91

Assurance, 110, 161, 420

Baptism, 12

Beatitudes, 62

Beauty, 27, 48, 60, 165, 196, 318, 356, 406, 418, 465, 480

Bence, Evelyn, 23–24, 55–56, 203–204, 247–248, 272–273, 293–294, 320–321, 416–417, 446–447, 523–524

Bentsen, Erika, 40–41, 70–71, 87–88, 158–159, 211–212, 234–235, 263–264, 421–422, 524

Bible, 19, 26, 29, 35–36, 48–49, 81, 103, 107, 117, 123, 142, 167–168, 209, 221, 277, 298, 321, 325, 328–329, 331, 335, 352, 360, 368, 376, 387, 420, 448, 461, 489, 510; King James Version (KJV), 447, 458; The Message (MSG), 331

Bible study, 5, 42, 61, 125, 212, 254, 357

Biblical figures: David, 35–36, 107; Israelites, 298; James (brother of Jesus), 172, 357–358; Jarha, 387; Jonathan, 107, 387; Joseph (father of Jesus), 505, 508; Joseph (Old Testament), 121; Joshua, 298; Luke, 209, 428–429; Mary (mother of Jesus), 505, 508; Mephibosheth, 387: Pharisee, 271; Rahab, 298; Samaritans, 239, 414, 466; Sarah, 121; Saul, 35, 107, 387; Wise Men (Magi), 9, 494, 500. *See also* Disciples. *See also* Prophets

Biblical sites: Bethlehem, 487, 505; Emmaus, 331; Galilee, 149; Jacob's Well, 466; Judea, 510; Nazareth, 505; Promised Land, 298; Sela Hammahlekoth (Rock of Escape), 36; Thessalonica, 160; Tyre, 368

Bill, J. Brent, 85–86, 351–352, 474–475, 486–487, 495–496, 505–506, 509–511, 524–525

Birthdays, 168, 198, 201, 269–270, 313–314, 353–354, 420, 444, 453, 507

Blecker, Rhoda, 34–35, 86–87, 92–94, 165–166, 227–228, 385–386, 425–426, 514–515, 525

Blessings, 13, 41, 48, 57, 108, 174, 179, 186, 201, 242–243, 358, 363, 438, 444, 447, 473, 484, 497

Books: *The Book of Common Prayer*, 249–250, 447; *A Christmas Carol*, 489; *Life Together*, 152; *Little House on the Prairie*, 238; *The Little Prince*, 320; *Not the Way It's Supposed to Be*, 492; *The Secret of Red Gate Farm*, 491; *Whistling in the Dark*, 294

Cancer. *See* Illness

Choir, 58, 199, 245, 254, 424, 484–485

Christmas, 25, 99, 326, 360, 384, 453–454, 473–474, 479, 486–489, 491–492, 495–496, 499–500, 503, 506–511

Christmas Eve, 507, 509–510

Church, 17, 52–53, 56, 58, 74–76, 81, 90, 94, 103, 105, 108, 115, 123, 136–137, 145, 148, 150, 153, 155, 160, 176, 186, 191, 202, 204, 217, 244–245, 254, 293, 318, 323, 325–326, 401, 407, 411, 416, 424, 430–431, 447, 451, 461, 465, 471, 473, 479, 502–503, 507, 509

Ciancanelli, Sabra, 30–31, 69–70, 90–91, 110–111, 139–140, 194–195, 236–237, 268–269, 329–331, 377–378, 417–418, 473–474, 526

Civil rights movement, 28

Collins, Mark, 46–47, 248–250, 378–379, 517–518, 526–527

Comfort, 267, 357, 443, 473

Communion, 325326

Compassion, 91, 139, 181, 290, 333, 358, 412

Confidence, 329, 371, 383, 394, 519

Contentment, 40, 296, 447, 489

Courage, 183–184, 264, 459, 472

COVID-19 pandemic, 35, 73, 145–146, 150, 153, 156, 173, 198, 228, 236, 268, 272, 293, 350

Creation, 77, 131, 133, 138, 163, 195–196, 312–313, 387

Crucifixion, 51, 454

Diaz, Pablo, 52–53, 172–173, 252–253, 437–438, 498–499, 527–528

Dignity, 323

Dilworth, John, 24–25, 191–192, 325–326, 366–367, 445–446, 528

Discernment, 191, 326–327

Disciples (Apostles), 42, 51–52, 120, 148–149, 151, 283; Paul, 25, 101, 147, 160, 168, 468; Peter, 100

Divorce, 122, 349

Easter, 93, 153–157, 164, 326

Eliasen, Logan, 7–8, 60–61, 123–124, 259–260, 350–351, 392–393, 454–455, 507–509, 528–529

Eliasen, Shawnelle, 67–69, 175–184, 310–312, 357–358, 394–396, 529

Emancipation Proclamation, 241

Encouragement, 236, 264, 276–278, 360, 378, 400, 423, 461–462

Epiphany, 9, 500, 517

Faith, 7, 11, 27, 35, 62, 75, 79–80, 86, 100–101, 114, 119, 120, 129, 132, 147, 150–153, 155, 176, 199, 203, 230, 233, 235, 251, 253, 260–261, 284, 298, 310, 329, 331, 335–343, 356, 367–368, 374, 395, 401, 405, 420, 422, 437, 442, 444, 466–467, 493, 496

Family, 3–4, 16–17, 25, 28–29, 35, 56, 73, 75–76, 89, 106–107, 115–116, 122, 126, 132, 135, 141, 150, 154, 167, 176, 183, 186–187, 197, 205–208, 218, 223, 231–232, 239, 243, 250–251, 277, 288–290, 300, 306, 308, 310–311, 317, 319, 326, 363–365, 379, 386–387, 396–398, 409, 413, 419, 454, 455, 471, 493, 499–500, 504, 507–509, 513, 516

Father's Day, 235–236

Fear, 71, 105, 137, 145, 176, 180, 203, 206, 220, 226, 267–268, 285, 310, 320–321, 329, 333, 388, 394, 452, 502

Fellowship, 57, 245, 254

"Filled with Holy Anticipation" series, 474–475, 486–487, 495–496, 505–506, 509–510

Forgiveness, 193, 221, 328, 403, 436

Friendship, 46, 57, 59, 107, 112, 135, 149, 173–174, 323, 445–446

Garcia, Nicole, 65–66, 122–123, 280–281, 371–372, 530

Generosity, 228, 345

Glory, 61, 79, 224, 296

God, 2, 5, 7, 10, 12, 16–17, 19–21, 34–37, 48–49, 53, 62, 65, 67, 73–82, 86–87, 89, 94–95, 99–100–101, 108, 110–112, 114–117, 119–121, 123, 125–126, 131–132, 135–138, 144–148, 150, 158–159, 162–163, 172, 174, 178, 182, 187, 190, 192, 197, 200–202, 217, 219–225, 227, 229–231, 233, 243, 248, 261, 268, 270, 277–278, 283–284, 289–299, 307, 309–310, 313, 318, 323, 327–328, 331, 333–336, 338, 341–345, 352, 359–361, 363, 367–371, 376–377, 380–383, 385, 388, 394, 401–403, 409–410, 413–415, 420, 427, 432, 436–437, 440–442, 447–448, 453, 457, 464, 473–475, 478, 480–481, 484, 491–493, 499, 504, 511, 515, 519

Good Friday, 152–153

Gospel, 68, 100–101, 109

Gossip, 278, 436

Graduations, 111, 227, 248, 454

Gratitude, 12, 114, 270, 274, 353–354, 418, 439–440, 451, 493

Great Commission, 149

Grief, 34, 75, 92, 196, 507

Grinnan, Edward, 26–27, 91–92, 98–99, 131–133, 173–174, 222–223, 265–267, 309–310, 354–355, 398–400, 441–442, 483–484, 530–531

Hamlin, Rick, 18–19, 58–59, 94–95, 141–142, 184–185, 244–246, 271–272, 316–317, 365–366, 404–405, 467–468, 484–486, 531–532

Harmony, 247

Hartke, Lynne, 64–65, 133–134, 238–239, 264–265, 299–300, 405–406, 429–430, 465–466, 532

Heaven, 6, 78–79, 135, 136, 143, 144, 147, 175, 187, 200, 206, 235, 247, 269, 271, 291, 293, 323, 369, 409, 411, 430, 491, 500, 504

Hendricks, Carla, 3–4, 27–28, 134–135, 218–219, 314–315, 363–365, 413–414, 487–488, 533

Henry, Kim Taylor, 20–21, 95–96, 210–211, 292–293, 376–377, 533–534

Holy Saturday, 153–154

Holy Spirit, 62, 86, 147–148, 163, 168, 192, 248, 322, 352, 395, 405, 416, 481

Holy Week, 145–146, 151

Homelessness, 13, 92, 102, 209, 290, 323, 412

Hope, 2, 135, 157, 209, 213, 241, 251, 263, 277, 340, 374, 493, 495–496, 498

Humility, 151, 419

Humor, 57, 188, 262, 274

Hurricanes, 146, 287, 317, 369, 380–381, 416. *See also* Storms

Hymns: "Be Still My Soul," 324; "Christ the Lord Is Risen Today," 155; "Come, Thou Long Expected Jesus," 496; "Crown Him with Many Crowns," 468; "I Shall Not Be Moved," 325; "Just as I Am," 254. *See also* Songs

Illnesses: addiction, 132, 230, 335–336; AIDS (acquired immunodeficiency syndrome), 354; ALS (amyotrophic lateral sclerosis), 407; arthritis, 226; cancer, 38, 50, 78, 279–280, 342, 345, 384, 438, 444, 453, 494–495, 500; chronic pain, 24–25, 261; coma, 117; dementia, 441, 478; depression, 226,

452; heart conditions, 32–33, 329, 407, 438; kidney failure, 335, 337, 340, 342; leprosy (Hansen's disease), 213; lupus, 91; seizure, 345; tumors, 50, 100, 335–336, 487; vasculitis, 226

Independence Day (Fourth of July), 259, 263–264

Indigenous people, 98

Intimacy, 5, 178, 217, 432

Iran hostage crisis, 354

Jackson, Leanne, 174–175, 296–297, 410–411, 478–479, 534–535

Janoso, Erin, 51–52, 104–106, 138–139, 273–275, 312–313, 361–362, 431–433, 518–519, 535

Jesus Christ, 9, 27, 33, 37, 42, 50–52, 55, 68, 80, 92, 100–101, 103–104, 107, 109, 120, 139, 149–151, 153–154, 160, 163–164, 166–167, 172, 191–193, 199, 209–211, 213, 217, 222, 224–225, 239–241, 253, 266, 271, 281, 283–284, 290–292, 299, 326, 328–329, 331–332, 351, 355, 358, 367–368, 403, 410, 414–415, 427–429, 443, 453, 460, 467, 485–487, 500, 503, 506–507, 511

Jesus Prayer, 271

Jewish traditions: Elul, 93; Seder, 151; Rosh Hashanah, 93, 385; Sabbath (Shabbat), 48, 217–218, 425; Yom Kippur, 93, 385

"Journeying with Jesus" series, 103–104, 149–150, 192–193, 239–240, 283–284, 328–329, 367–369, 414–415

Joy, 4, 9, 11, 16, 21, 25, 27, 53, 77, 108–109, 138, 140, 148, 195, 212, 235, 284, 292, 363, 371, 375, 453, 486, 489, 491, 493, 499, 507, 511

Judgment, 124, 139, 304, 388, 436, 472, 481

Juneteenth, 240–242

Justice, 148, 492

Kappel, Ashley, 36–38, 78–79, 142–143, 199–200, 306–307, 370–371, 393–394, 456–457, 503–505, 536

Keller, Jenny Lynn, 255–256, 260–261, 276–278, 285–287, 295–296, 308–309, 317–318, 326–328, 536

Kidd, Brock, 28–30, 130–131, 275–276, 400–401, 459–461, 488–490, 512–513, 537

Kidd, Pam, 2–3, 22–23, 116–118, 187–188, 288–289, 322–324, 401–402, 447–449, 537–538

Kindness, 139, 168, 240, 306, 345, 367, 407, 465

Kirk, Patty, 35–36, 79–80, 106–107, 208–209, 297–299, 386–387, 427–429, 466–467, 538

Knapp, Carol, 103–104, 149–150, 192–193, 239–240, 261–263, 283–284, 328–329, 267–369, 414–415, 539

Kuykendall, Carol, 53–54, 217–218, 279–280, 382–383, 499–501, 539–540

Kuyper, Vicki, 12–14, 71–72, 162–163, 185–186, 246–247, 333–335, 381–382, 402–404, 439–441, 480–481, 540–541

Labor Day, 349–350

Last Supper, 454

Law of Moses, 193

Lent, 92–93

"Life Lessons from the Beach" series, 255–256, 260–261, 276–278, 285–287, 295–296, 308–309, 317–318, 326–328

Light of Christ, 153–154, 328, 443, 459, 475, 486–487, 510

Livezey, Lisa, 56–57, 204–205, 321–322, 344–346, 494–495, 541

Lord's Prayer, 114, 232

Lorenz, Patricia, 15–16, 73–74, 102–103, 164–165, 188–189, 232–234, 287–288,

349–350, 383–385, 406–408, 453–454, 541–542

Love, 19, 28, 36–37, 49, 52, 55, 68, 92, 94, 111–112, 117, 120, 135, 139, 150–151, 177, 179, 181, 186, 193, 200, 202, 208–209, 213, 224, 235–236, 251, 261, 266, 285–286, 290, 296–299, 311–312, 333, 345, 367–368, 386–387, 402–403, 412–413, 422, 437, 441, 445, 461, 471, 473–475, 487, 493, 510

*Macbeth*, 160

Macomber, Debbie, 61–62, 120–122, 219–222, 291–292, 420–421, 470–471, 542–543

MacPherson, Erin, 96–97, 284–285, 501–502, 543

Marriage, 68, 123, 172, 192–193, 209, 312, 422

Martin Luther King Jr. Day, 27–28

Mass, 102, 164

Maundy Thursday, 150–152

McCollors, Tia, 4–6, 111–112, 143–144, 250–251, 409–410, 463–464, 543–544

Meditation, 210–211

Memorial Day, 205–207

Messner, Roberta, 38–39, 230–231, 335–343, 544–545

Meyer, Gabrielle, 115–116, 226–227, 387–388, 452–453, 545

Military, United States, 207, 449, 482–483, 504; Air Force, 384; Army, 449; Navy, 384

Ministry, 14, 39, 52–53 103, 116, 152, 172, 208–209, 331, 438–439

Miracles, 20, 29, 43, 65, 147, 157, 220, 402, 454, 511

Mother's Day, 177, 185–186, 188

Neighbors, 24, 81, 88, 113, 195, 203–204, 240, 248–249, 259, 277, 314, 316, 320, 349, 354–355, 368

New Year, 6–7, 517–518; New Year's Day, 2–3, 453; New Year's Eve, 518–519

Nobel Peace Prize, 27–28

Oberammergau Passion Play, 366

Ondov, Rebecca, 10–11, 48–49, 202–203, 243–244, 289–290, 358–359, 430–431, 461–462, 546

Palm Sunday, 144–146

Parables, 191–192, 240, 271

Patience, 95–96, 121, 139, 249

Peace, 21, 33, 49, 98–99, 120, 147–148, 210–211, 224, 246–247, 363, 367, 370, 377, 407, 409, 418, 447, 453, 456, 492. *See also* Serenity

Podcasts, 35–36, 284, 298, 387

Prejudice, 22

Presidents' Day, 66–67

Prophets, 146, 148, 201, 204, 209; Abraham, 121, 307, 437; Anna, 209; Elijah, 146–147; Elisha, 79–80; Joel, 201; Micah, 204, 387. *See also* Biblical figures

Provision, God's, 40, 144–146, 181–182, 342

Purpose, 207, 295–296, 328, 360, 384, 388, 400–401

Rainbows, 135, 369–370

Redmond, Shirley Raye, 32–34, 167–169, 212–213, 491–492, 546–547

Resentment, 124, 333

Resilience, 16, 133

Resurrection, 156–157

Rue, Ginger, 14–15, 119–120, 160–161, 251–252, 355–356, 444–445, 547

Ruiz, Adam, 50–51, 99–100, 253–255, 332–333, 458–459, 492–494, 548

Saints: St. Francis, 266; Mother Teresa, 345

Salvation Army, 148

Sampson, Kenneth, 305–306, 438–439, 449–450, 481–483, 548–549

Satan, 328

Schantz, Daniel, 16–17, 62–63, 109–110, 135–136, 242–243, 304–305, 324–325, 418–419, 457–458, 549

Schilling, Gail Thorell, 75–76, 144–146, 117–121, 150–157, 424–425, 549–550

Schwab, Penney, 19–20, 107–109, 198–199, 436–437, 479–480, 502–503, 550–551

Secret Service, 66

"Seemingly Insignificant" series, 35–36, 79–80, 106–107, 208–209, 297–299, 386–387, 427–429, 466–467

Serenity, 99, 247, 287, 339. *See also* Peace

Sermon on the Mount, 495

"Sheltered in Grace" series, 144–146, 150–157

Snow, 13, 23, 40–41, 64, 89, 141, 145, 159, 287, 291, 426–427, 449–450, 505, 510, 516

Sobriety, 132

Songs: "Angels Among Us," 366–367; "Away in a Manger," 485; "In the Wee Small Hours of the Morning," 324; "Mysteries of Love," 354; "O Little Town of Bethlehem," 485; "Puttin' On the Ritz," 424; "Silent Night," 485; "There Are Angels Hovering 'Round," 511; "When I Fall in Love," 324; "Wildwood Flower," 38. *See also* Hymns

Storm, Buck, 66–67, 89–90, 205–207, 224–226, 380–381, 469–470, 490–491, 551

Storms, 76, 137–138, 159, 165, 189, 267–268, 285, 313, 370, 397, 448, 469, 505–506. *See also* Hurricanes

Strandberg, Jolynda, 113–115, 161–162, 207–208, 231–232, 396–397, 506–507, 552

Stress, 52, 176, 201, 330. *See also* Anxiety

Sunday school, 340, 342, 503

Sweeney, Jon M., 9–10, 57–58, 112–113, 195–196, 282–283, 313–314, 426–427, 552

Tau Herculids (meteor shower), 429

Teen Missions International, 149

Ten Commandments, 62

Thanksgiving Day, 430, 461–462, 467–468, 470–471, 473, 478, 517

Thompson, Rachel, 137–138, 318–320, 374–375, 422–423, 552–553

Thompson, Stephanie, 42–43, 81–82, 125–126, 166–167, 225–226, 353–354, 497–498, 553–554

Tithing, 271, 275–276, 304

Treasures, 68, 144, 194, 260, 317–318, 366, 398, 473

Triangulum Galaxy, 344

Trust, 33, 120–121, 177–178, 232, 259–260, 280, 285, 320, 328, 336–337, 341, 381, 394, 403, 442, 444, 464

Truth, 32, 46–47, 50–51, 147, 176, 232, 255–256, 341, 344, 358, 368, 459, 492

Turk, Marilyn, 6–7, 77–78, 118–119, 157–158, 189–191, 359–360, 554–555

Valentin, Karen, 31–32, 47–48, 129–130, 269–270, 362–363, 408–409, 462–463, 516–517, 555

Veterans Day, 449–450

Volunteerism, 76, 94, 116, 218–219, 233–234, 293, 411, 430

Walker, Scott, 229–230, 267–268, 343–344, 373–374, 397–398, 556

Wars: War in Afghanistan, 234; World War II, 220, 384

Wheelock, Jacqueline Freeman, 39–40, 100–102, 146–147, 200–201, 240–242, 331–332, 369–370, 442–443, 556–557

"When Change Comes" series, 175–184

"When Doubt Became Faith" series, 335–343

Williams, Gayle T., 221–222, 235–236, 450–451, 513–514, 557–558

Wisdom, 54, 68, 111–112, 191, 235, 279, 312, 414

Word of God, 10, 251, 255, 329, 395, 420, 444, 448, 464, 495

Worry, 80, 137, 267, 310

Worship, 5, 16, 94, 114, 124, 136, 145, 155, 293, 325, 407, 498, 503

## A NOTE FROM THE EDITORS

We hope you enjoyed *Walking in Grace,* published by Guideposts. For over seventy-five years, Guideposts, a nonprofit organization, has been driven by a vision of a world filled with hope. We aspire to be the voice of a trusted friend, a friend who makes you feel more hopeful and connected.

By making a purchase from Guideposts, you join our community in touching millions of lives, inspiring them to believe that all things are possible through faith, hope, and prayer. Your continued support allows us to provide uplifting resources to those in need. Whether through our communities, websites, apps, or publications, we inspire our audiences, bring them together, and comfort, uplift, entertain, and guide them. Visit us at guideposts.org to learn more.

We would love to hear from you. Write us at Guideposts, P.O. Box 5815, Harlan, Iowa 51593 or call us at (800) 932-2145. Did you love *Walking in Grace*? Leave a review for this product on guideposts.org/shop. Your feedback helps others in our community find relevant products.

*Find inspiration, find faith, find Guideposts.*

## Shop our best sellers and favorites at
# guideposts.org/shop
Or scan the QR code to go directly to our Shop